HAPPINESS
#4

SHUZO OSHIMI

HAPPINESS #4 CONTENTS

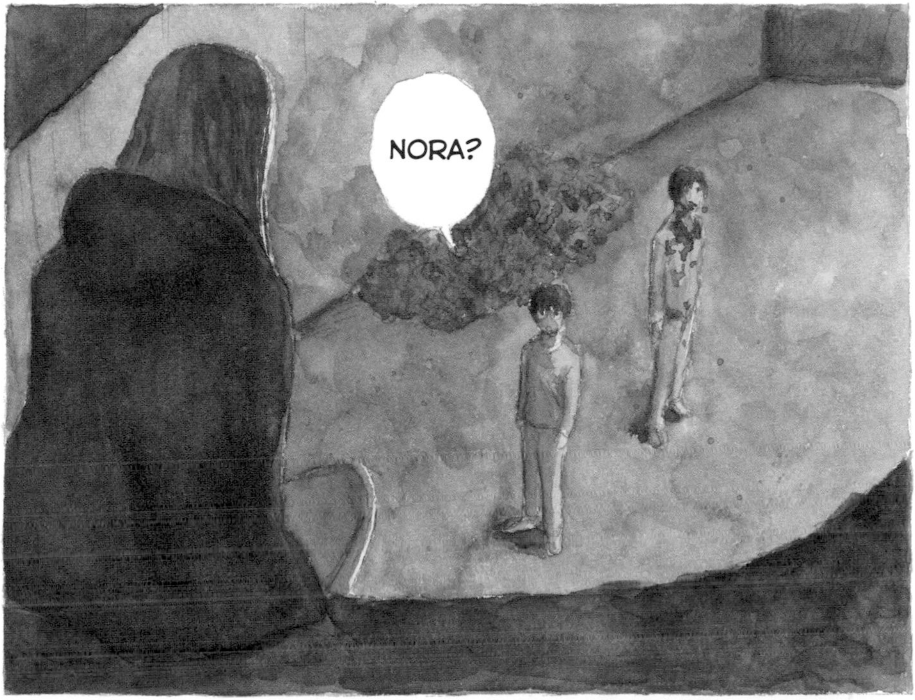
NORA?
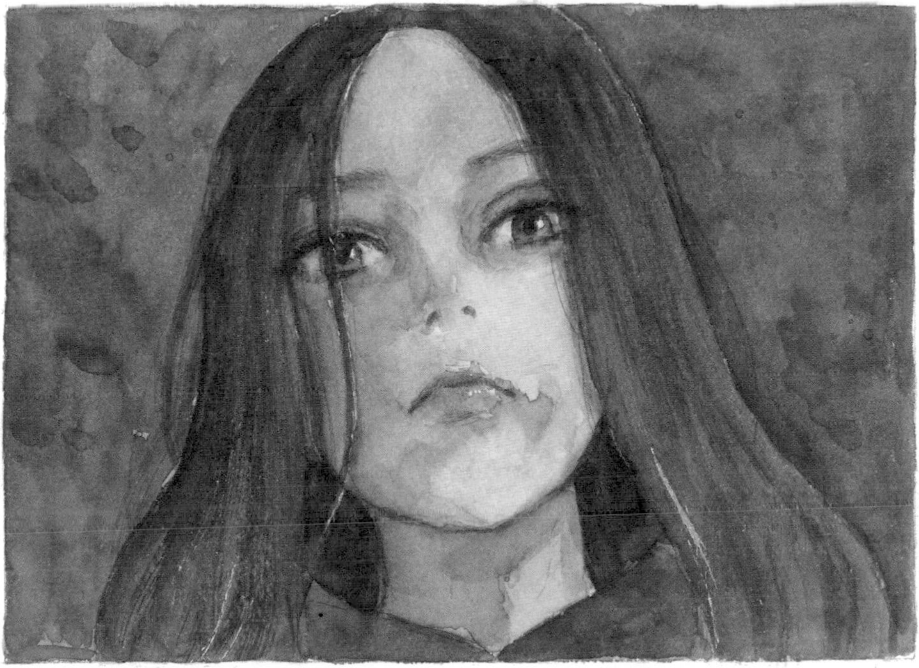

Chapter 16: Separation

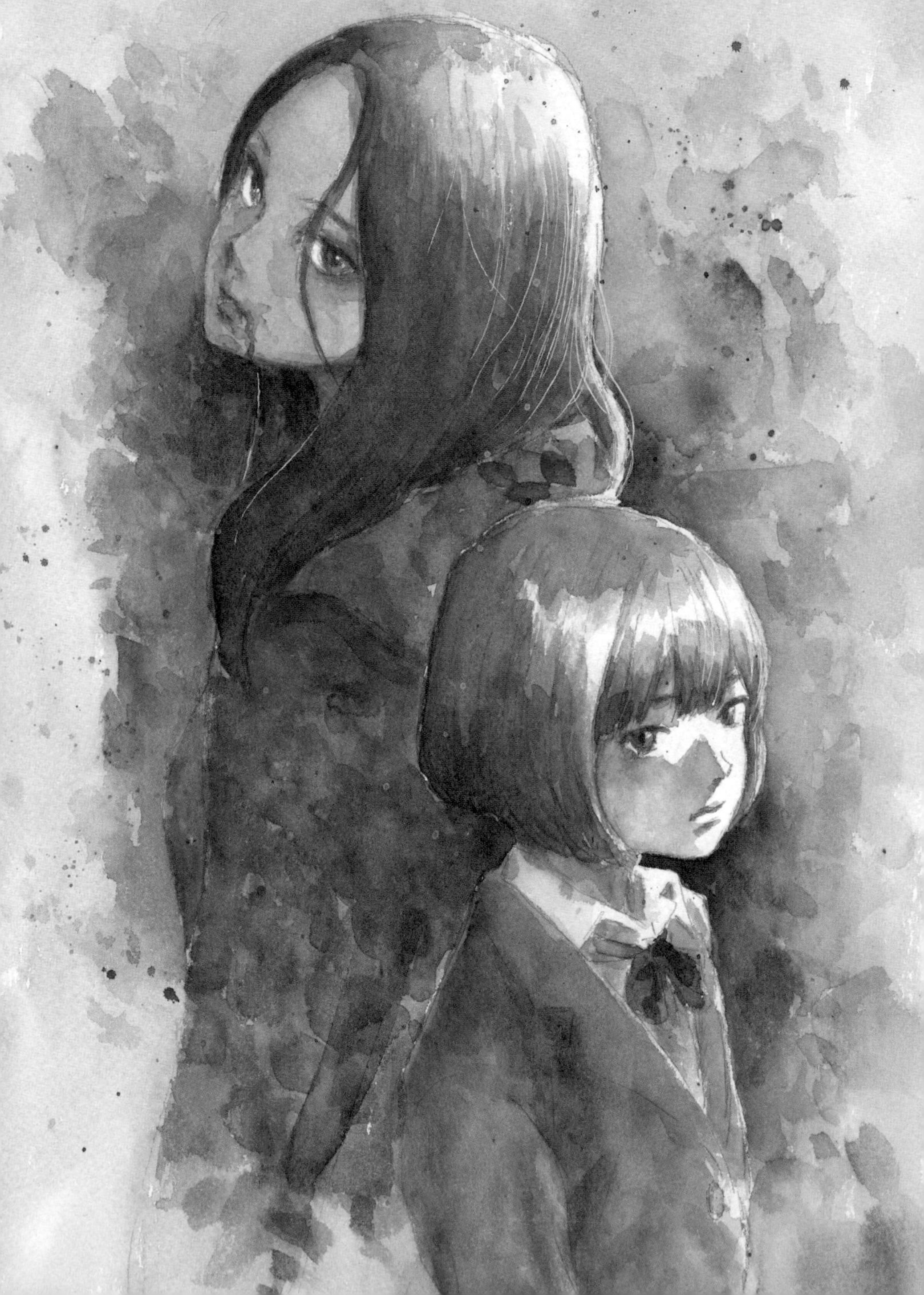

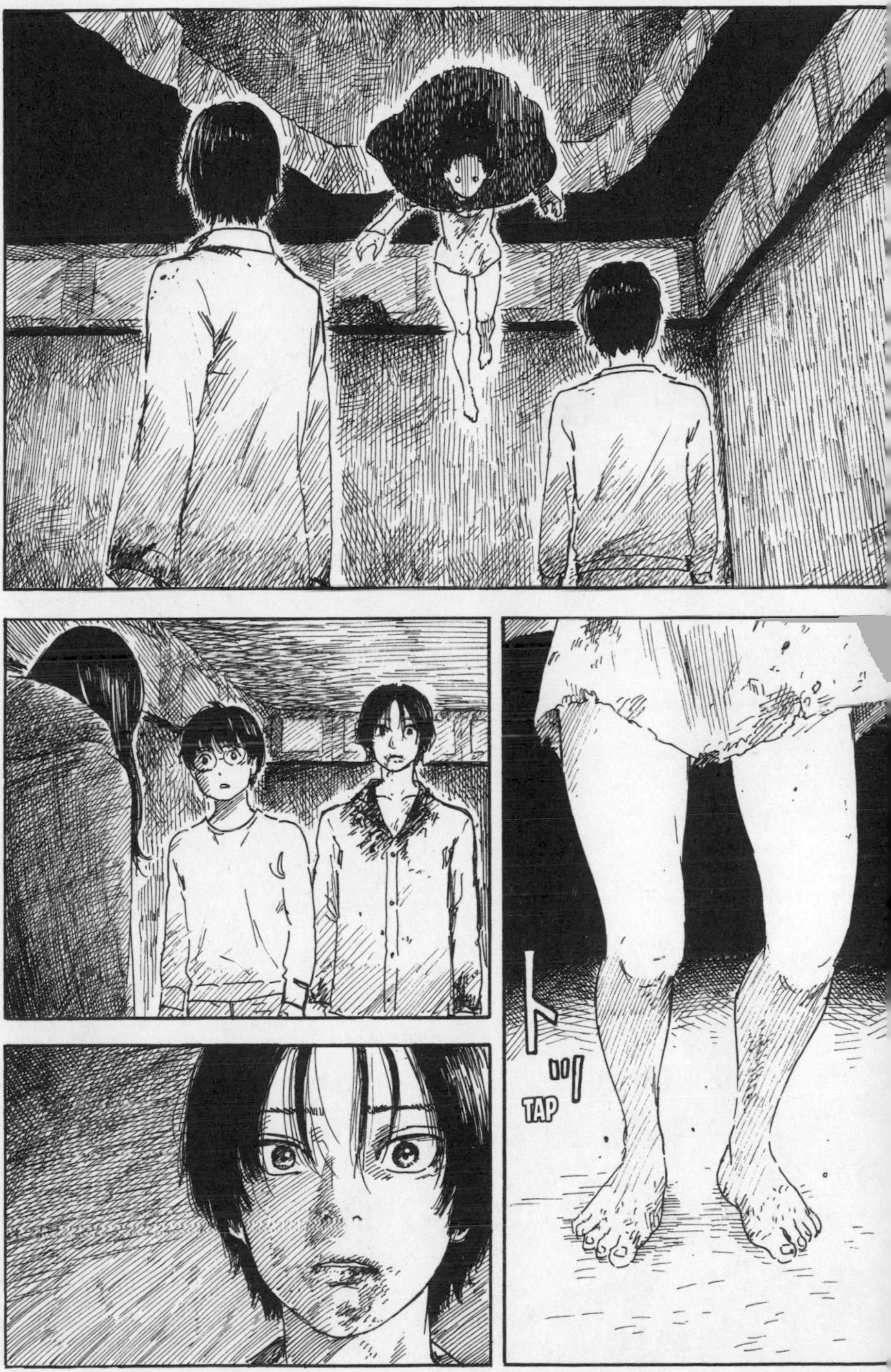
トッ
TAP

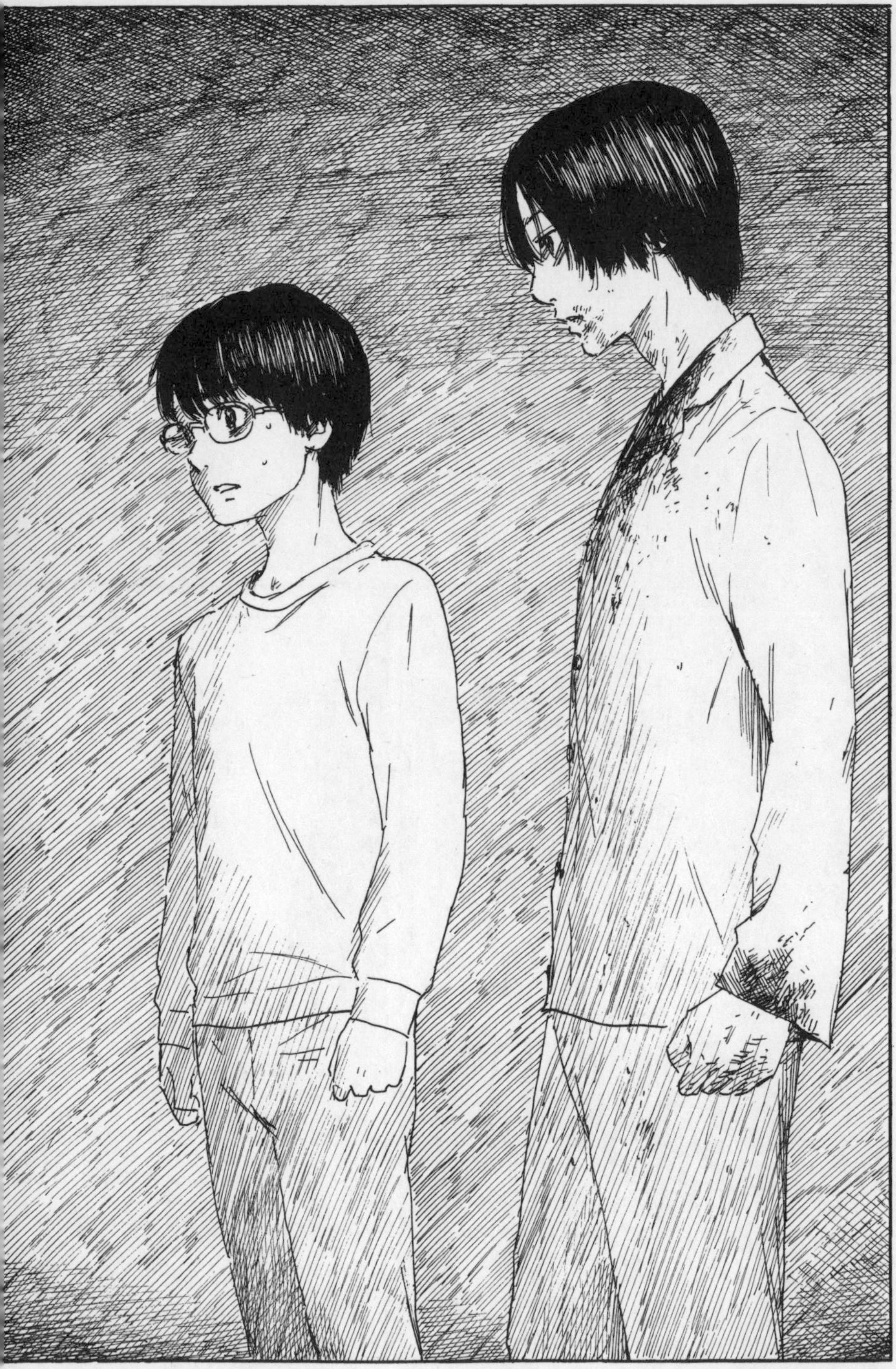

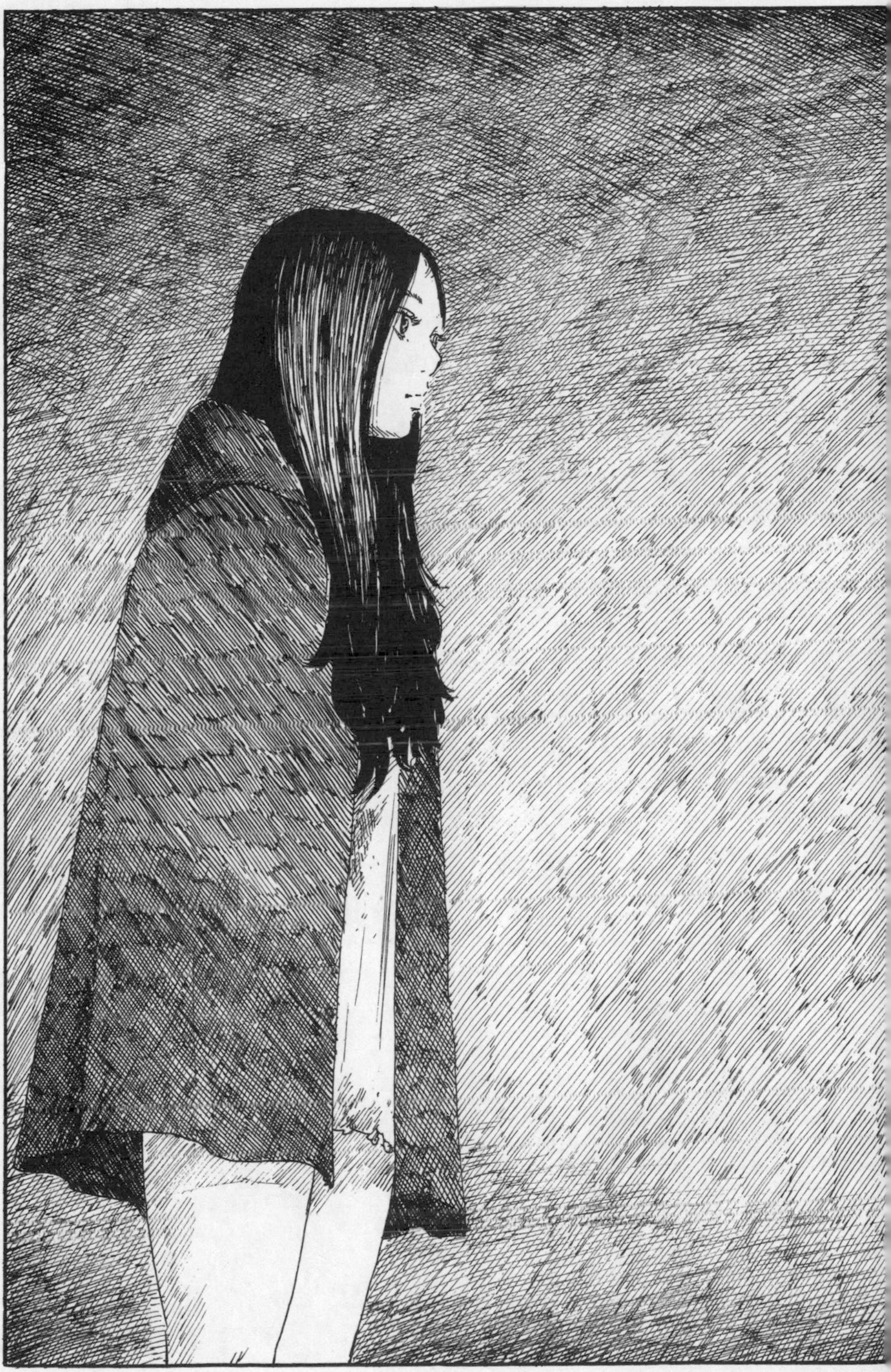

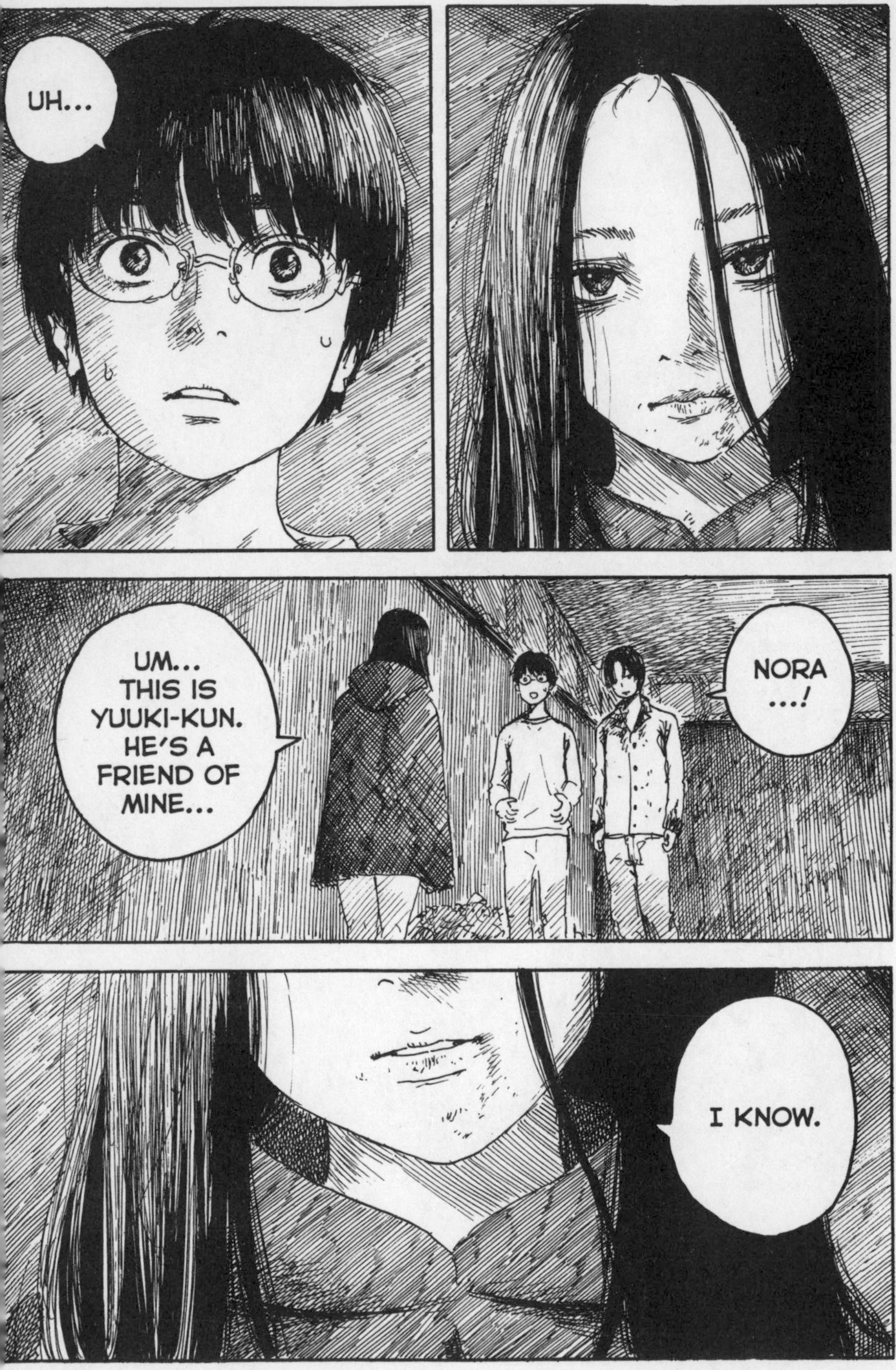
UH...
NORA ...!
UM... THIS IS YUUKI-KUN. HE'S A FRIEND OF MINE...
I KNOW.

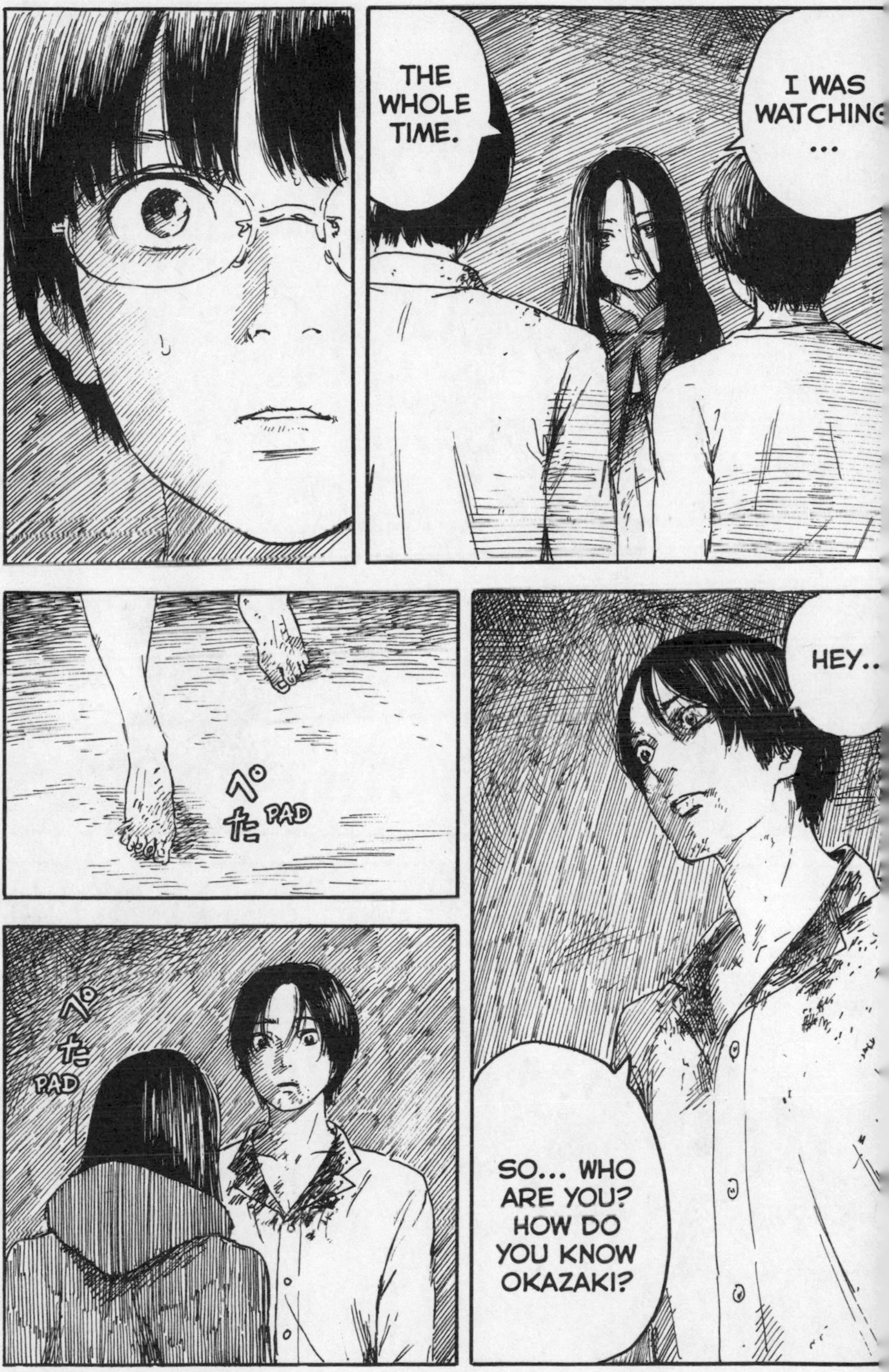
I WAS WATCHING ...
THE WHOLE TIME.
HEY...
SO... WHO ARE YOU? HOW DO YOU KNOW OKAZAKI?
ぺた PAD
ぺた PAD

SNIF ...
SNIFF SNIFF
SNF
SNF ...
...WHAT THE HELL ARE YOU DOING?!
WE NEED TO GET OUT OF HERE, NOW!

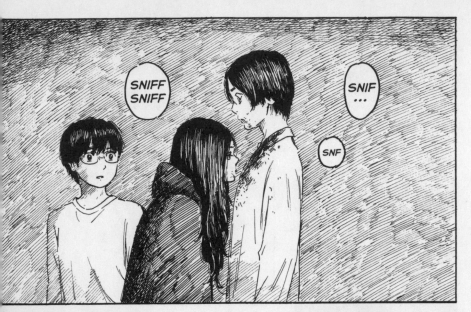

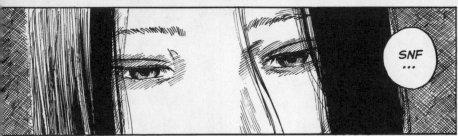

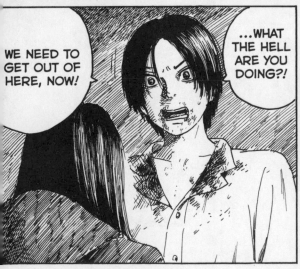

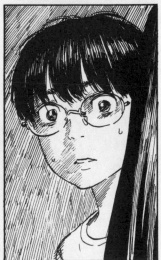

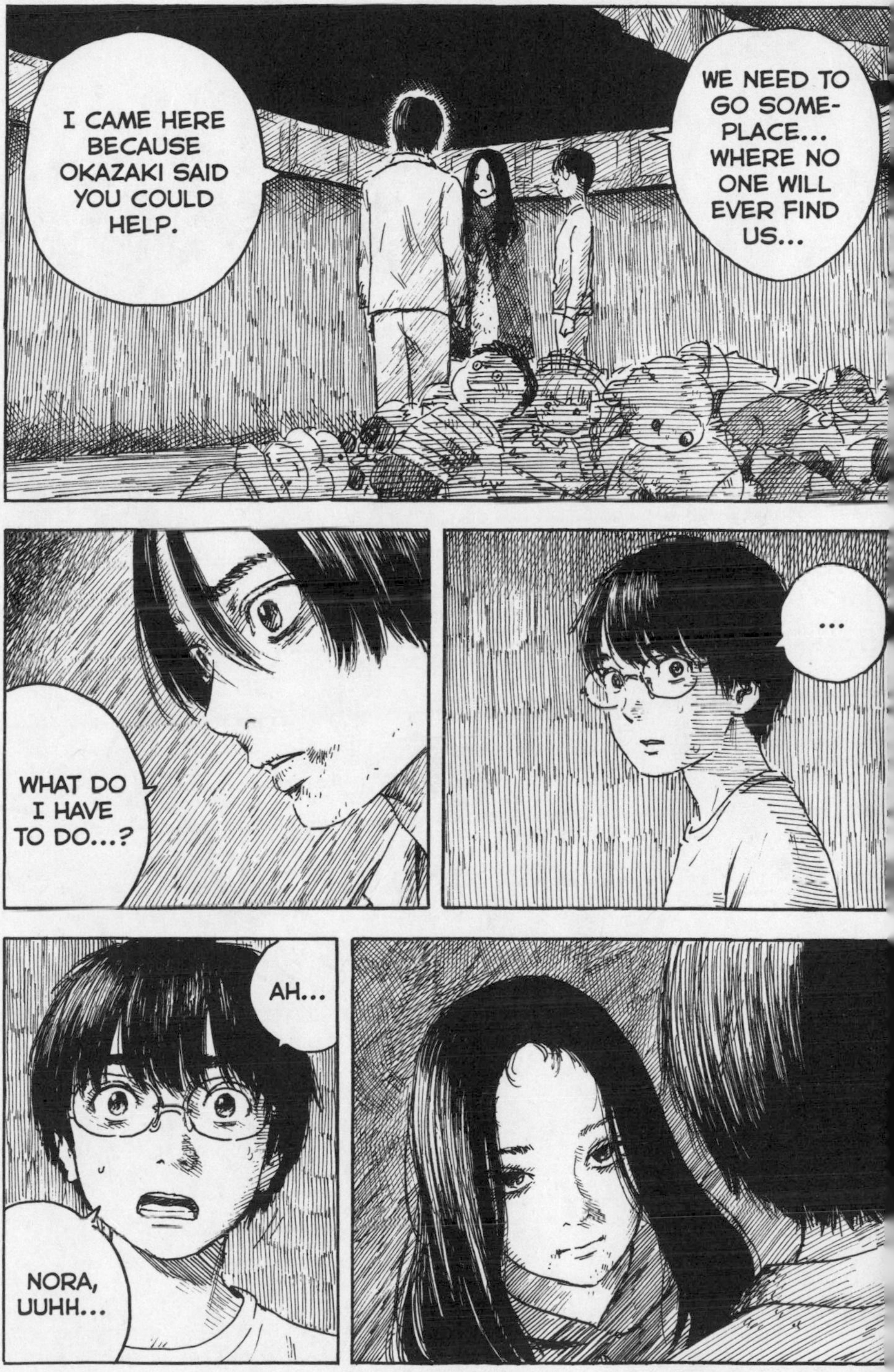
WE NEED TO GO SOME-PLACE... WHERE NO ONE WILL EVER FIND US...
I CAME HERE BECAUSE OKAZAKI SAID YOU COULD HELP.
...
WHAT DO I HAVE TO DO...?
AH...
NORA, UUHH...

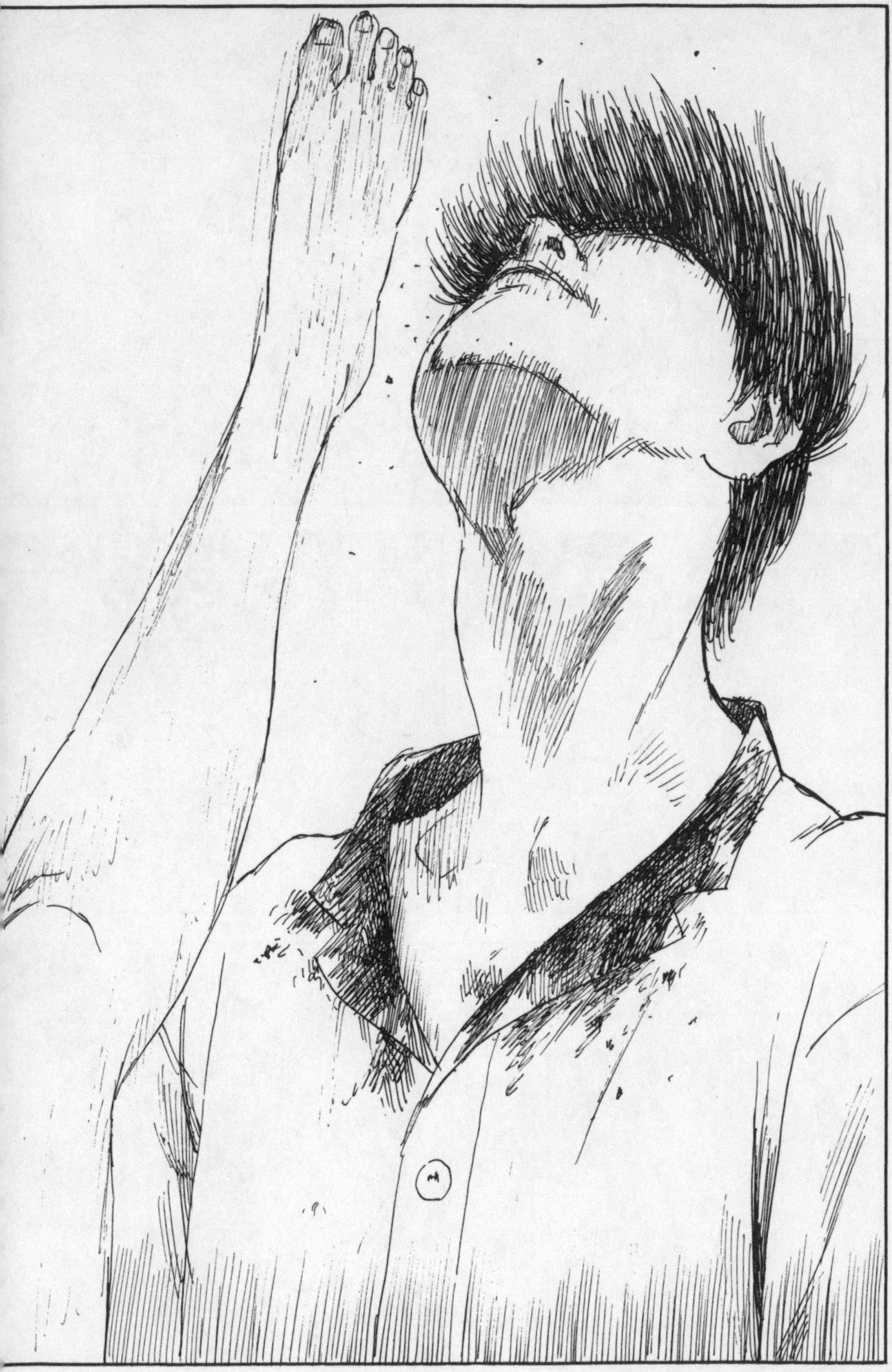

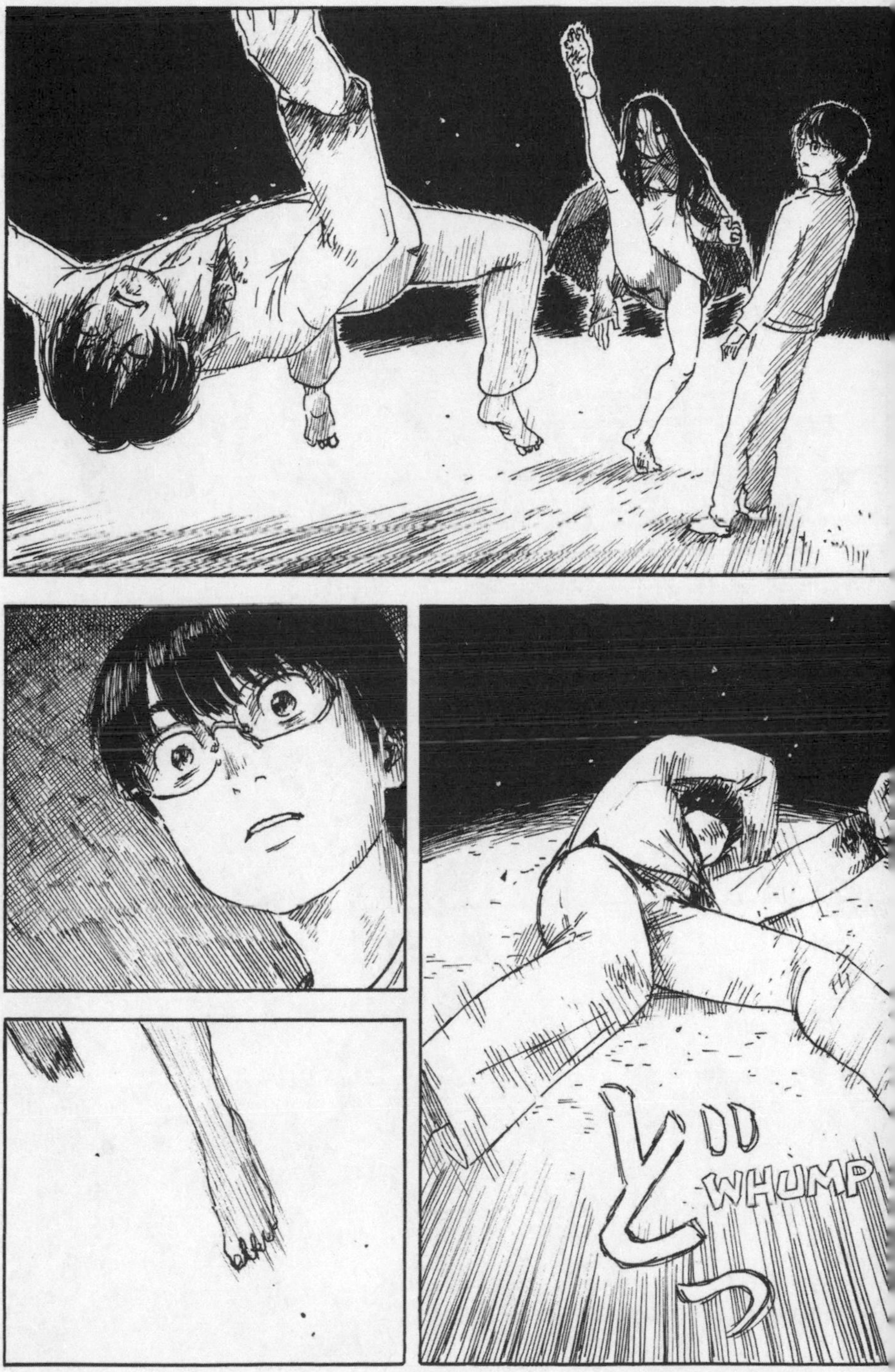
どっ
WHUMP

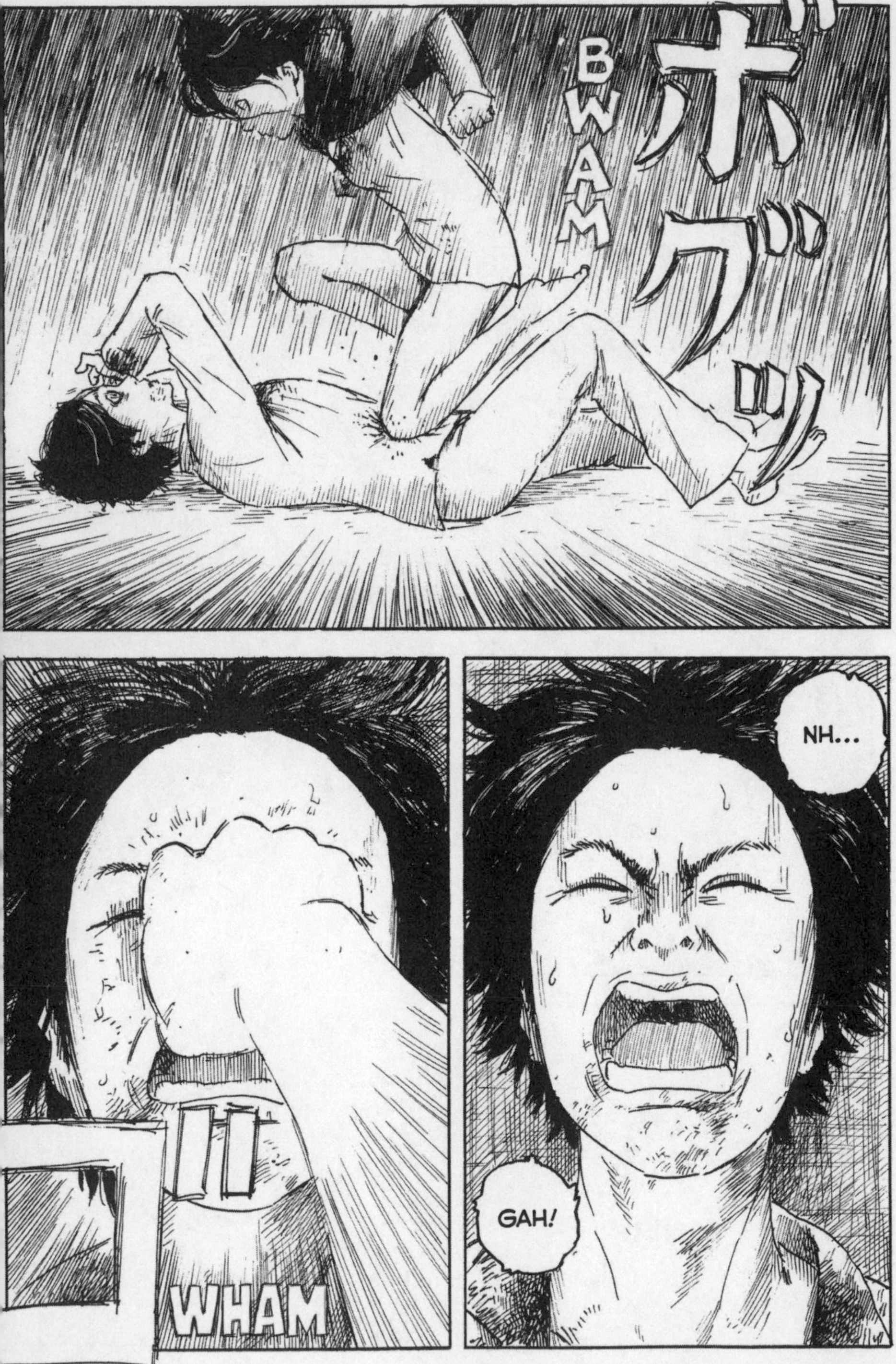

ボグッ
BWAM
NH...
GAH!
WHAM

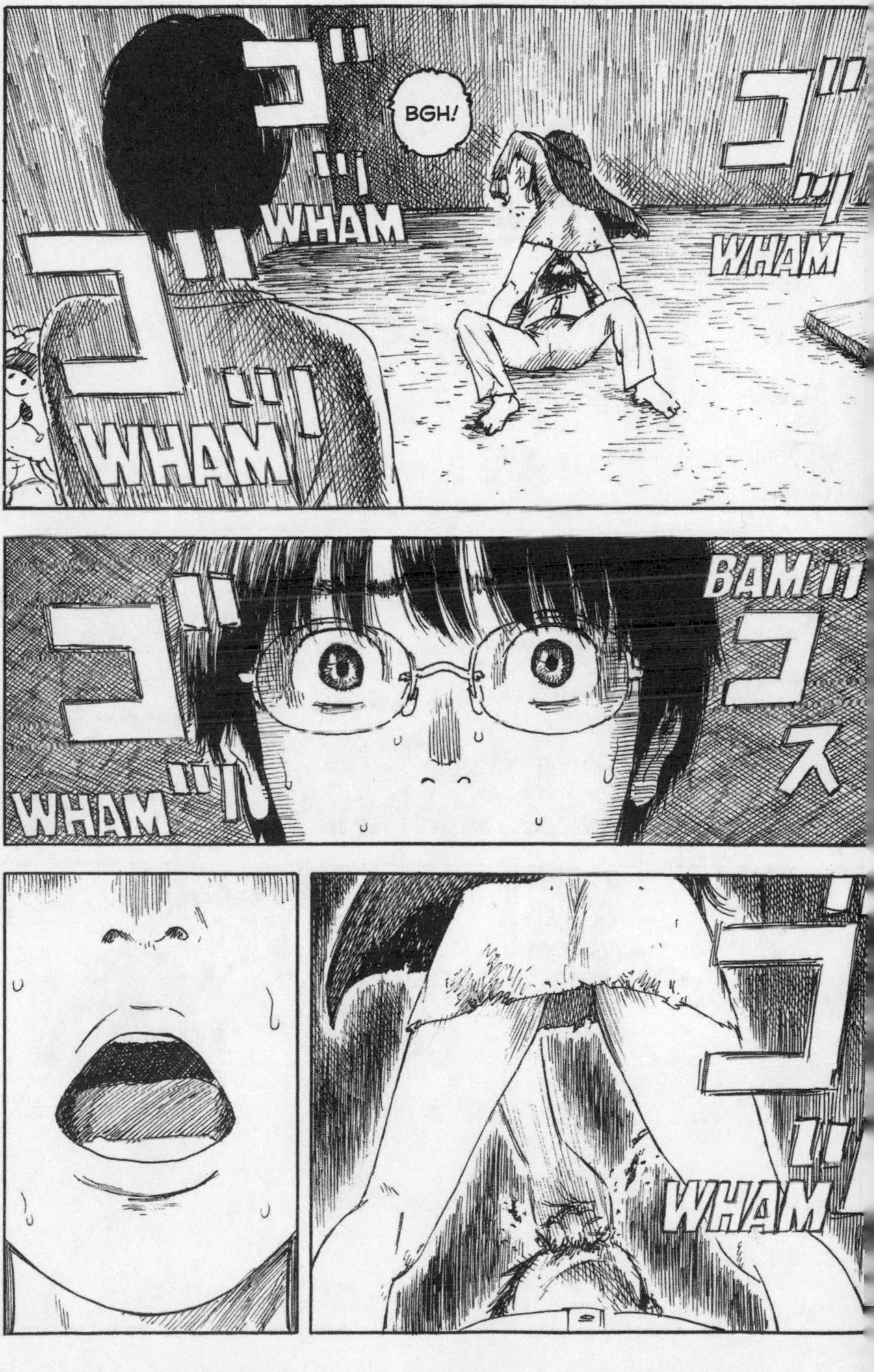
WHAM
BGH!
WHAM
WHAM
BAM!!
WHAM
WHAM

NORA!!
STOP!!
UGH ...
MAKOTO.

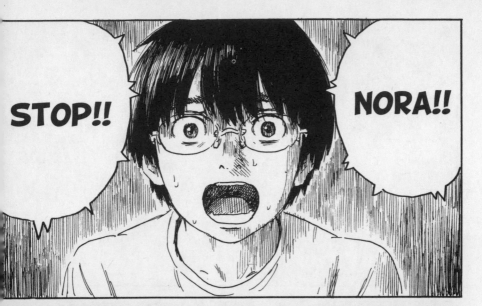

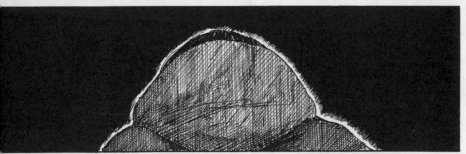

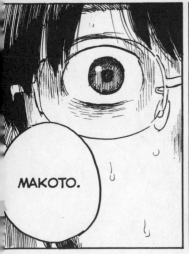

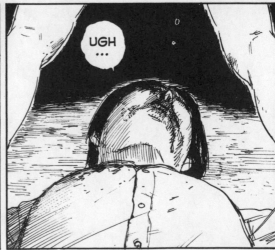

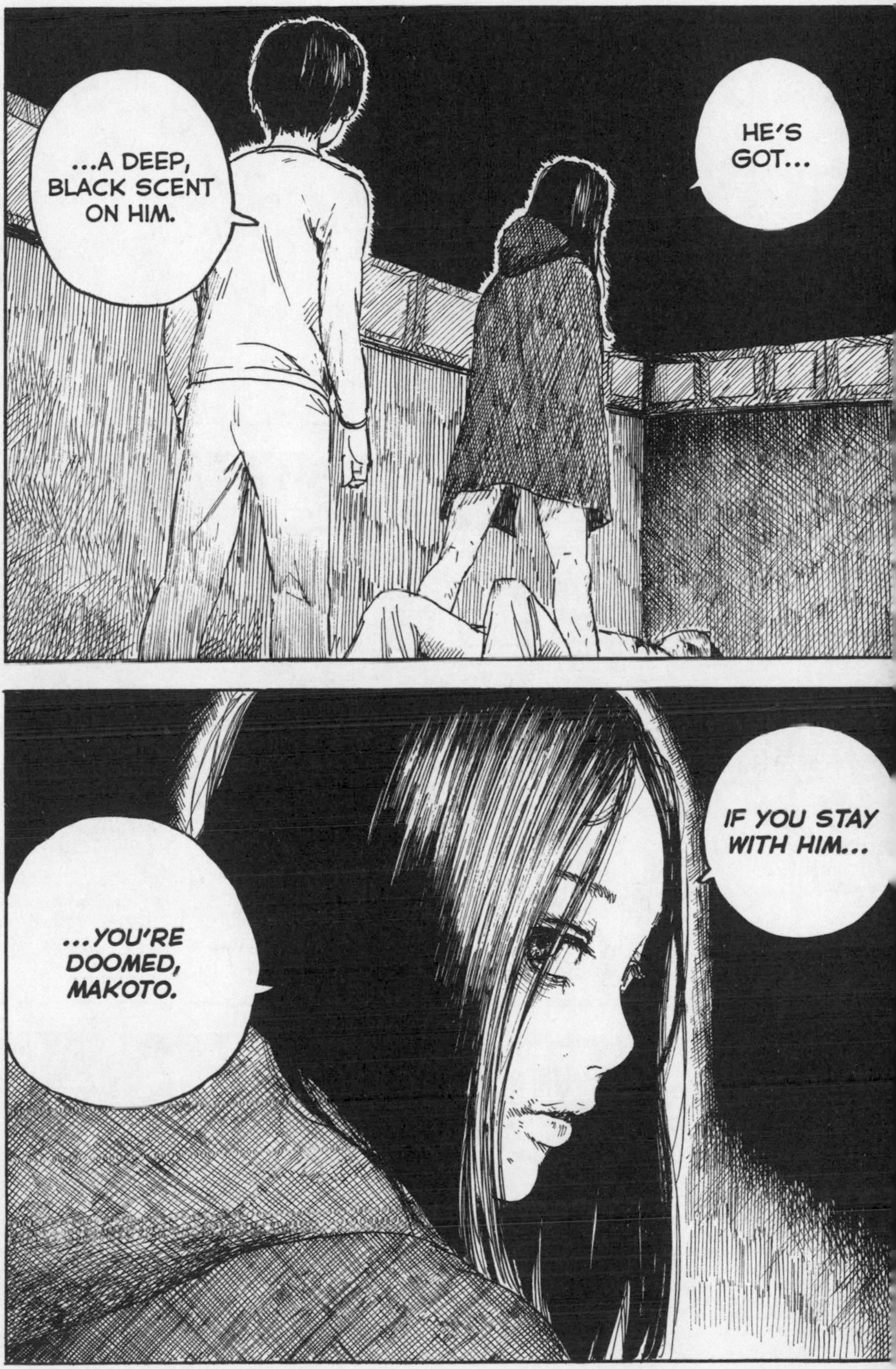
HE'S GOT...
...A DEEP, BLACK SCENT ON HIM.
IF YOU STAY WITH HIM...
...YOU'RE DOOMED, MAKOTO.

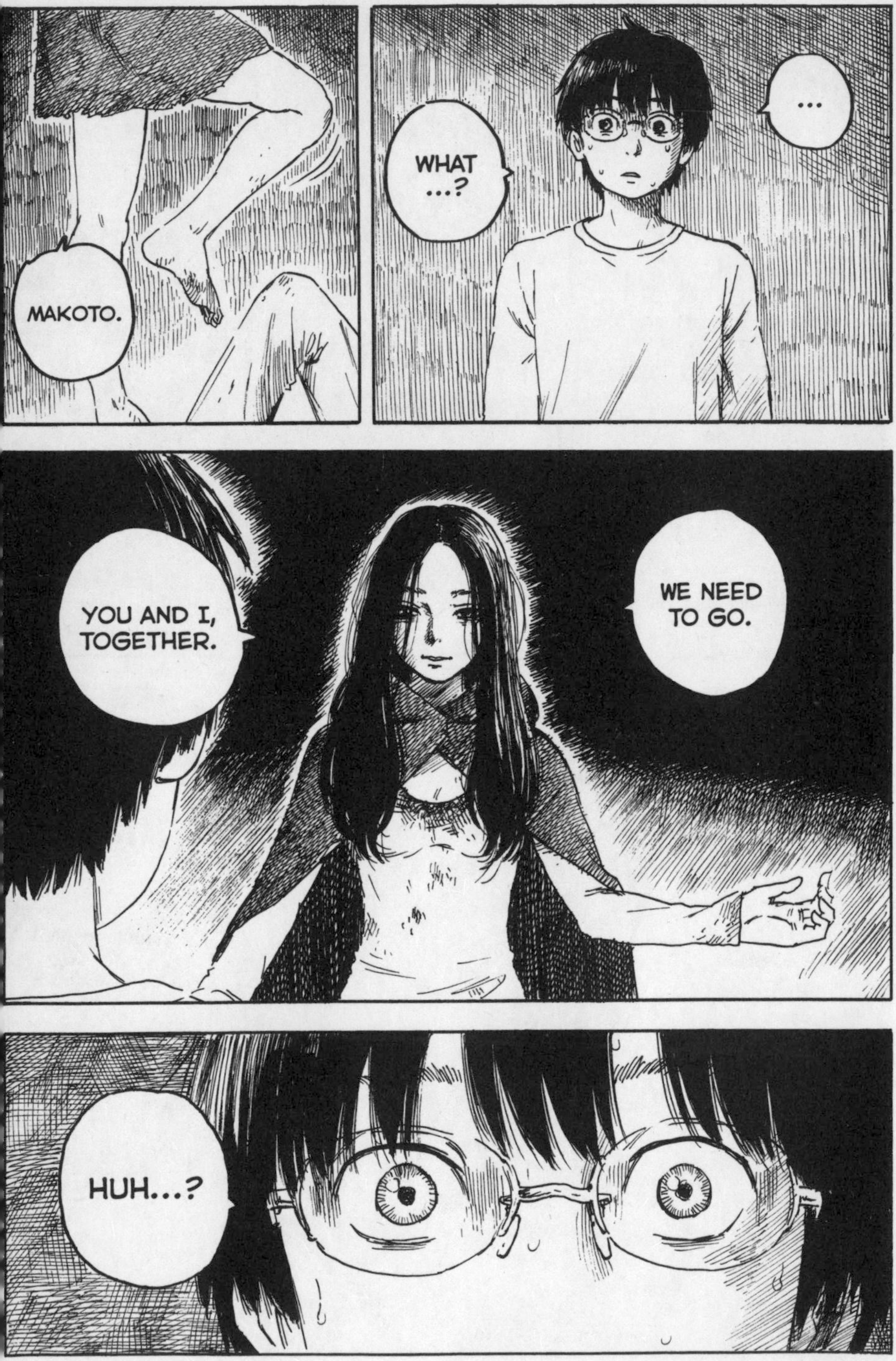
...
WHAT ...?
MAKOTO.
WE NEED TO GO.
YOU AND I, TOGETHER.
HUH...?

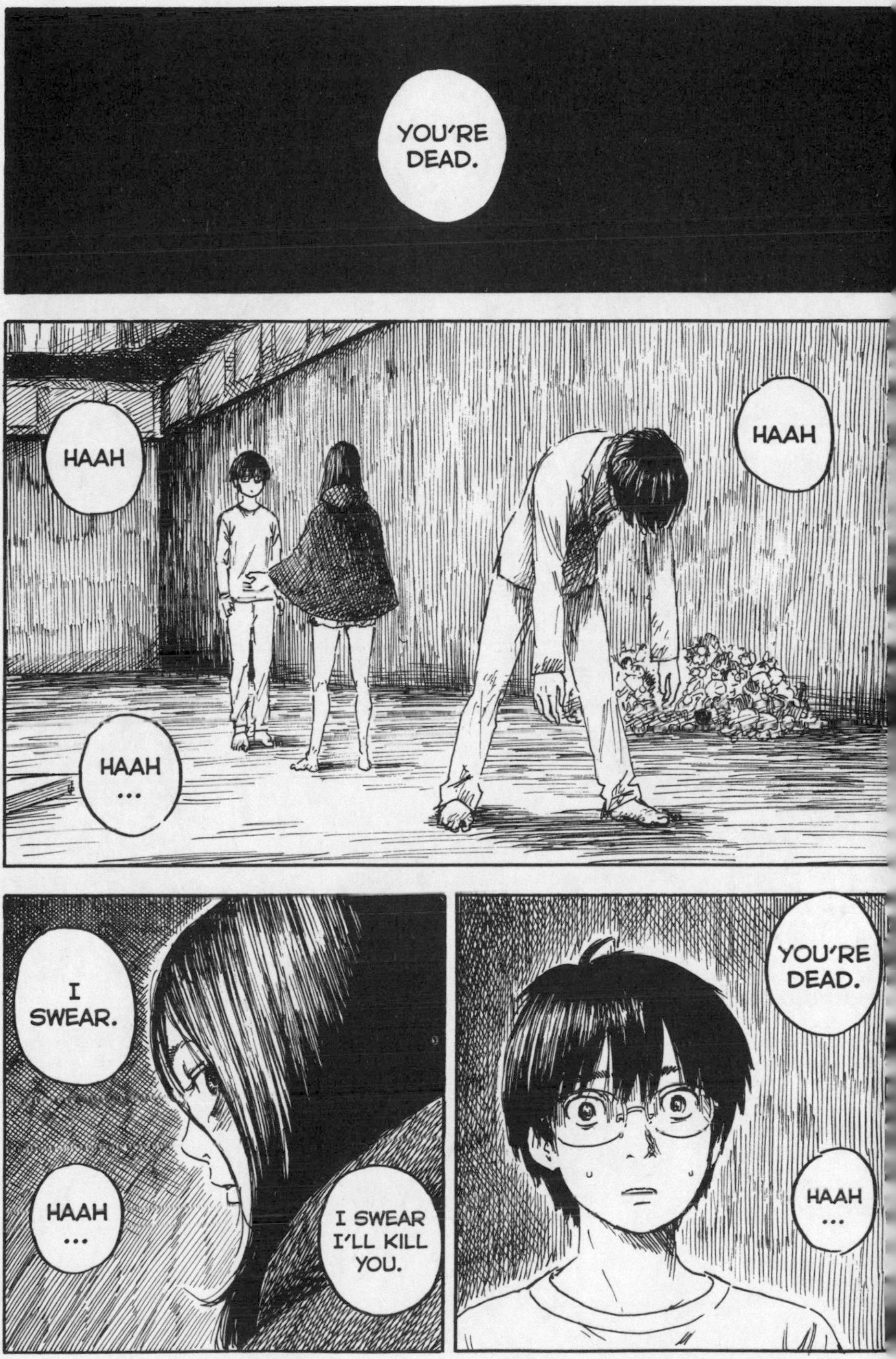

YOU'RE DEAD.
HAAH
HAAH
HAAH ...
YOU'RE DEAD.
HAAH ...
I SWEAR.
I SWEAR I'LL KILL YOU.
HAAH ...

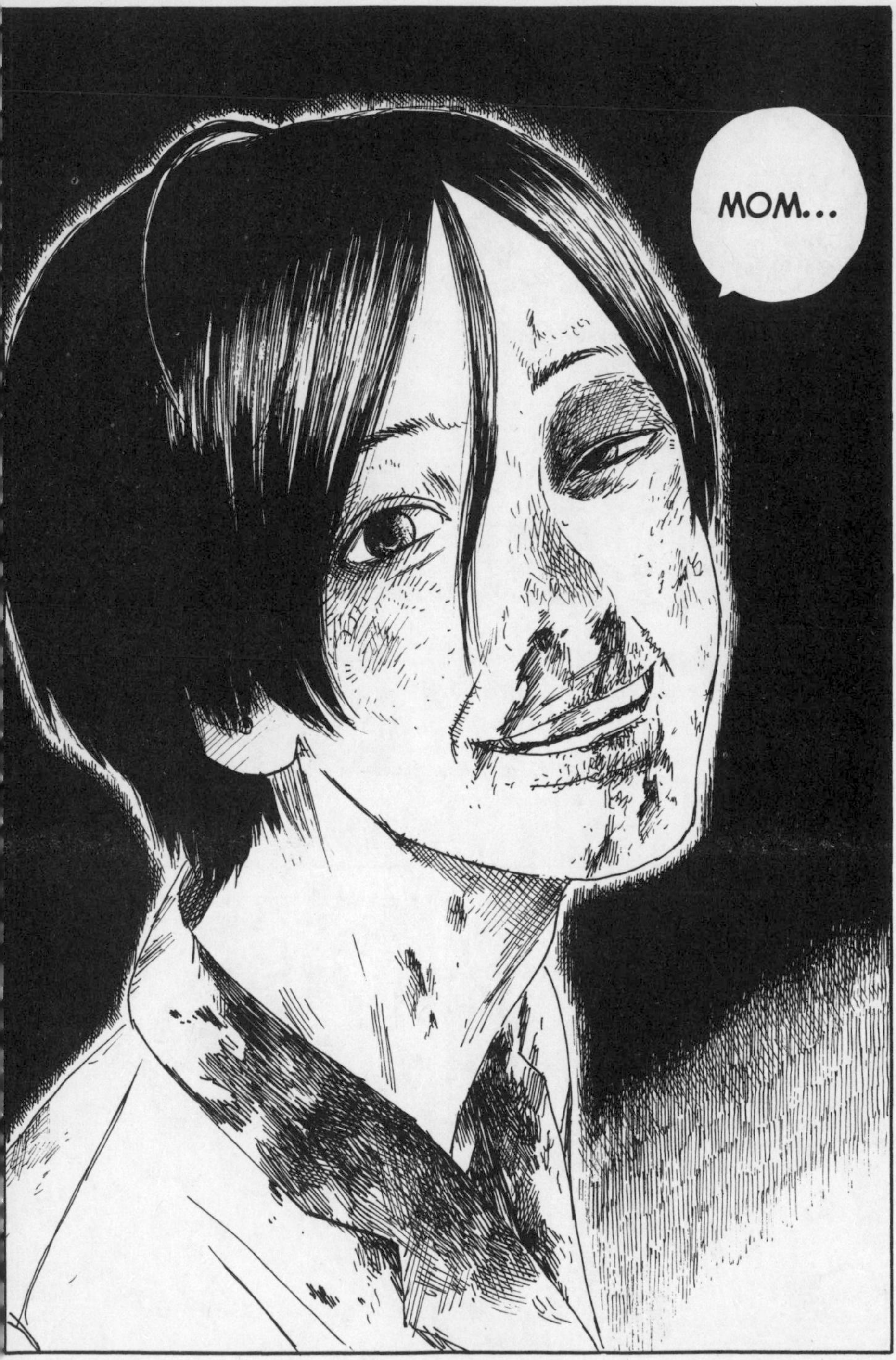
MOM...

びくっ
TWITCH

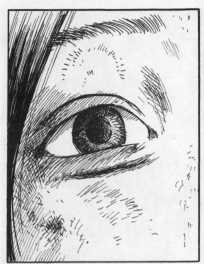

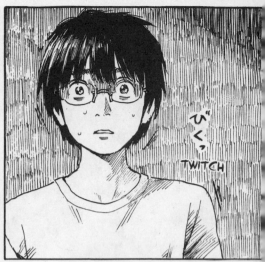

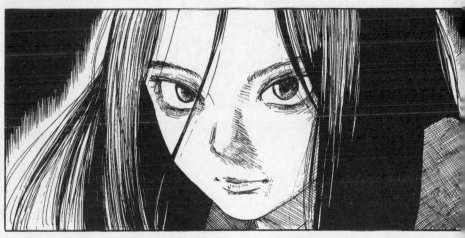

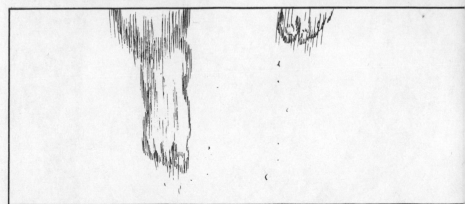

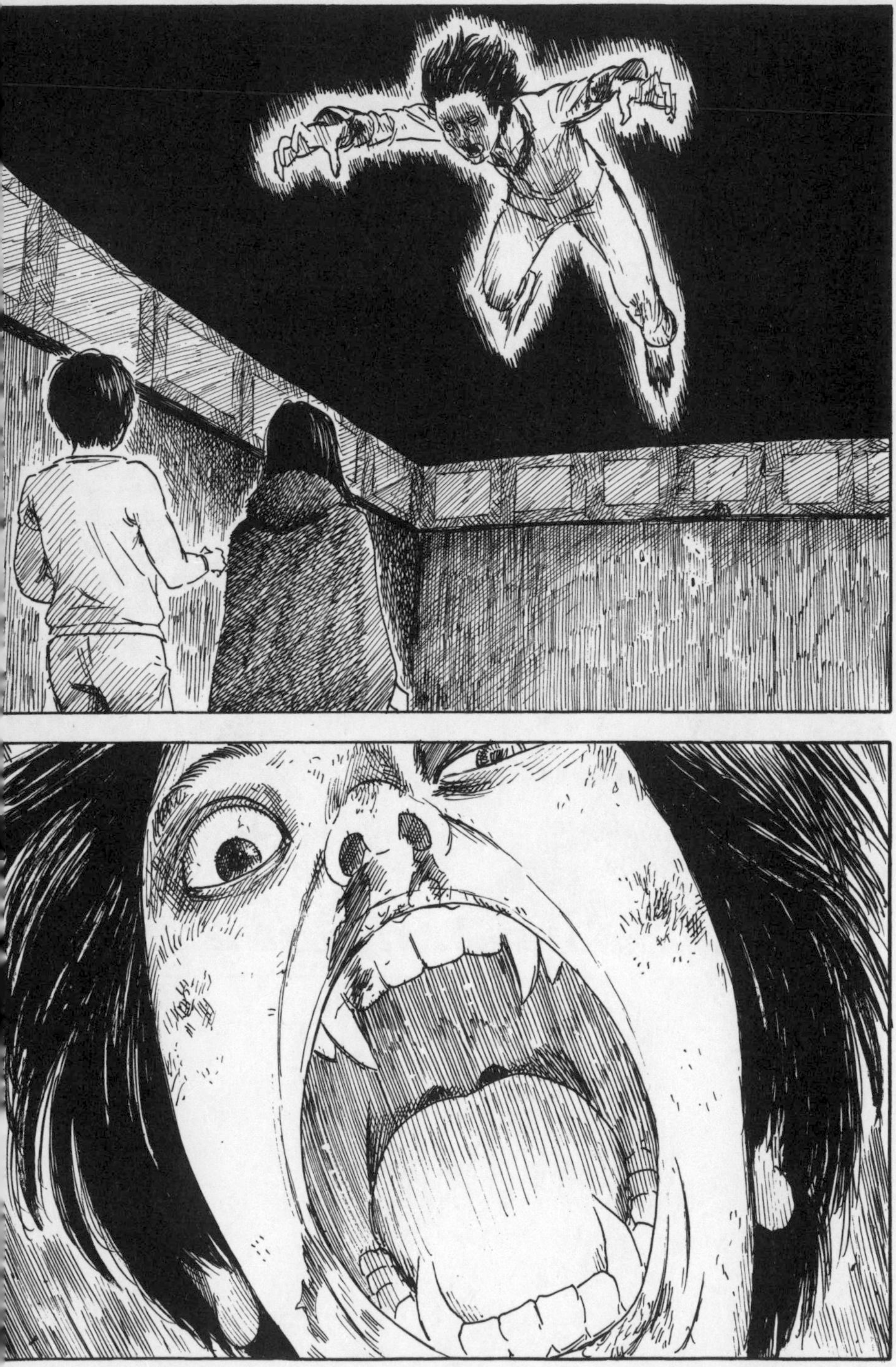

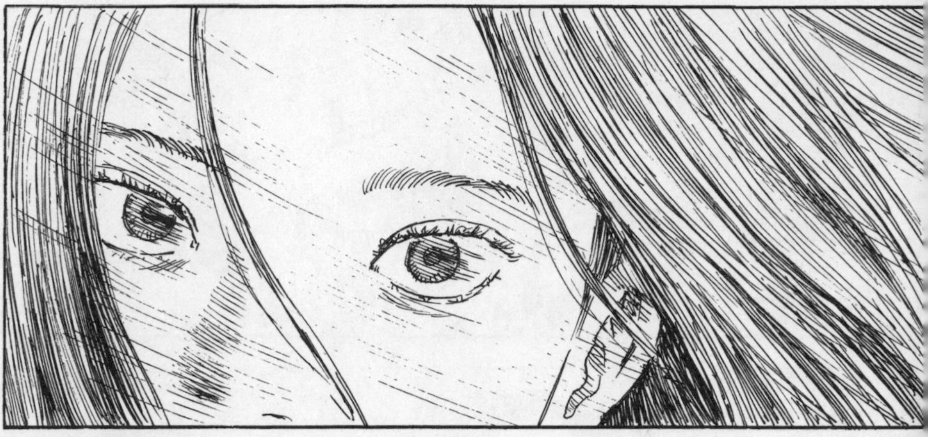
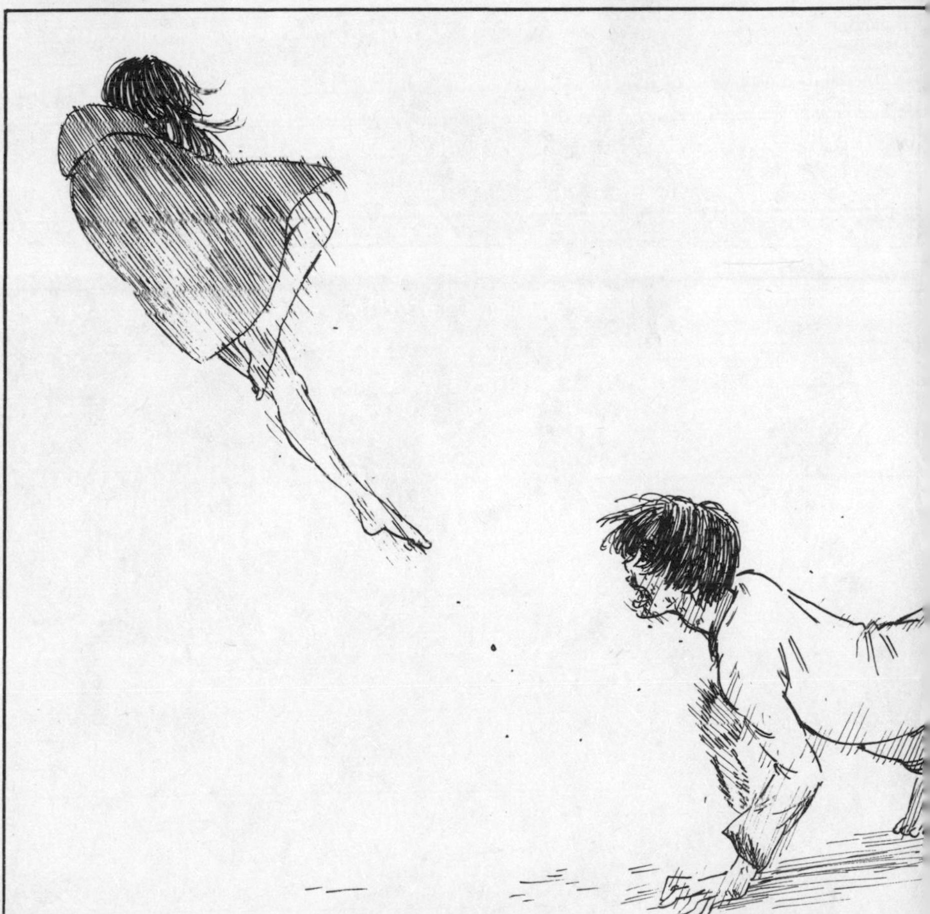

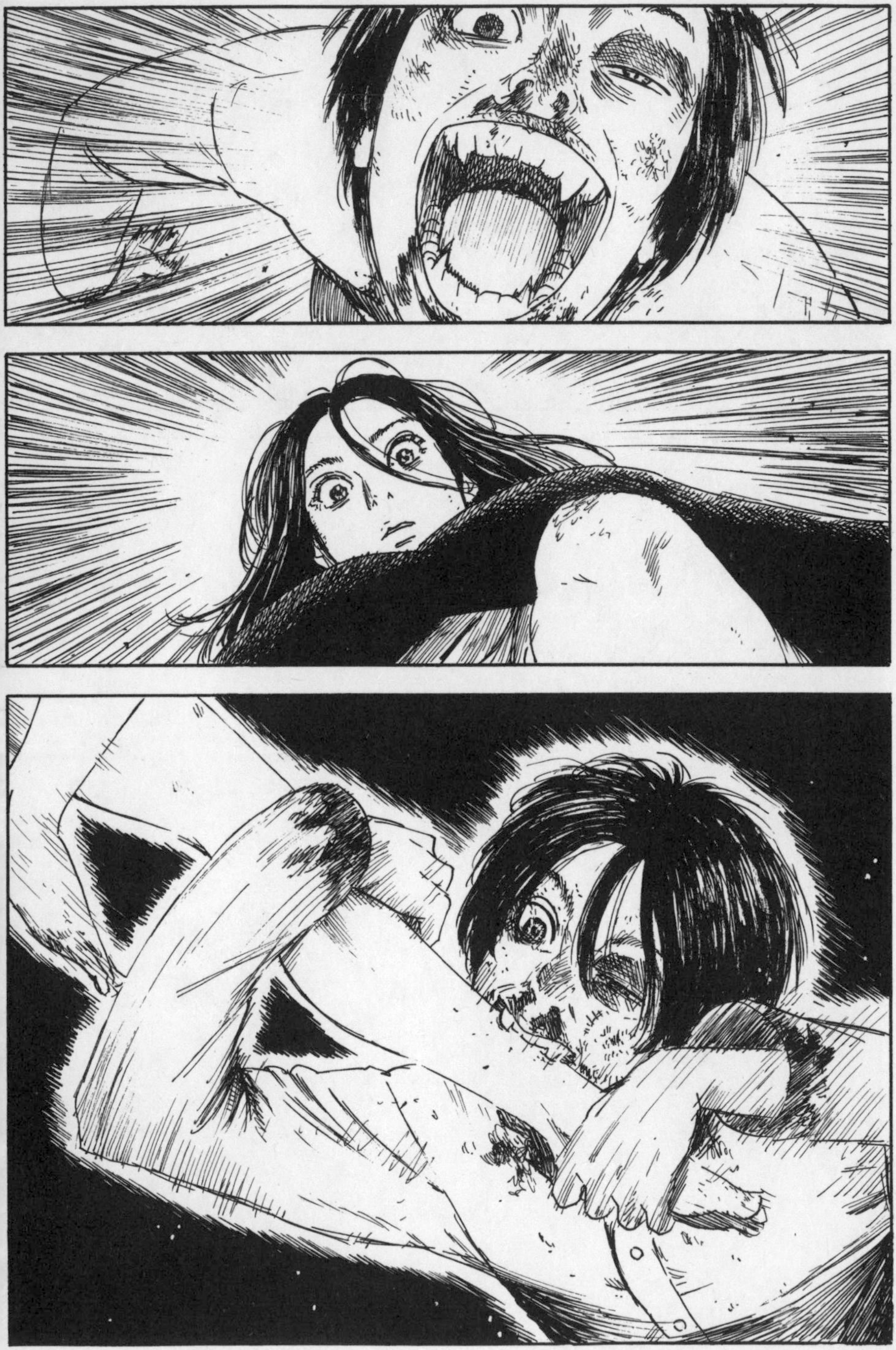

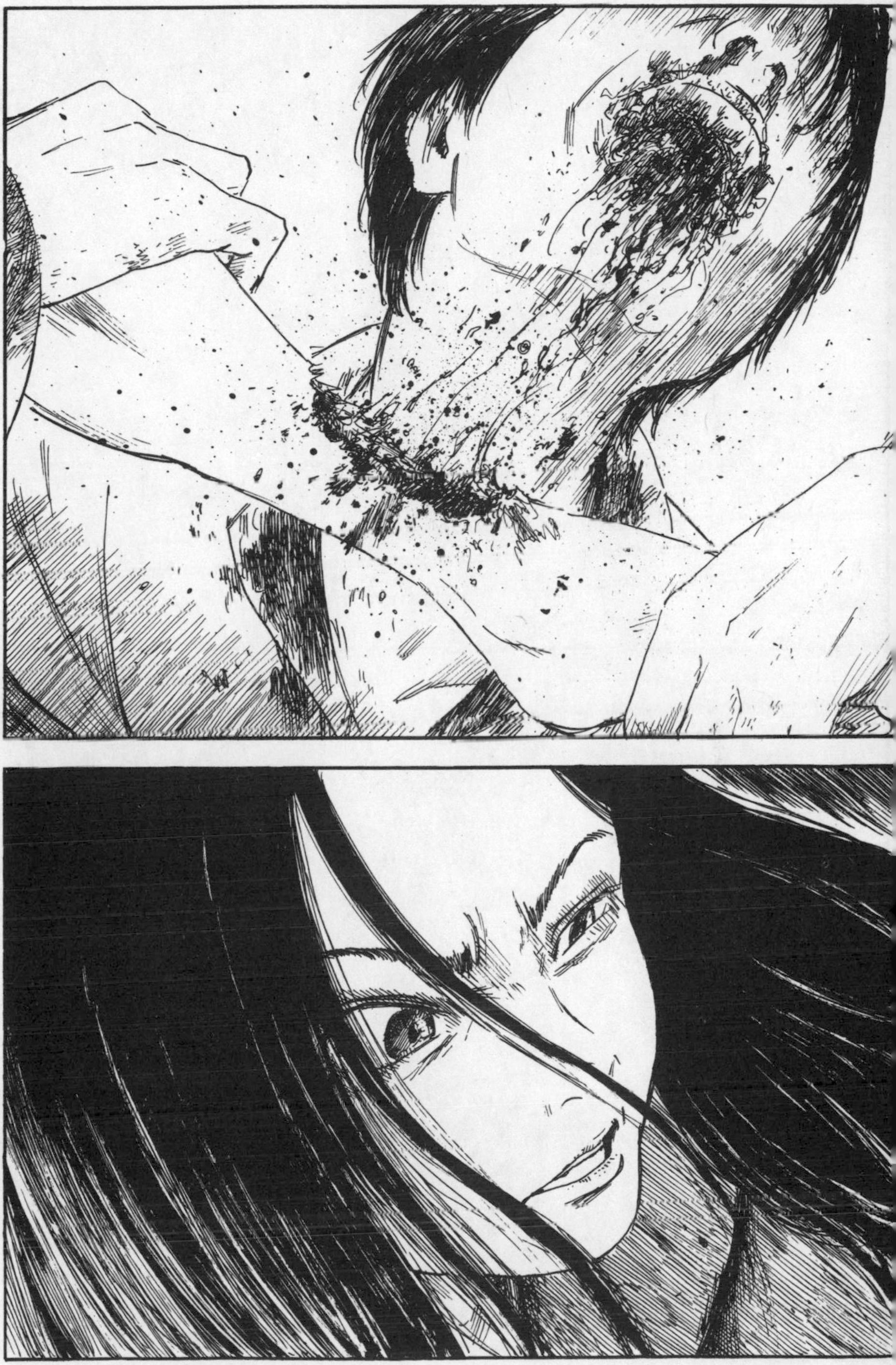

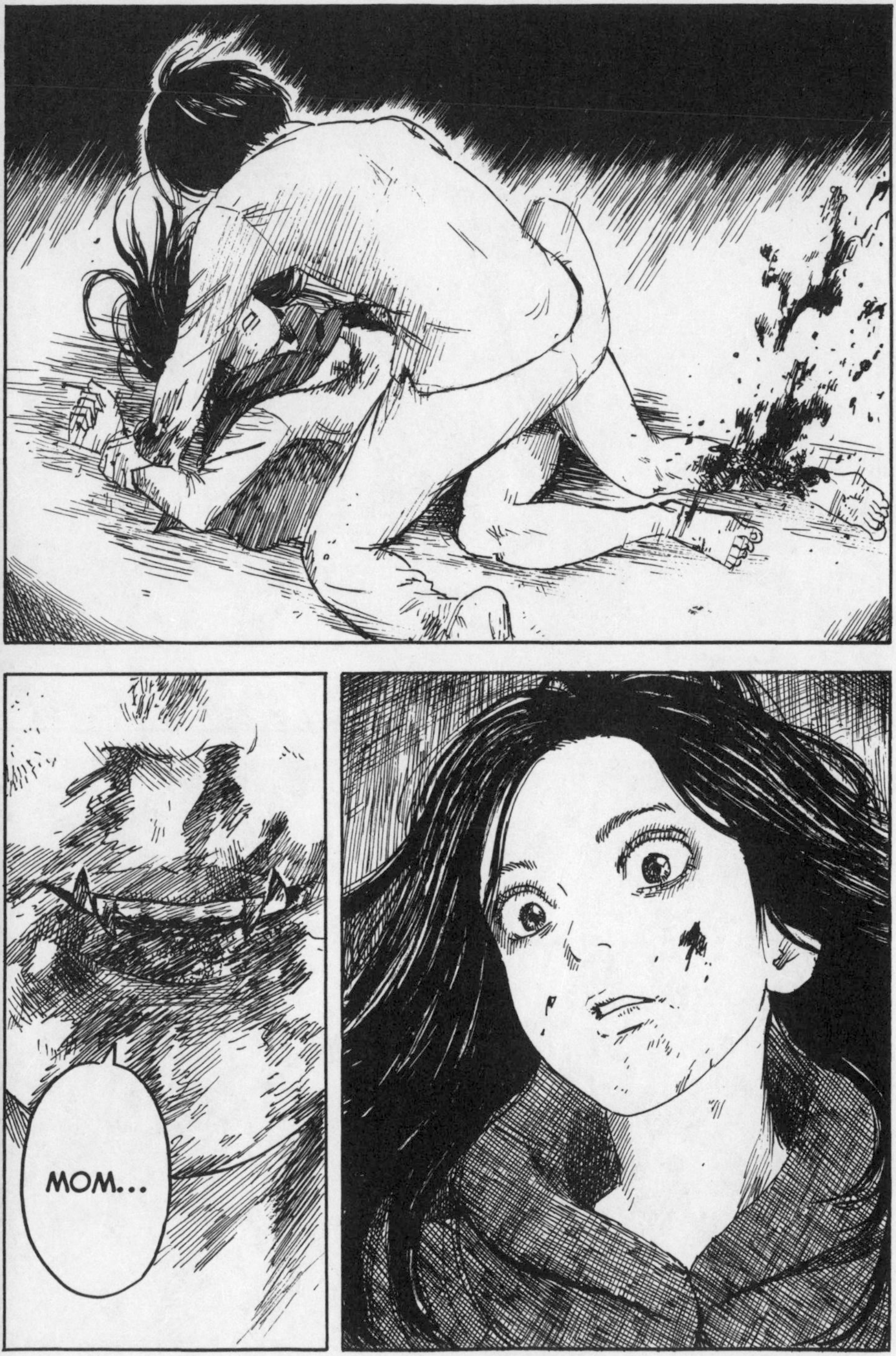
MOM...

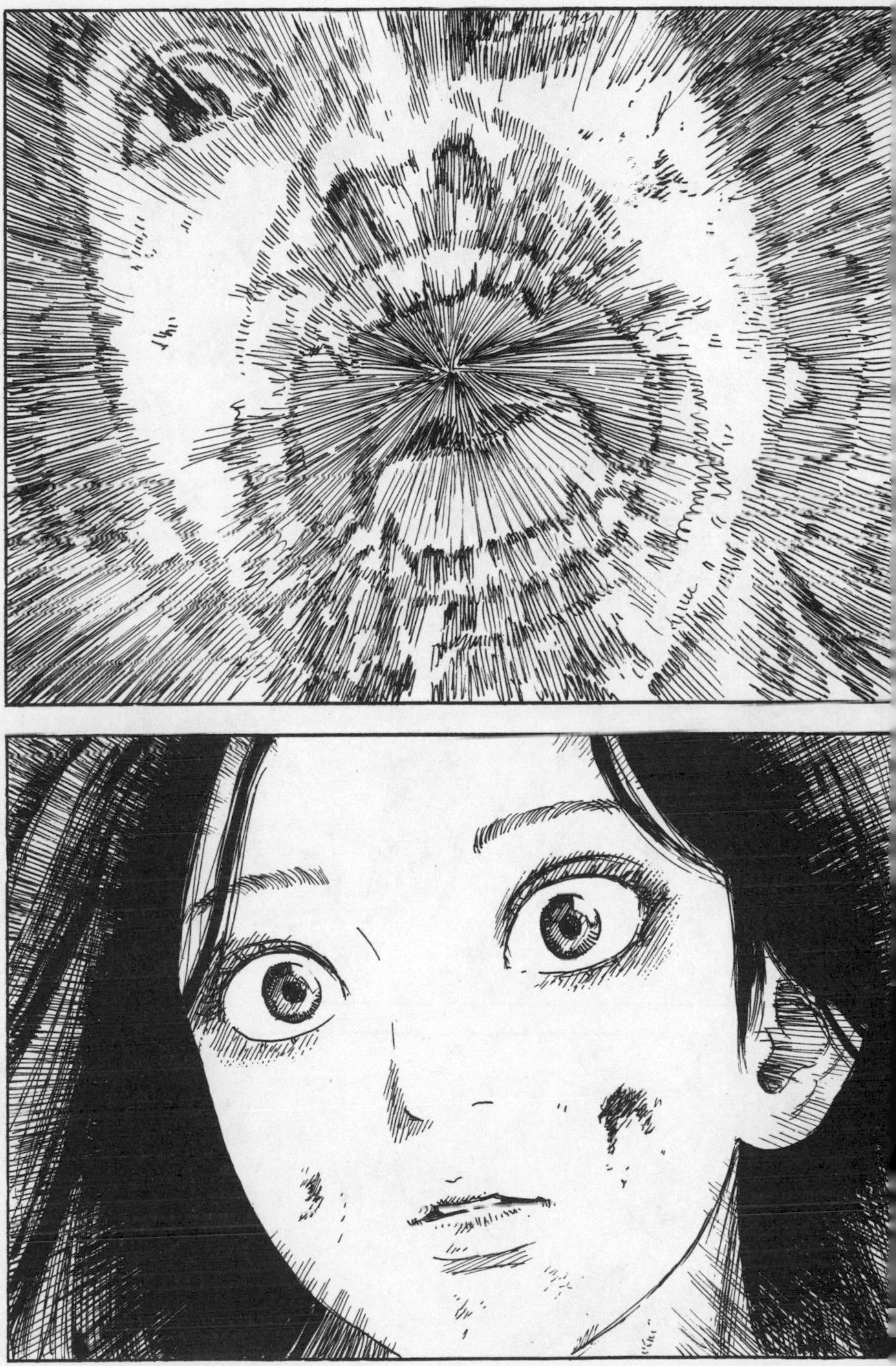

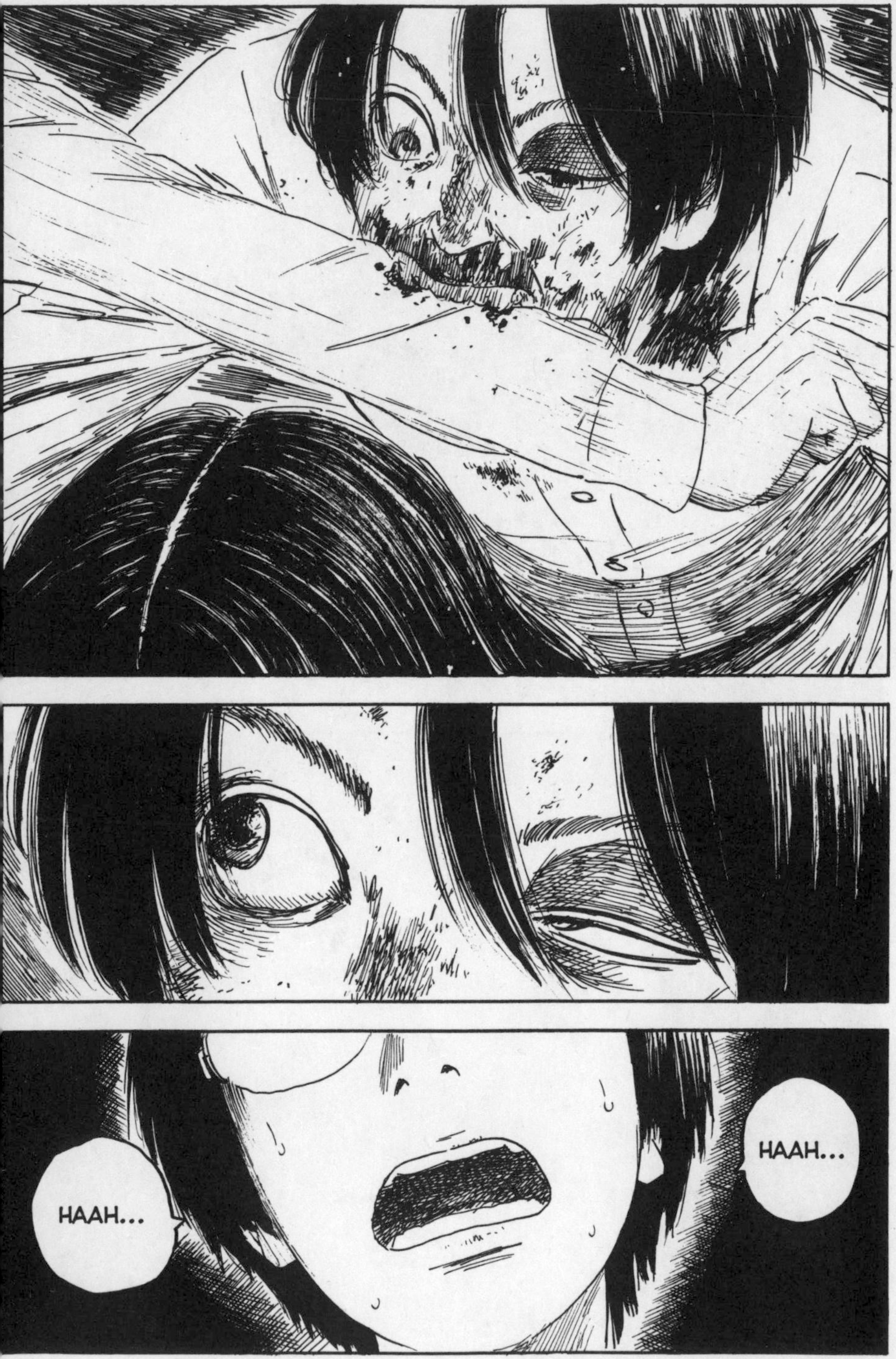
HAAH...
HAAH...

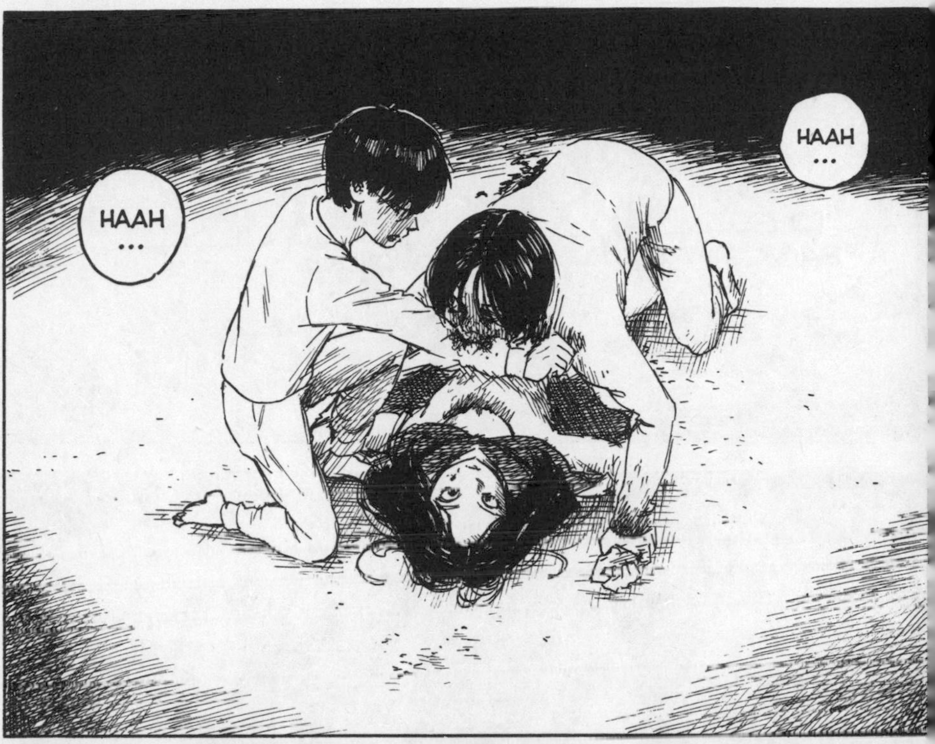
HAAH ...
HAAH ...

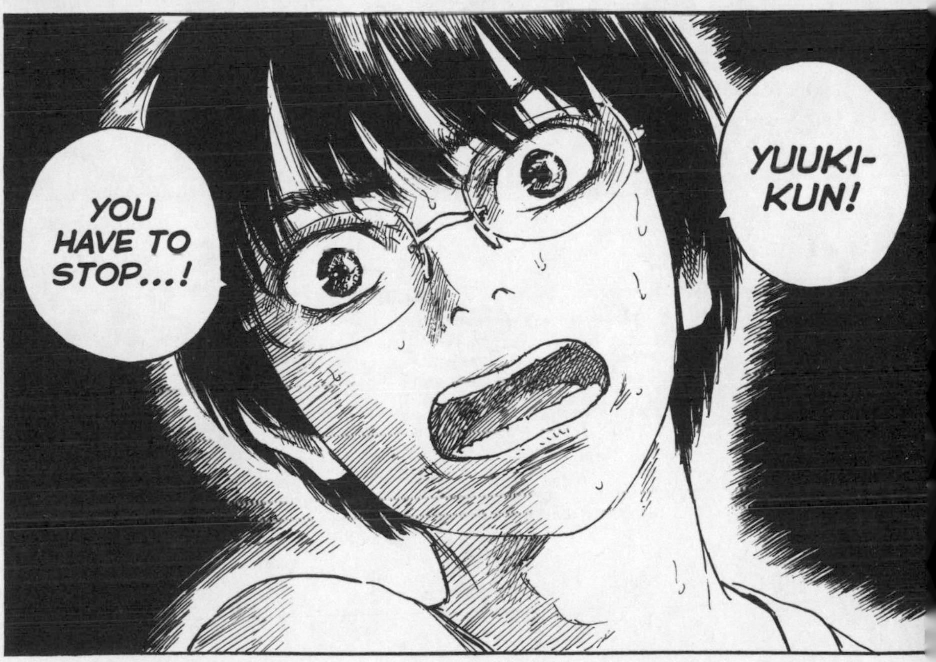
YUUKI-KUN!
YOU HAVE TO STOP...!

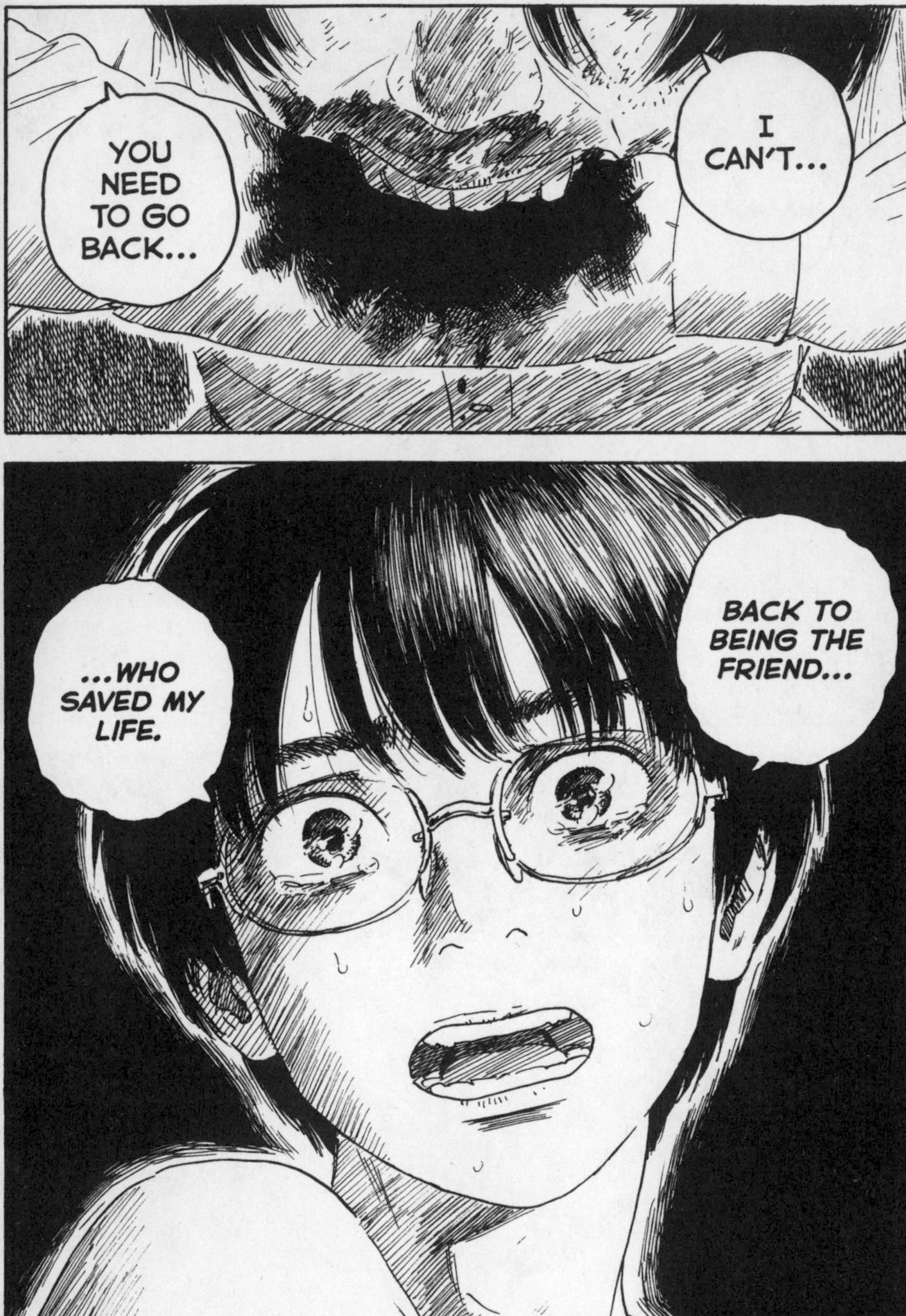
I CAN'T...
YOU NEED TO GO BACK...
BACK TO BEING THE FRIEND...
...WHO SAVED MY LIFE.

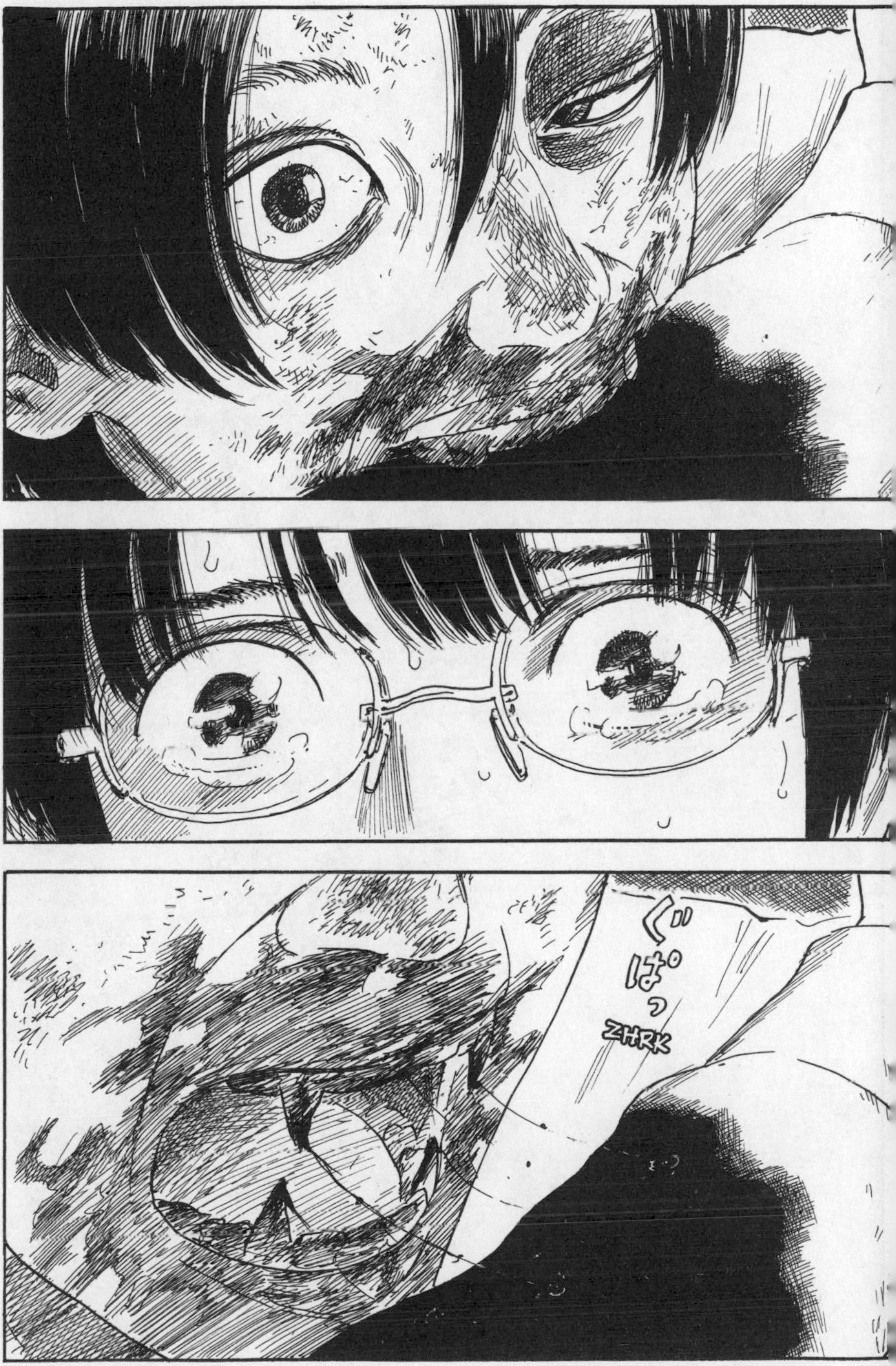
ぐぱっ
ZHRK

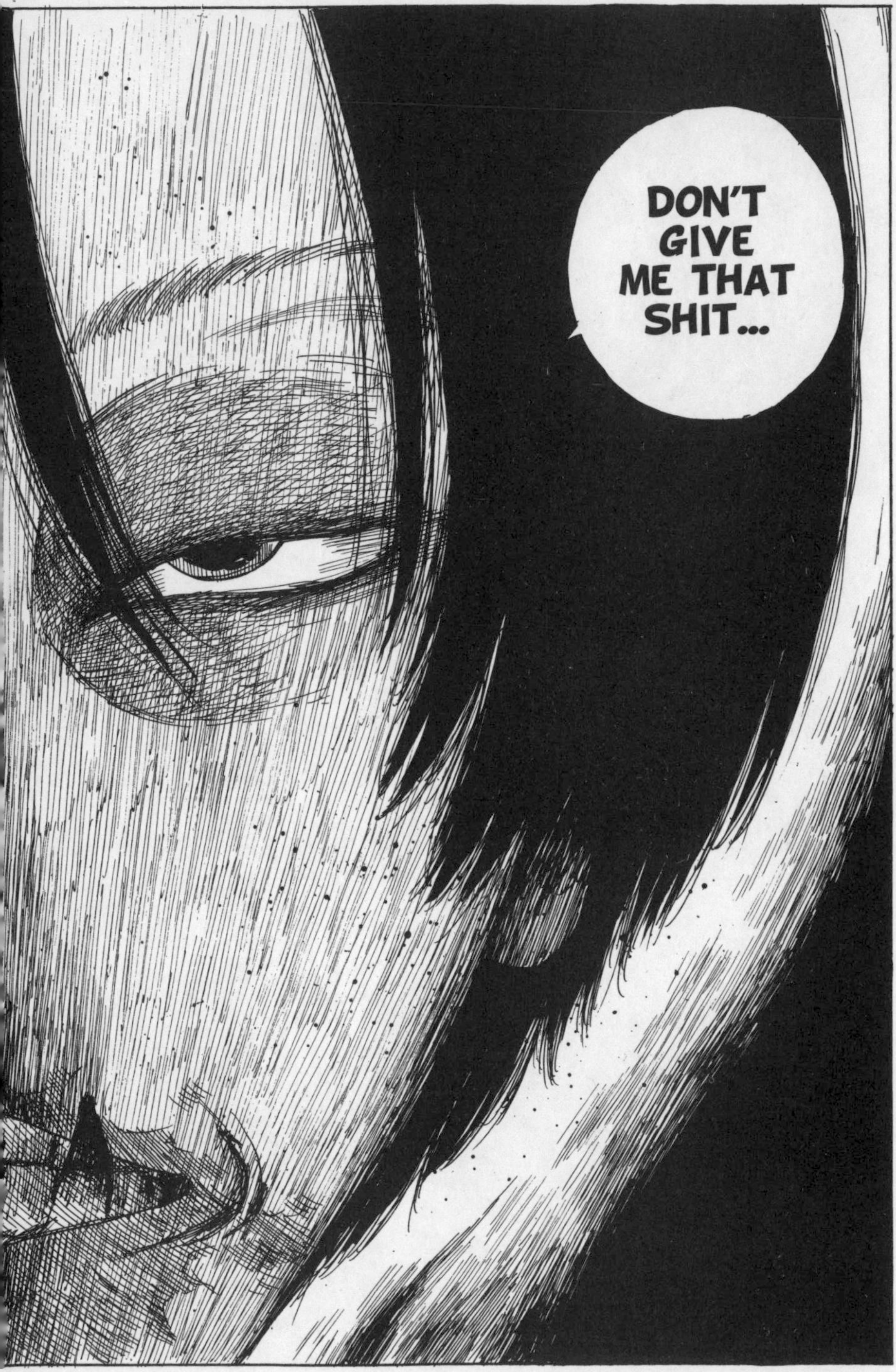
DON'T GIVE ME THAT SHIT...

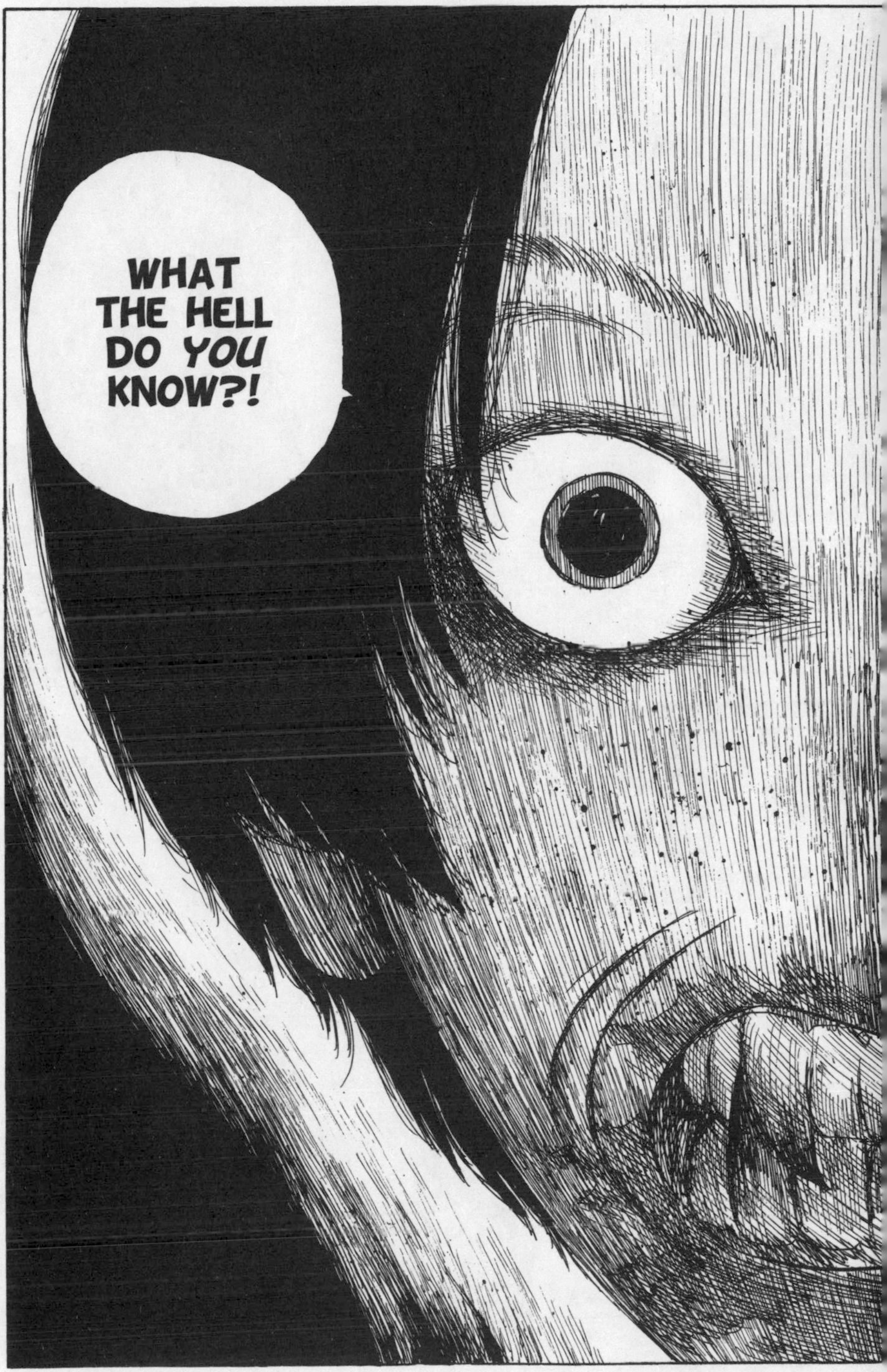
WHAT THE HELL DO YOU KNOW?!

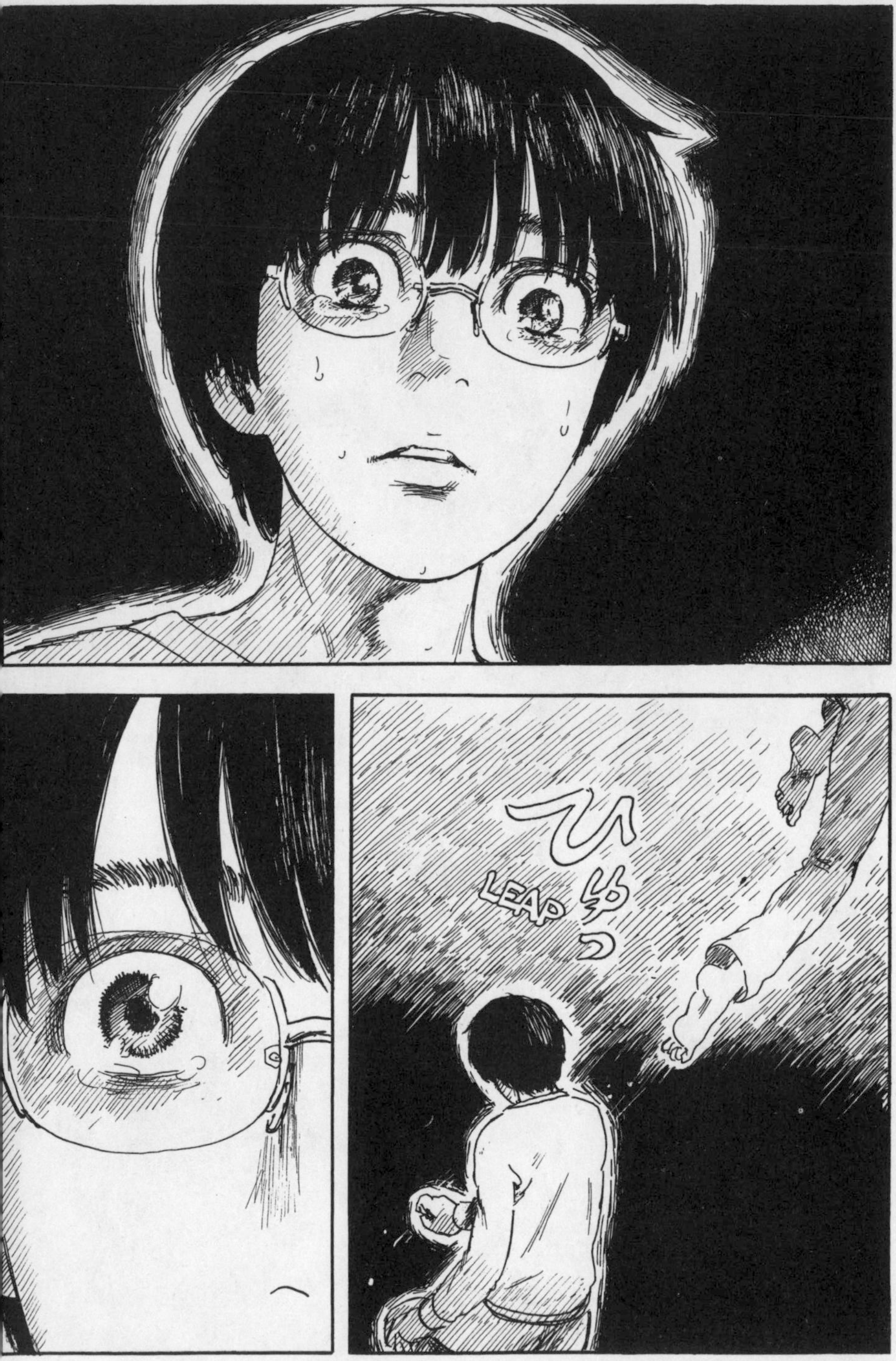
ひゅっ
LEAP

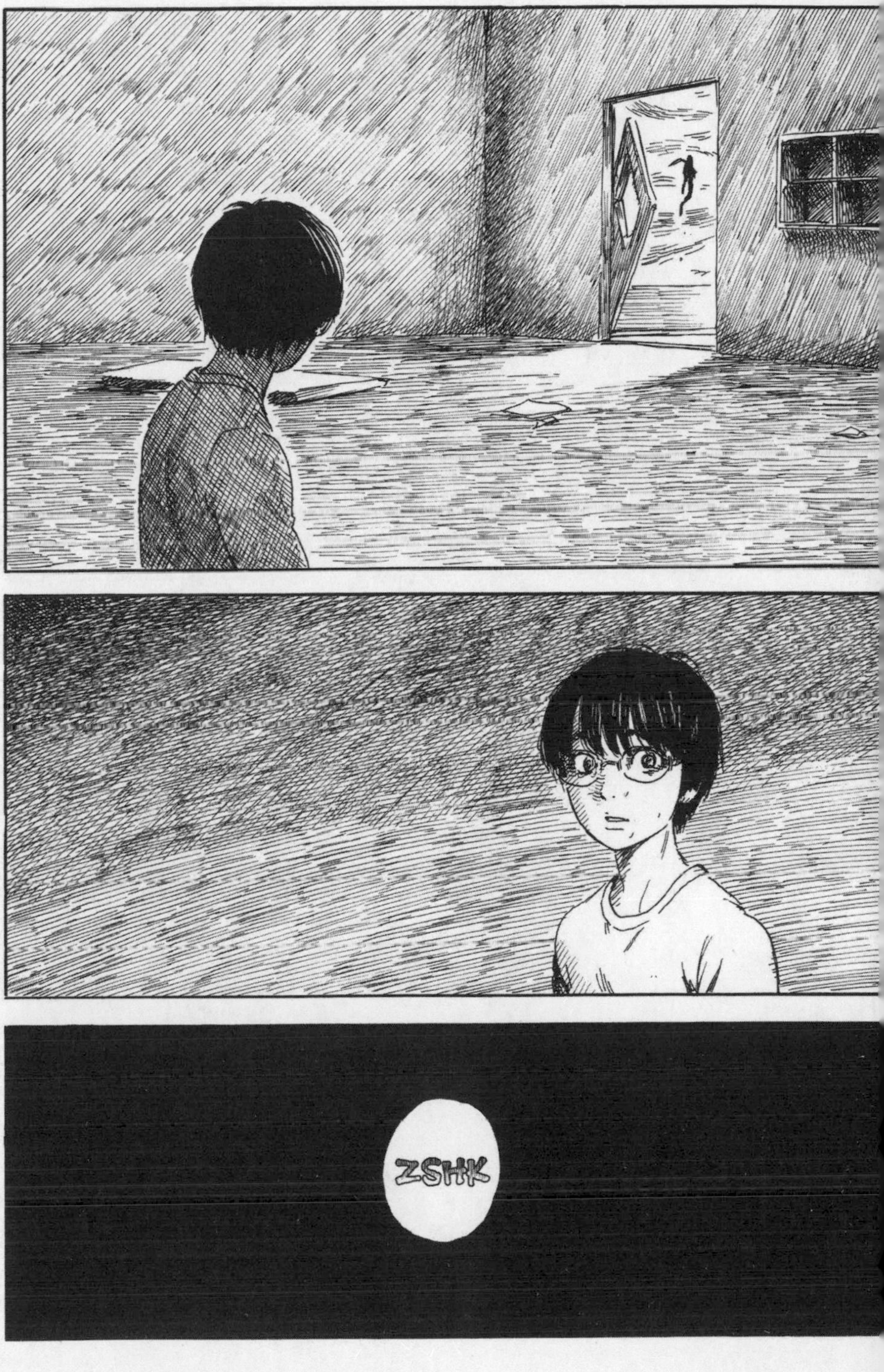
ZSHK

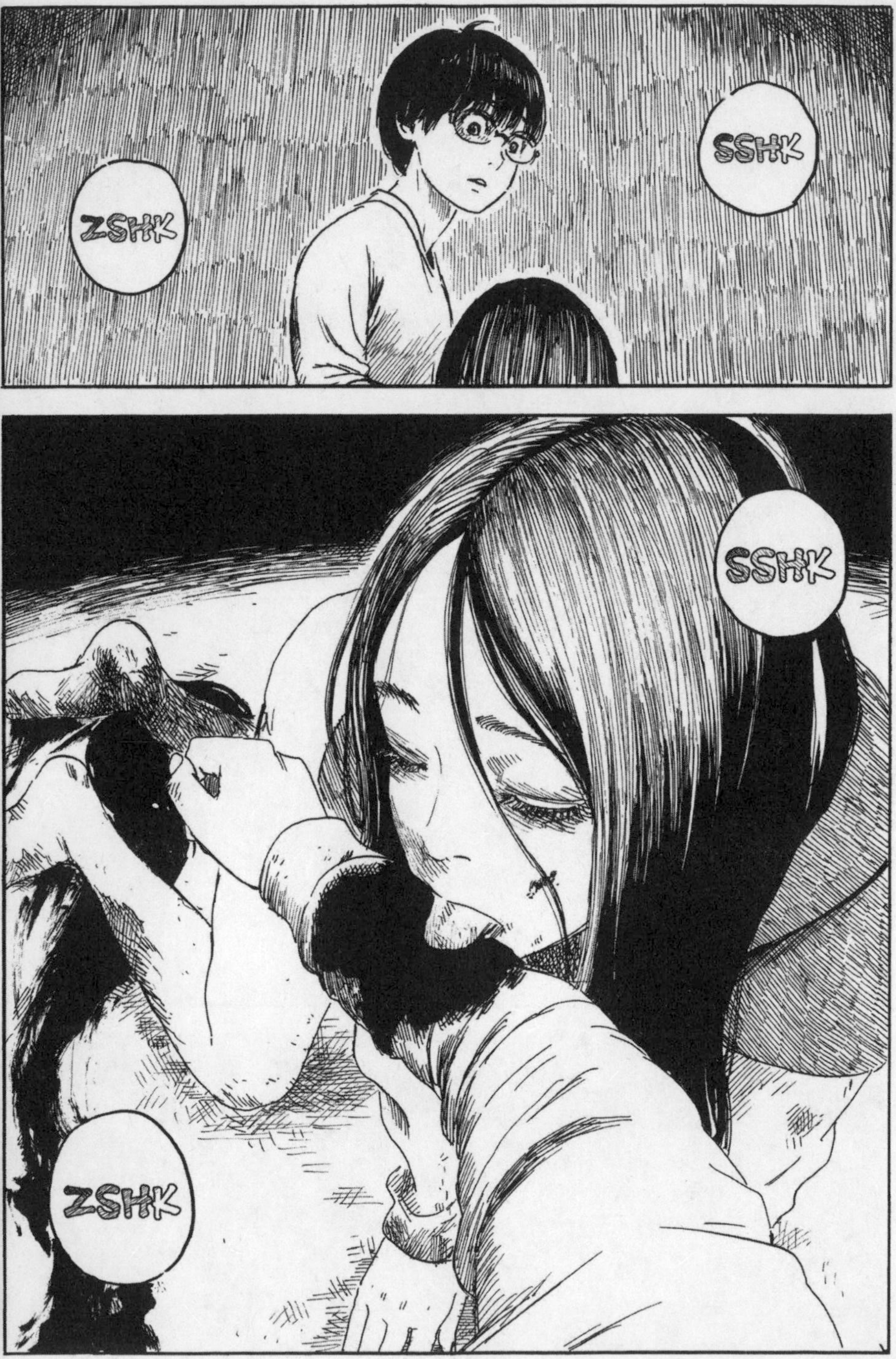
SSHK
ZSHK
SSHK
ZSHK

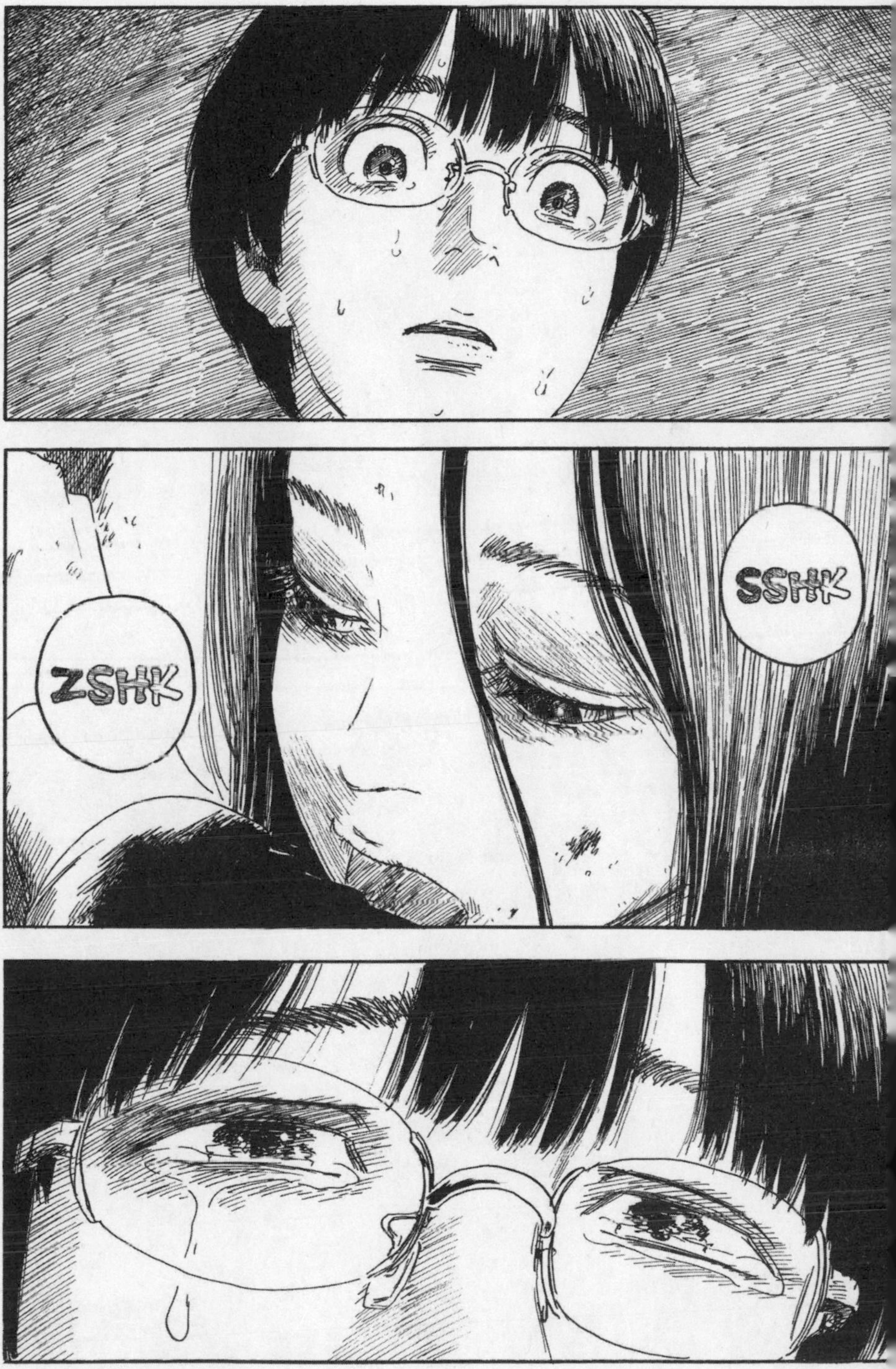
SSHK
ZSHK

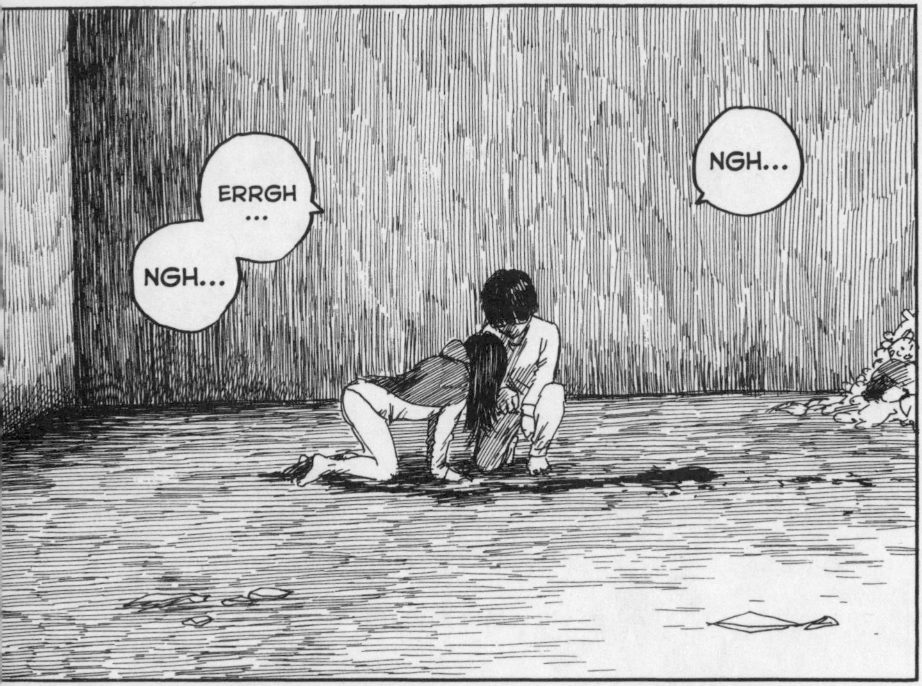
NGH...
ERRGH ...
NGH...

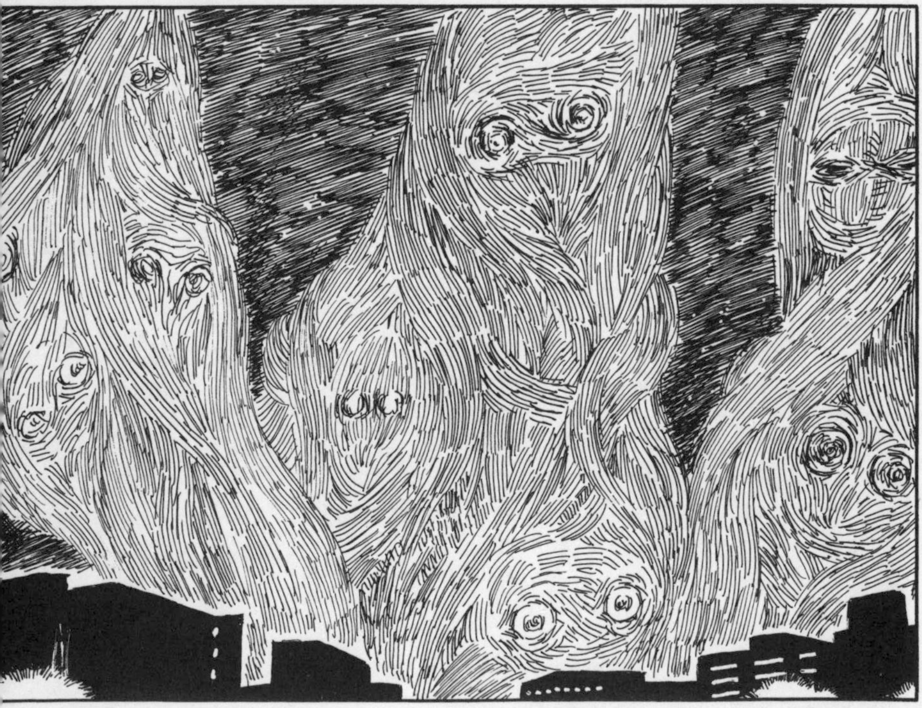

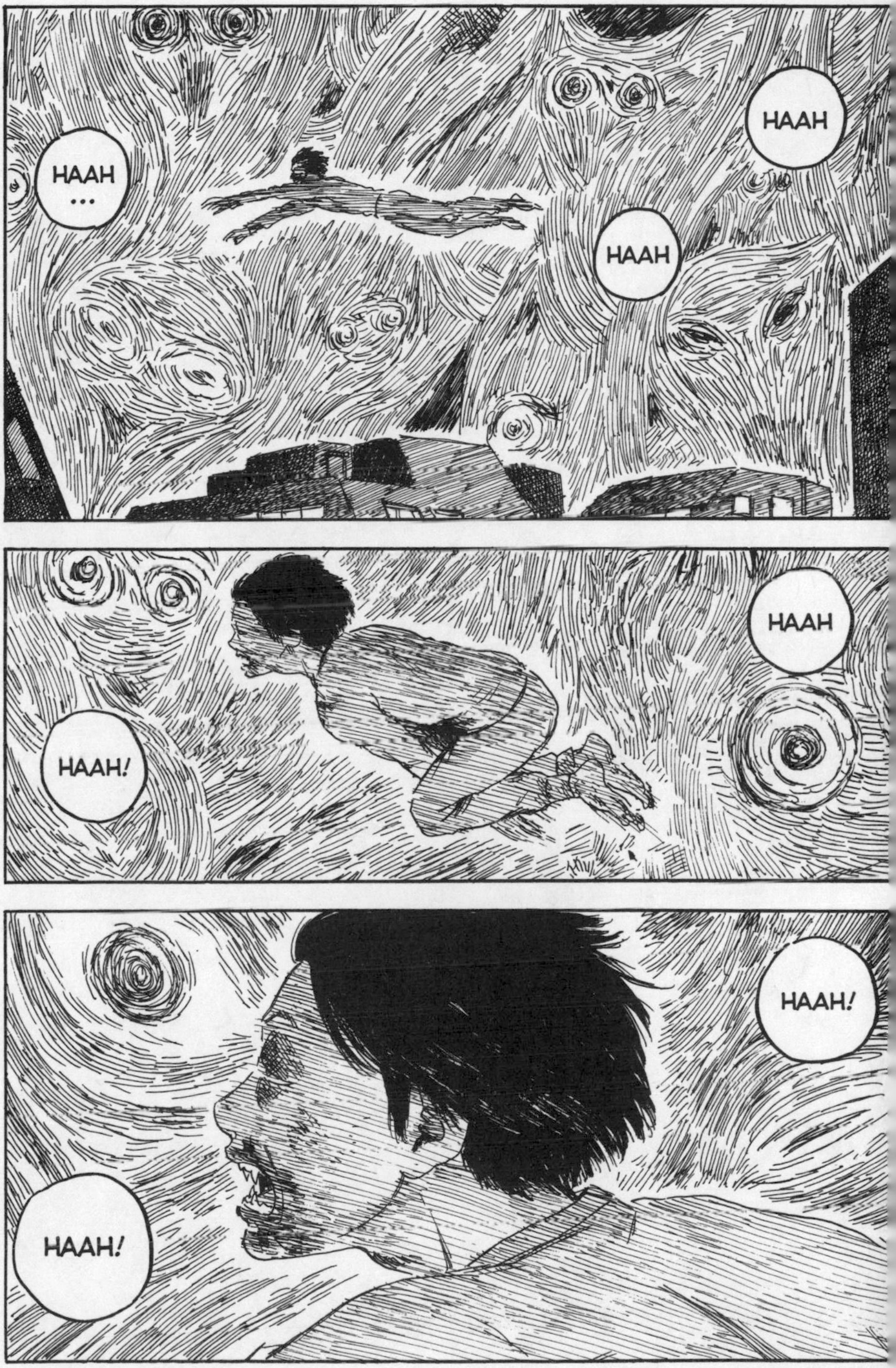
HAAH
HAAH
HAAH ...
HAAH
HAAH!
HAAH!
HAAH!

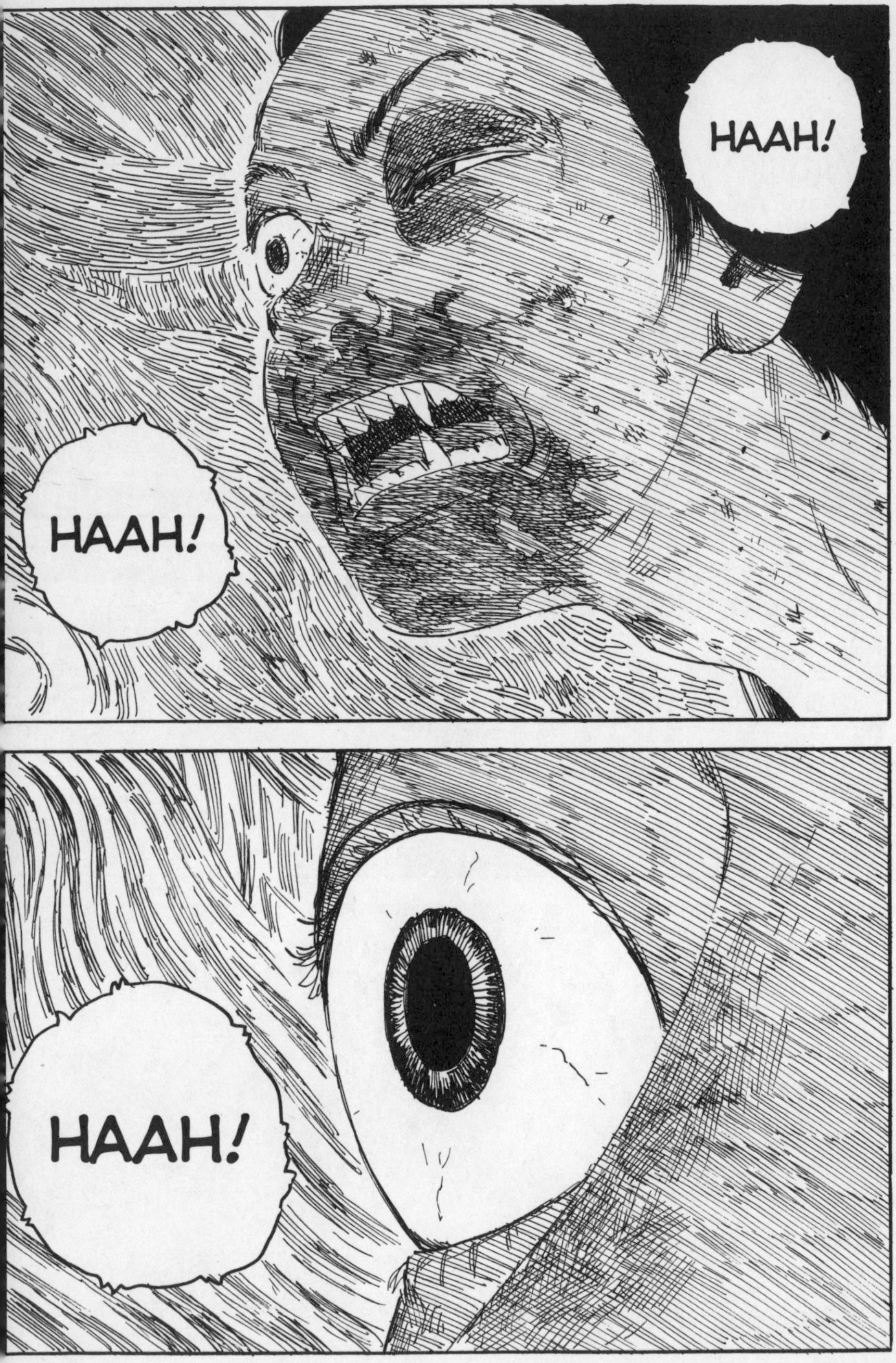
HAAH!
HAAH!
HAAH!

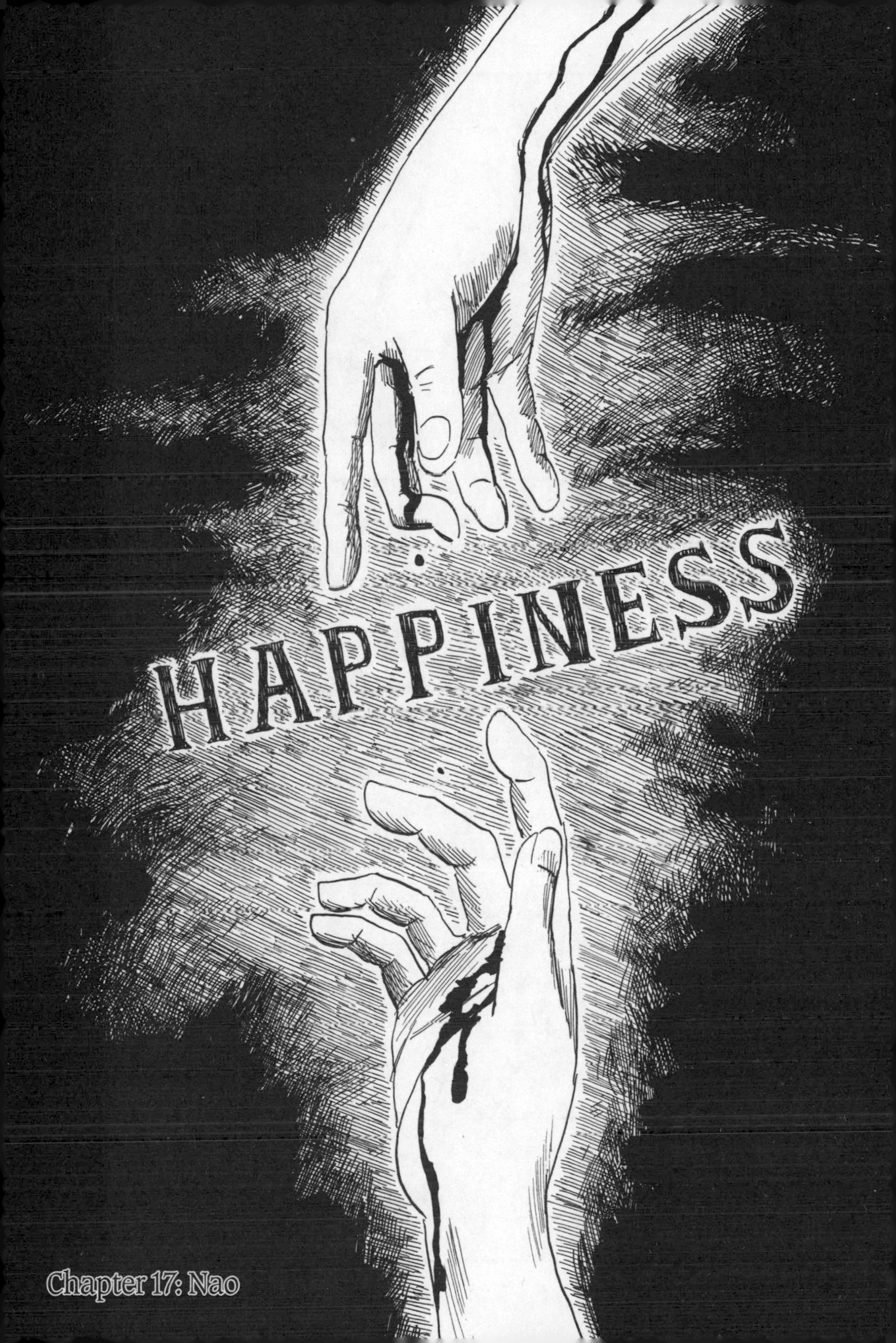
HAPPINESS
Chapter 17: Nao

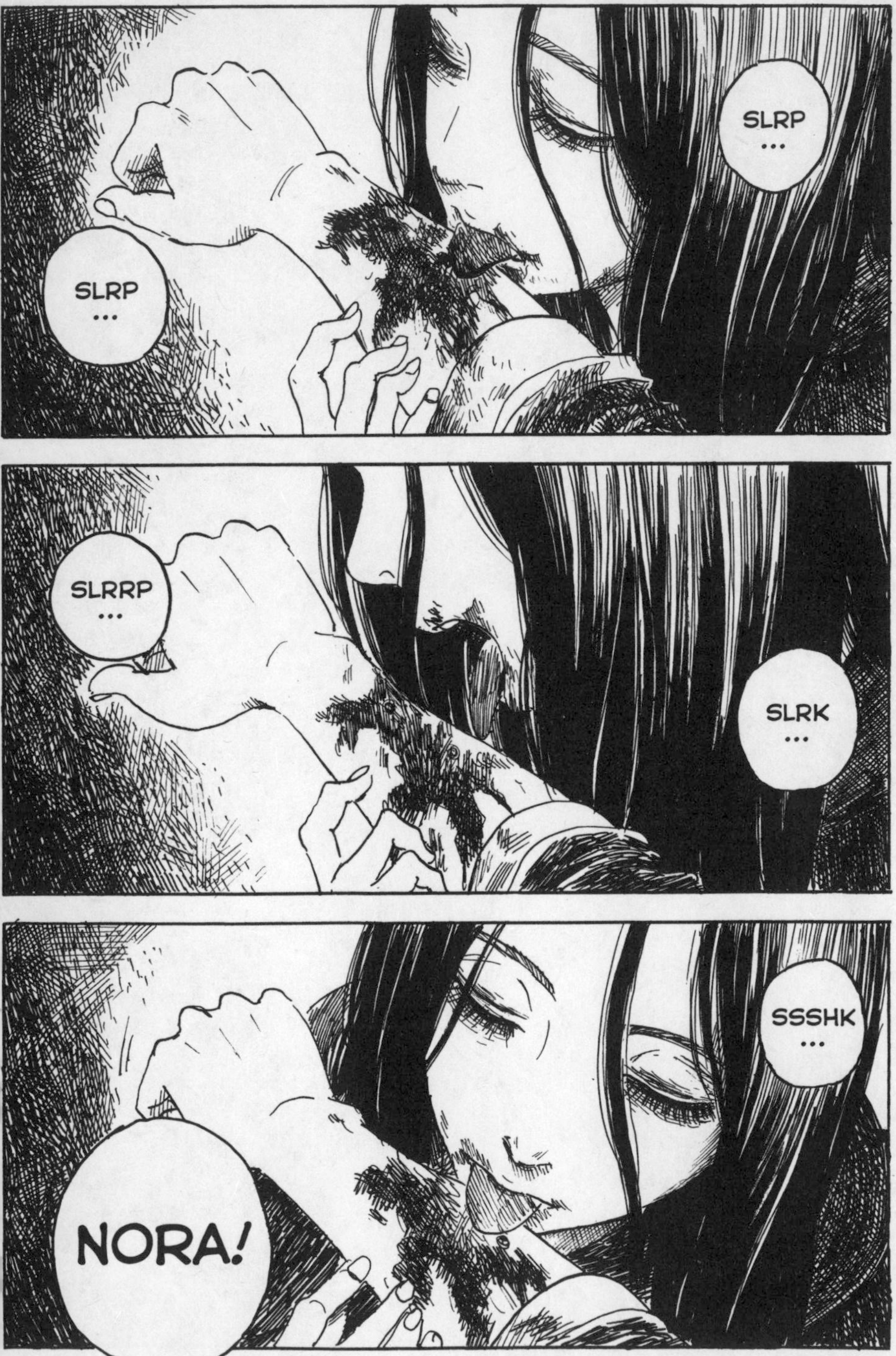
SLRP ...
SLRP ...
SLRK ...
SLRRP ...
SSSHK ...
NORA!

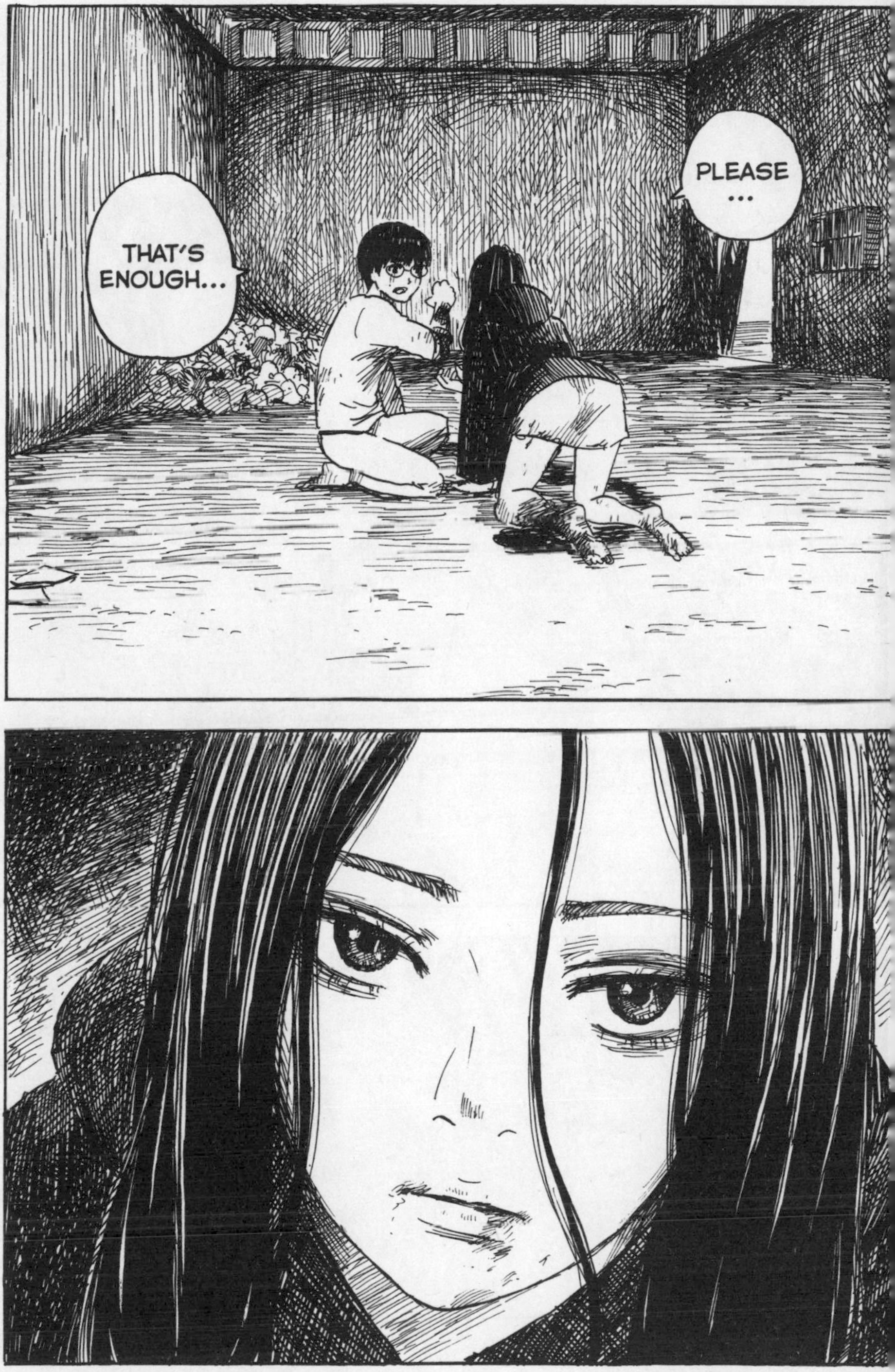
PLEASE ...
THAT'S ENOUGH...

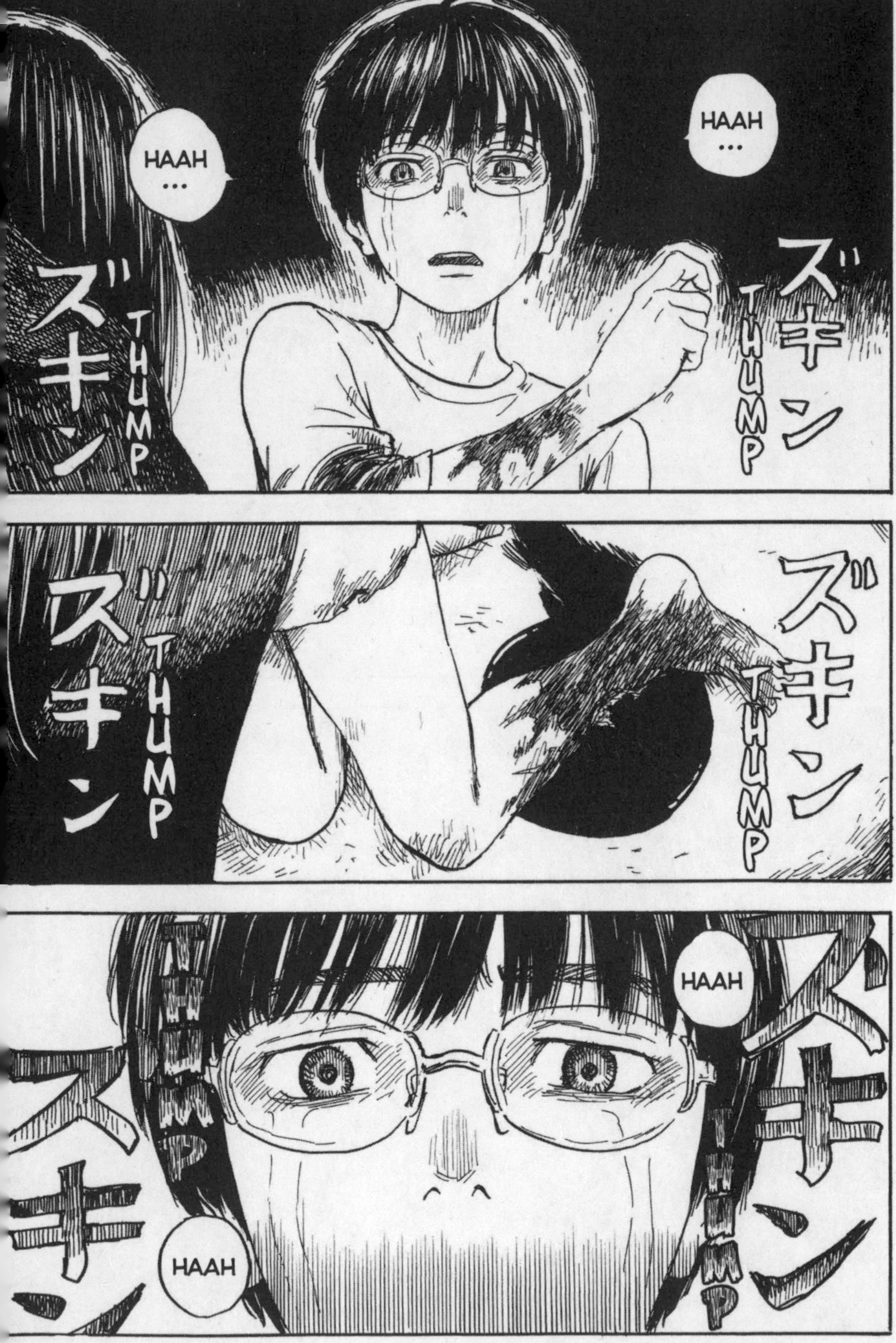
HAAH ...
ズキン
THUMP
HAAH ...
ズキン
THUMP
ズキン
THUMP
ズキン
THUMP
HAAH
ズキン
THUMP
HAAH
THUMP

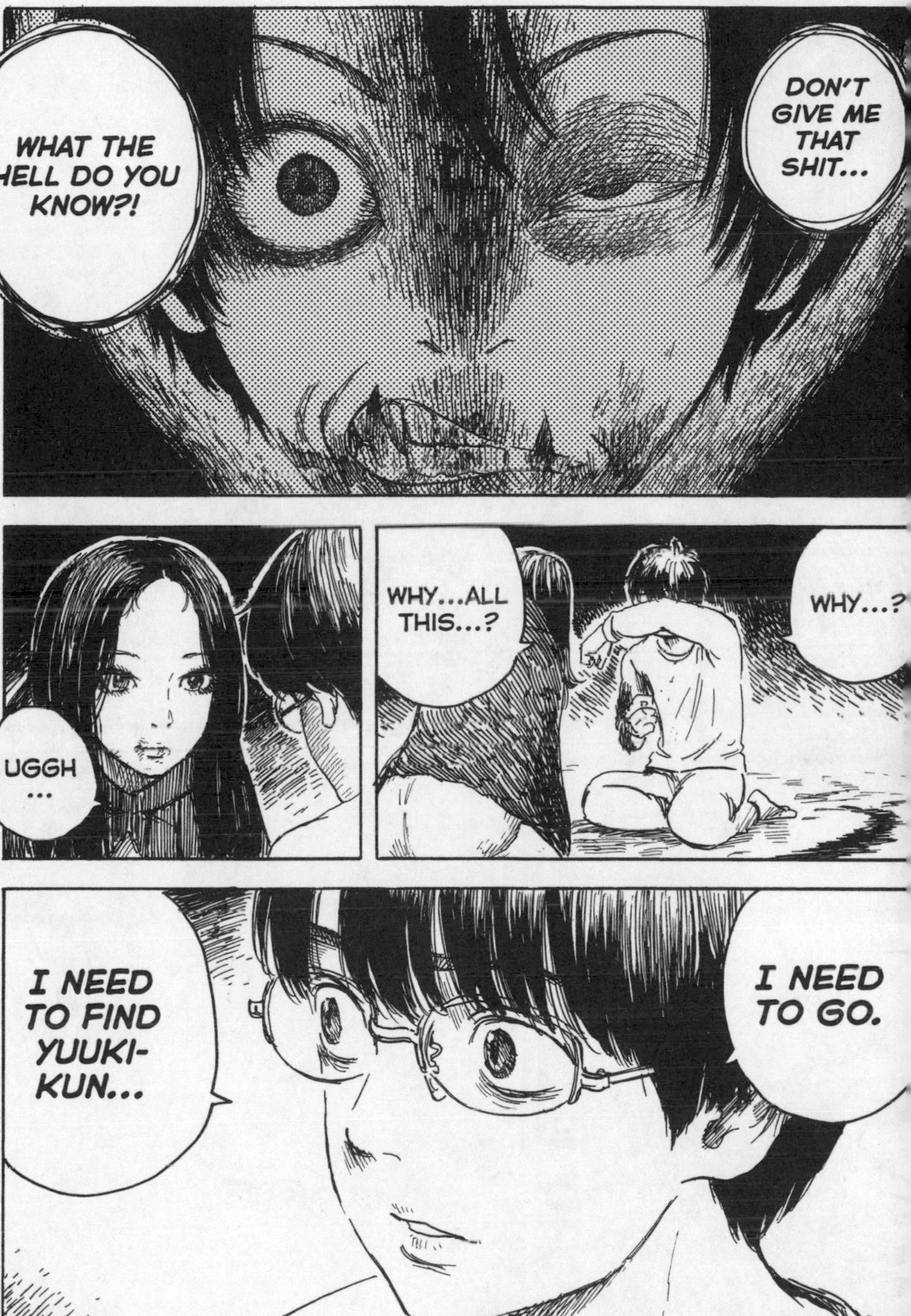
DON'T GIVE ME THAT SHIT...
WHAT THE HELL DO YOU KNOW?!
WHY...?
WHY...ALL THIS...?
UGGH ...
I NEED TO GO.
I NEED TO FIND YUUKI-KUN...

ぐっ
GRIP

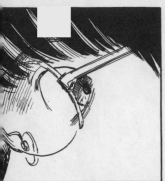

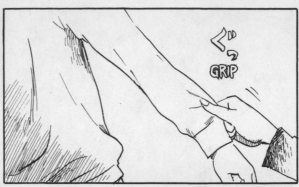

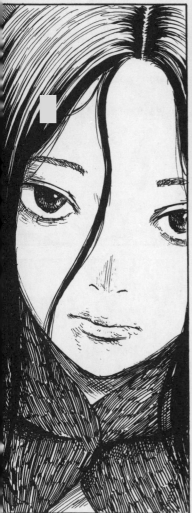

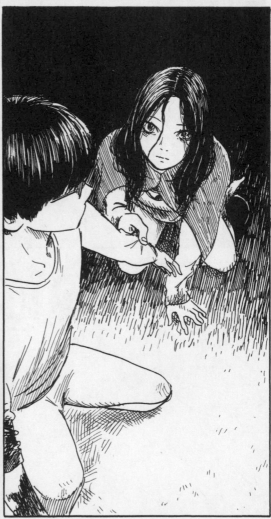

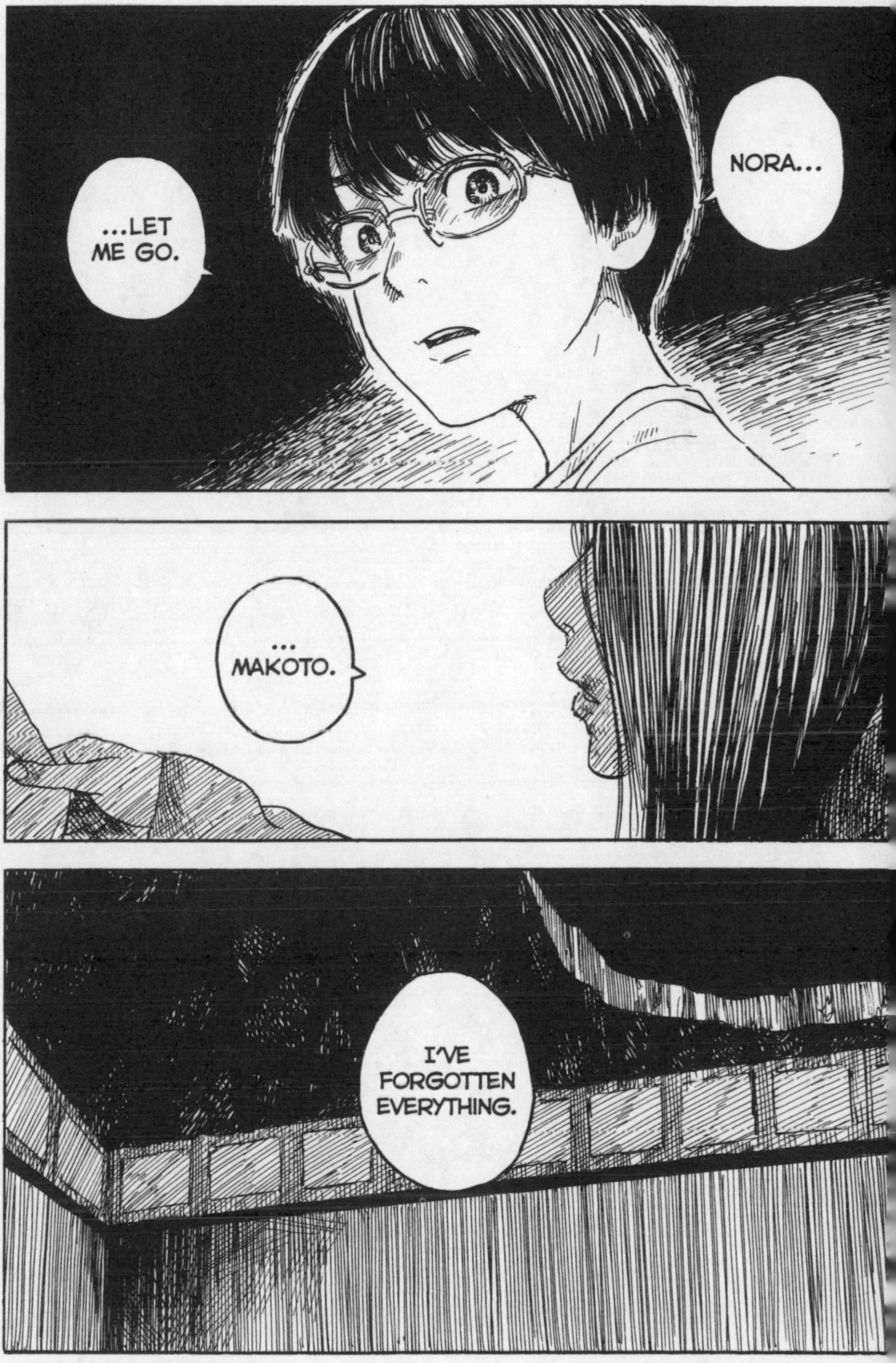
NORA...
...LET ME GO.
... MAKOTO.
I'VE FORGOTTEN EVERYTHING.

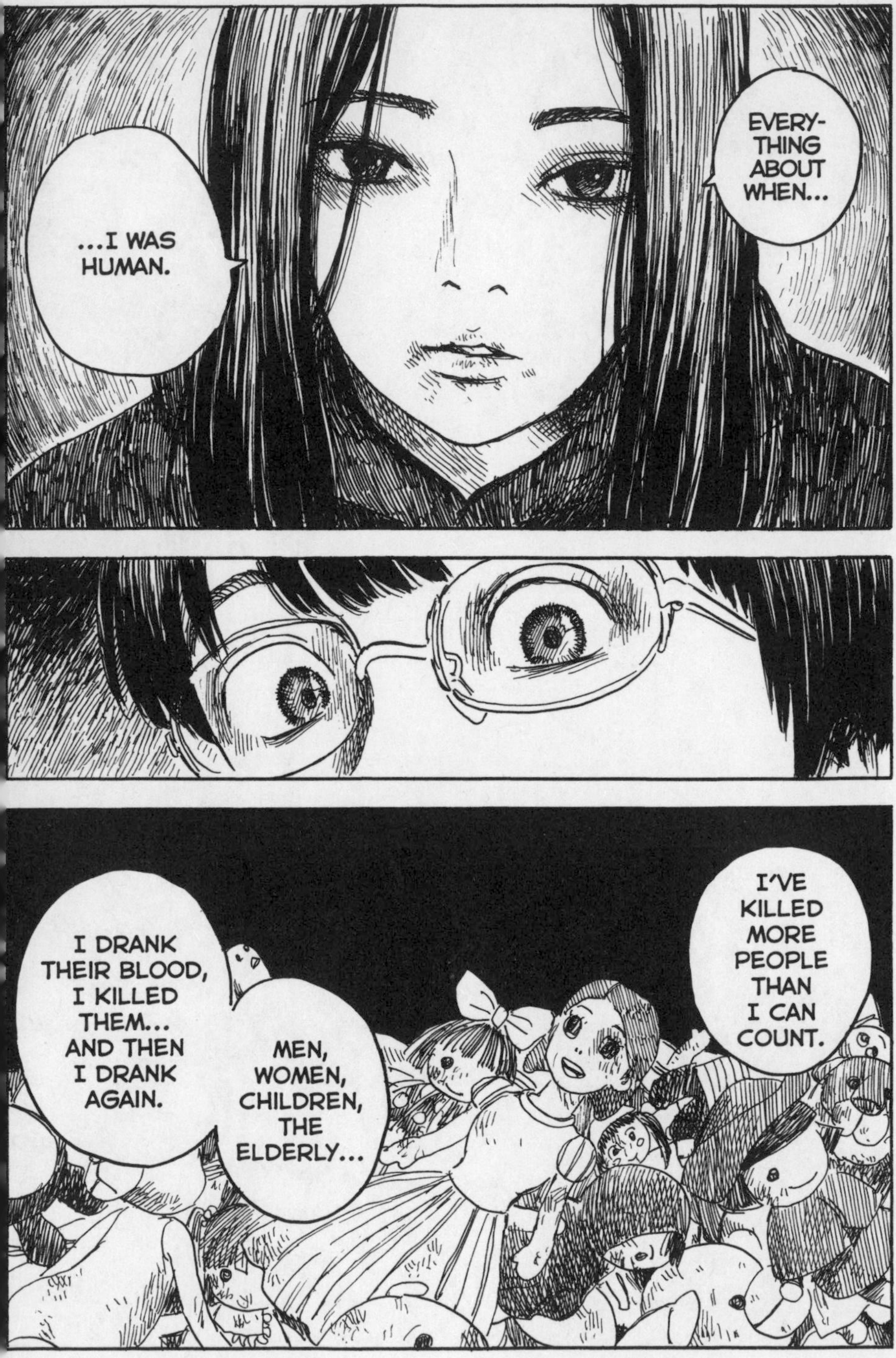
EVERY-THING ABOUT WHEN...
...I WAS HUMAN.
I'VE KILLED MORE PEOPLE THAN I CAN COUNT.
MEN, WOMEN, CHILDREN, THE ELDERLY...
I DRANK THEIR BLOOD, I KILLED THEM... AND THEN I DRANK AGAIN.

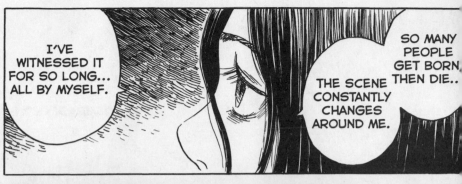

SO MANY PEOPLE GET BORN, THEN DIE...
THE SCENE CONSTANTLY CHANGES AROUND ME.
I'VE WITNESSED IT FOR SO LONG... ALL BY MYSELF.
EVERYTHING ABOUT MY LIFE AS A HUMAN...
IT'S ALL GONE SO FAR AWAY FROM ME.
BUT...
AFTER I ATTACKED YOU...
...AND DRANK YOUR BLOOD...
WHEN I LOOKED AT YOUR FACE...

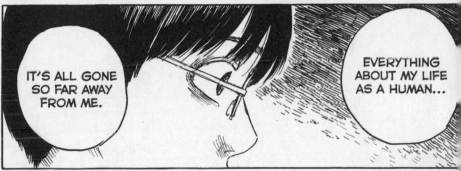

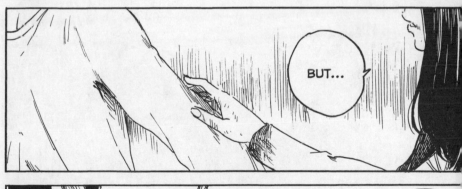

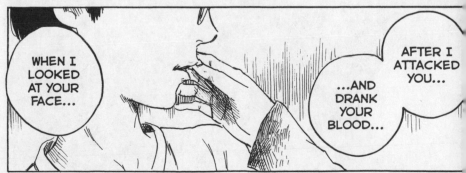

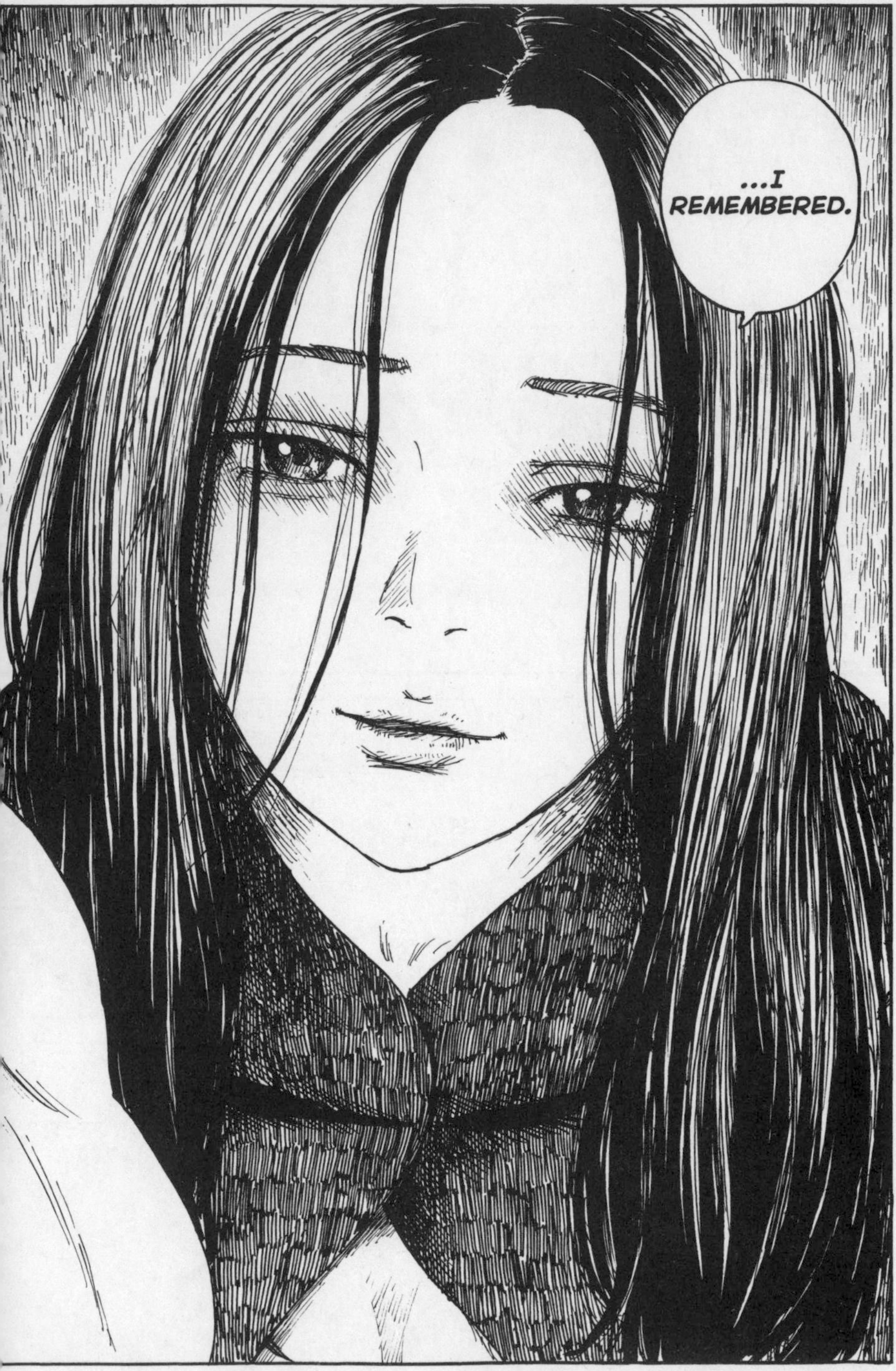
...I REMEMBERED.

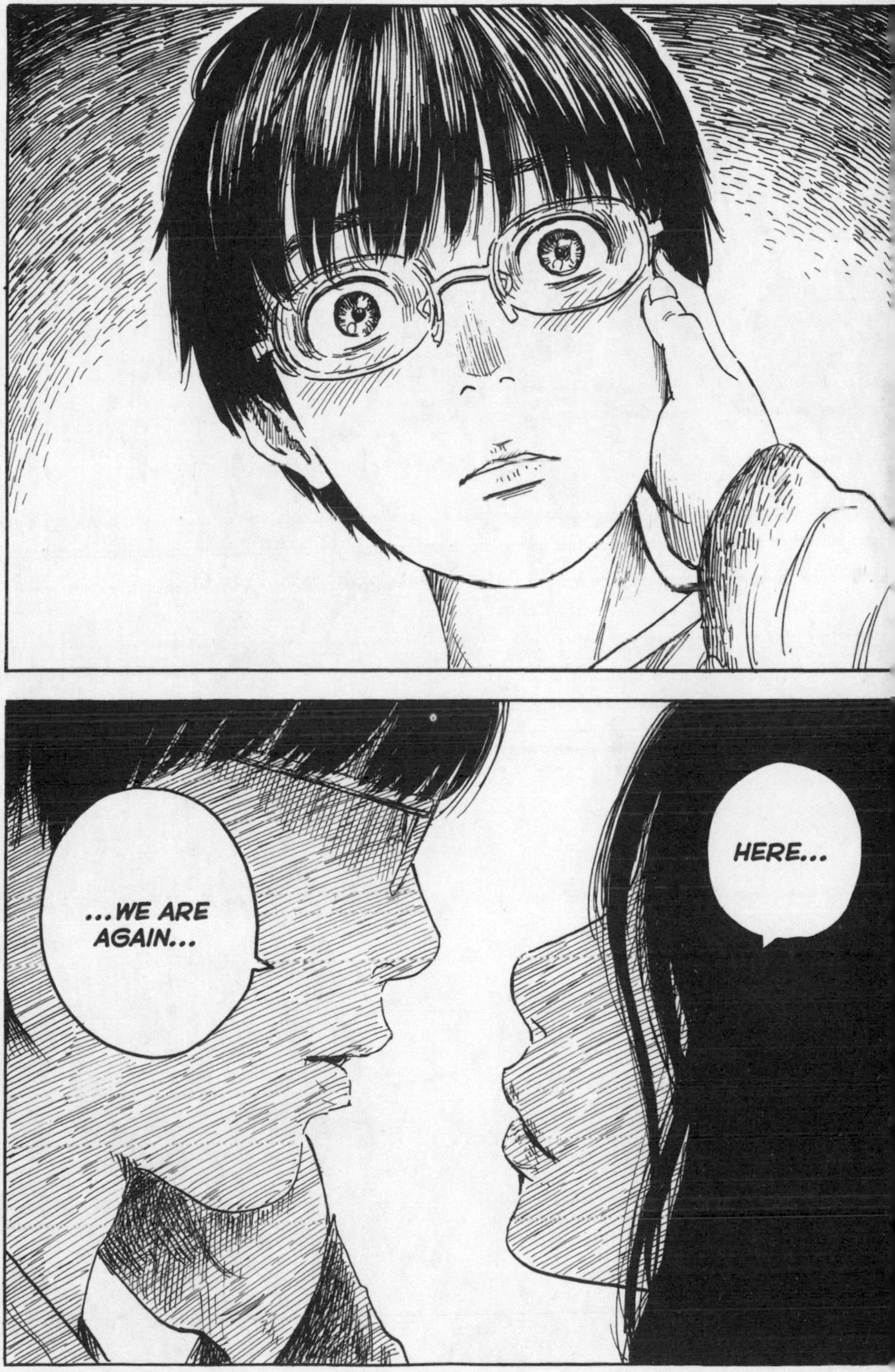
HERE...
...WE ARE AGAIN...

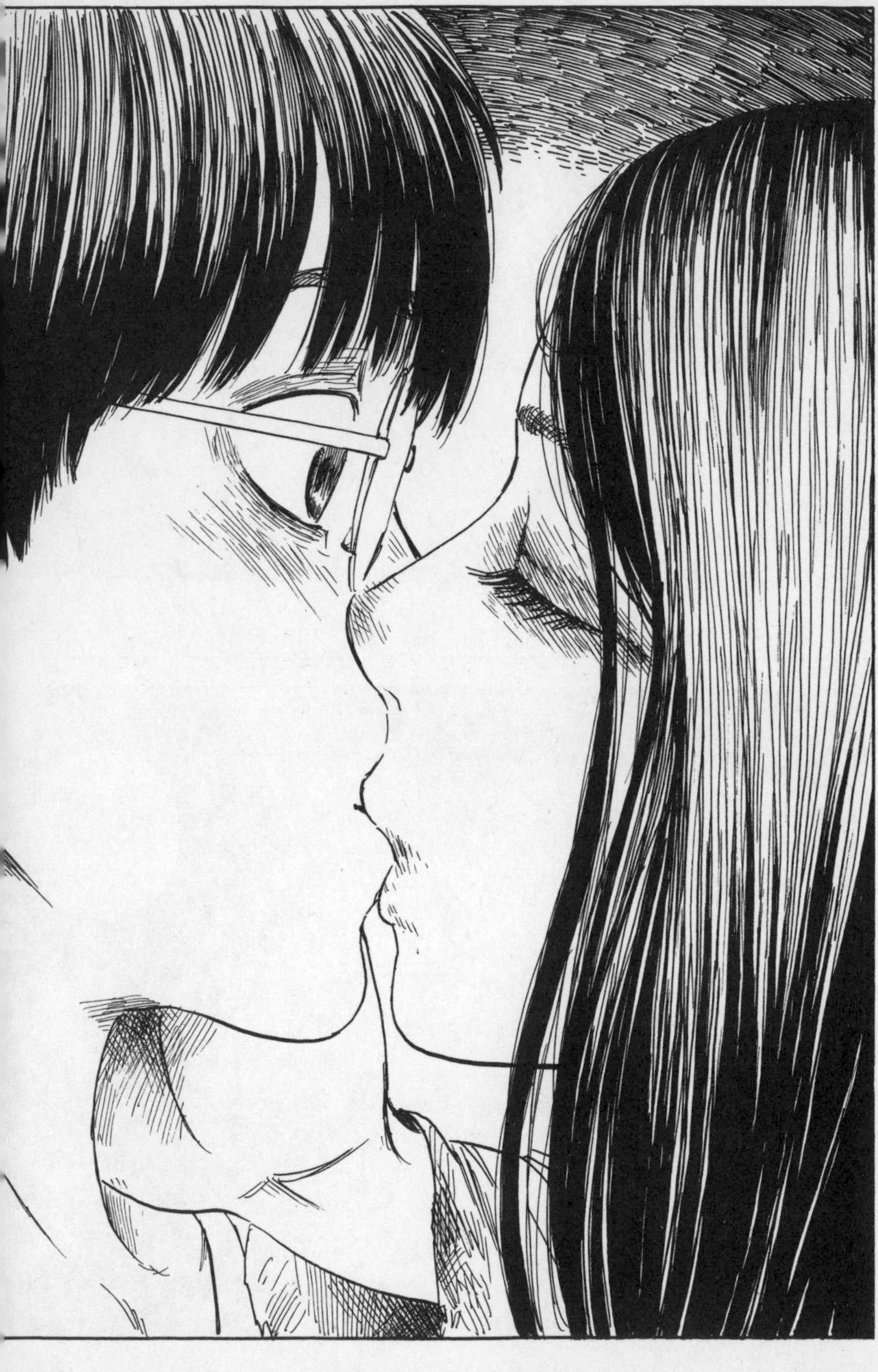

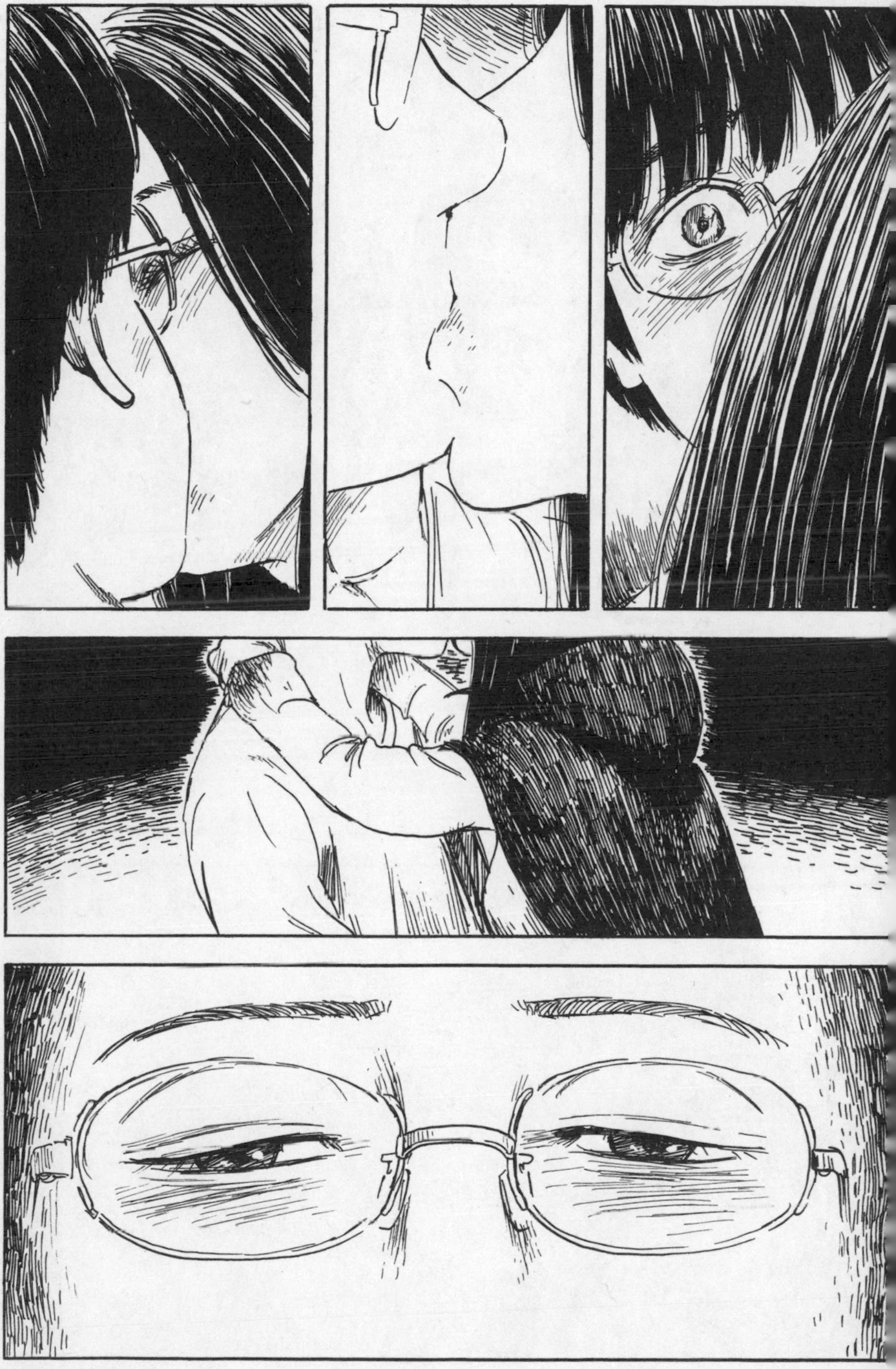

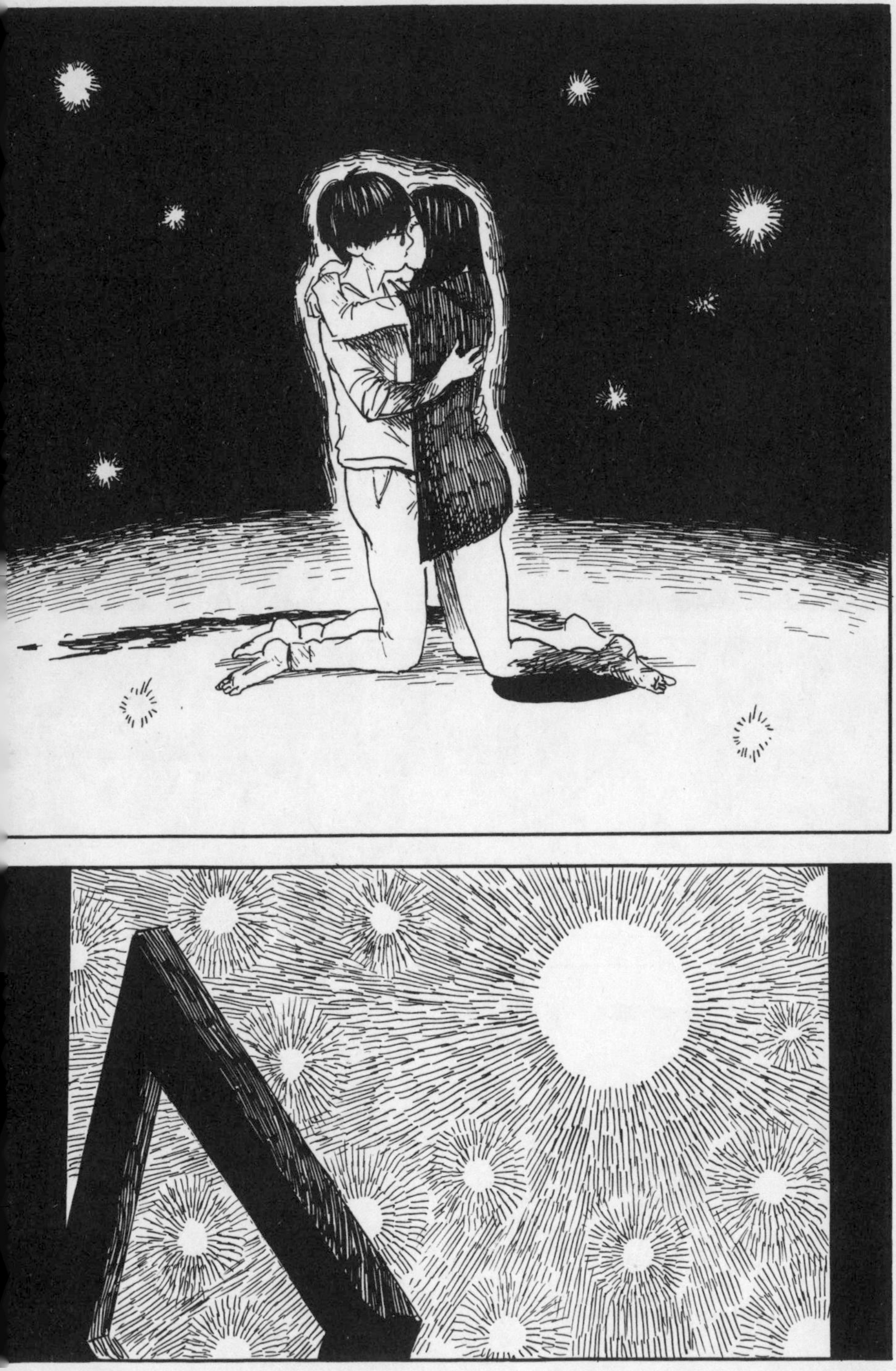

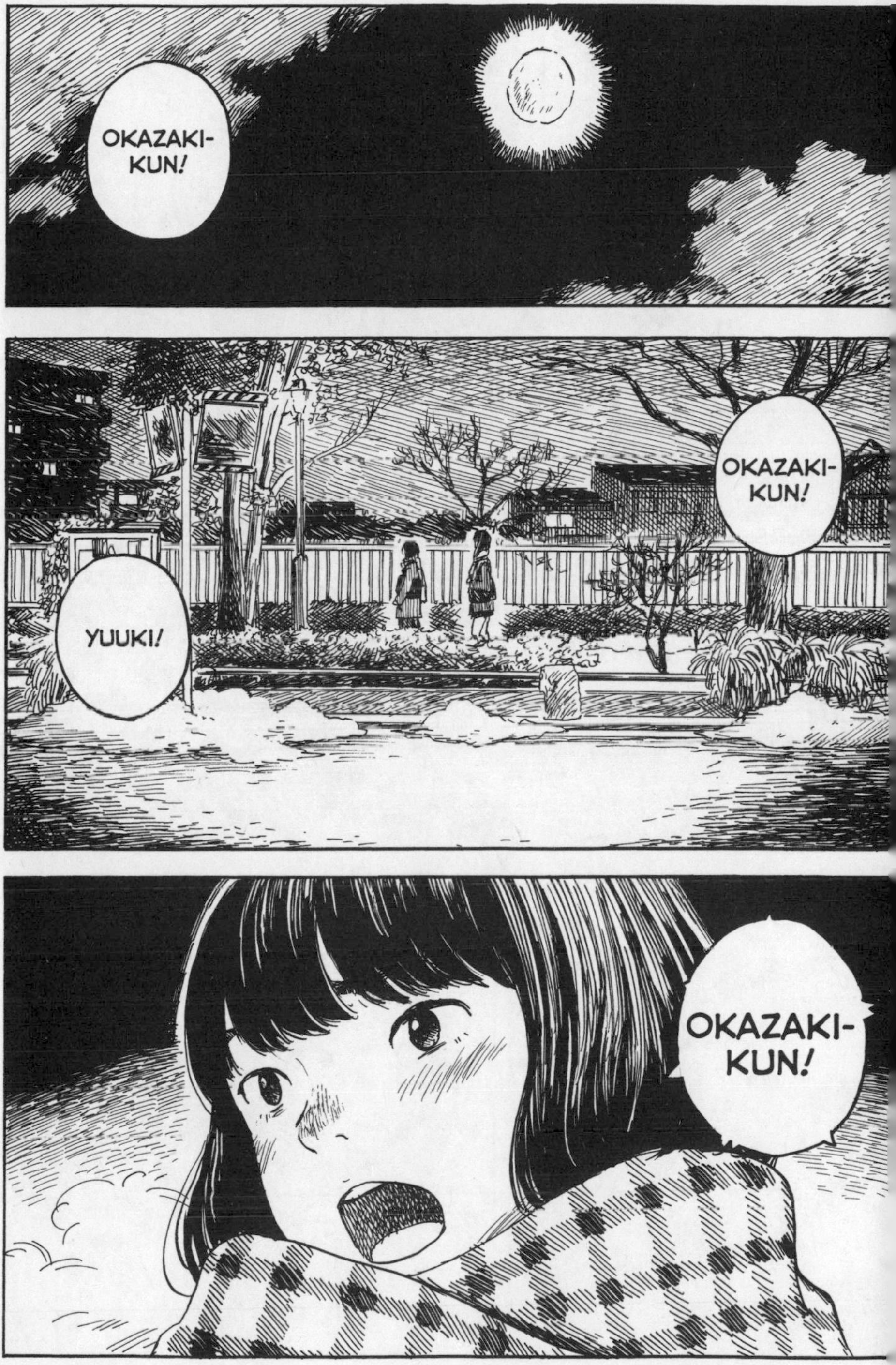
OKAZAKI-KUN!
OKAZAKI-KUN!
YUUKI!
OKAZAKI-KUN!

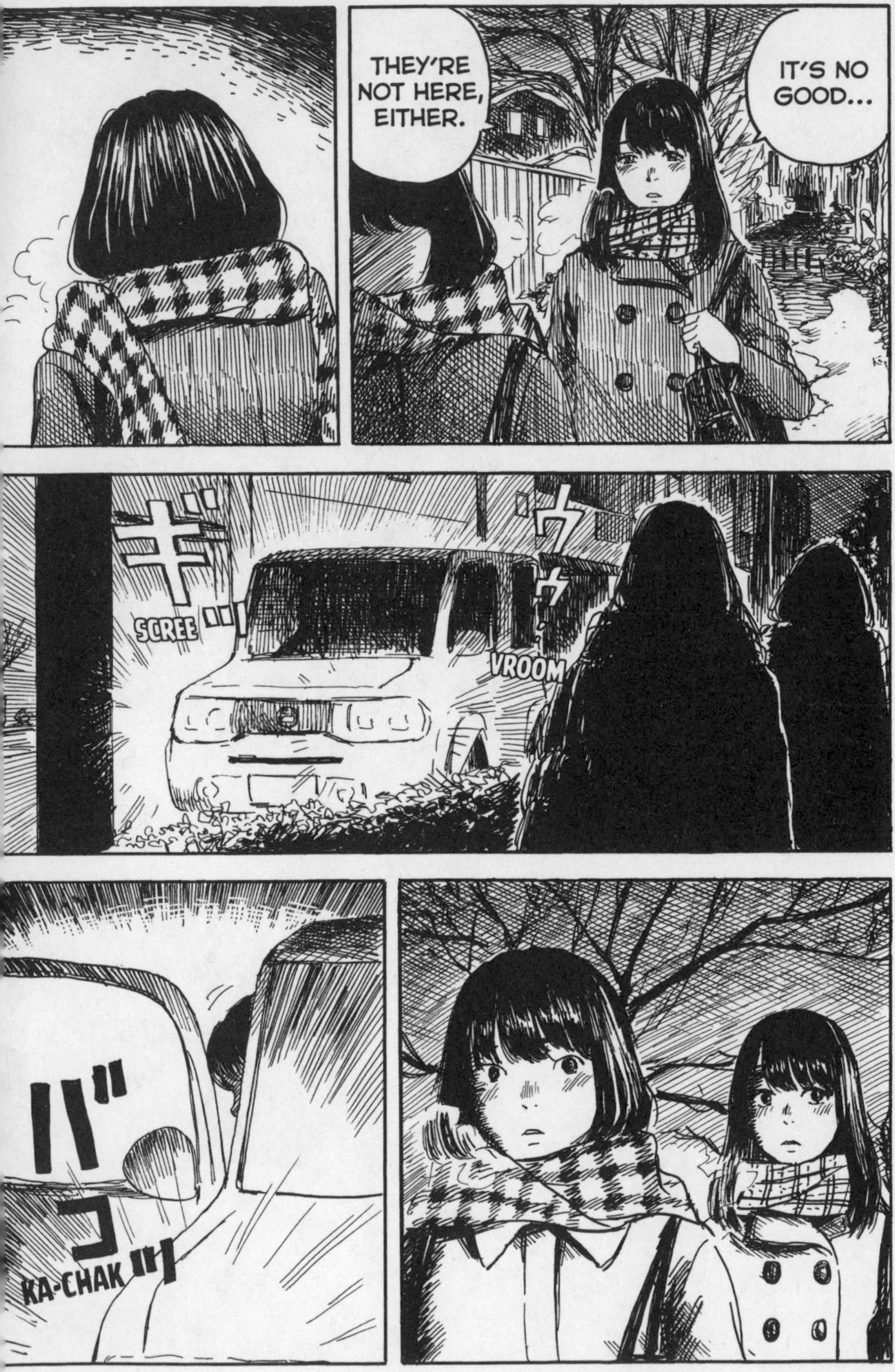
IT'S NO GOOD...
THEY'RE NOT HERE, EITHER.
VROOM
SCREE
バコ
KA-CHAK

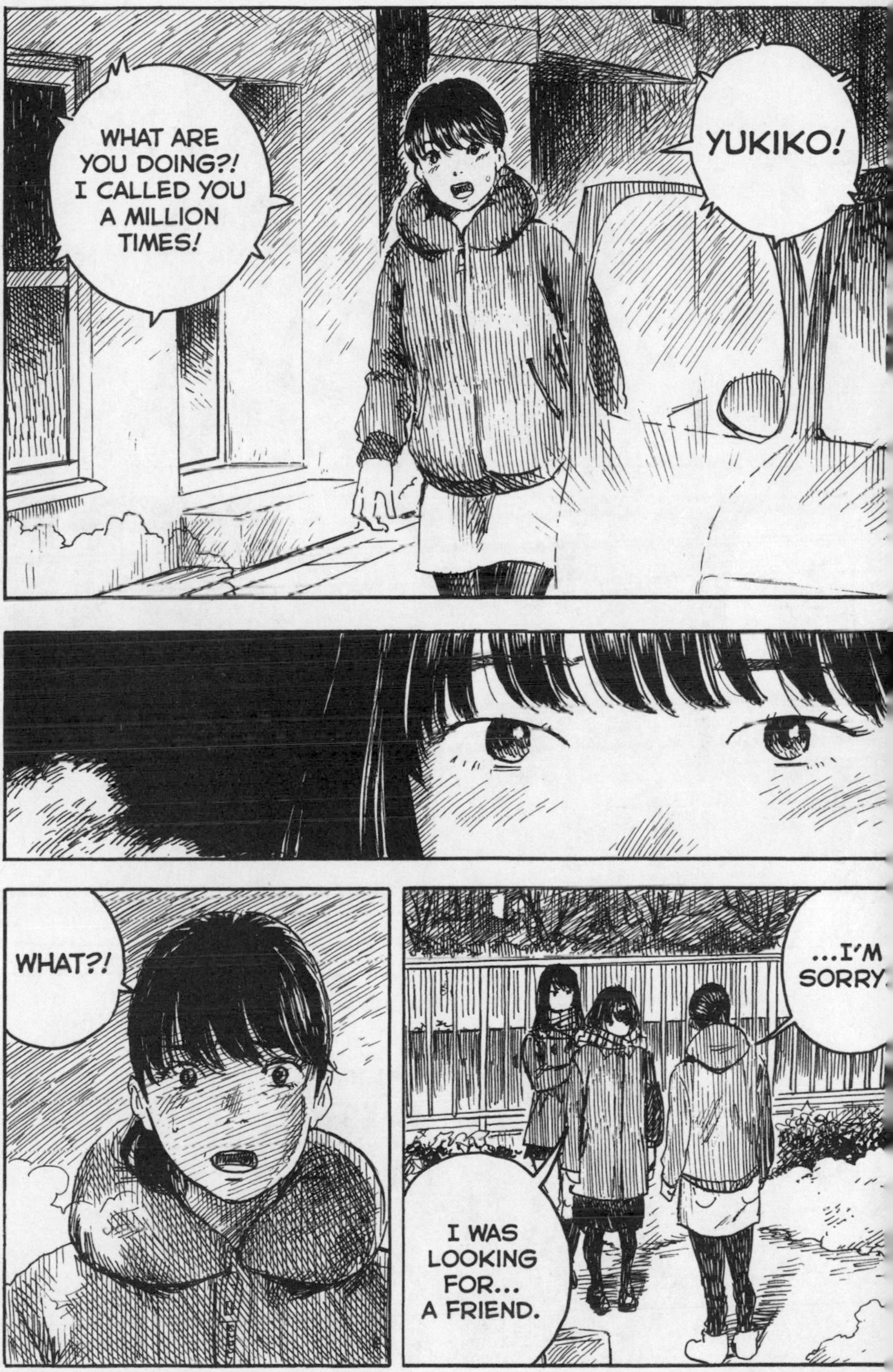
YUKIKO!
WHAT ARE YOU DOING?! I CALLED YOU A MILLION TIMES!
...I'M SORRY.
I WAS LOOKING FOR... A FRIEND.
WHAT?!

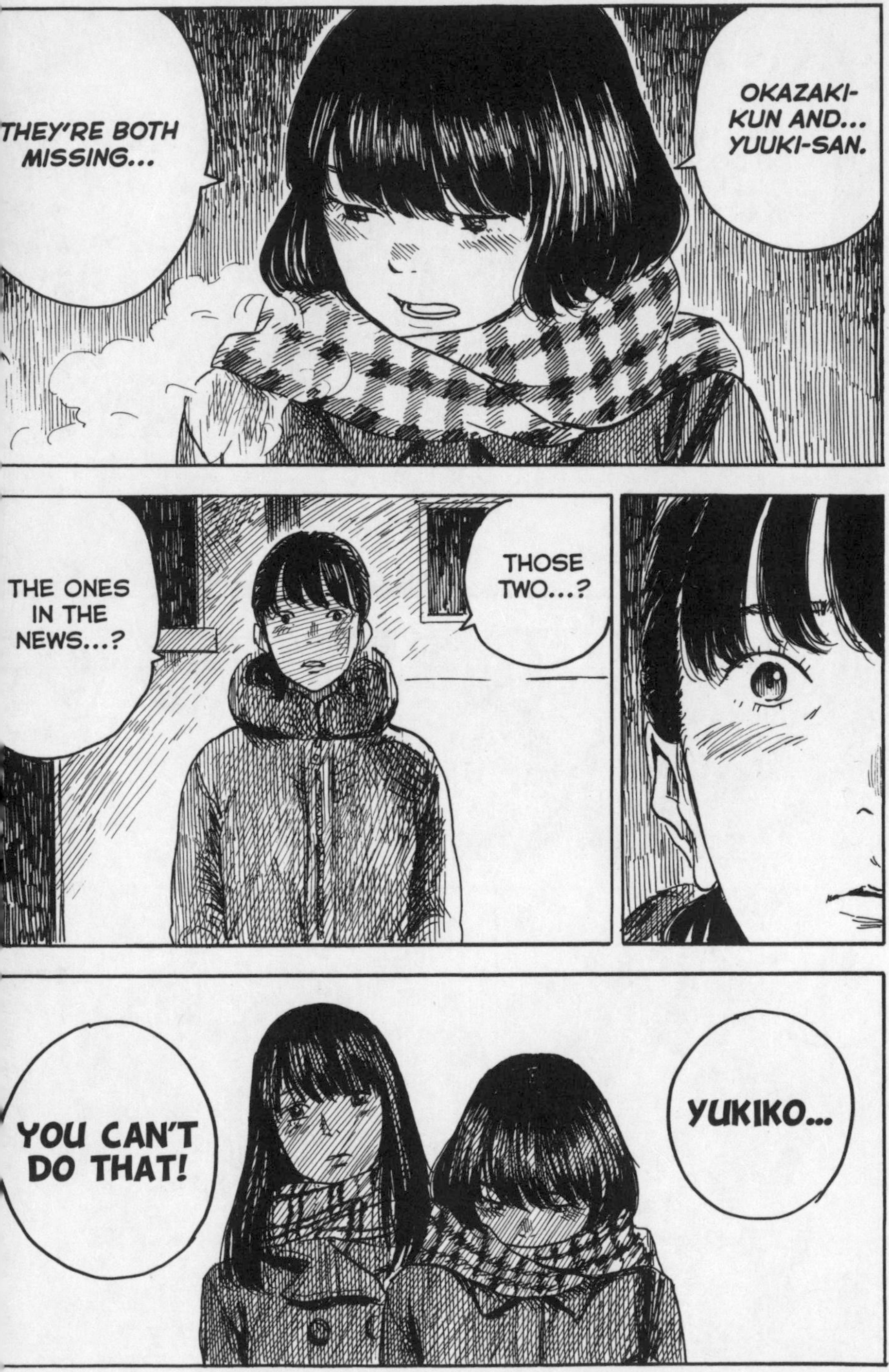
OKAZAKI-KUN AND... YUUKI-SAN.
THEY'RE BOTH MISSING...
THOSE TWO...?
THE ONES IN THE NEWS...?
YUKIKO...
YOU CAN'T DO THAT!

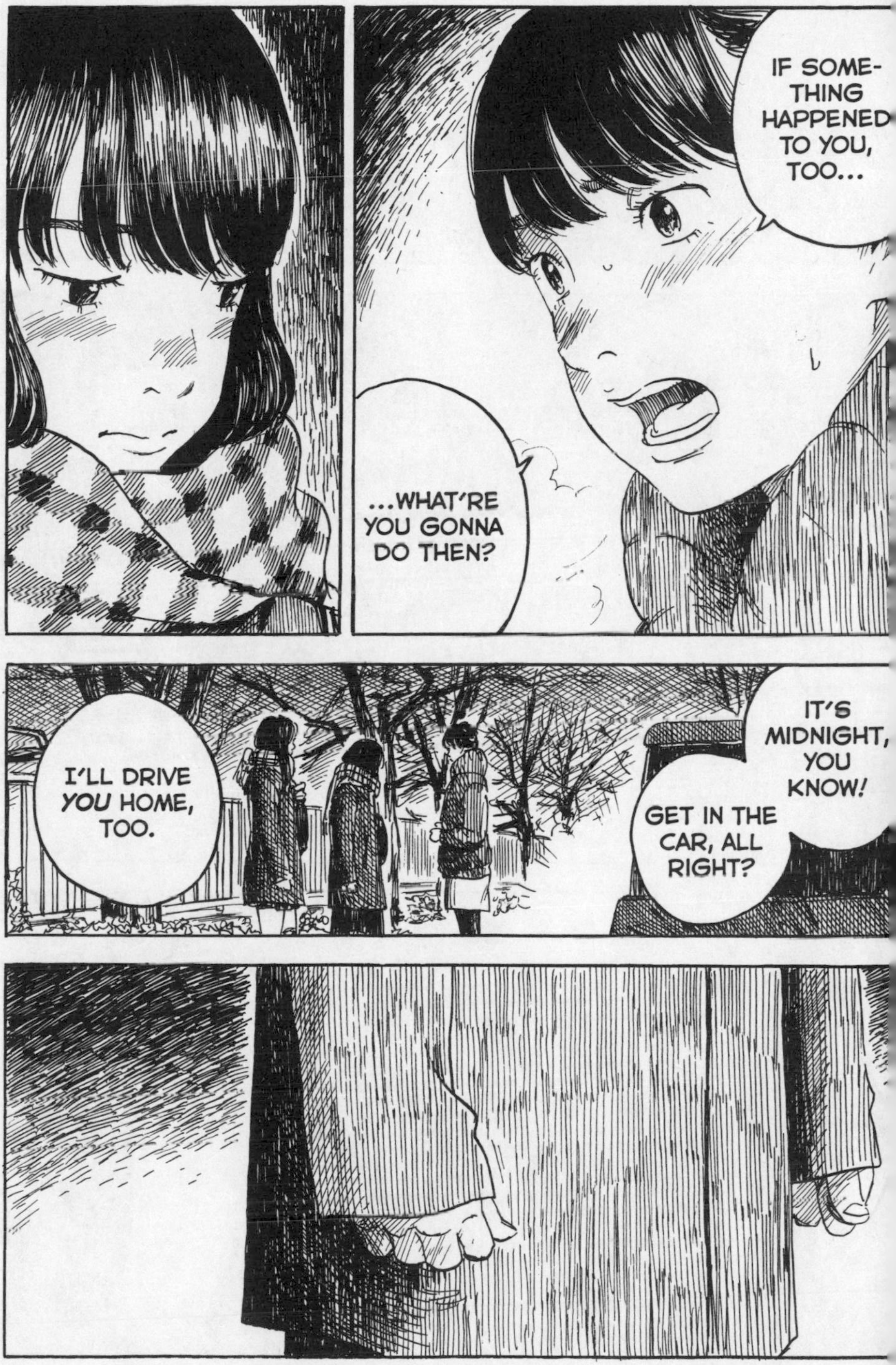
IF SOME-THING HAPPENED TO YOU, TOO...
...WHAT'RE YOU GONNA DO THEN?
IT'S MIDNIGHT, YOU KNOW!
GET IN THE CAR, ALL RIGHT?
I'LL DRIVE *YOU* HOME, TOO.

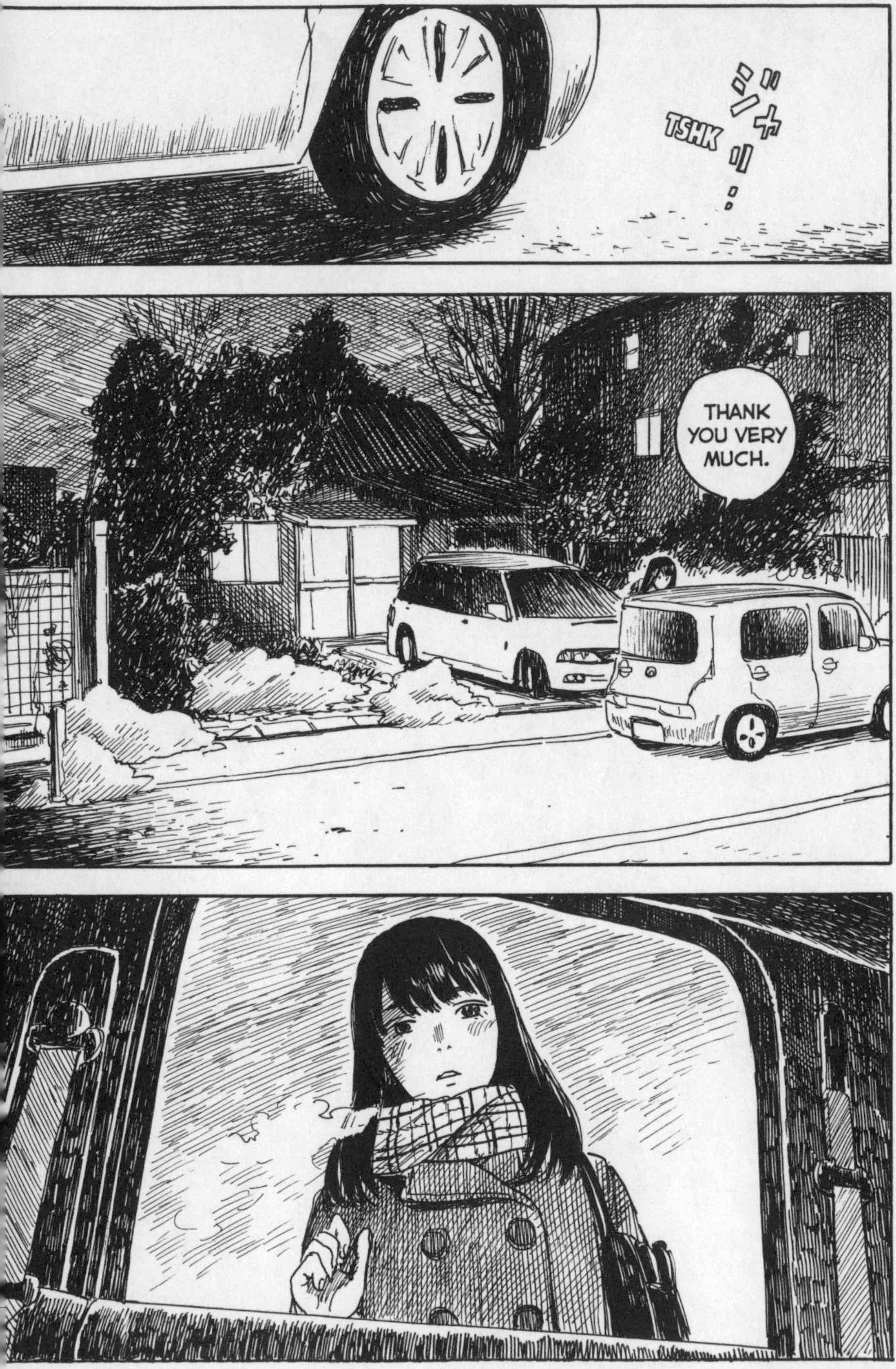
ジャリ・・
TSHK
THANK YOU VERY MUCH.

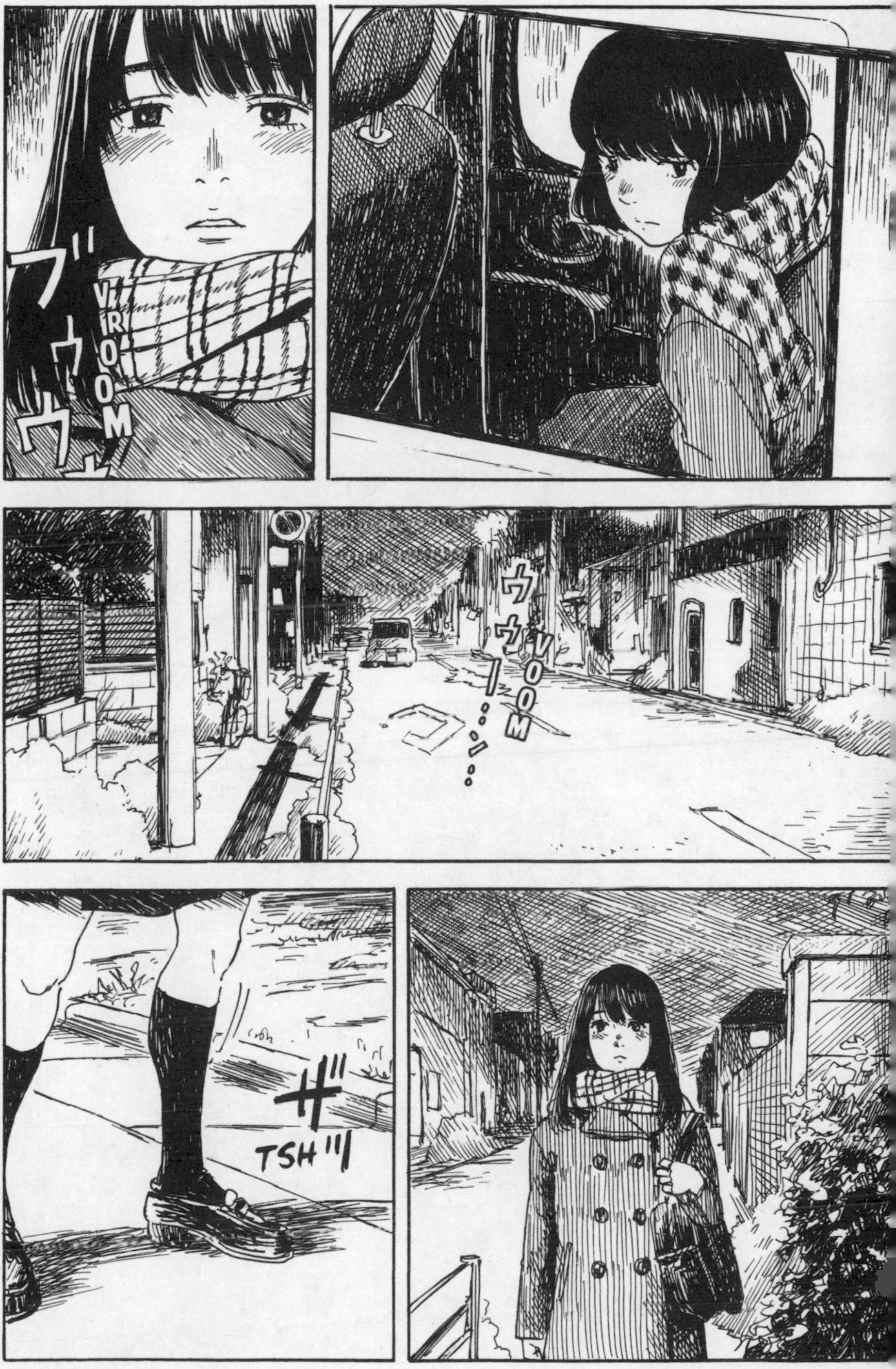

VROOM
ウウー…ン…
VROOM
TSH

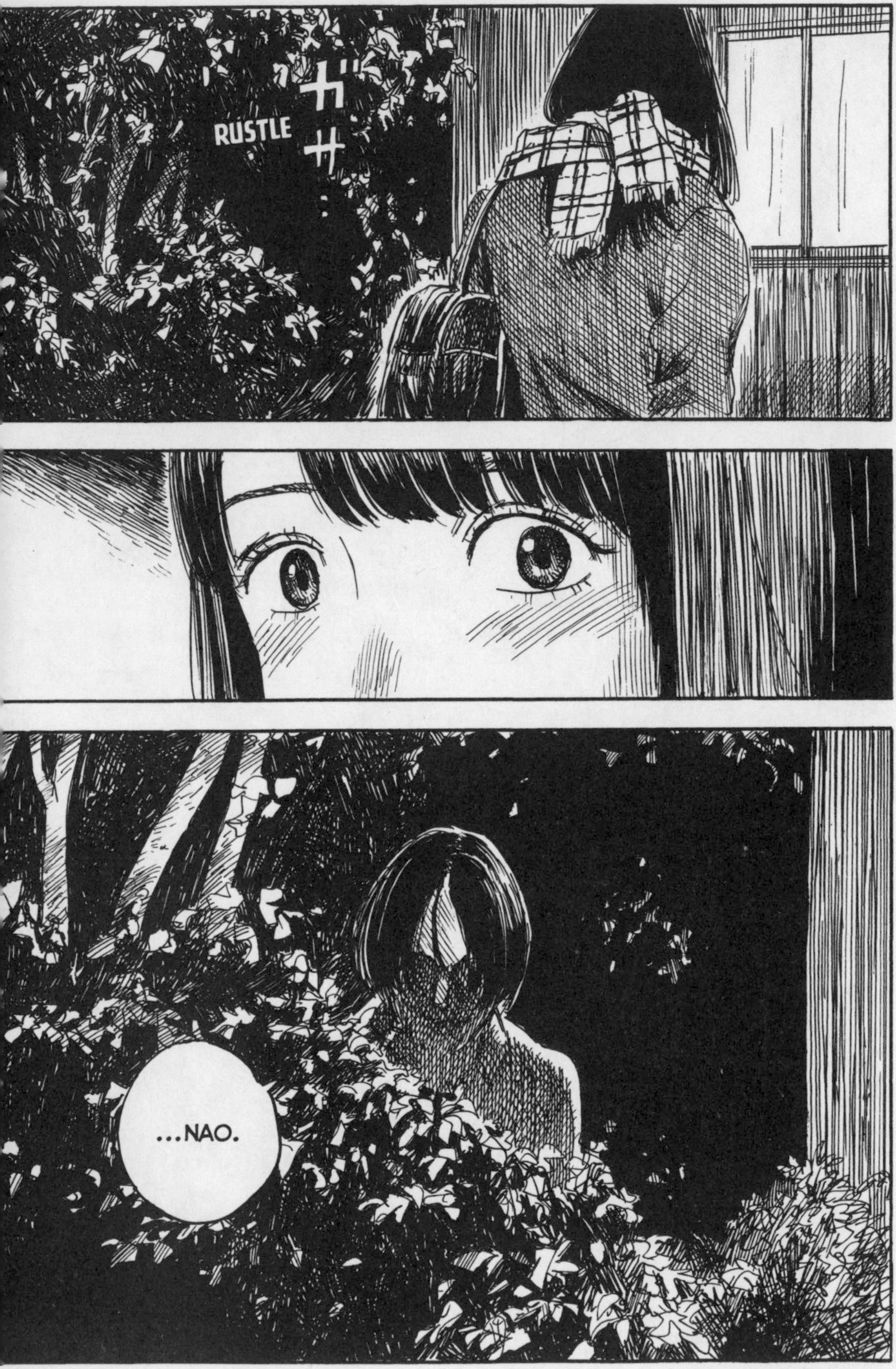
RUSTLE
ガサ
...NAO.

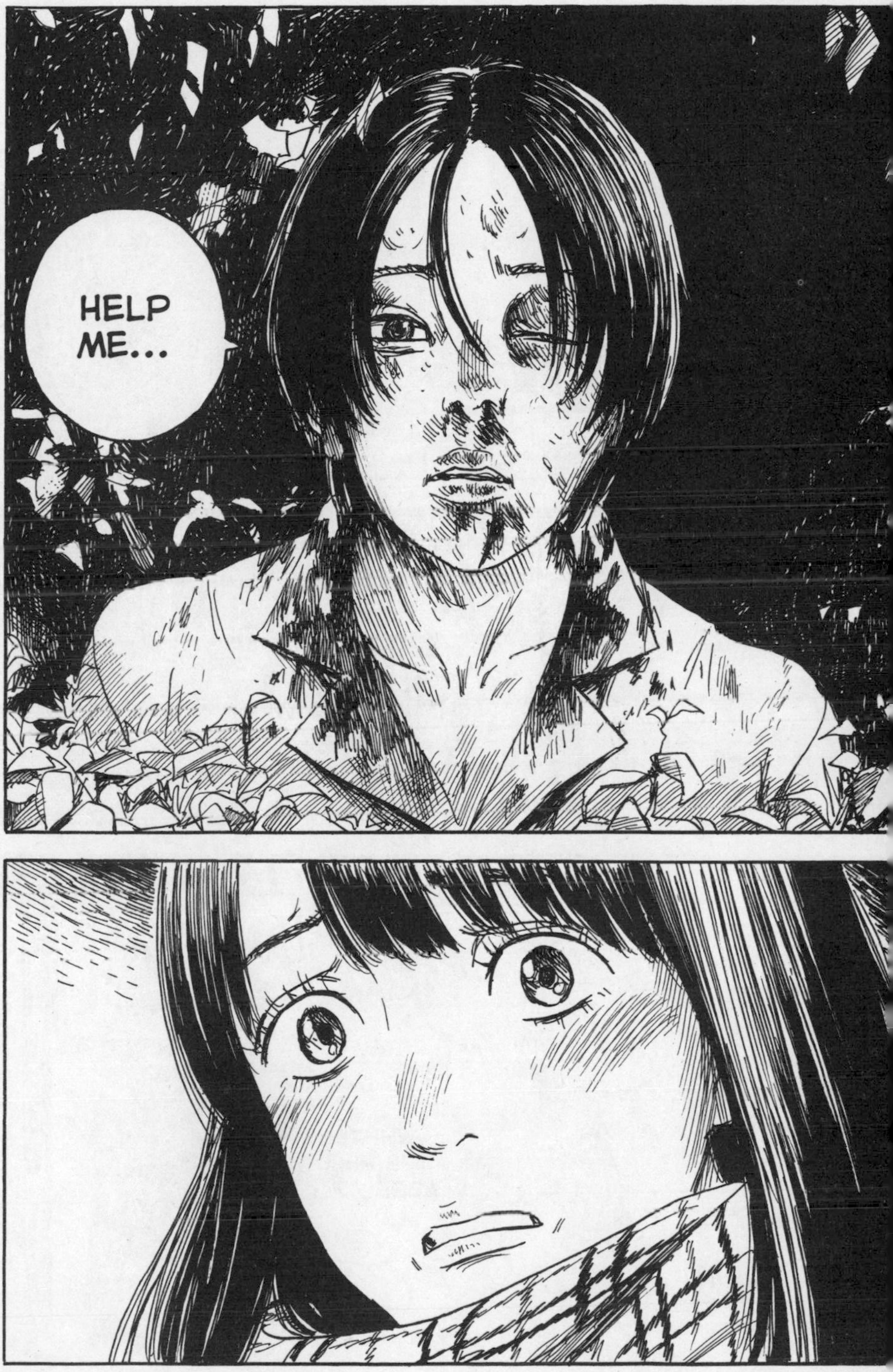
HELP ME...

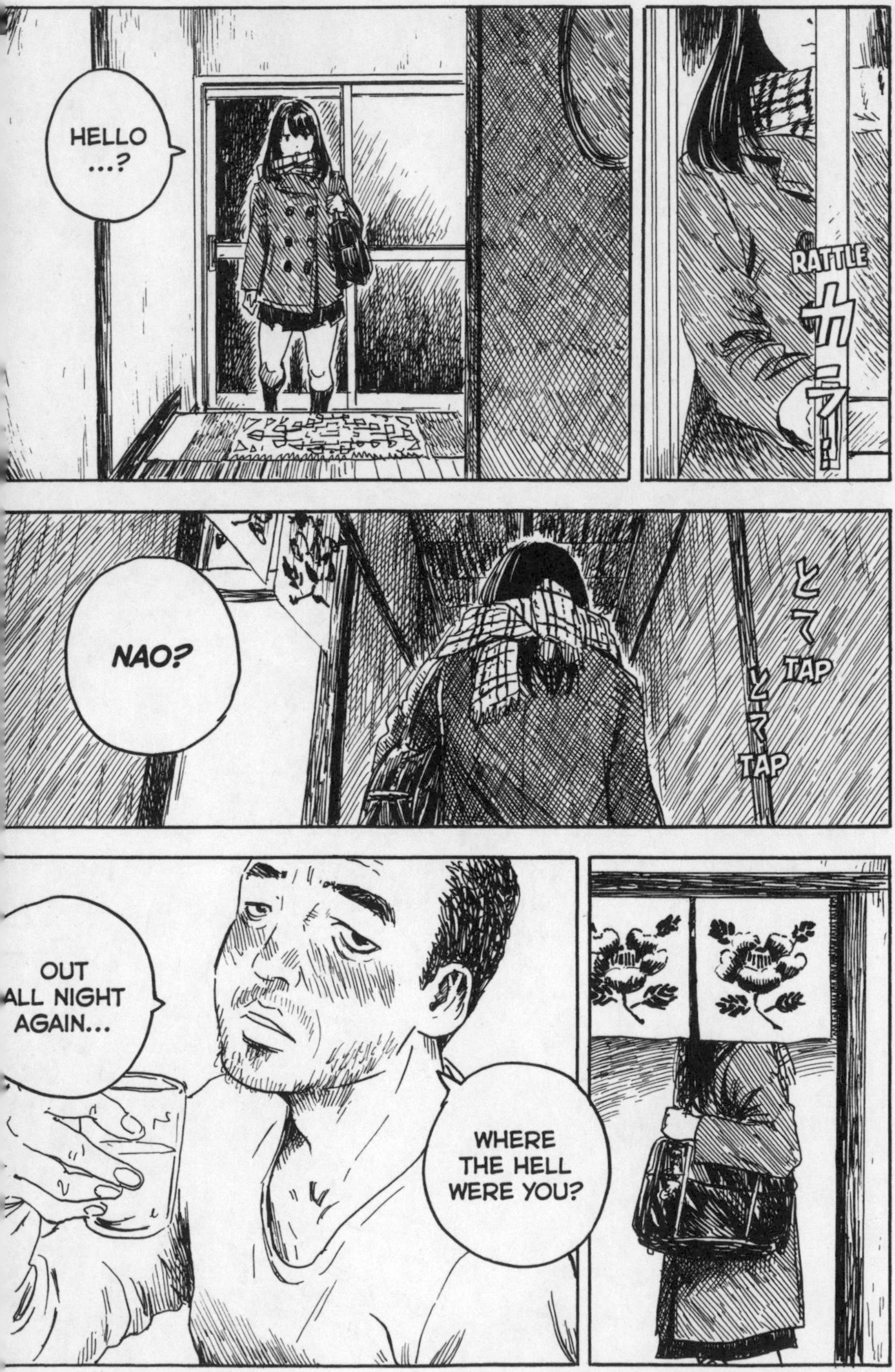
RATTLE
カラ
HELLO ...?
とて
TAP
とて
TAP
NAO?
OUT ALL NIGHT AGAIN...
WHERE THE HELL WERE YOU?

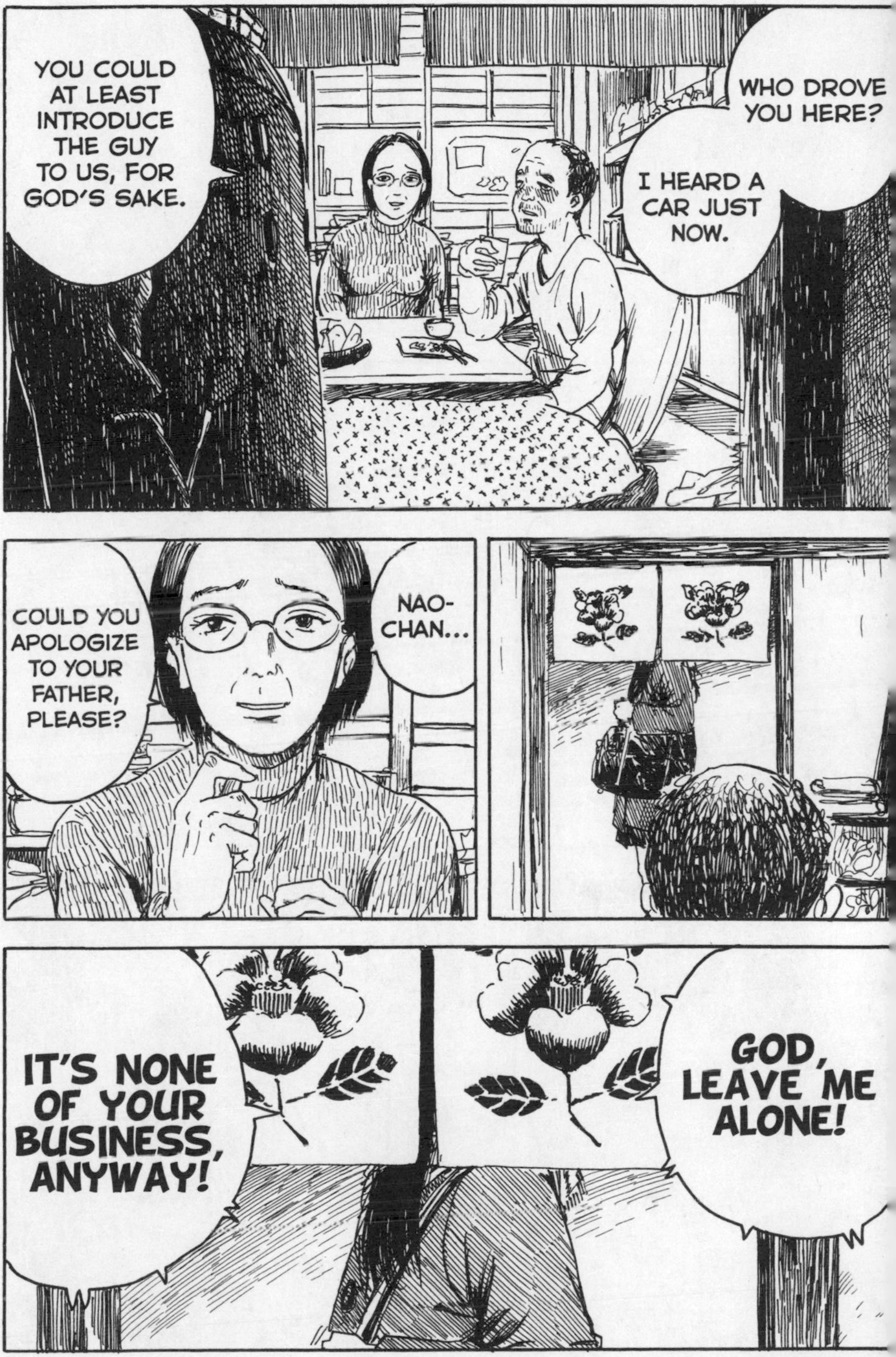
WHO DROVE YOU HERE?
I HEARD A CAR JUST NOW.
YOU COULD AT LEAST INTRODUCE THE GUY TO US, FOR GOD'S SAKE.
NAO-CHAN...
COULD YOU APOLOGIZE TO YOUR FATHER, PLEASE?
GOD, LEAVE ME ALONE!
IT'S NONE OF YOUR BUSINESS, ANYWAY!

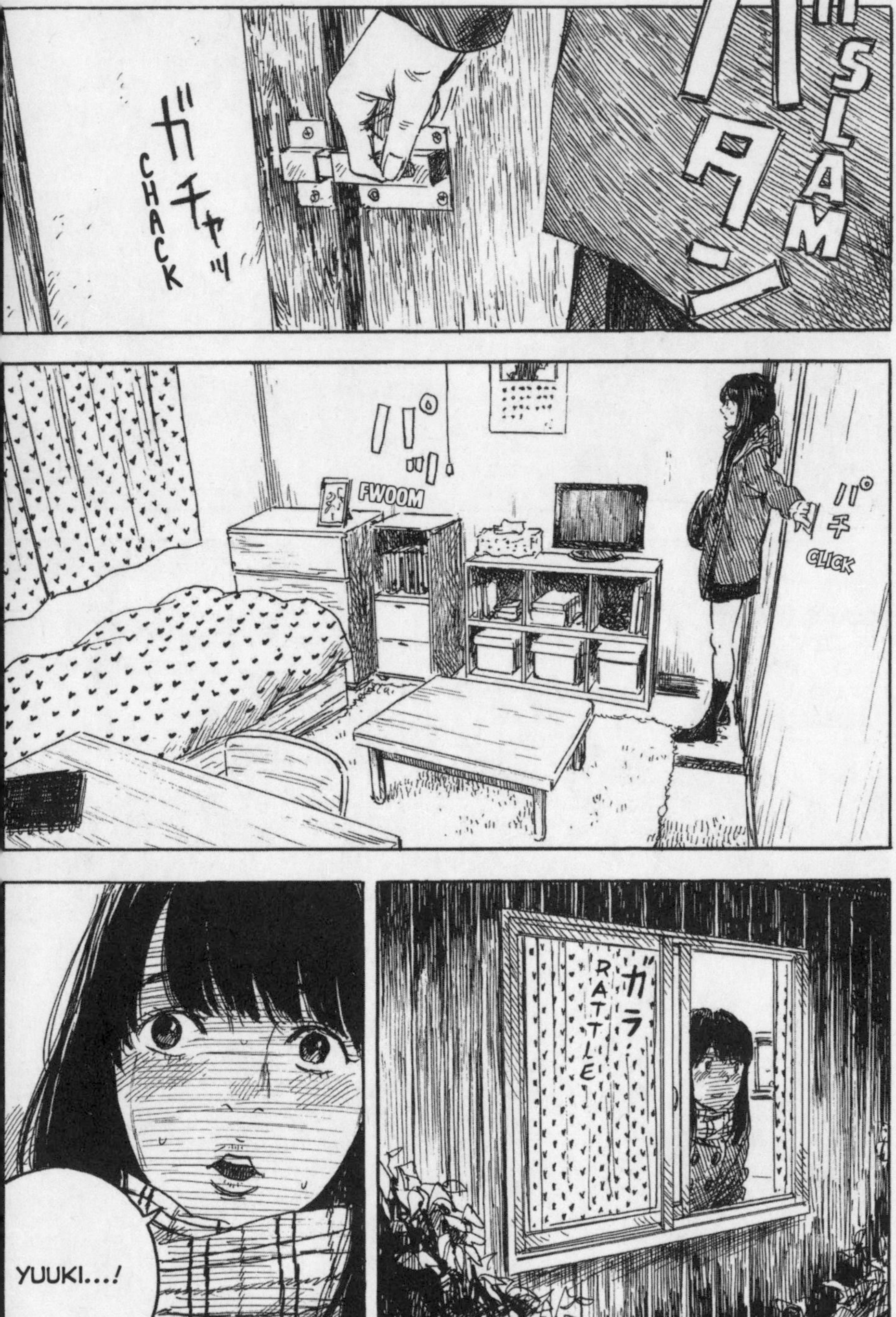
バタン
SLAM
ガチャッ
CHACK
パチ
CLICK
パッ
FWOOM
ガラ
RATTLE
YUUKI...!

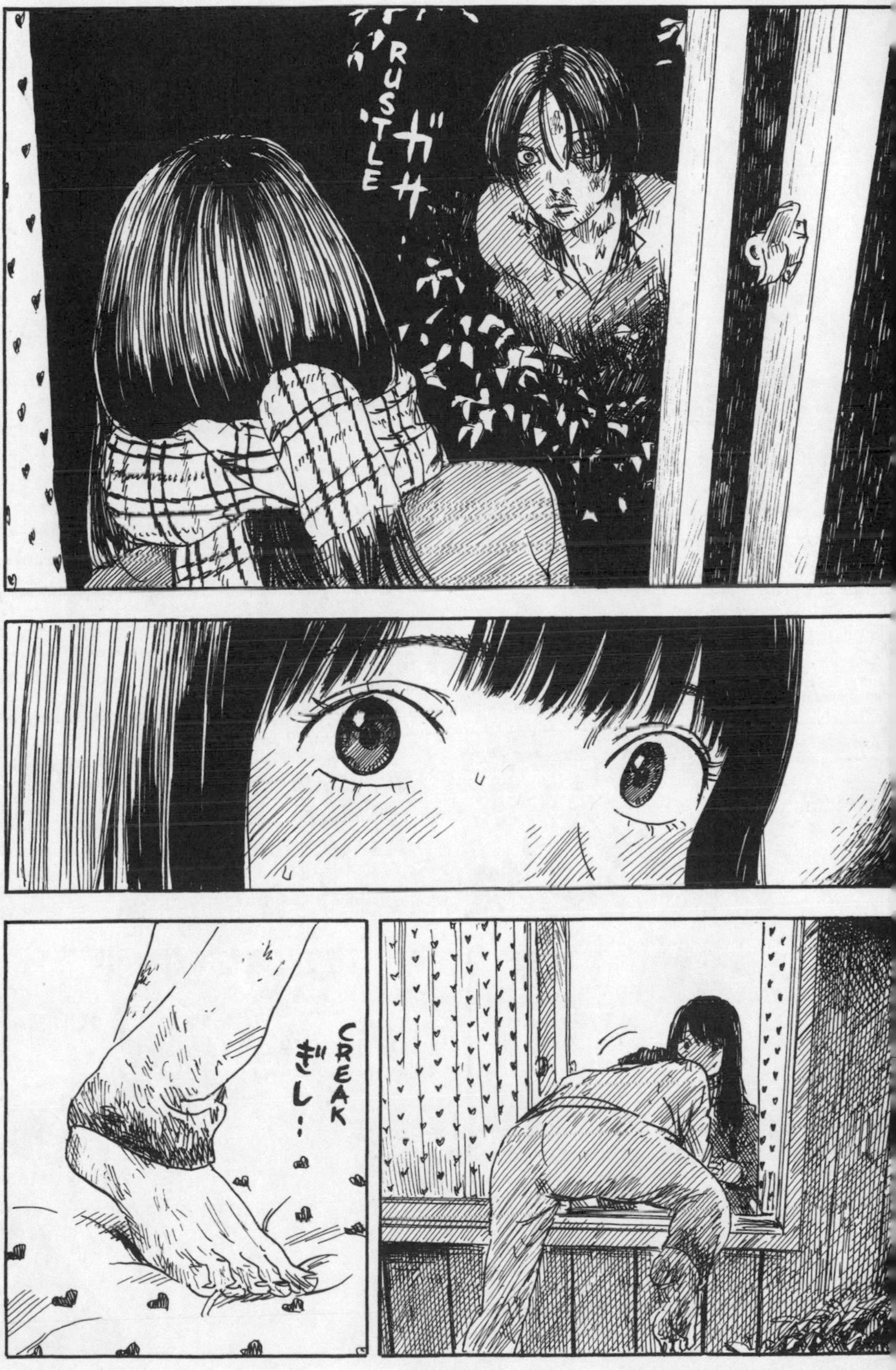
RUSTLE
ガサ
CREAK
ぎし

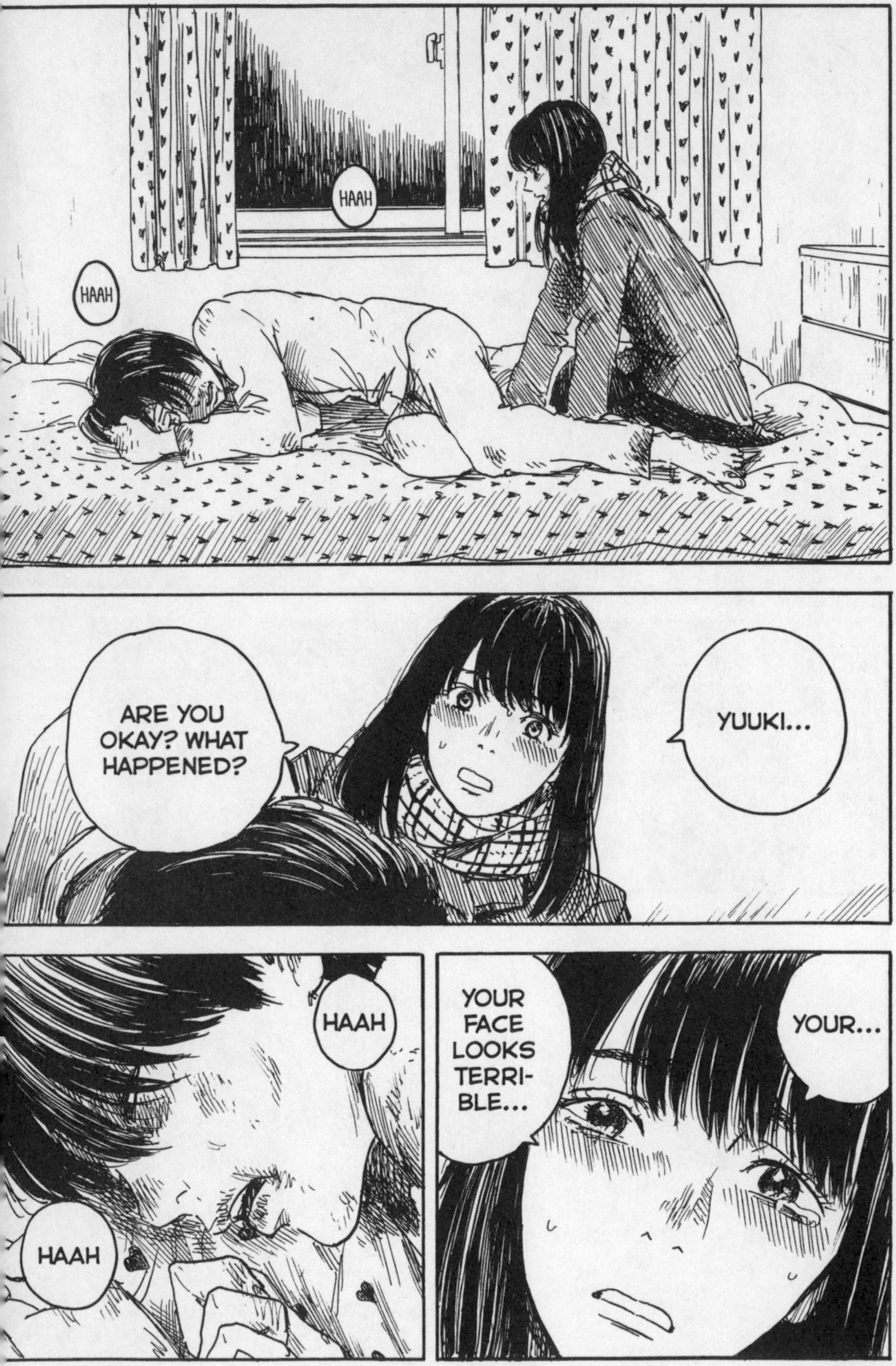
HAAH
HAAH
YUUKI...
ARE YOU OKAY? WHAT HAPPENED?
YOUR...
YOUR FACE LOOKS TERRI-BLE...
HAAH
HAAH

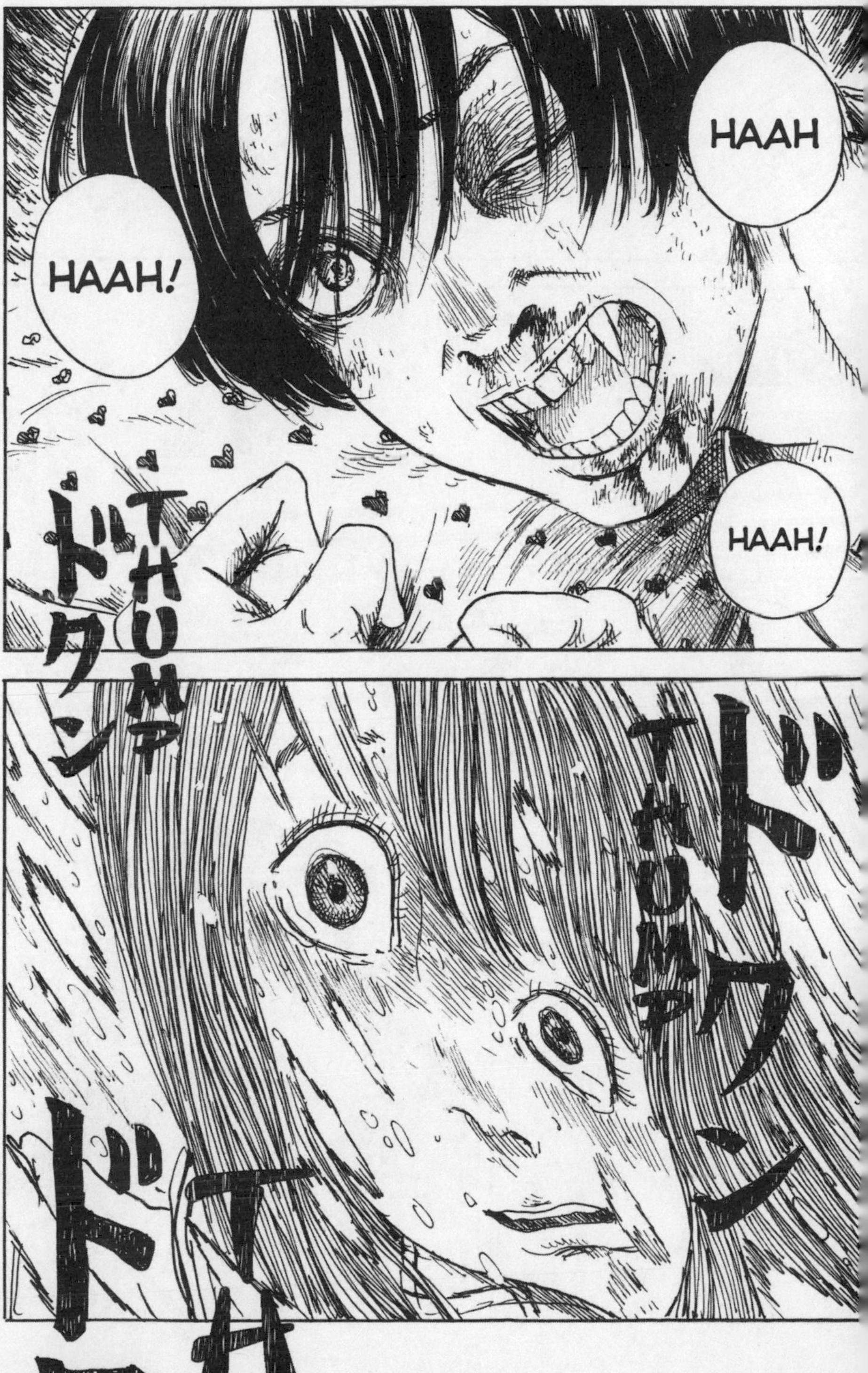
HAAH
HAAH!
HAAH!
THUMP
ドクン
THUMP
ドクン

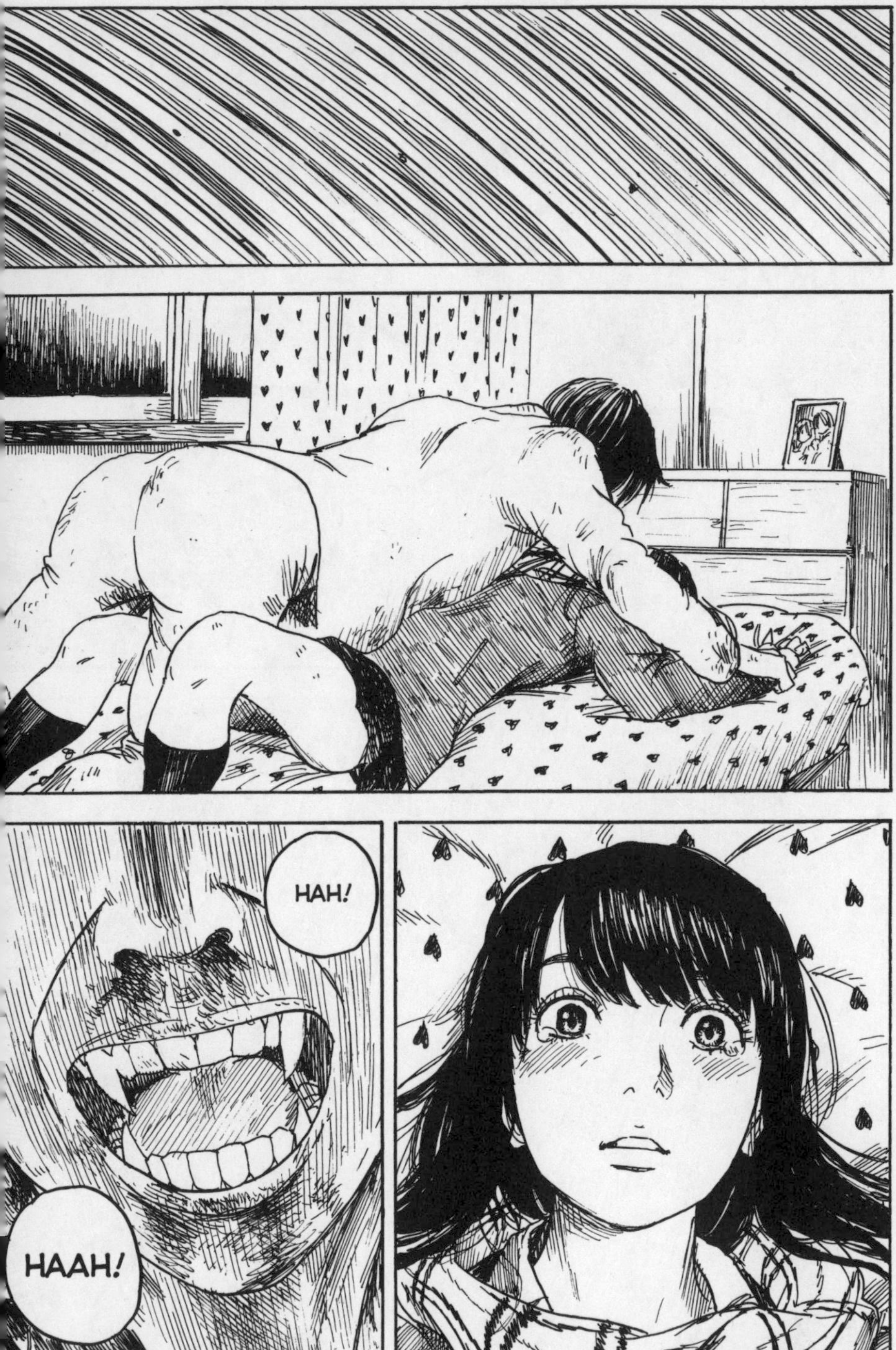
HAH!
HAAH!

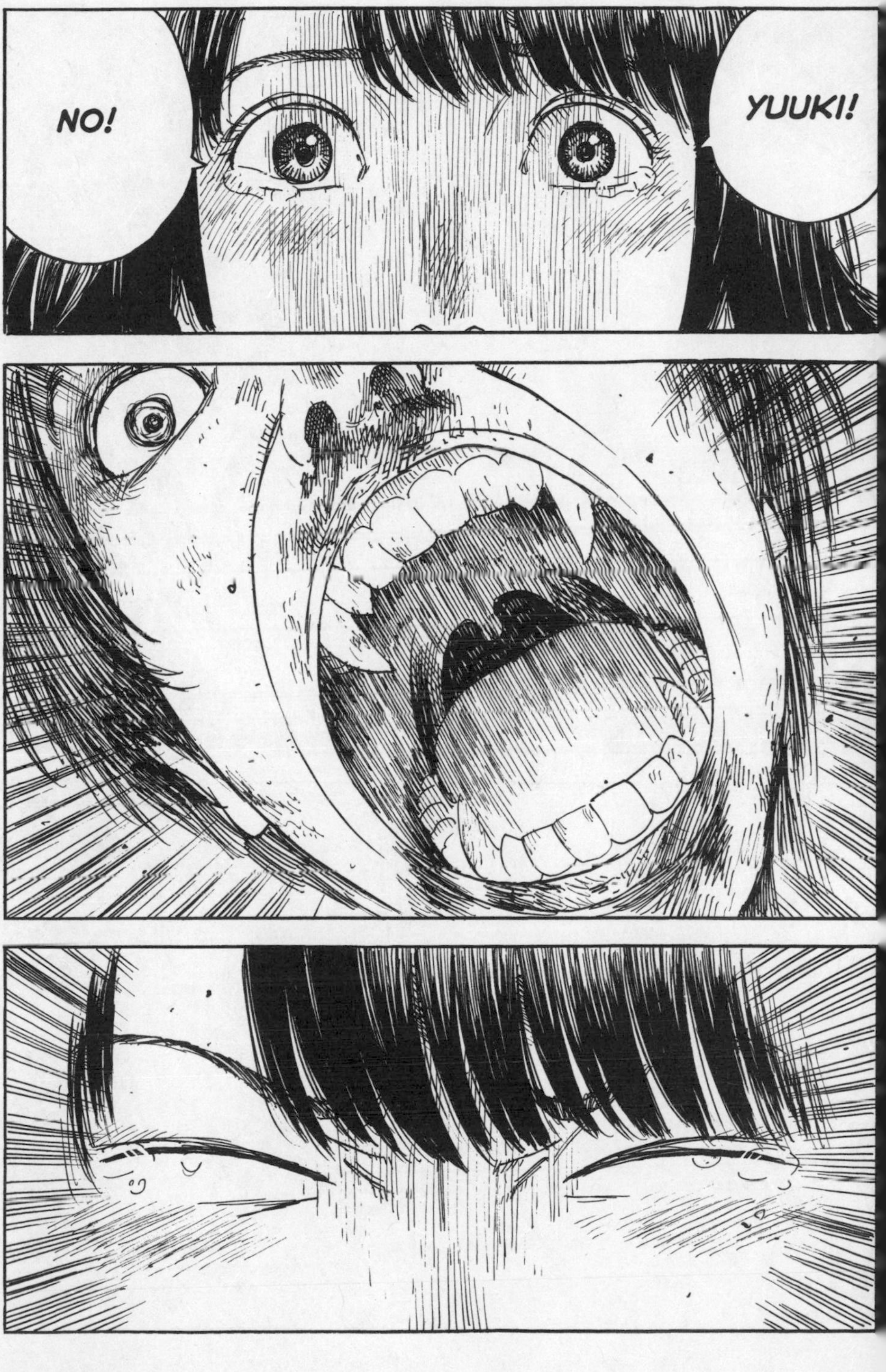
YUUKI!
NO!

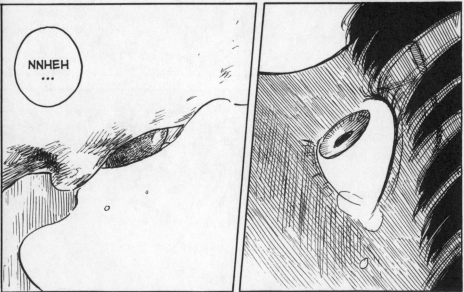

NNHEH
...

72

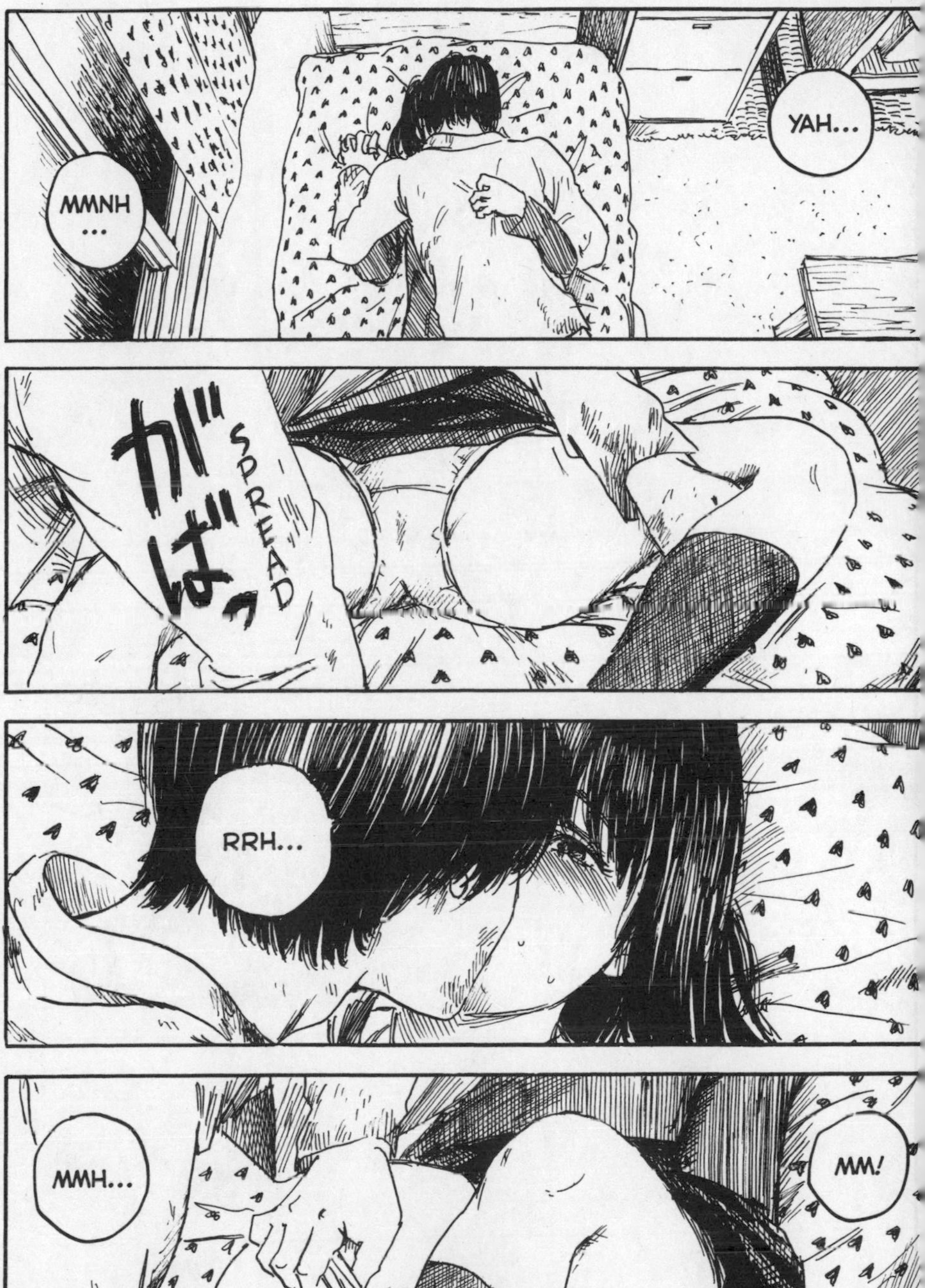
YAH...
MMNH ...
がばっ
SPREAD
RRH...
MM!
MMH...

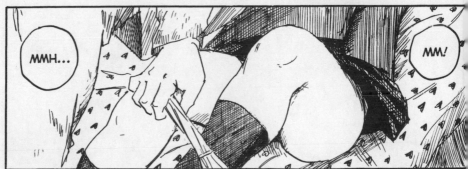

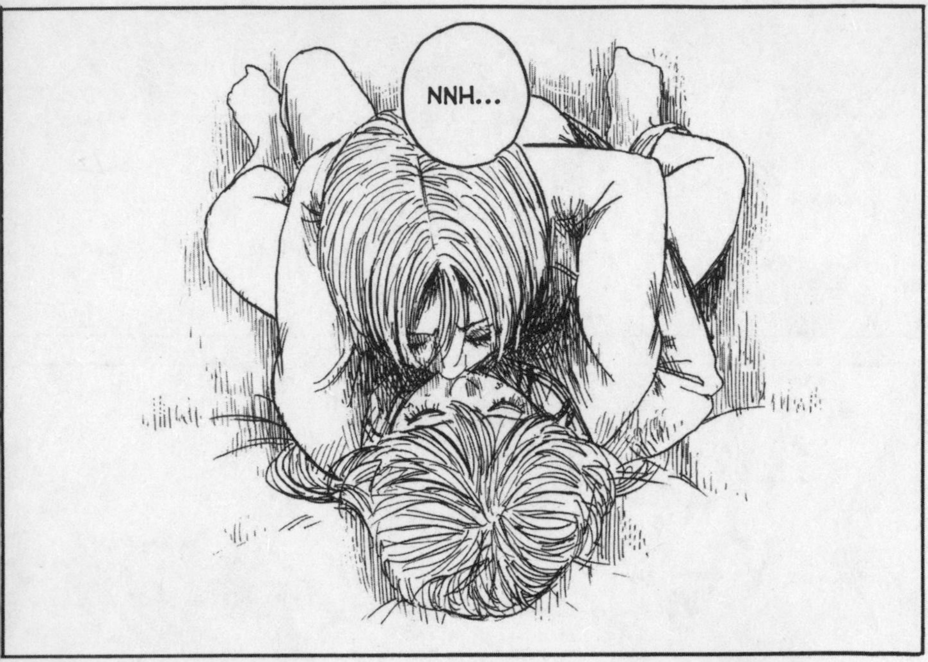
NNH...

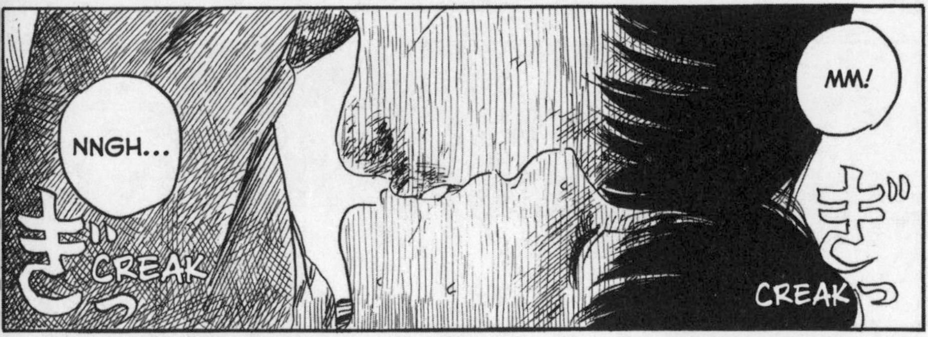
MM!
ぎっ
CREAK
NNGH...
ぎっ
CREAK

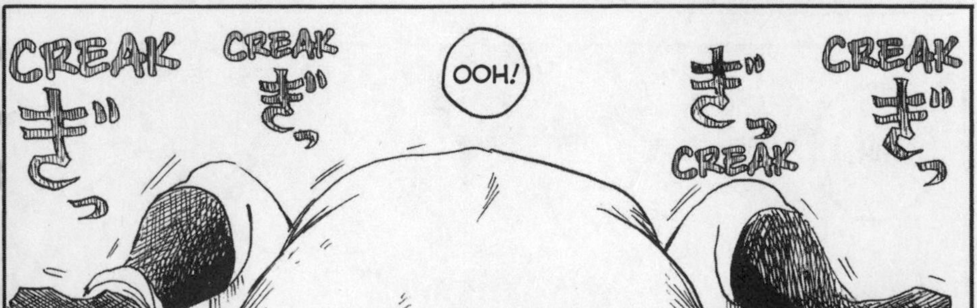
CREAK
ぎっ
ぎっ
CREAK
OOH!
CREAK
ぎっ
CREAK
ぎっ

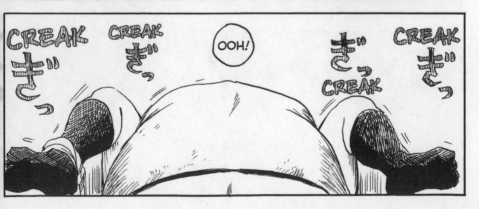

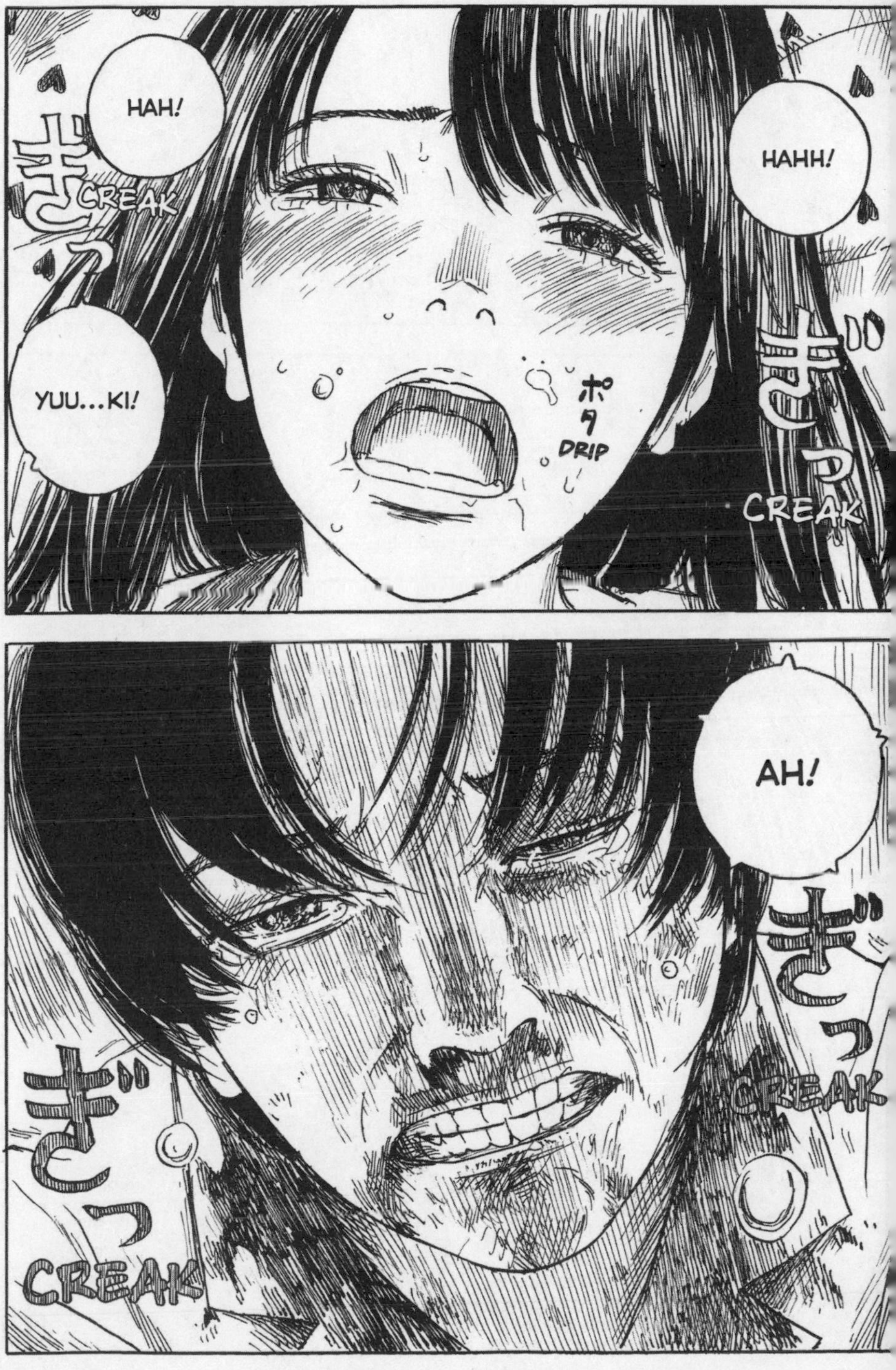
HAHH!
ぎっ
CREAK
ポタ
DRIP
HAH!
ぎっ
CREAK
YUU...KI!
AH!
ぎっ
CREAK
ぎっ
CREAK

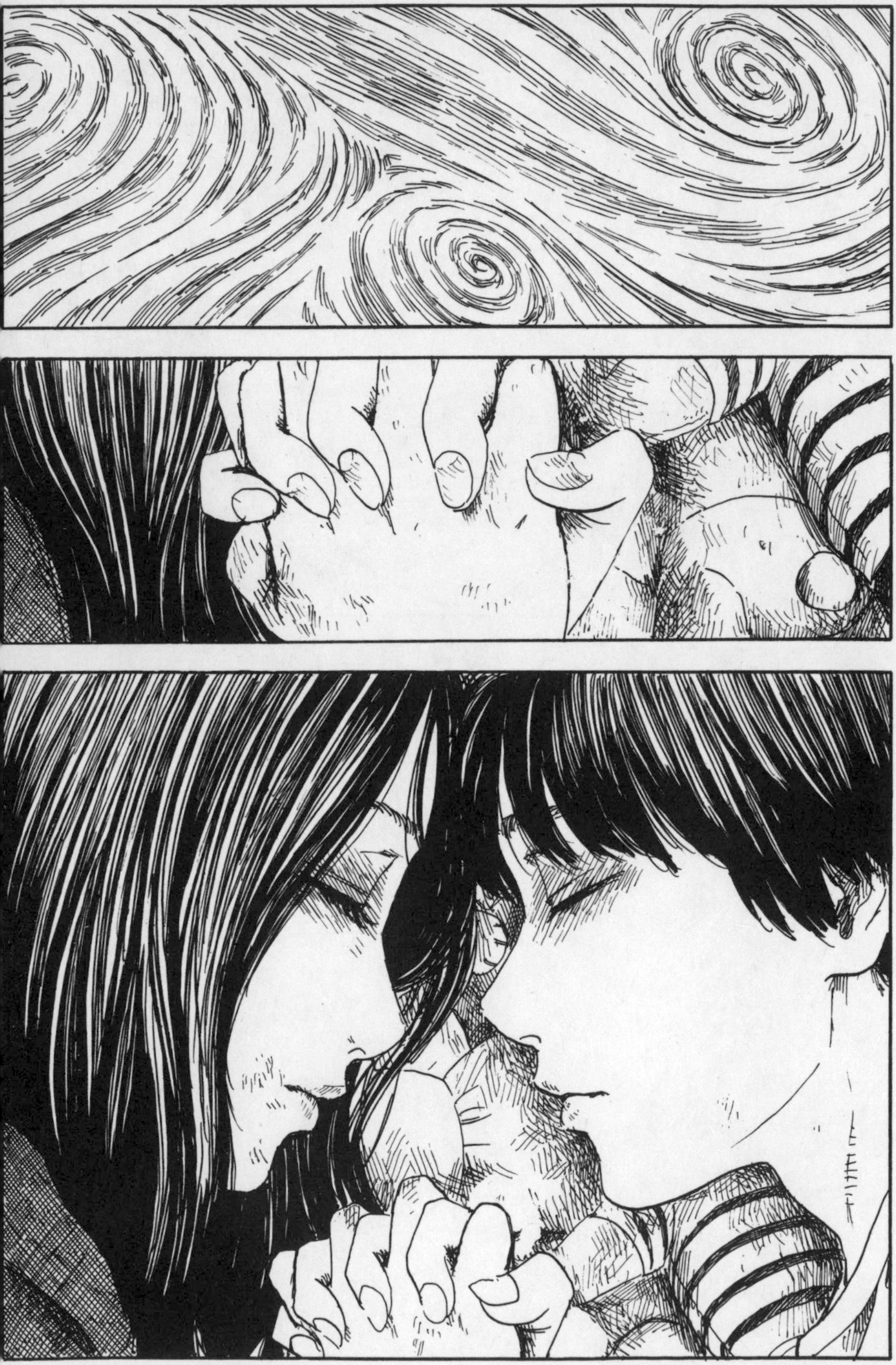

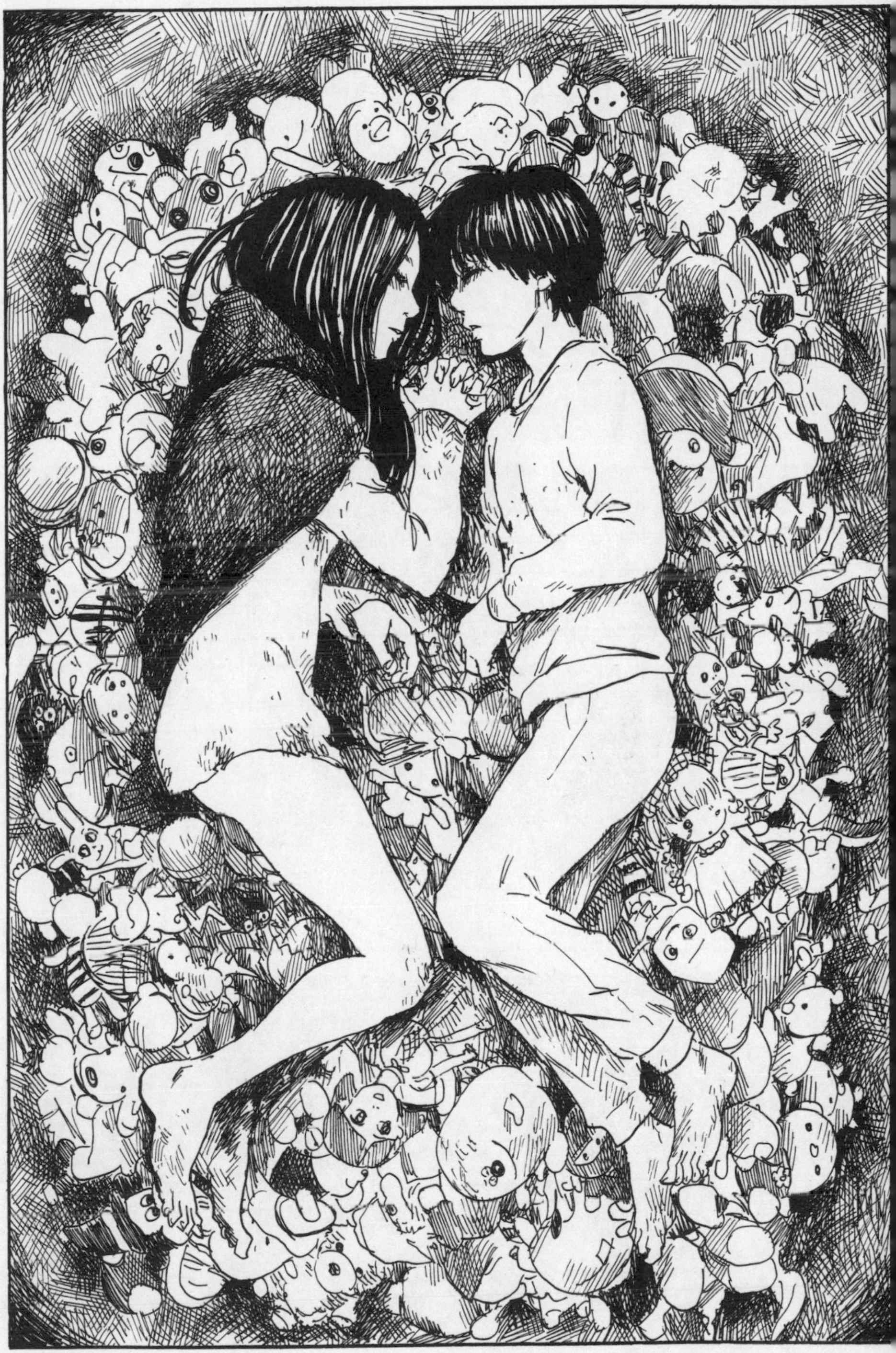

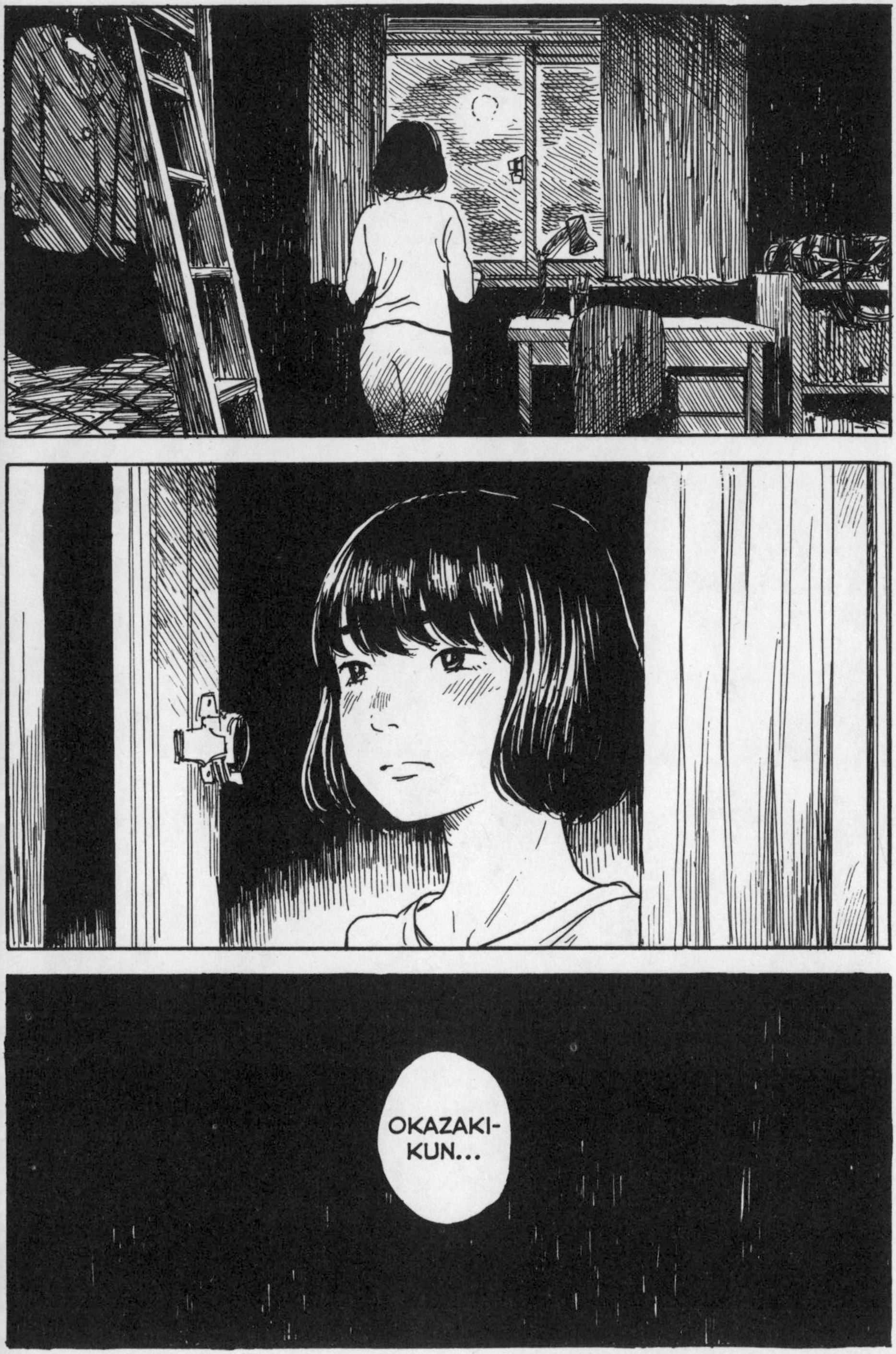
OKAZAKI-KUN...

Chapter 18: Sister and Brother

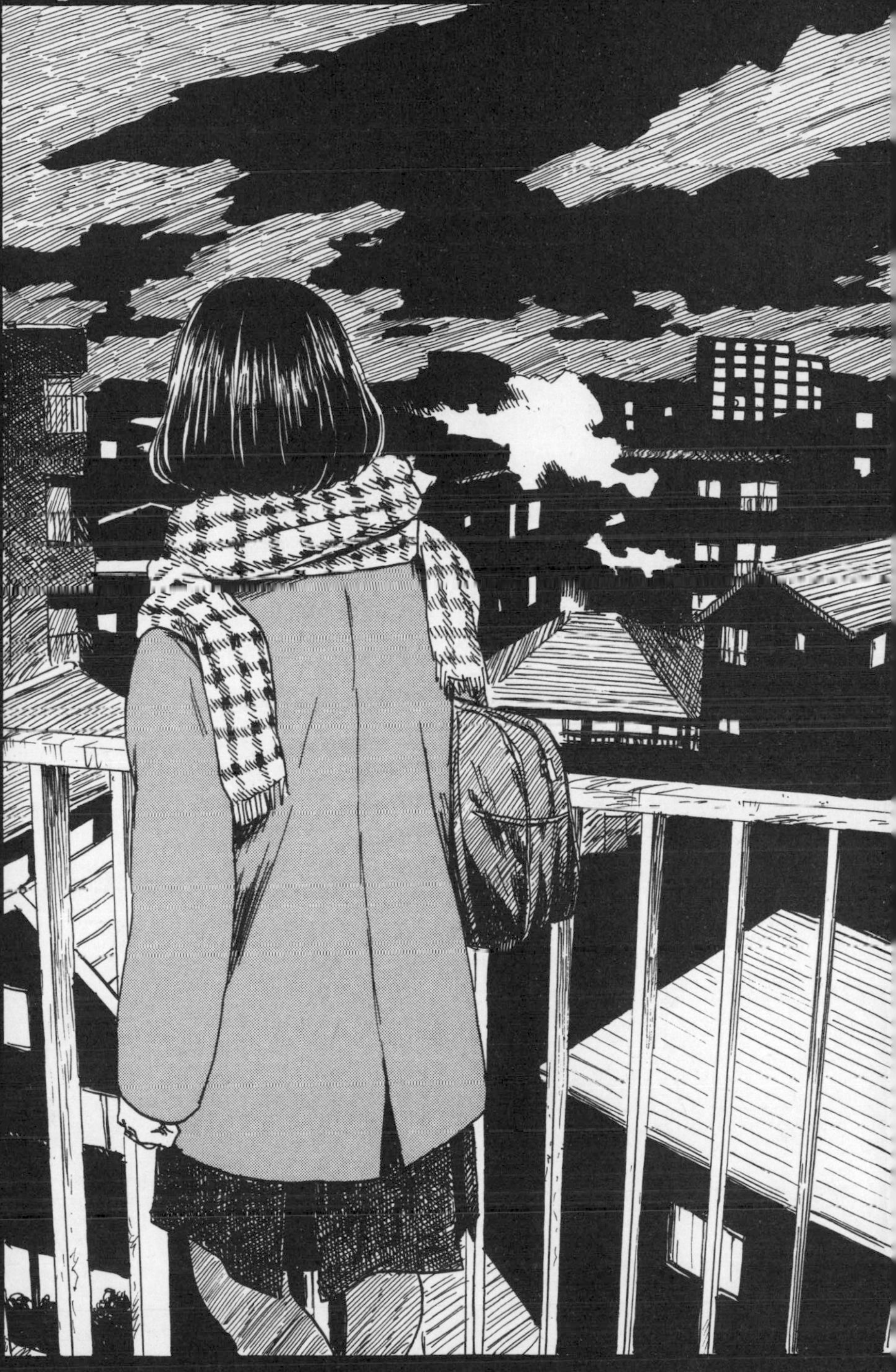

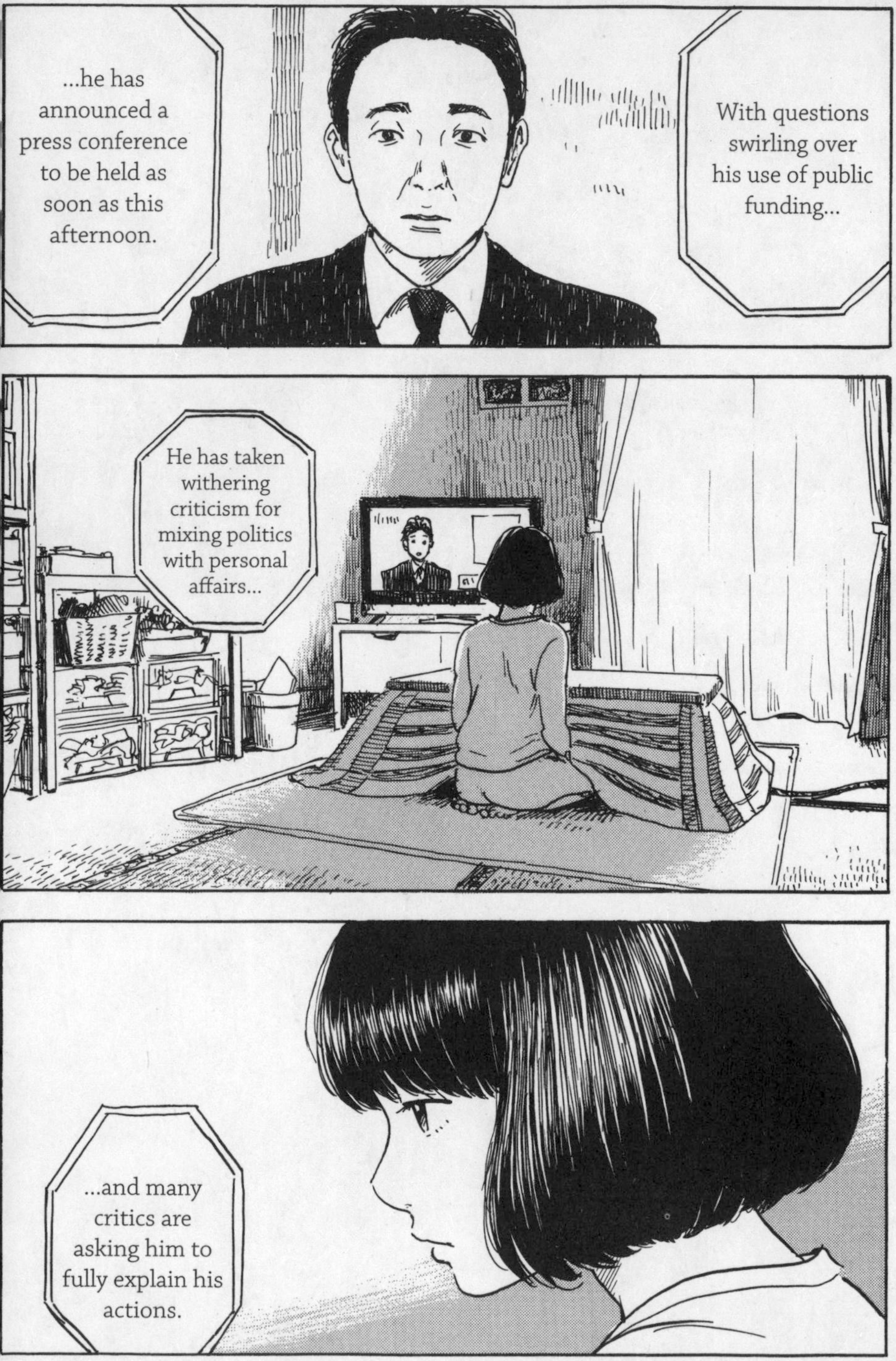
With questions swirling over his use of public funding...
...he has announced a press conference to be held as soon as this afternoon.
He has taken withering criticism for mixing politics with personal affairs...
...and many critics are asking him to fully explain his actions.

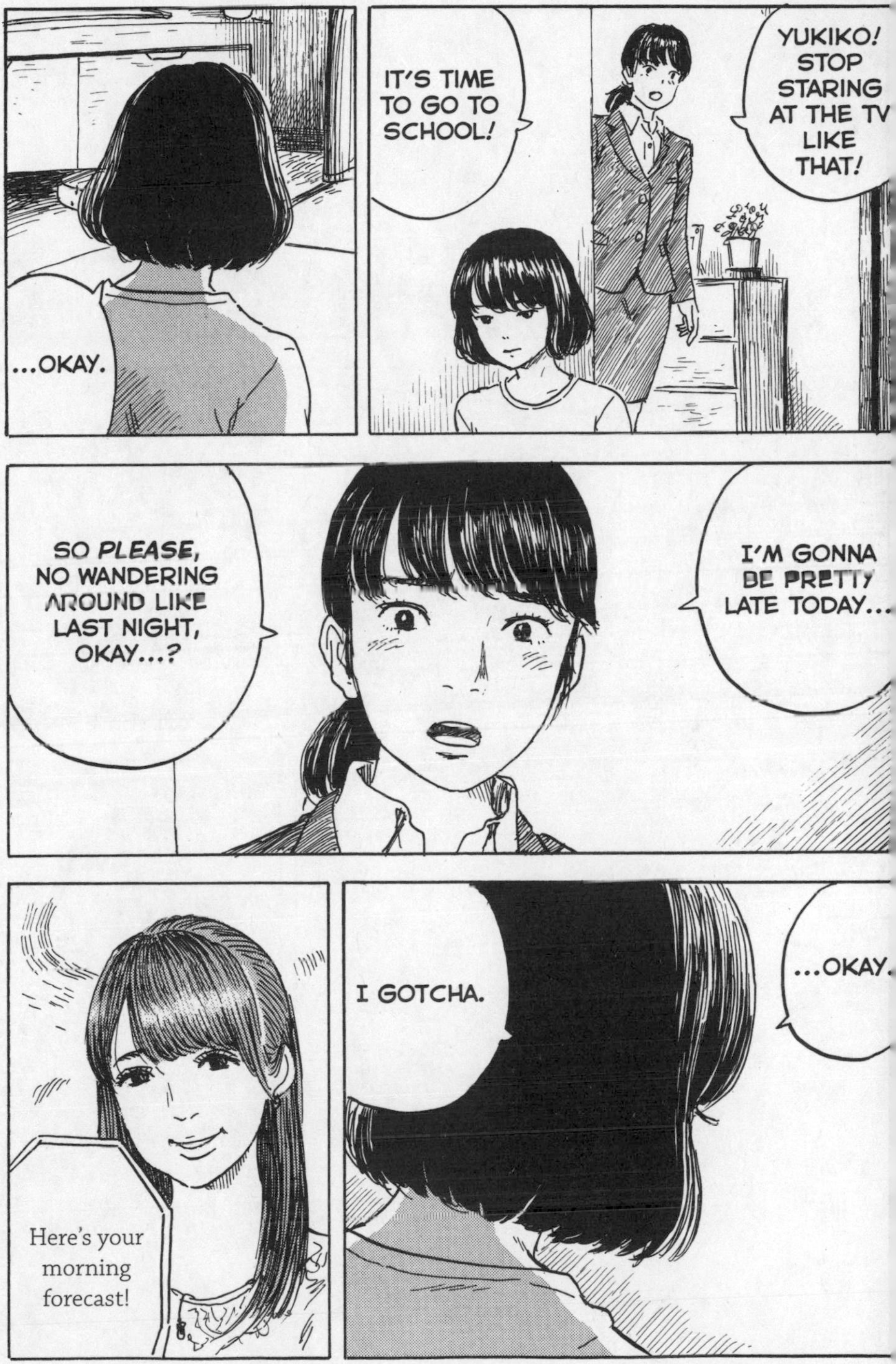
YUKIKO! STOP STARING AT THE TV LIKE THAT!
IT'S TIME TO GO TO SCHOOL!
...OKAY.
I'M GONNA BE PRETTY LATE TODAY...
SO *PLEASE*, NO WANDERING AROUND LIKE LAST NIGHT, OKAY...?
...OKAY.
I GOTCHA.
Here's your morning forecast!

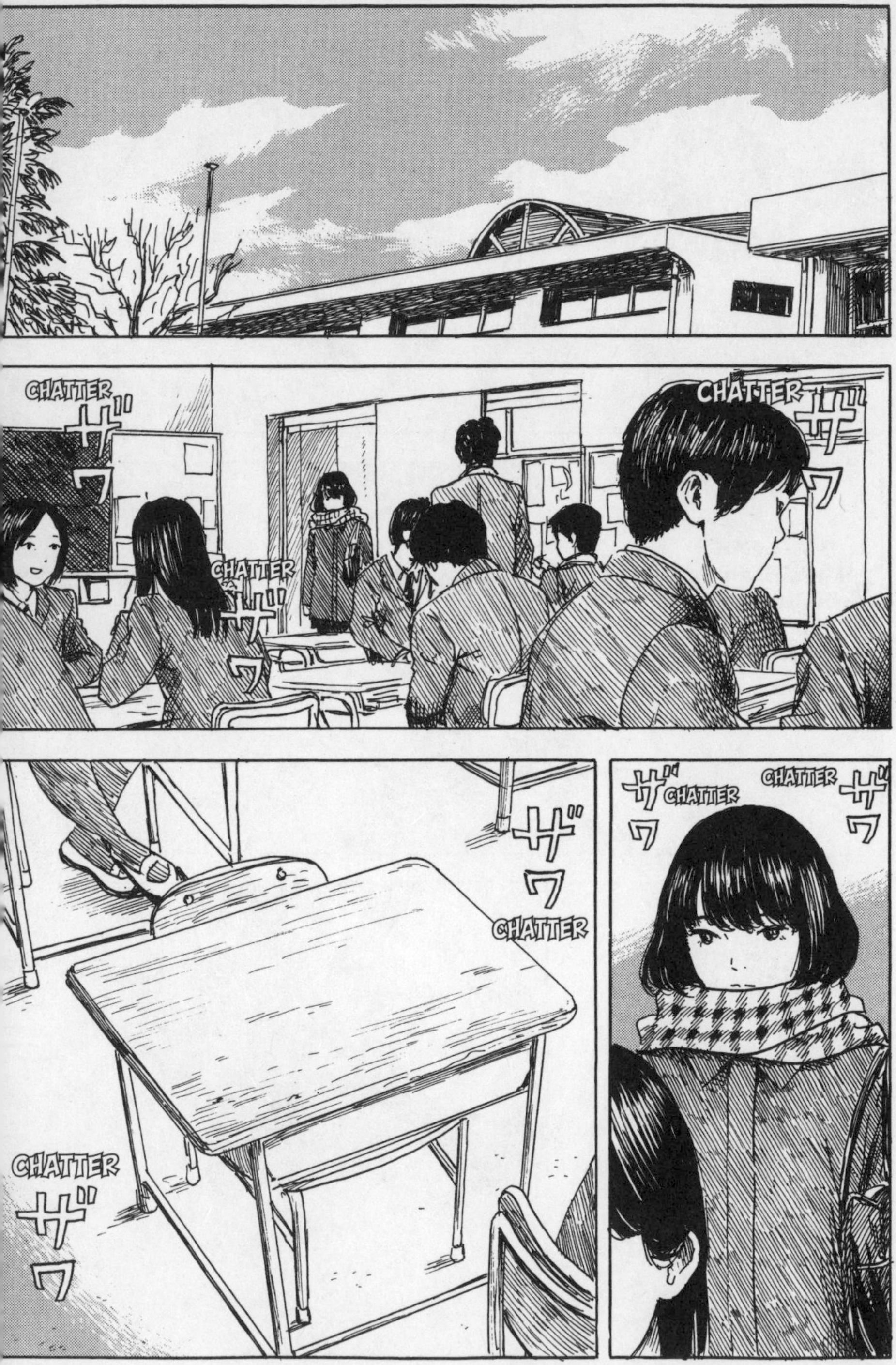
CHATTER
ザワ
CHATTER
ザワ
CHATTER
ザワ
CHATTER
ザワ
CHATTER
ザワ
ザワ
CHATTER
CHATTER
ザワ

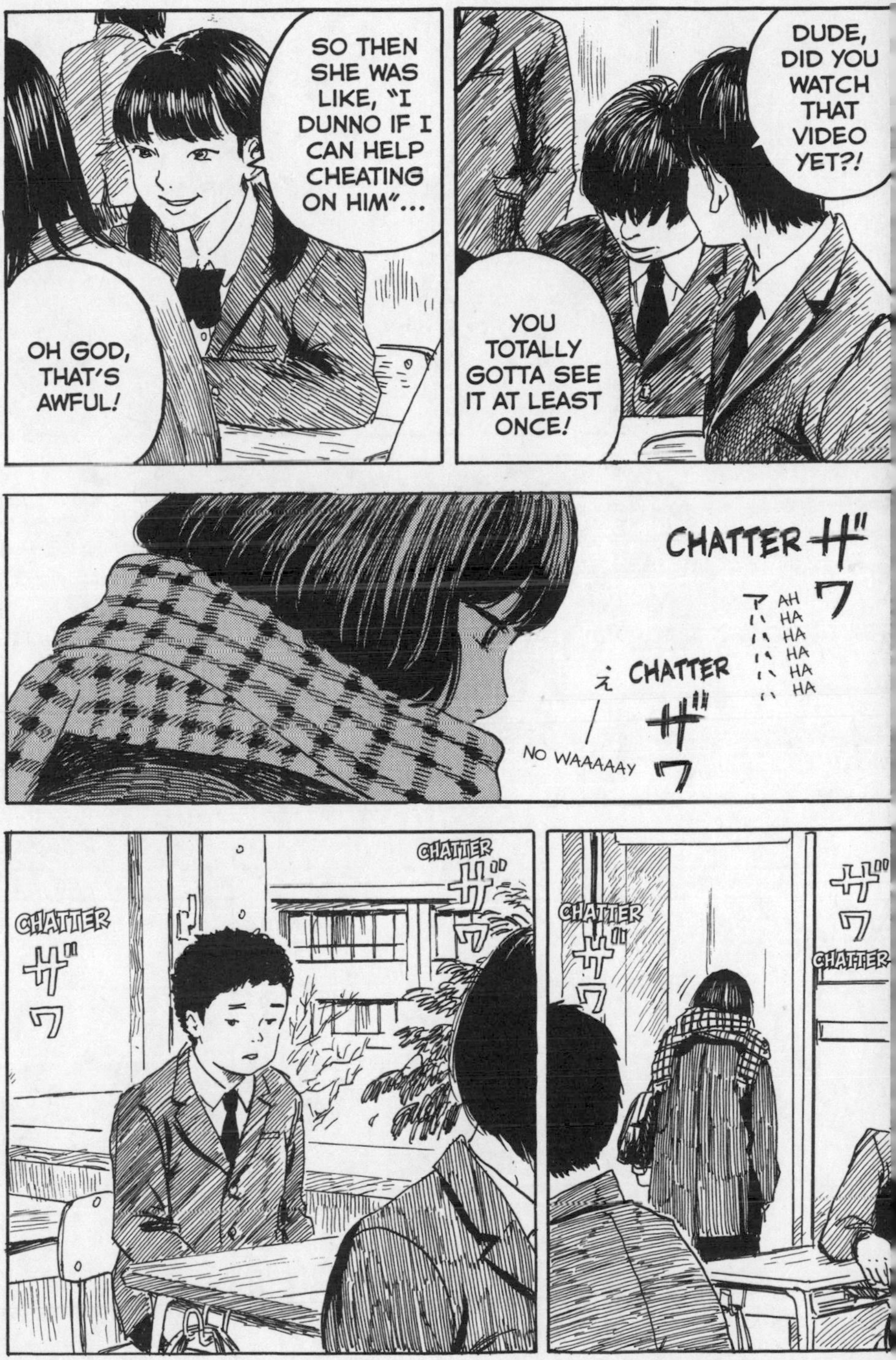

DUDE, DID YOU WATCH THAT VIDEO YET?!
YOU TOTALLY GOTTA SEE IT AT LEAST ONCE!
SO THEN SHE WAS LIKE, "I DUNNO IF I CAN HELP CHEATING ON HIM"...
OH GOD, THAT'S AWFUL!
CHATTER ザワ
AH HA HA HA HA HA
アハハハハハ
CHATTER ザワ
え
NO WAAAAAY
ザワ
CHATTER
CHATTER ザワ
CHATTER ザワ
CHATTER ザワ

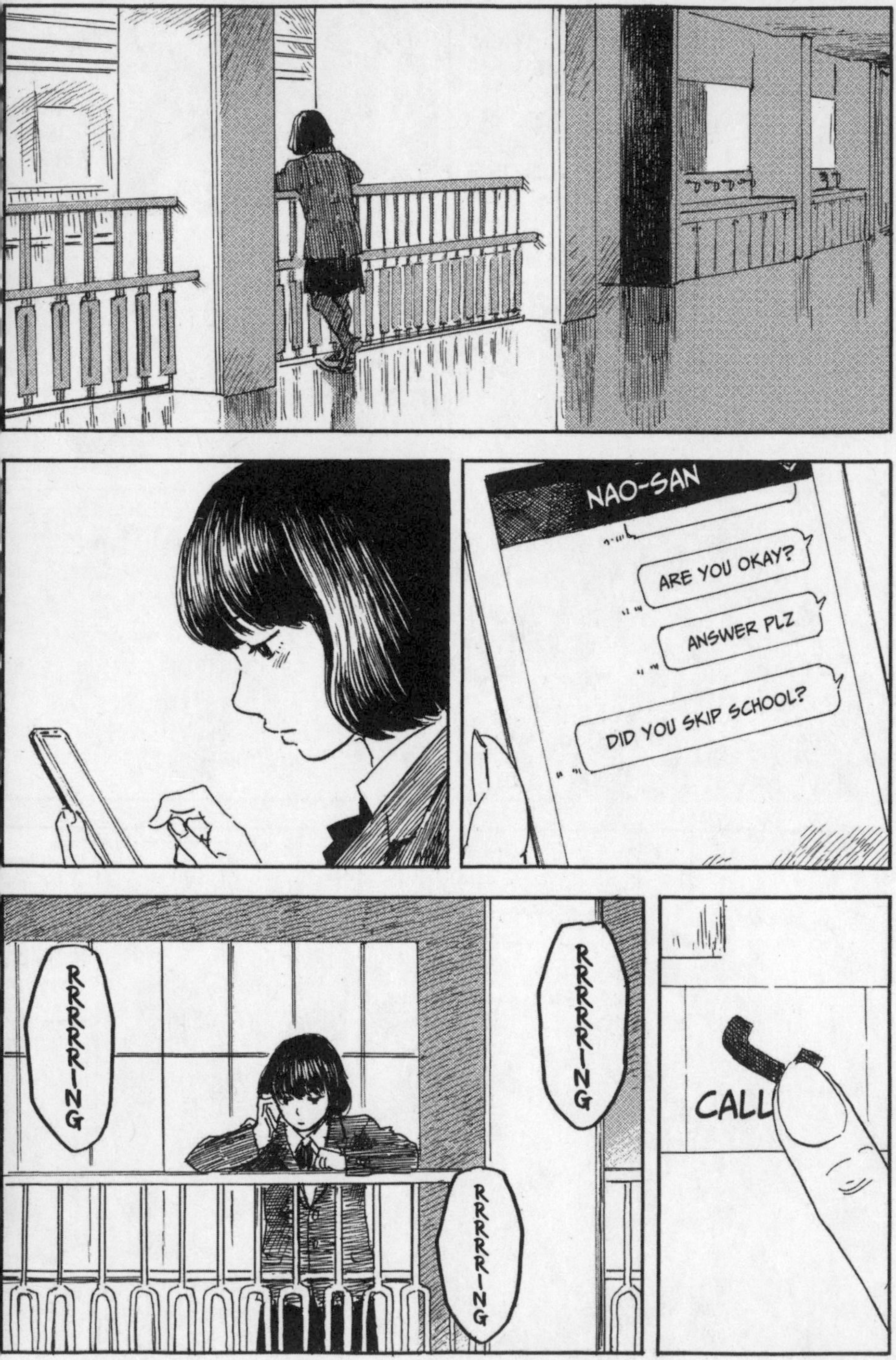
NAO-SAN
ARE YOU OKAY?
ANSWER PLZ
DID YOU SKIP SCHOOL?
CALL
RRRRRING
RRRRRING
RRRRRING

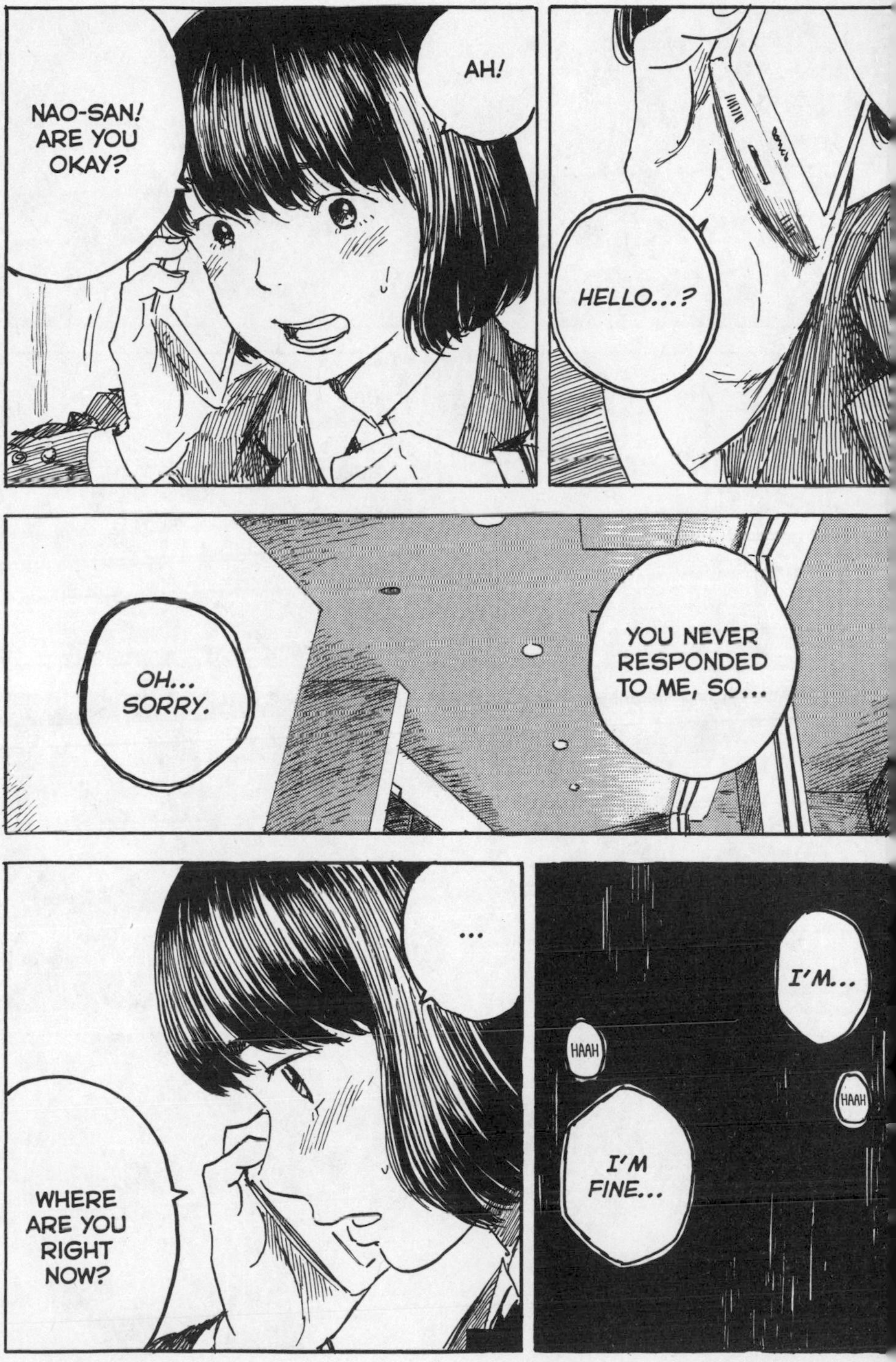
HELLO...?
AH!
NAO-SAN! ARE YOU OKAY?
YOU NEVER RESPONDED TO ME, SO...
OH... SORRY.
I'M...
HAAH
HAAH
I'M FINE...
...
WHERE ARE YOU RIGHT NOW?

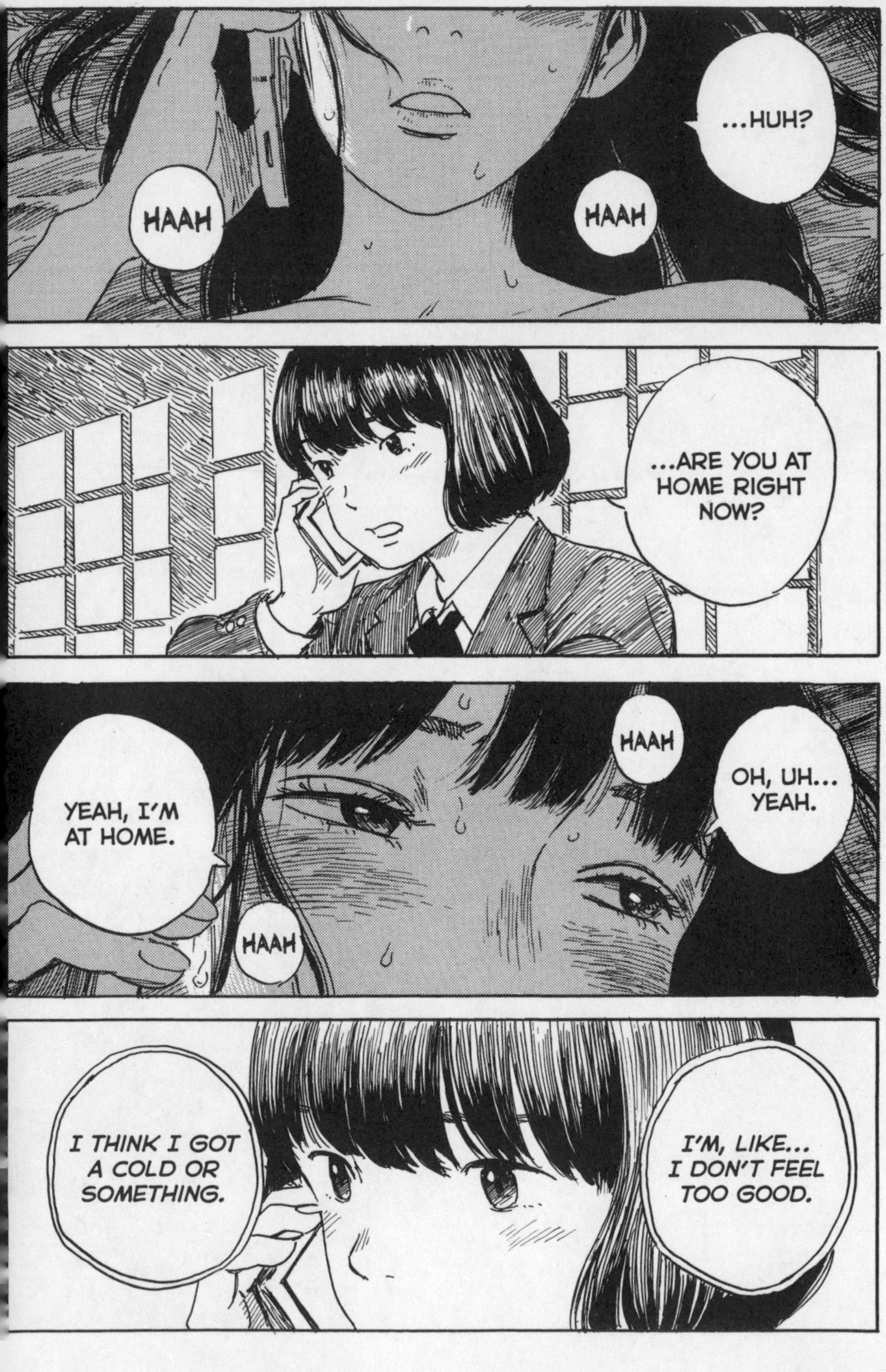
...HUH?
HAAH
HAAH
...ARE YOU AT HOME RIGHT NOW?
HAAH
OH, UH... YEAH.
YEAH, I'M AT HOME.
HAAH
I'M, LIKE... I DON'T FEEL TOO GOOD.
I THINK I GOT A COLD OR SOMETHING.

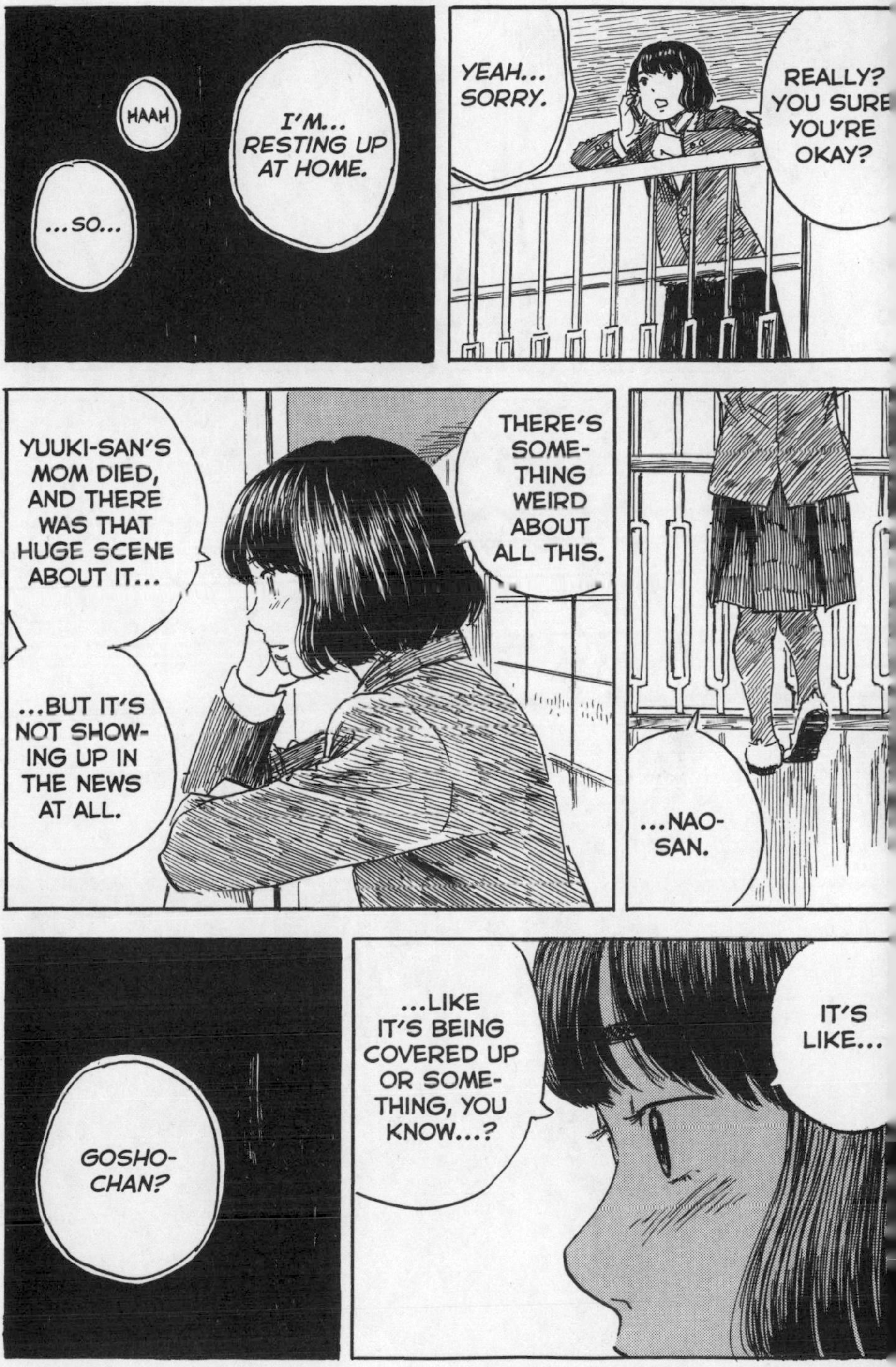
REALLY? YOU SURE YOU'RE OKAY?
YEAH... SORRY.
I'M... RESTING UP AT HOME.
HAAH
...SO...
...NAO-SAN.
THERE'S SOMETHING WEIRD ABOUT ALL THIS.
YUUKI-SAN'S MOM DIED, AND THERE WAS THAT HUGE SCENE ABOUT IT...
...BUT IT'S NOT SHOWING UP IN THE NEWS AT ALL.
IT'S LIKE...
...LIKE IT'S BEING COVERED UP OR SOMETHING, YOU KNOW...?
GOSHO-CHAN?

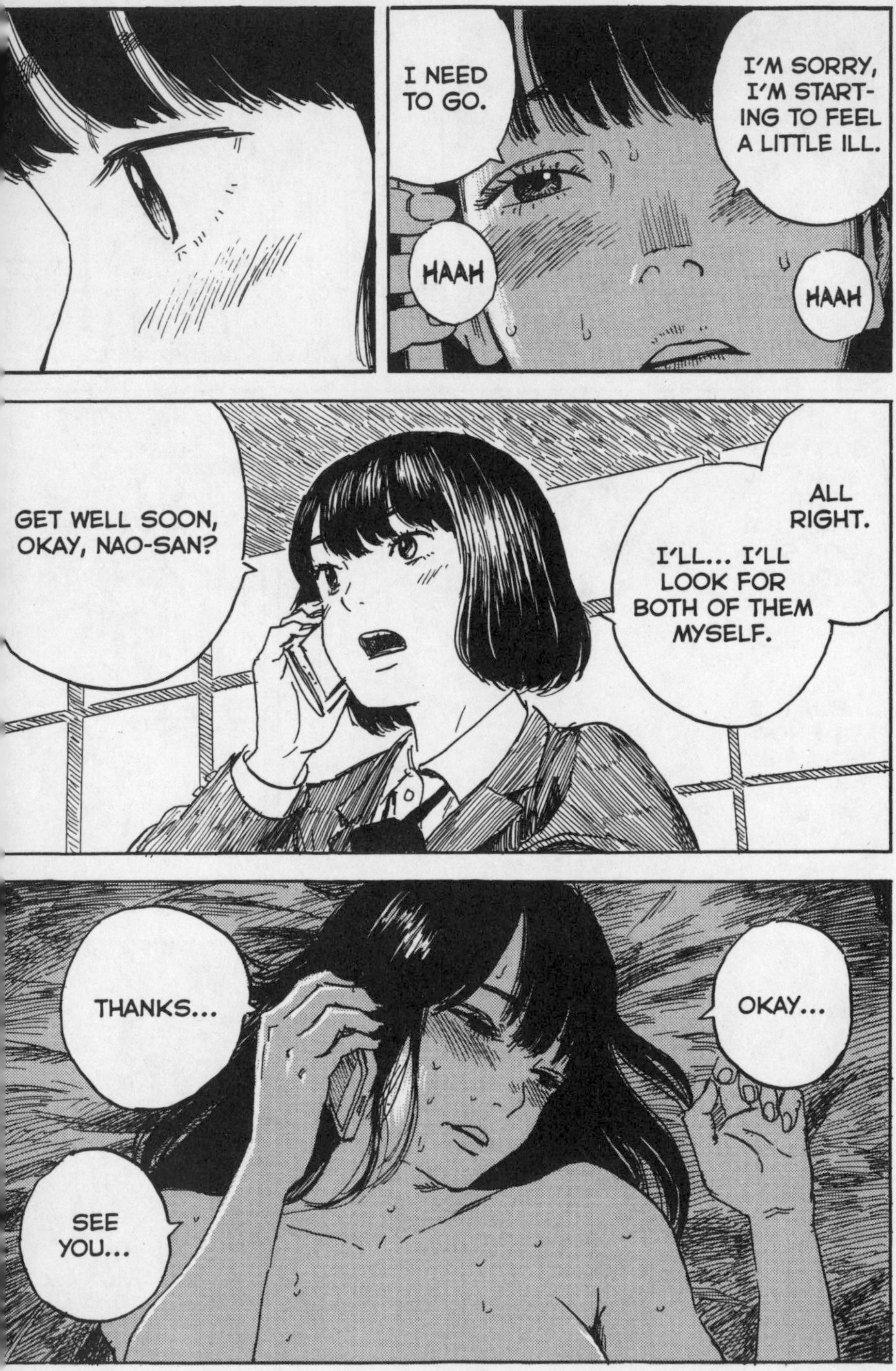
I'M SORRY, I'M STARTING TO FEEL A LITTLE ILL.
I NEED TO GO.
HAAH
HAAH
ALL RIGHT.
I'LL... I'LL LOOK FOR BOTH OF THEM MYSELF.
GET WELL SOON, OKAY, NAO-SAN?
OKAY...
THANKS...
SEE YOU...

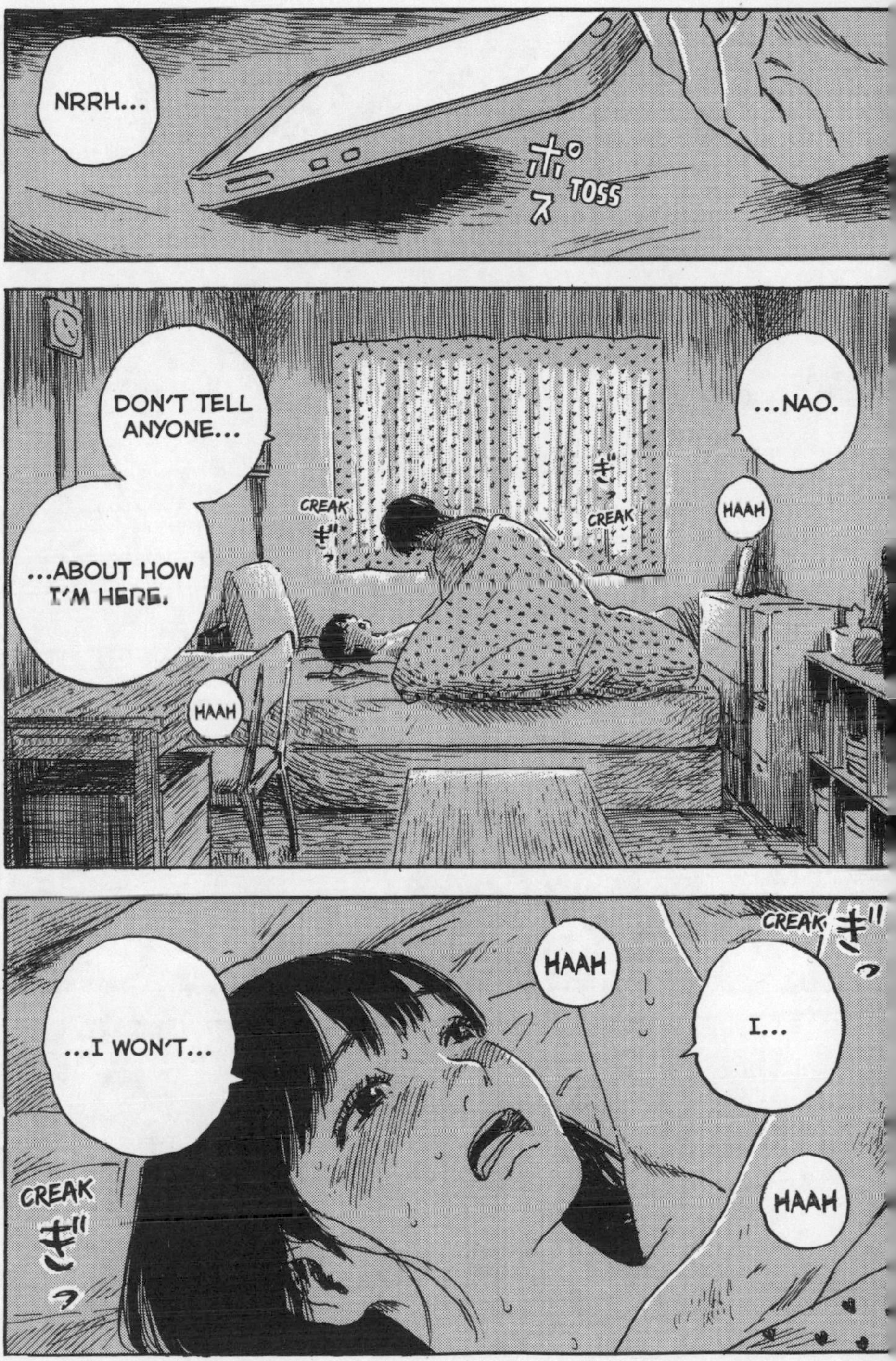
ポス
TOSS
NRRH...
...NAO.
HAAH
ぎっ
CREAK
DON'T TELL ANYONE...
CREAK
ぎっ
...ABOUT HOW I'M HERE.
HAAH
CREAK
ぎっ
I...
HAAH
...I WON'T...
HAAH
CREAK
ぎっ

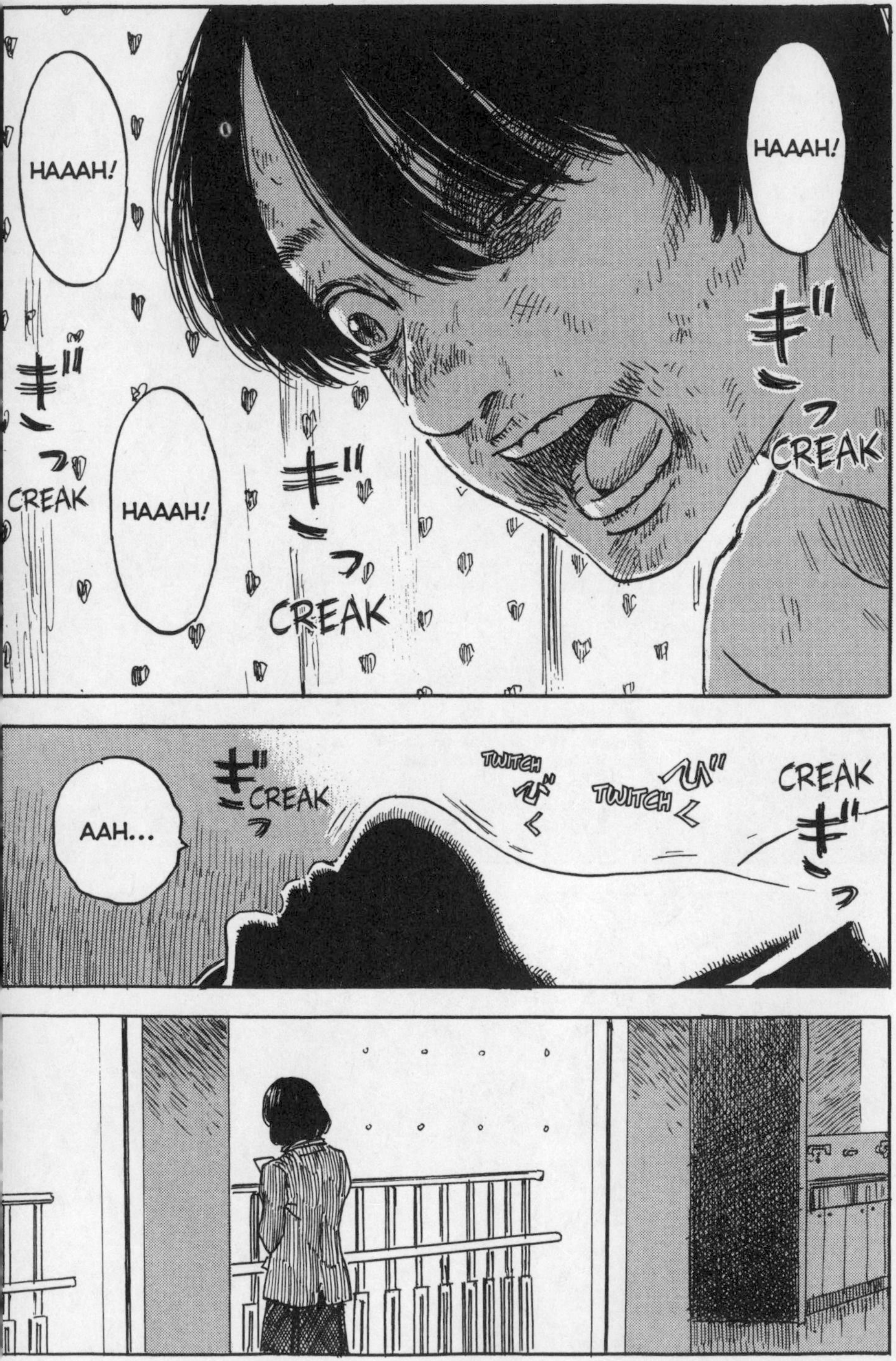
HAAAH!
ぎっ CREAK
ぎっ CREAK
HAAAH!
HAAAH!
ぎっ CREAK
CREAK ぎっ
びく TWITCH
びく TWITCH
ぎっ CREAK
AAH...

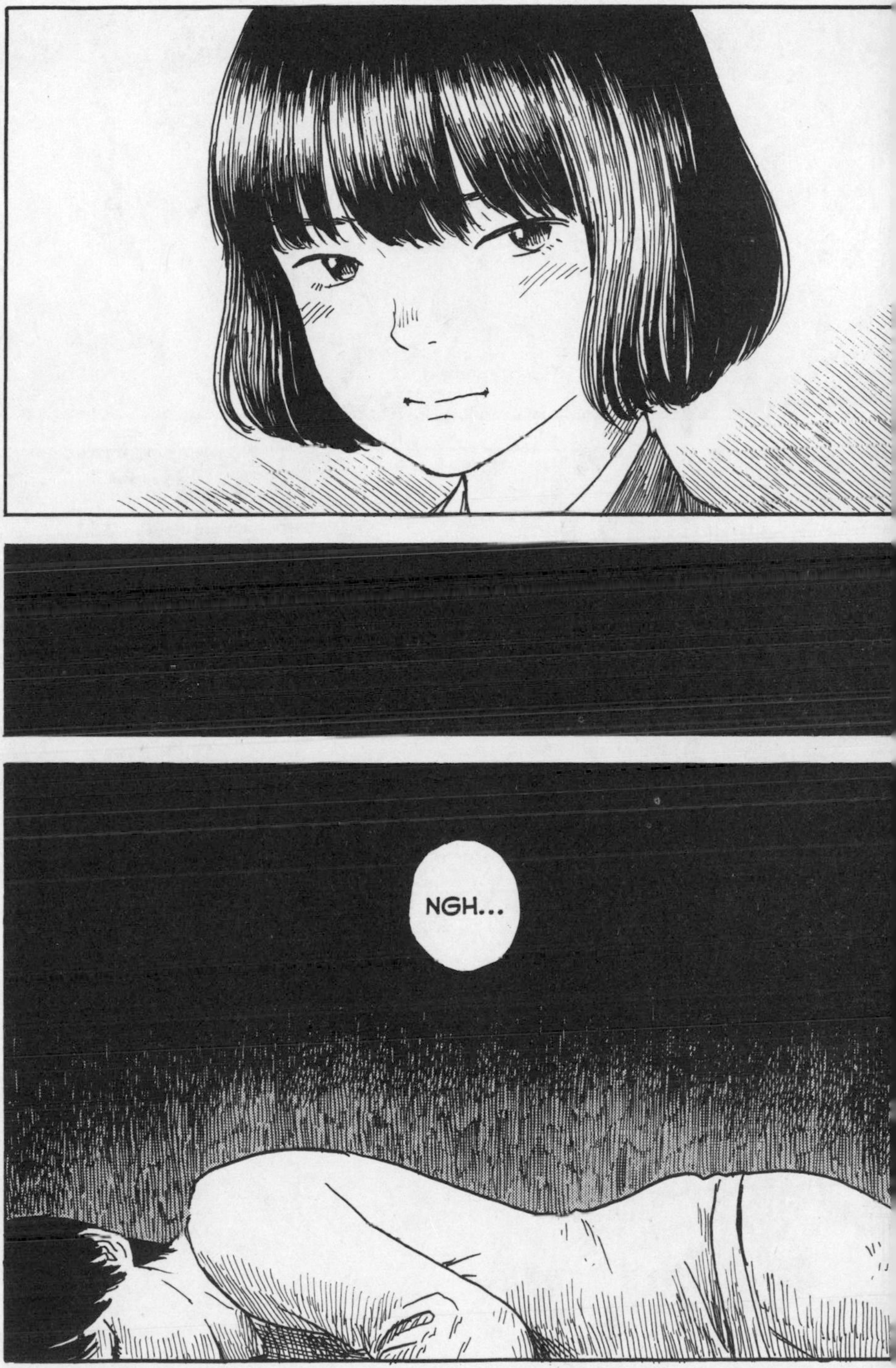
NGH...

ZZZ...
ZZZ...

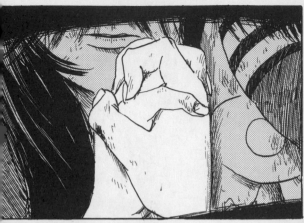

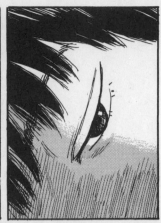

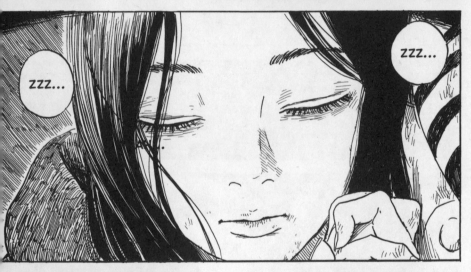

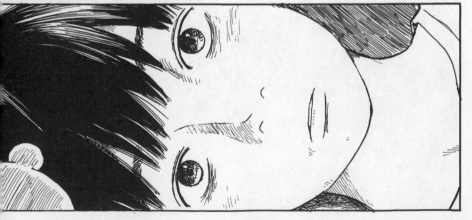

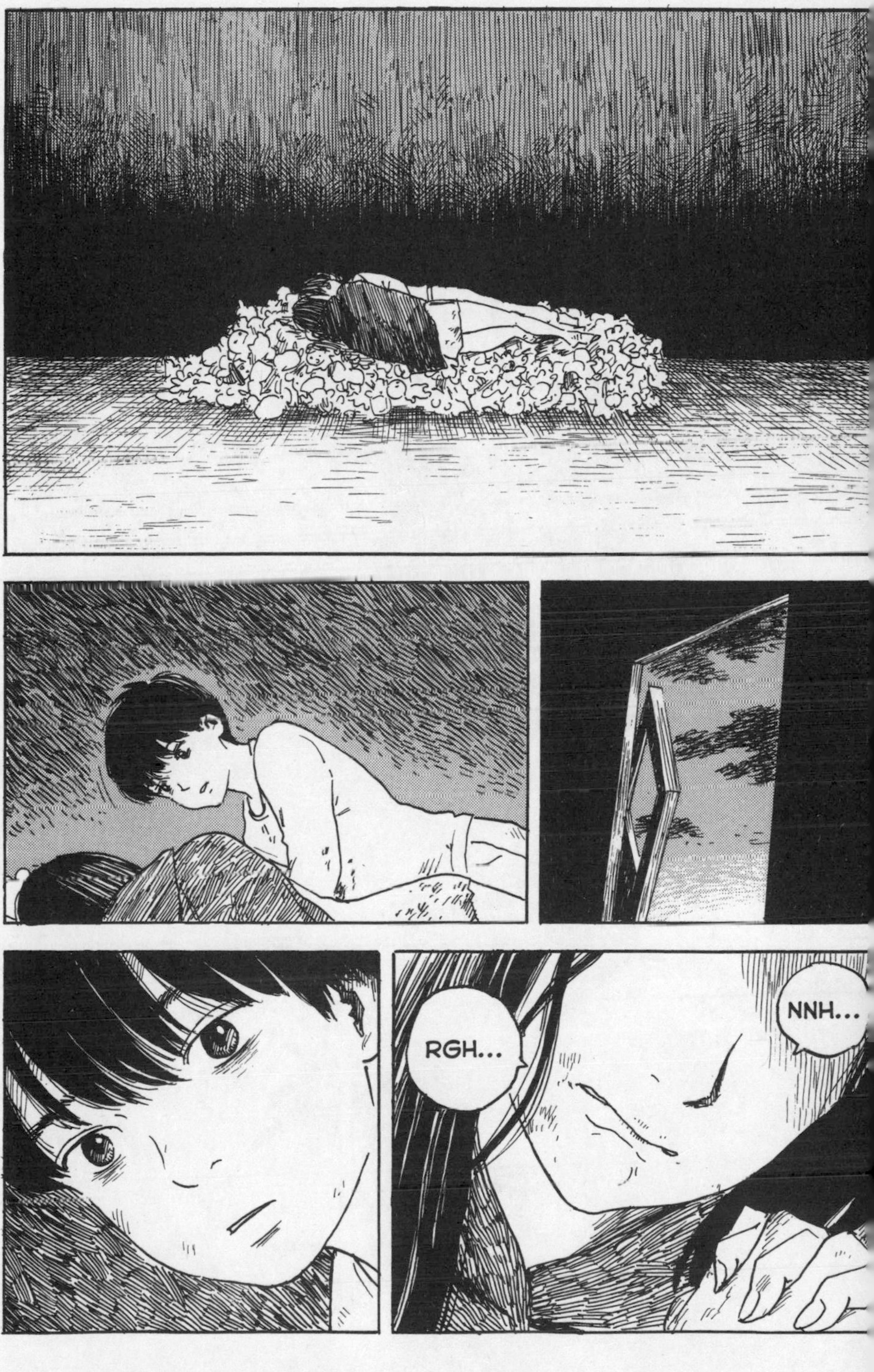
NNH...
RGH...

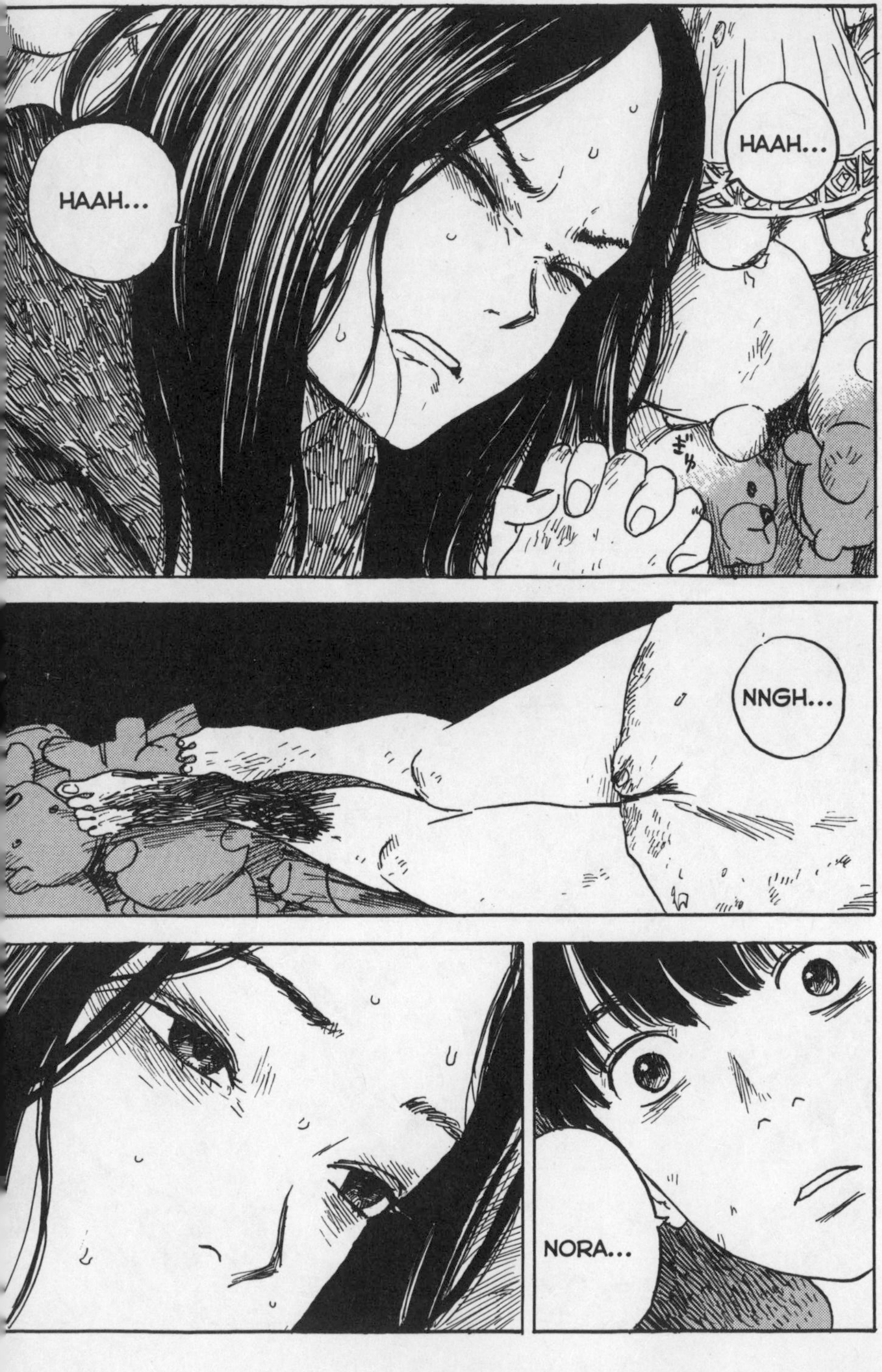
HAAH...
HAAH...
ぎゅ
NNGH...
NORA...

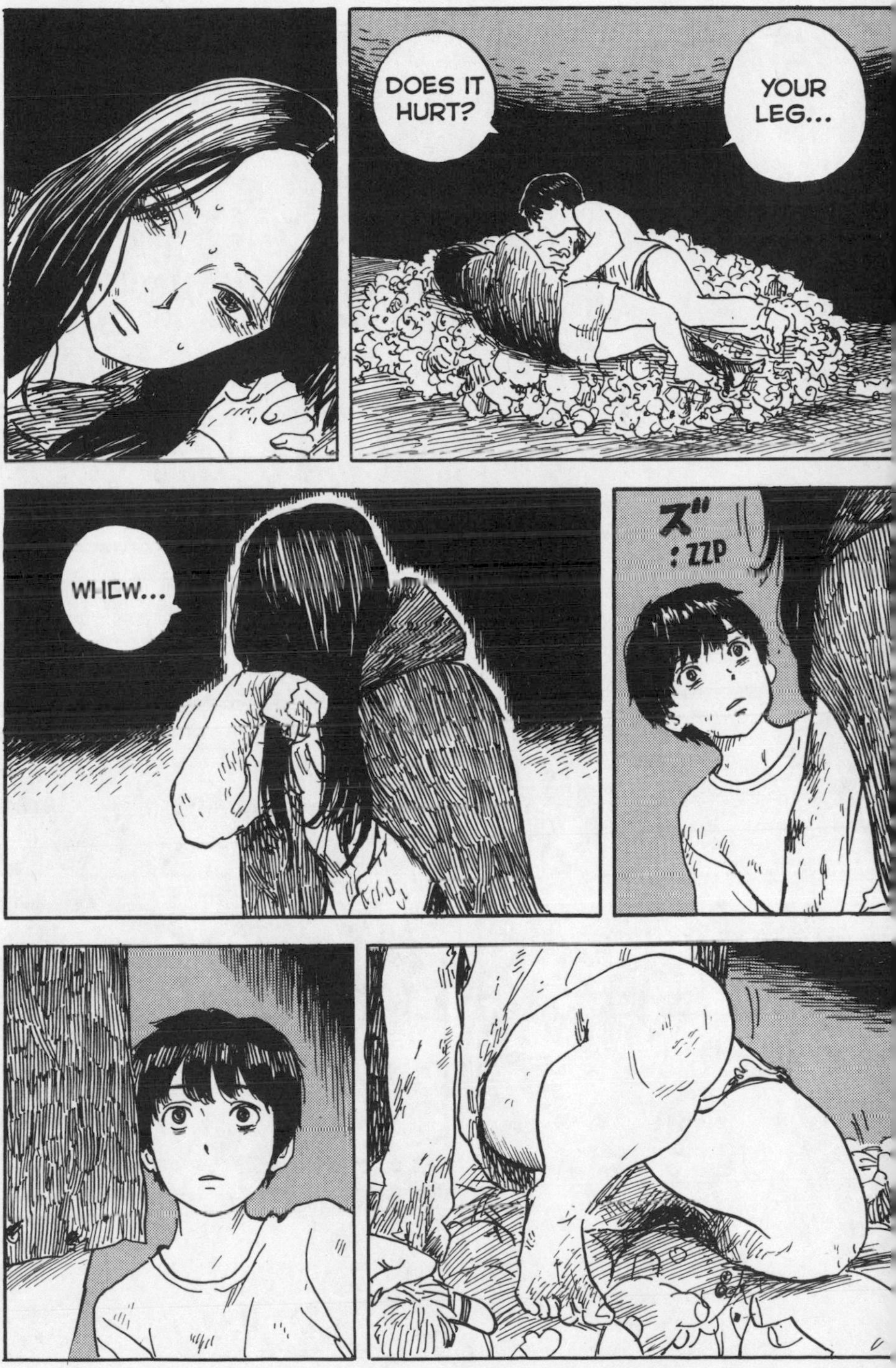
YOUR LEG...
DOES IT HURT?
ズ
: ZZP
WHEW...

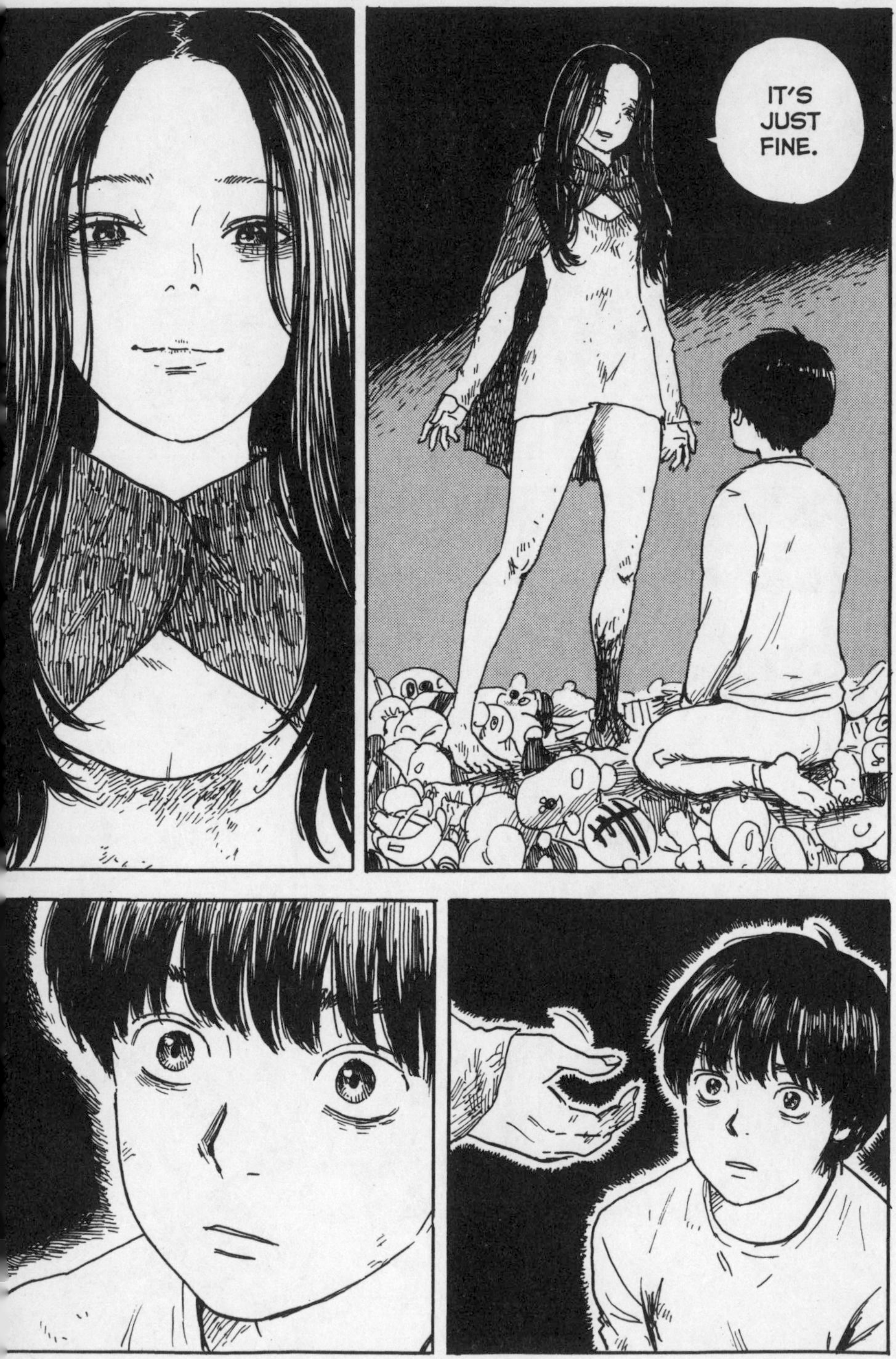
IT'S
JUST
FINE.

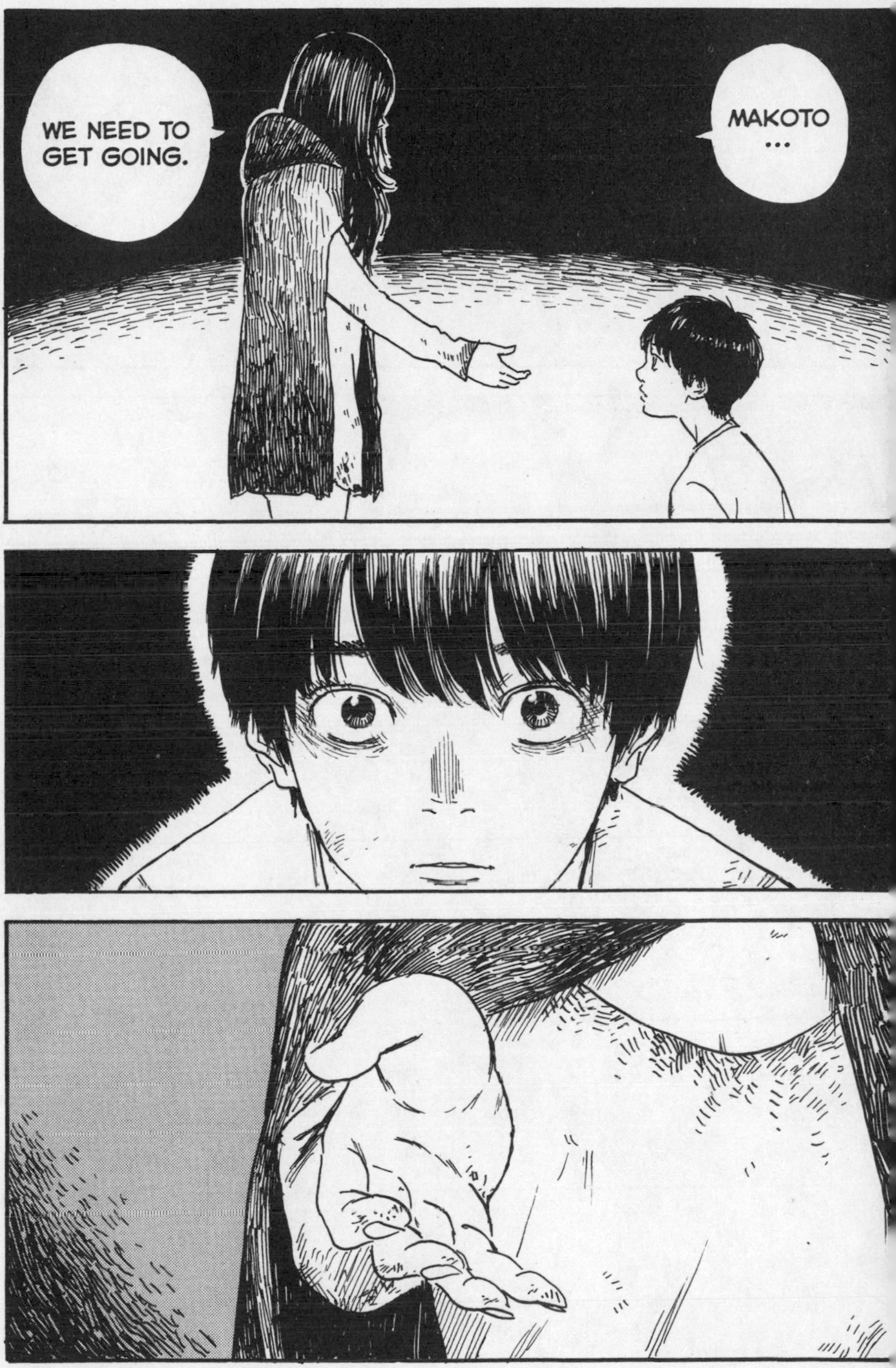
MAKOTO ...
WE NEED TO GET GOING.

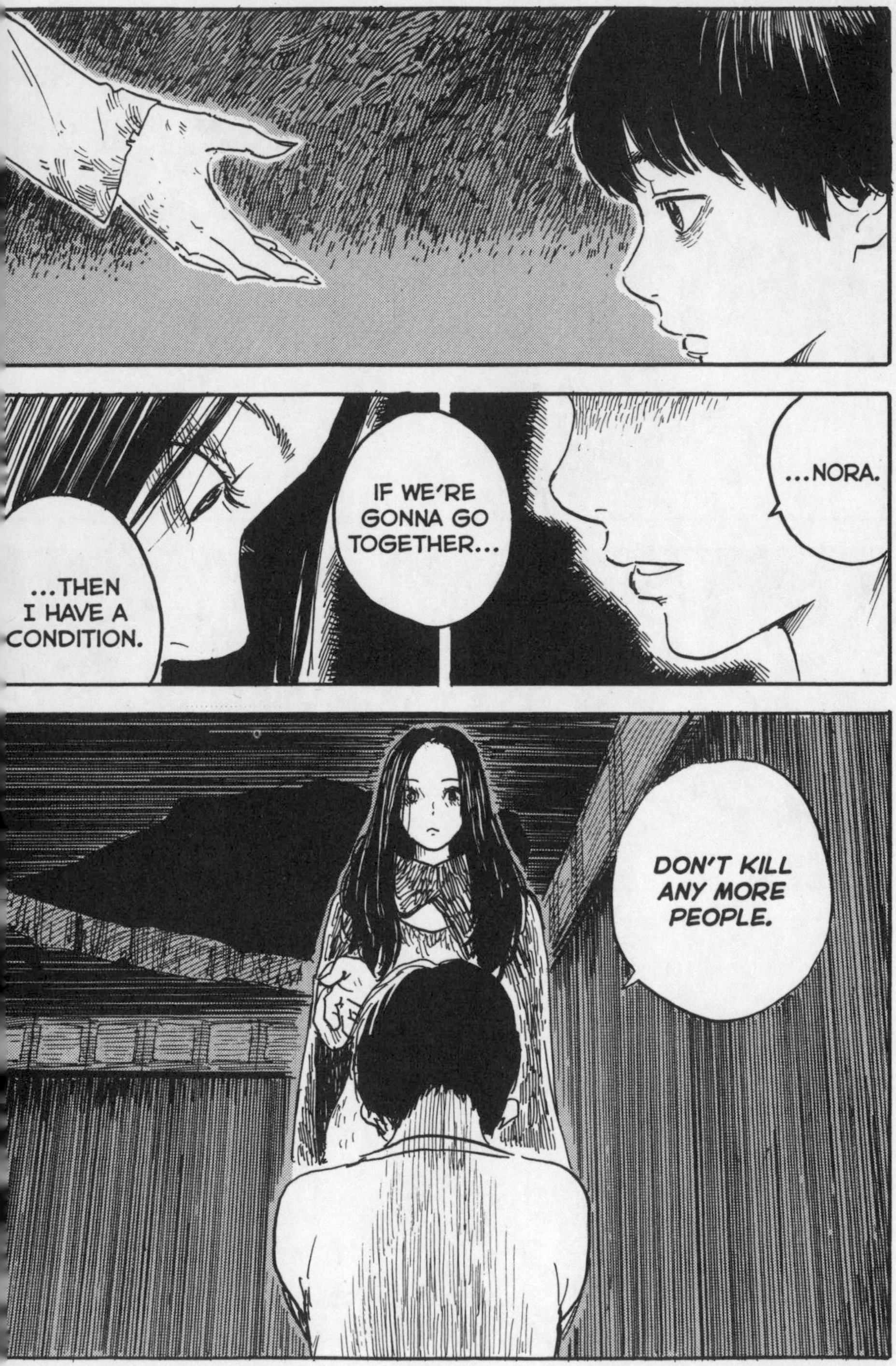
...NORA.
IF WE'RE GONNA GO TOGETHER...
...THEN I HAVE A CONDITION.
DON'T KILL ANY MORE PEOPLE.

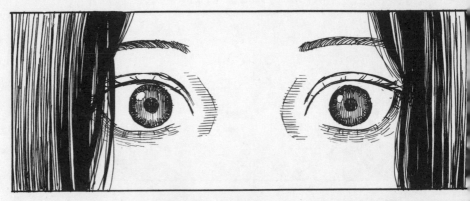

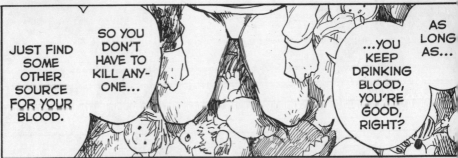

AS LONG AS...
...YOU KEEP DRINKING BLOOD, YOU'RE GOOD, RIGHT?
SO YOU DON'T HAVE TO KILL ANY-ONE...
JUST FIND SOME OTHER SOURCE FOR YOUR BLOOD.
IF YOU USED TO BE HUMAN, NORA...
...YOU NEED TO TRY AND GET BACK THERE AGAIN.

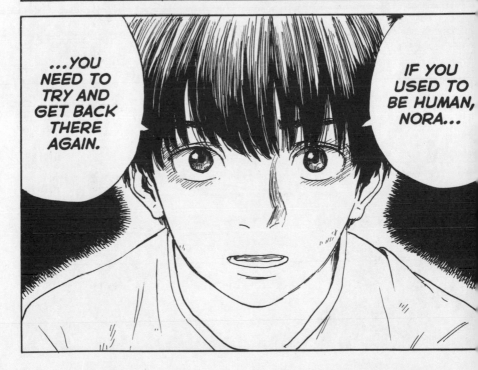

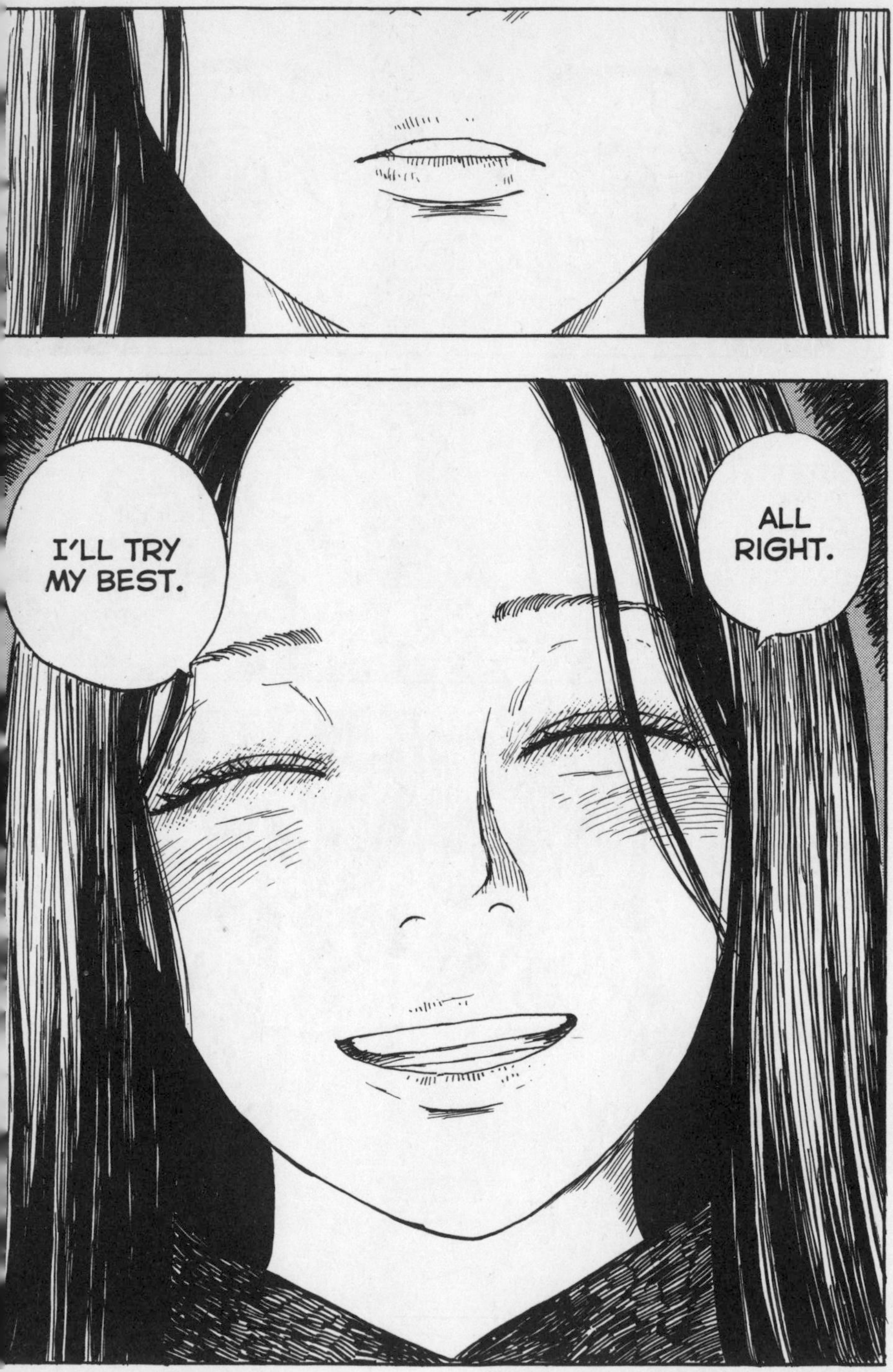
ALL RIGHT.
I'LL TRY MY BEST.

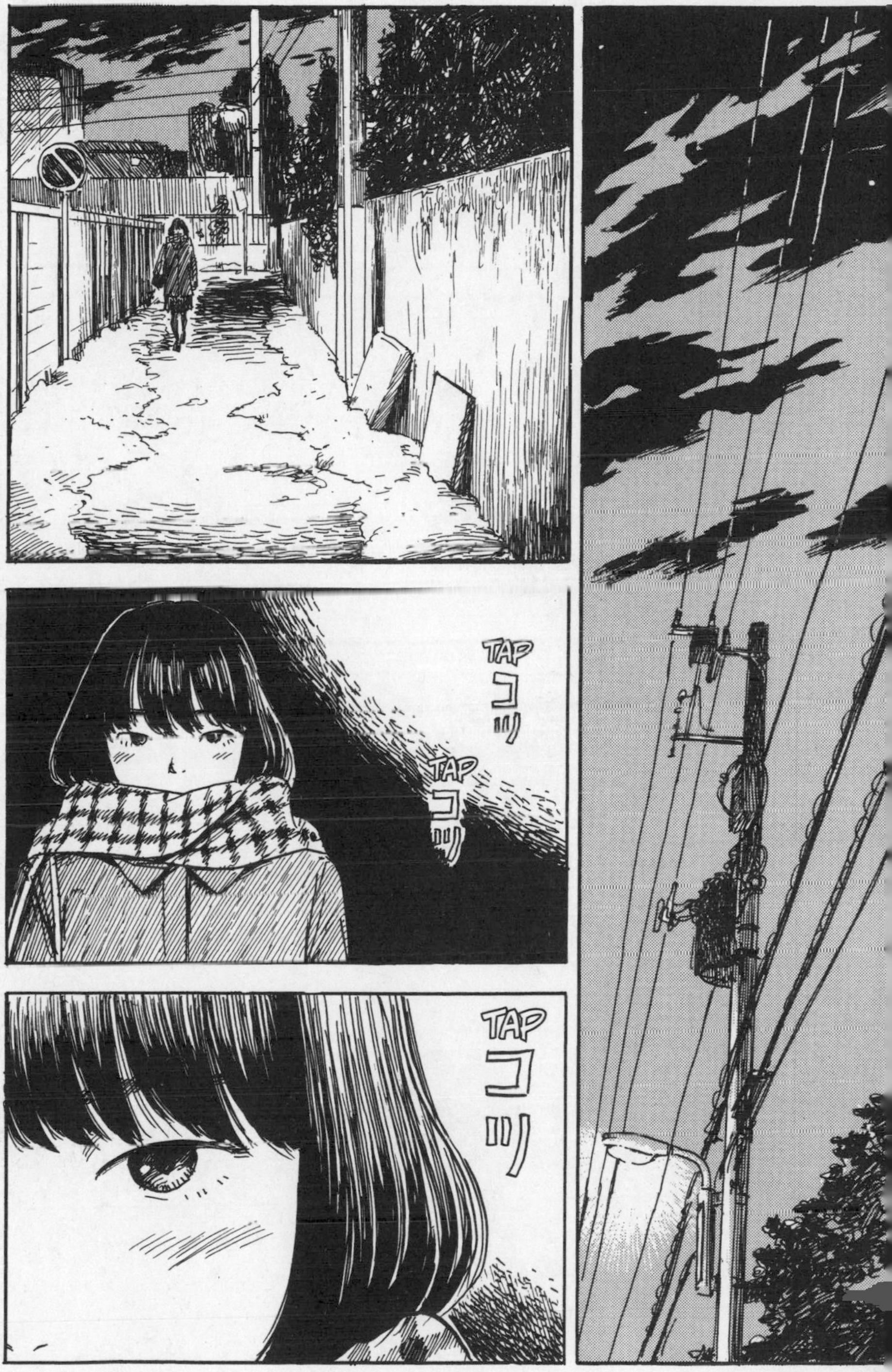
TAP
コッ
TAP
コッ
TAP
コッ

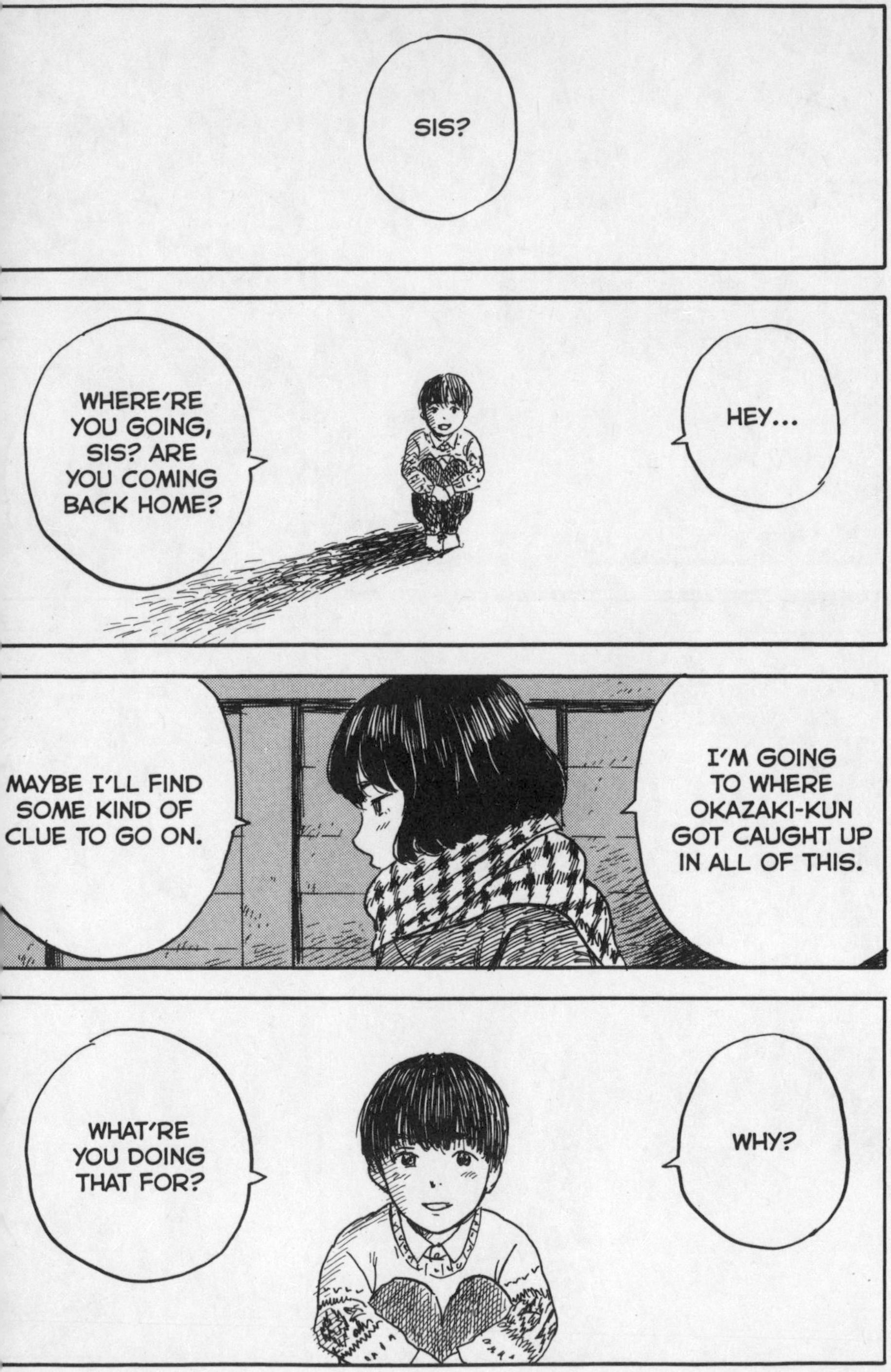
SIS?
HEY...
WHERE'RE YOU GOING, SIS? ARE YOU COMING BACK HOME?
I'M GOING TO WHERE OKAZAKI-KUN GOT CAUGHT UP IN ALL OF THIS.
MAYBE I'LL FIND SOME KIND OF CLUE TO GO ON.
WHY?
WHAT'RE YOU DOING THAT FOR?

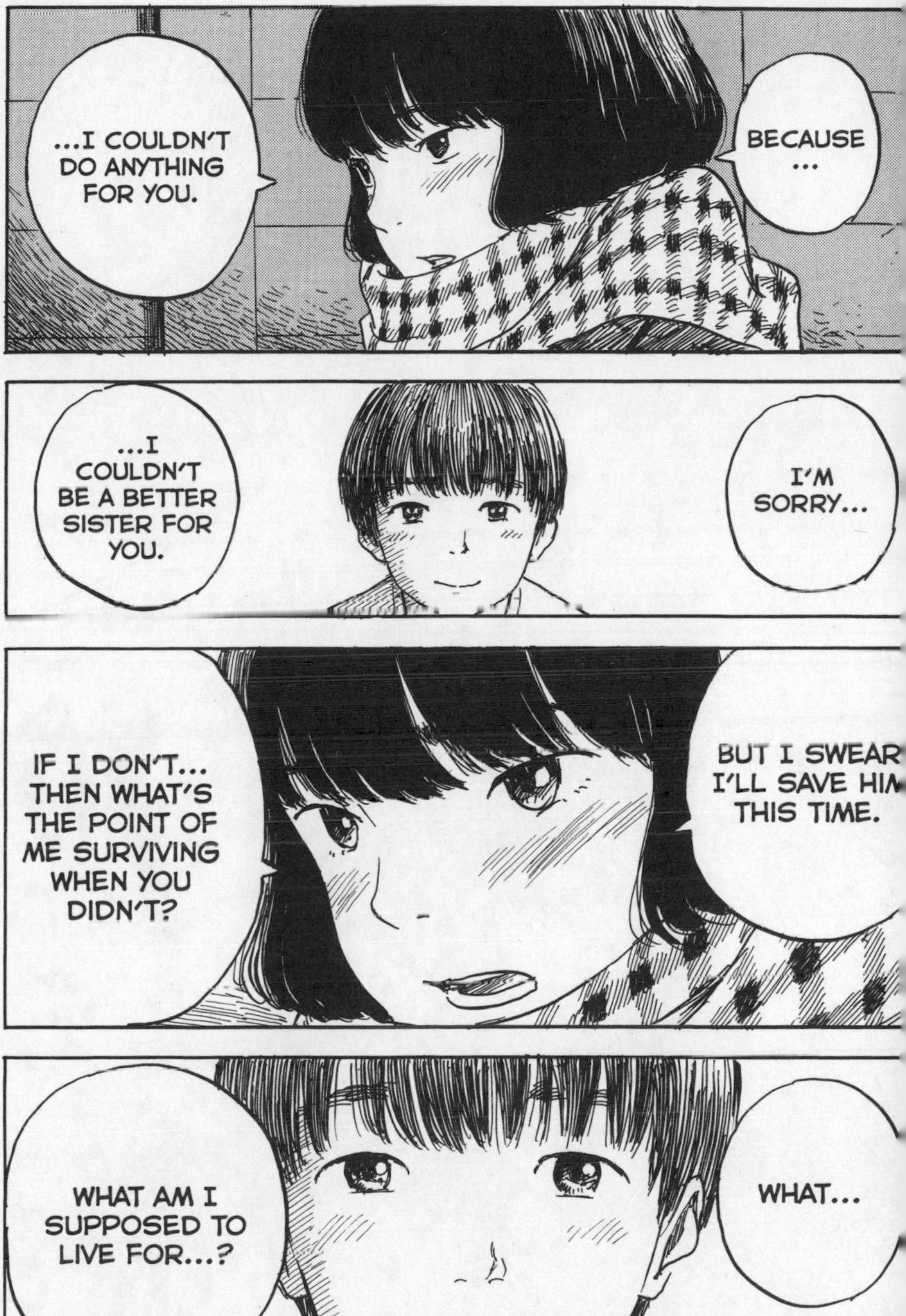
BECAUSE ...
...I COULDN'T DO ANYTHING FOR YOU.
I'M SORRY...
...I COULDN'T BE A BETTER SISTER FOR YOU.
BUT I SWEAR I'LL SAVE HIM THIS TIME.
IF I DON'T... THEN WHAT'S THE POINT OF ME SURVIVING WHEN YOU DIDN'T?
WHAT...
WHAT AM I SUPPOSED TO LIVE FOR...?

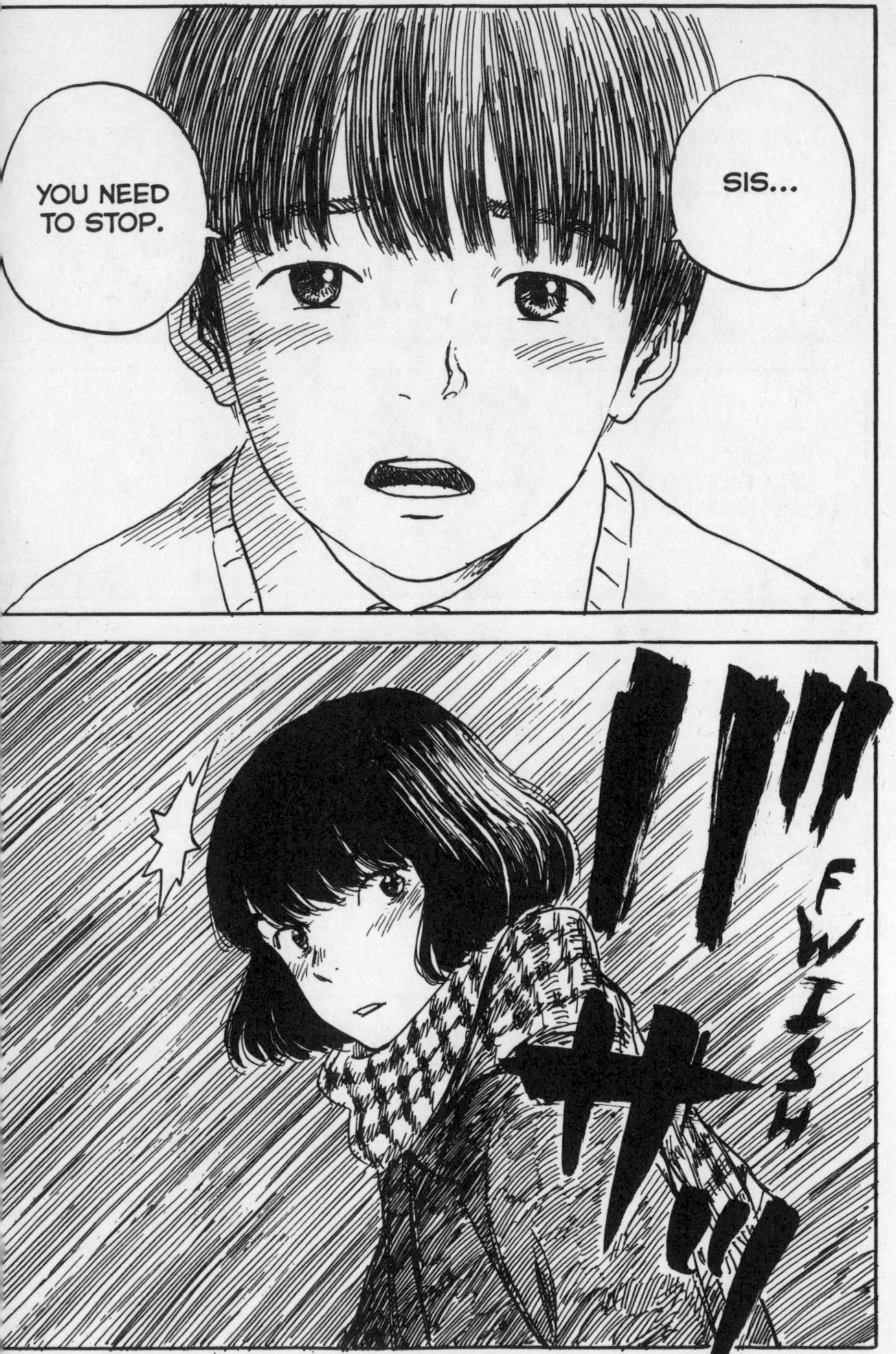
SIS...
YOU NEED TO STOP.
FWISH

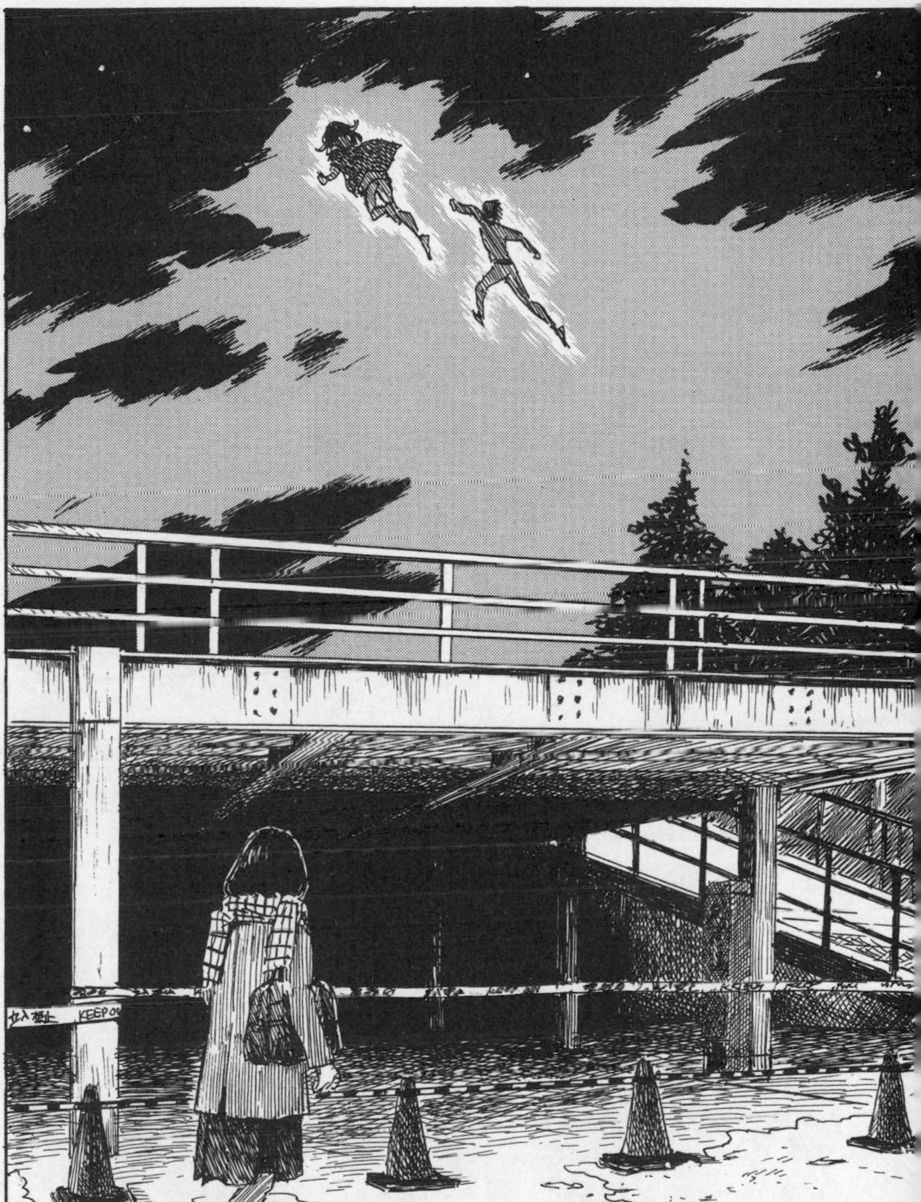
立入禁止

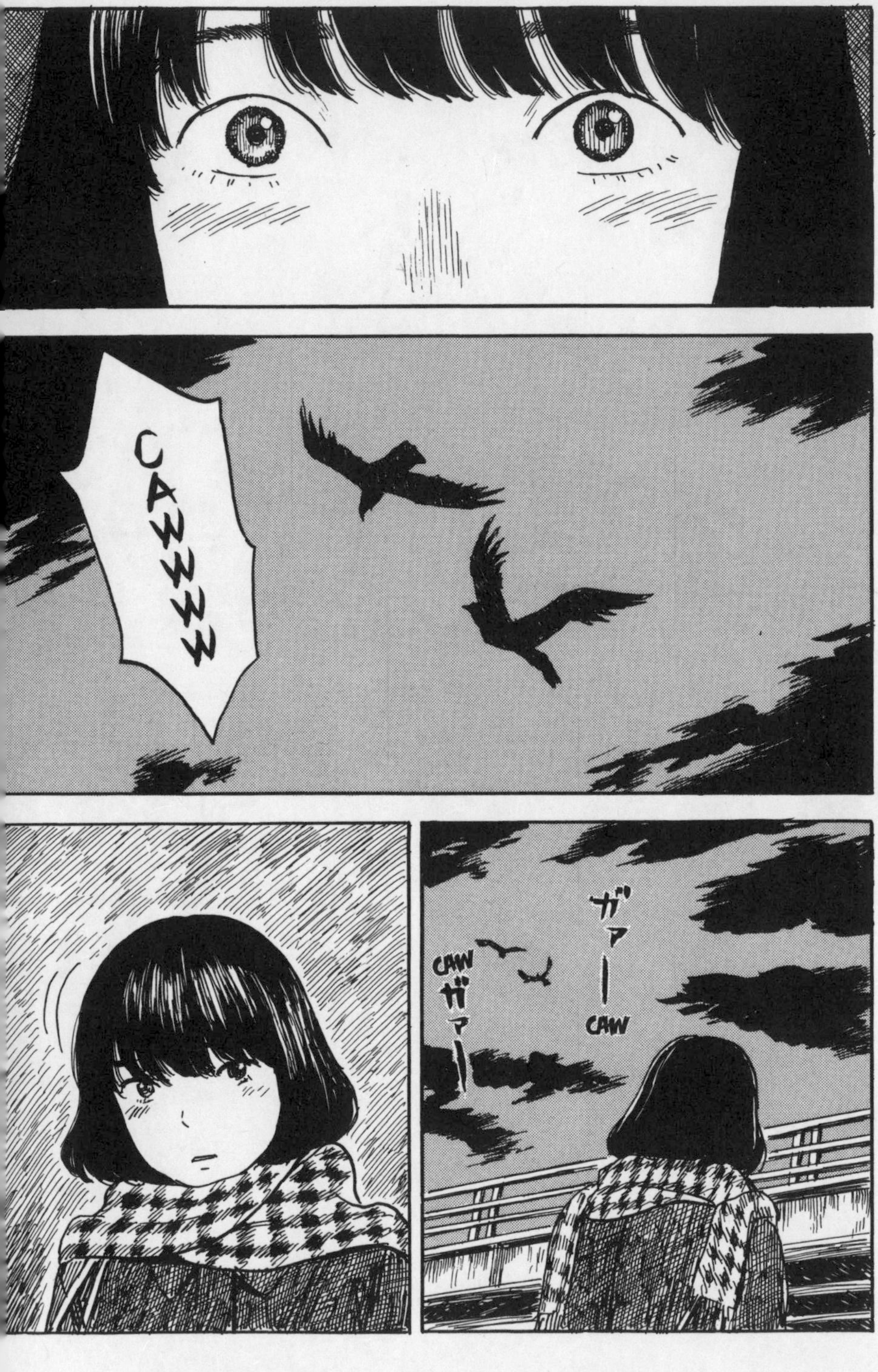
CAWWWW
ガァー
CAW
CAW
ガァー

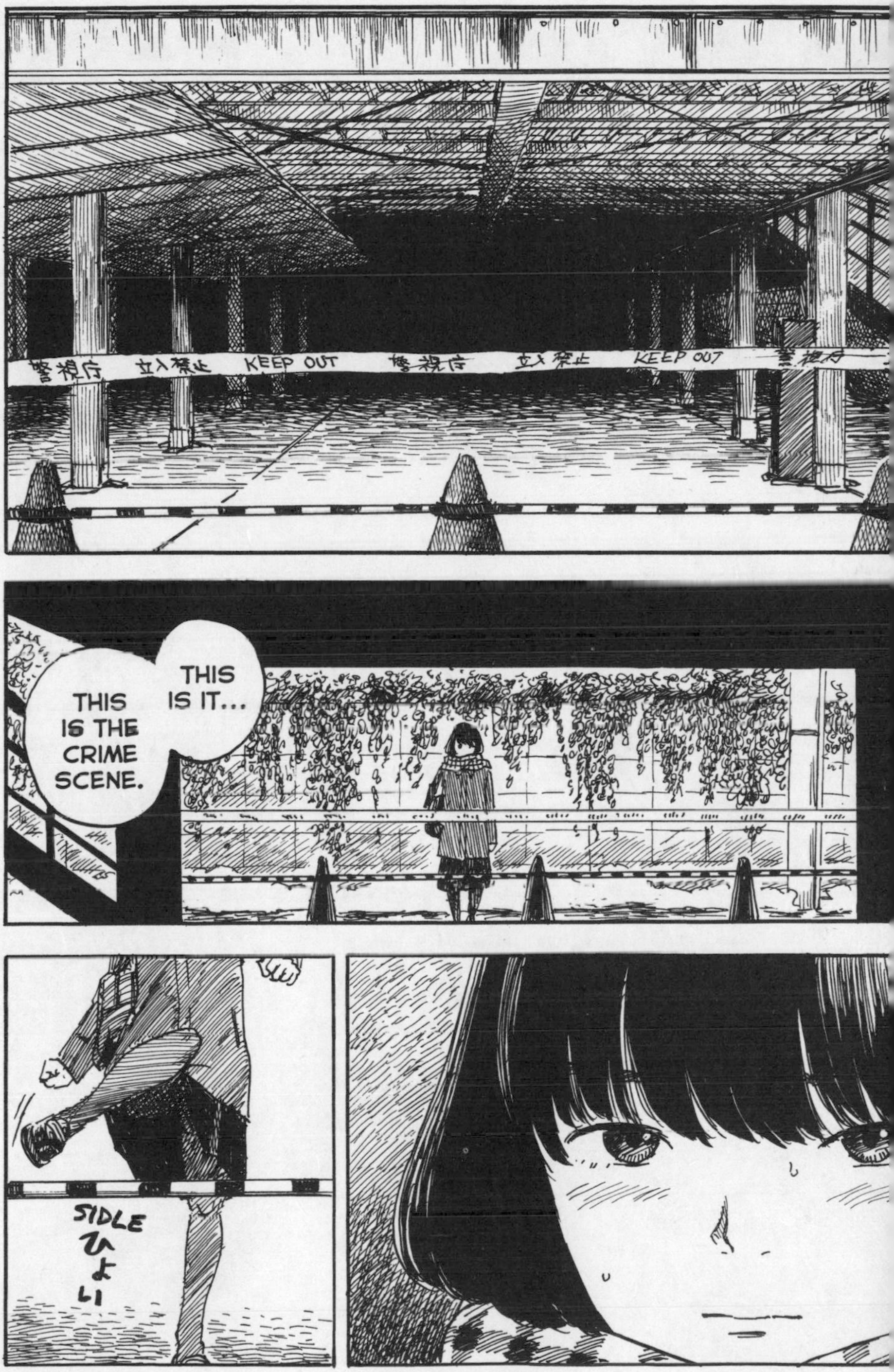
警視庁 立入禁止 KEEP OUT 警視庁 立入禁止 KEEP OUT 警視庁
THIS IS IT...
THIS IS THE CRIME SCENE.
SIDLE
ひょい

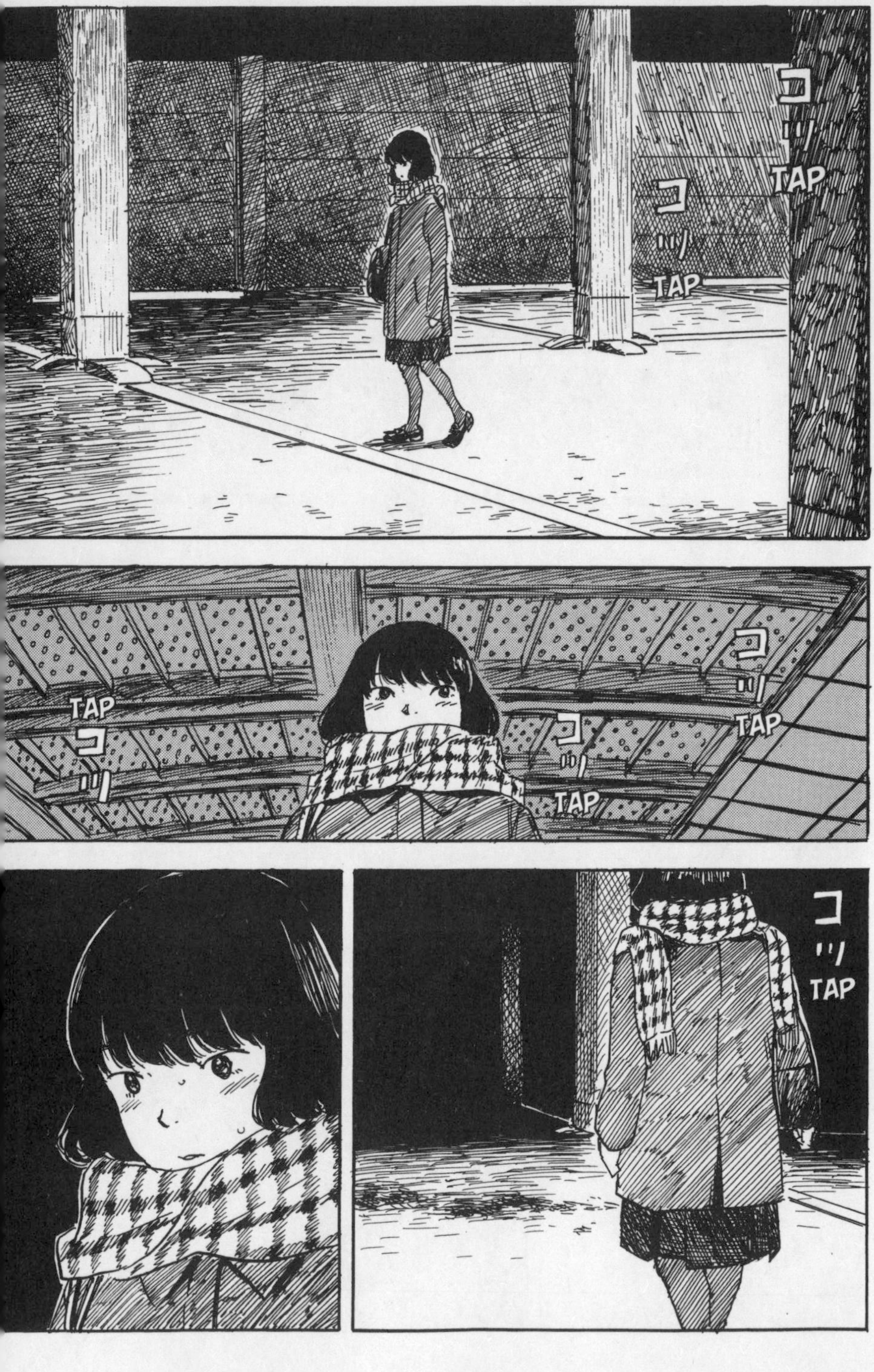

コッ TAP
コッ TAP
コッ TAP
コッ TAP
TAP コッ
コッ TAP

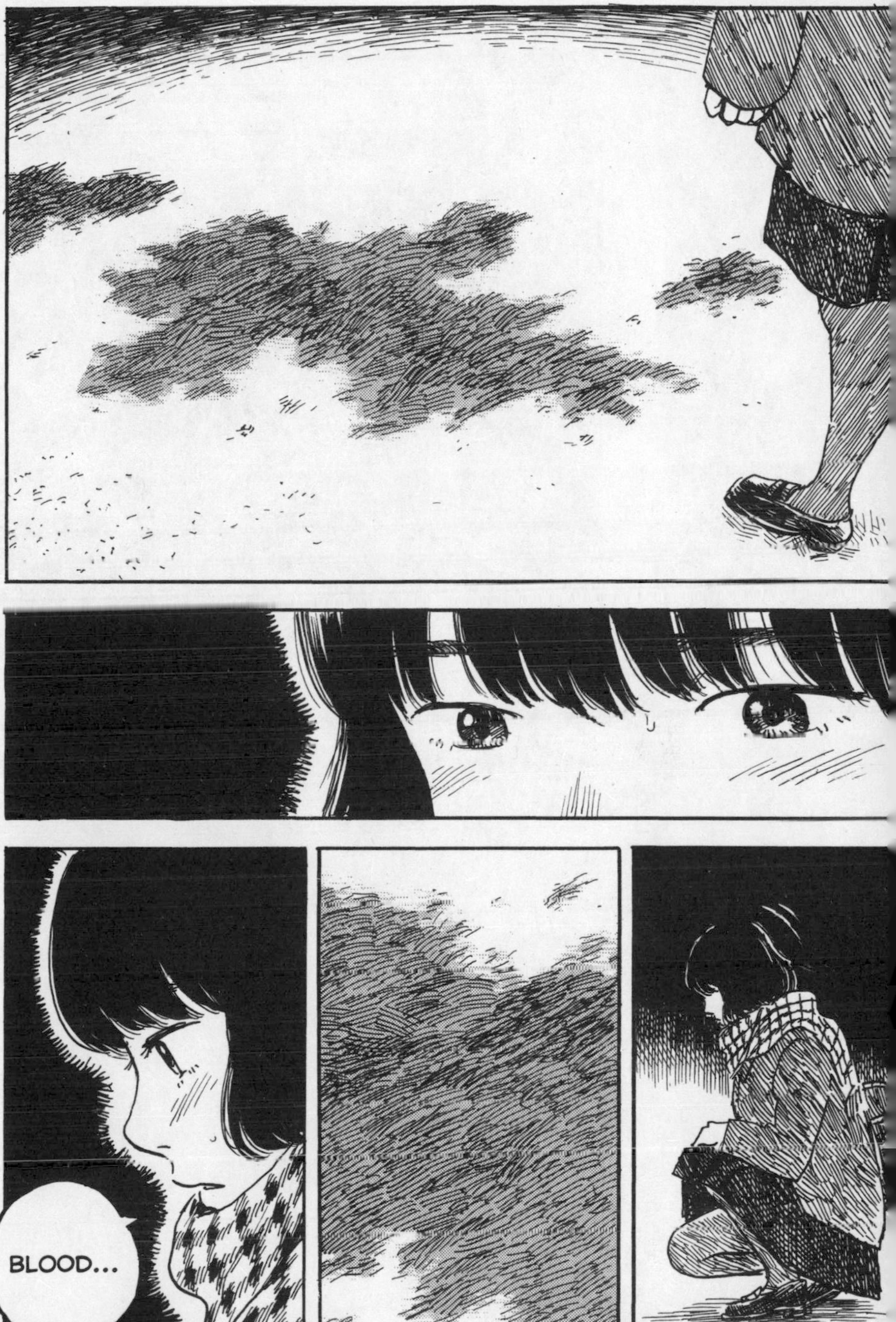
BLOOD...

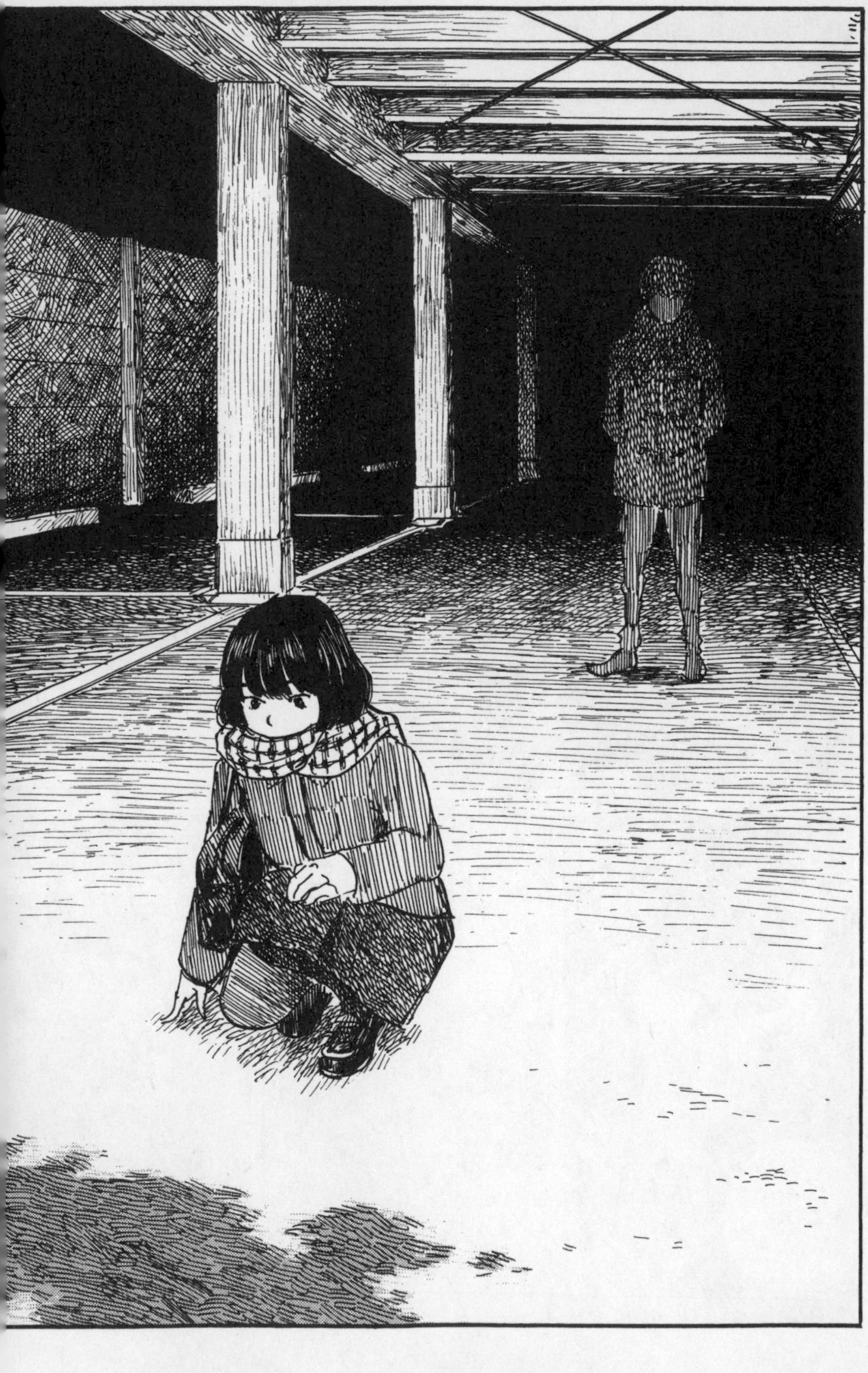

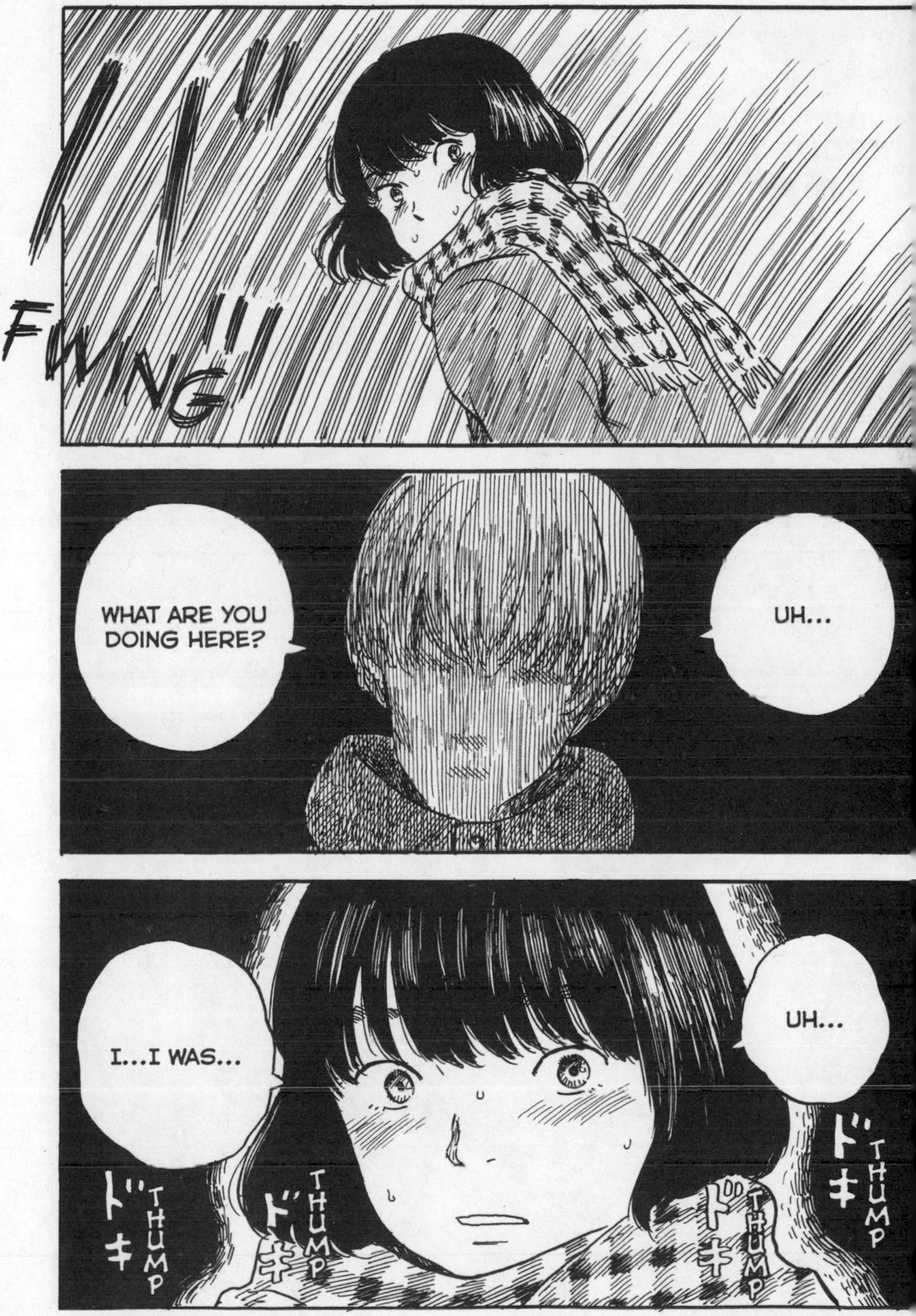
FWING!!
UH...
WHAT ARE YOU DOING HERE?
UH...
I...I WAS...
ドキ THUMP
ドキ THUMP THUMP
ドキ THUMP THUMP
ドキ THUMP

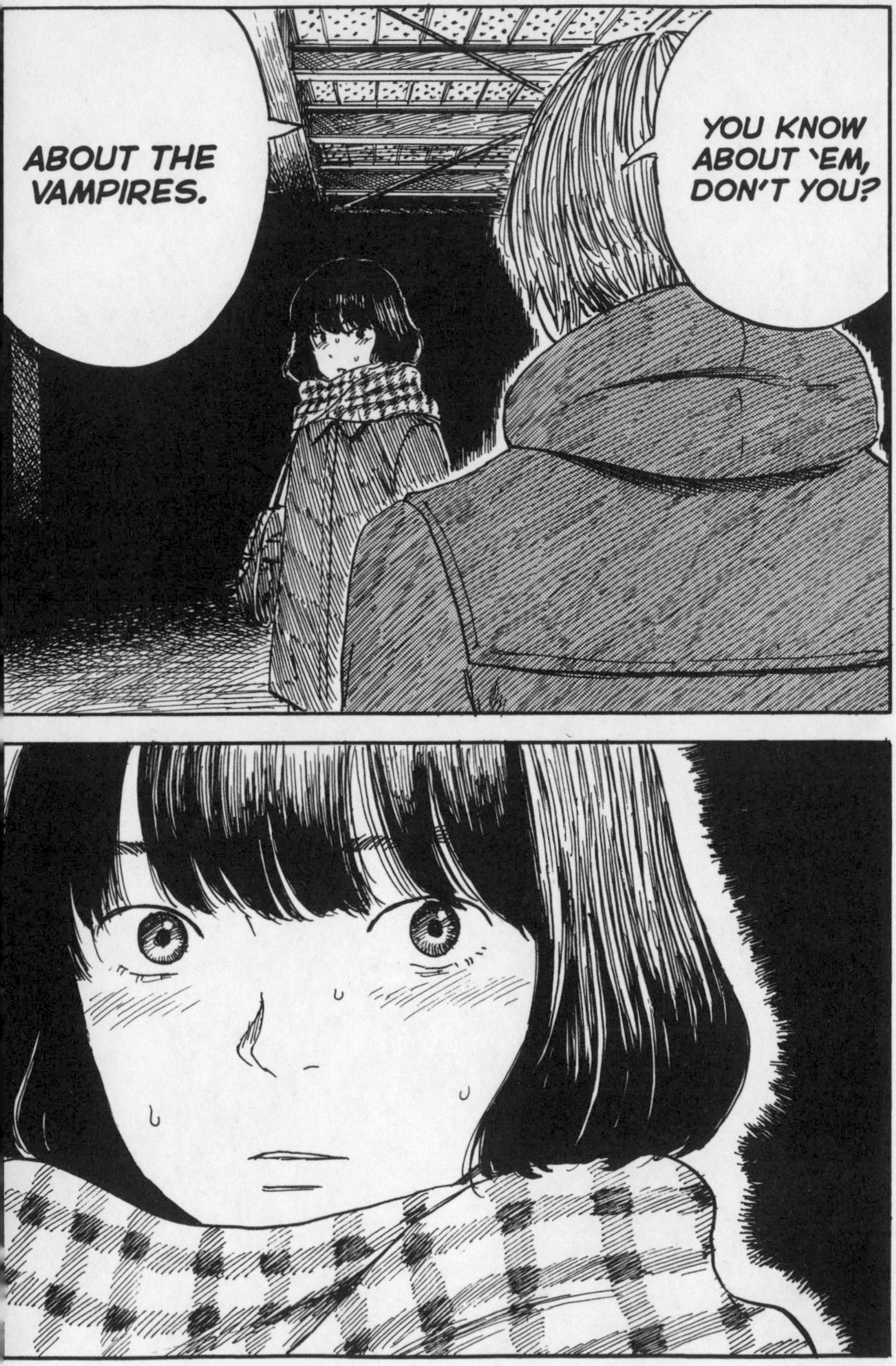
YOU KNOW ABOUT 'EM, DON'T YOU?
ABOUT THE VAMPIRES.

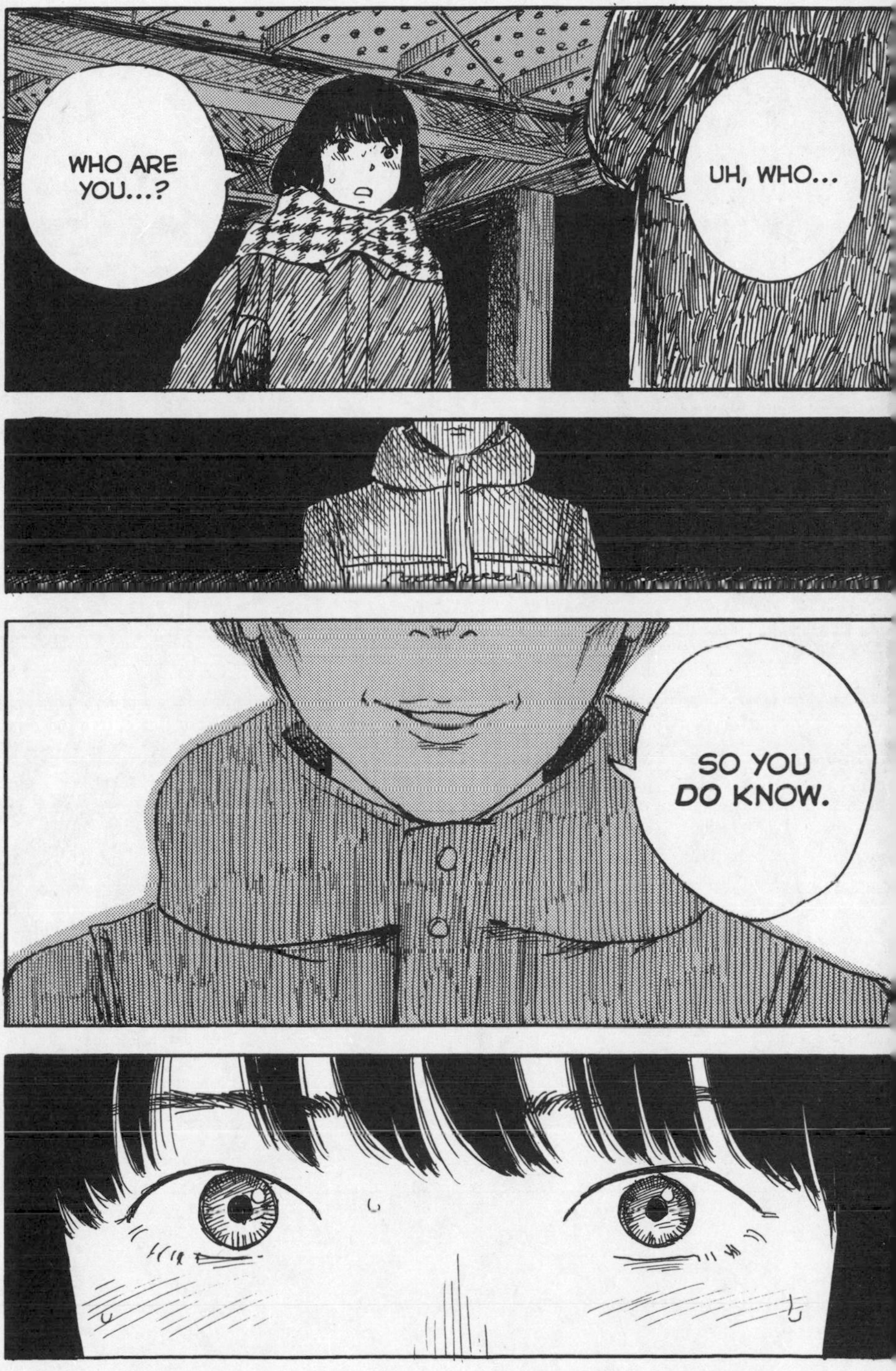
UH, WHO...
WHO ARE YOU...?
SO YOU *DO* KNOW.

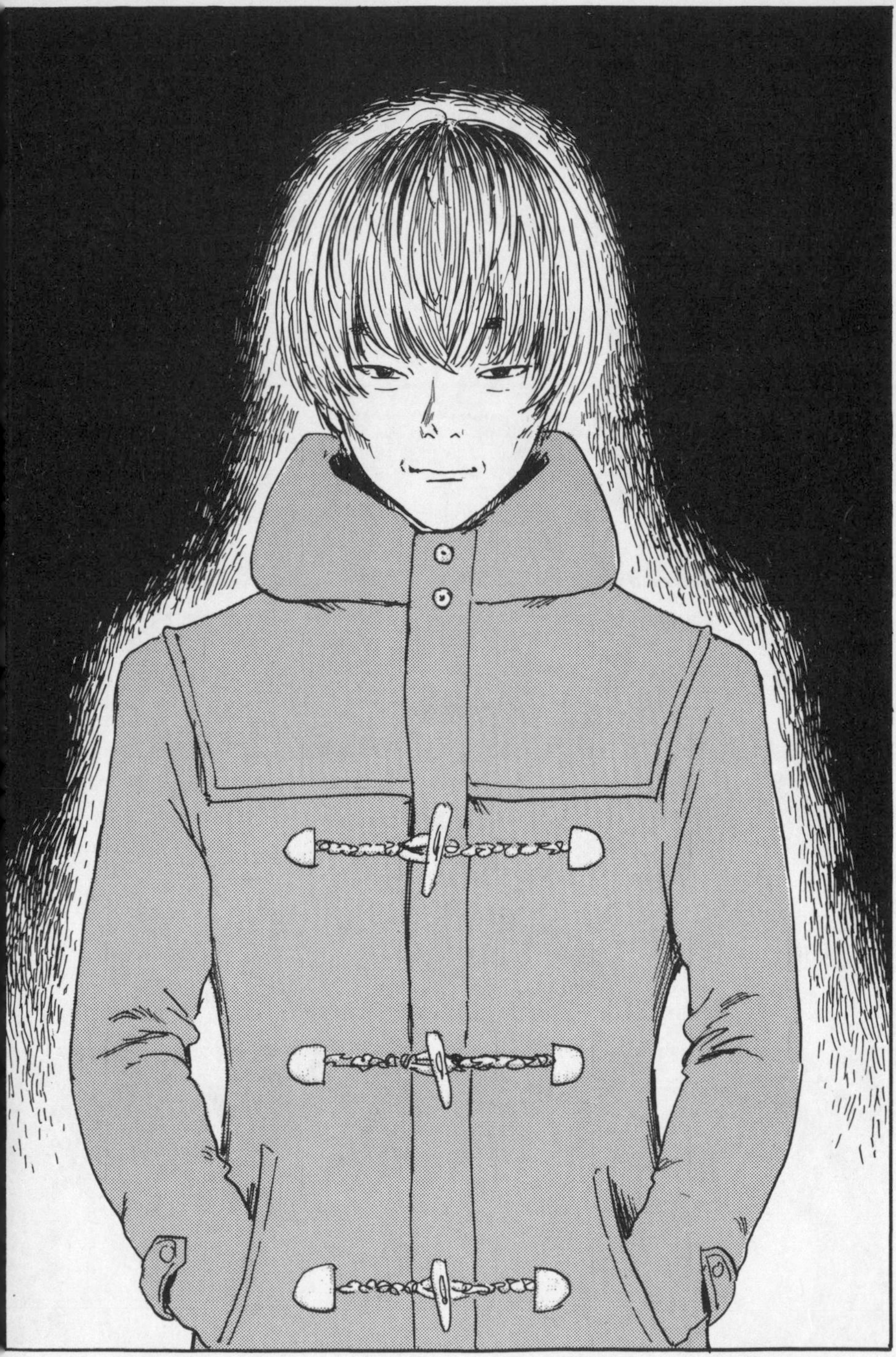

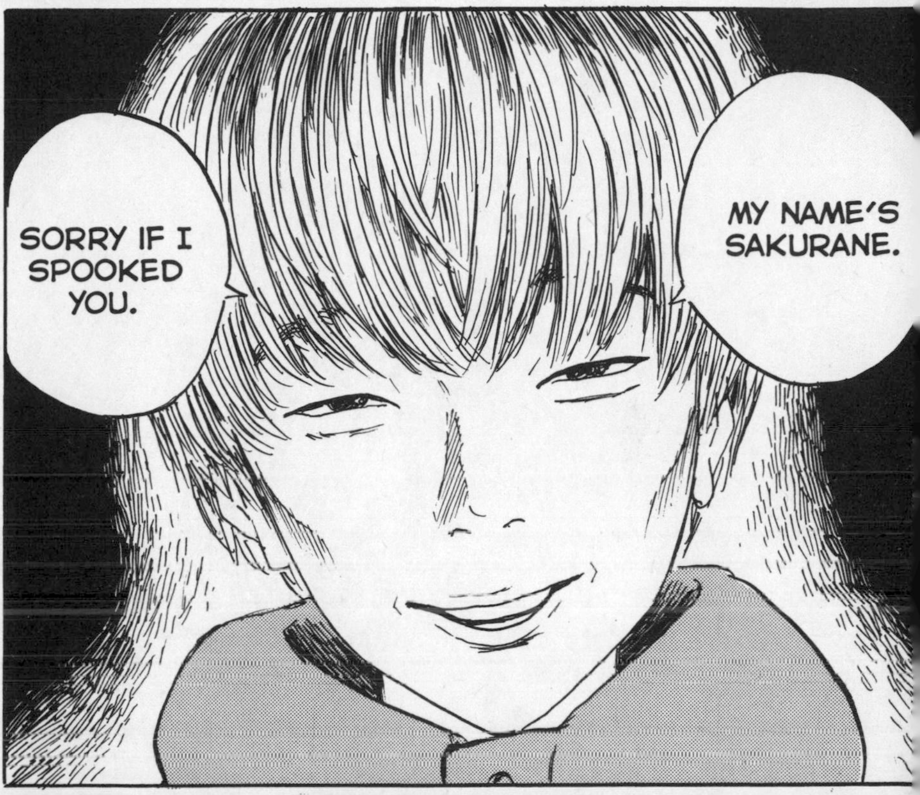
MY NAME'S SAKURANE.
SORRY IF I SPOOKED YOU.

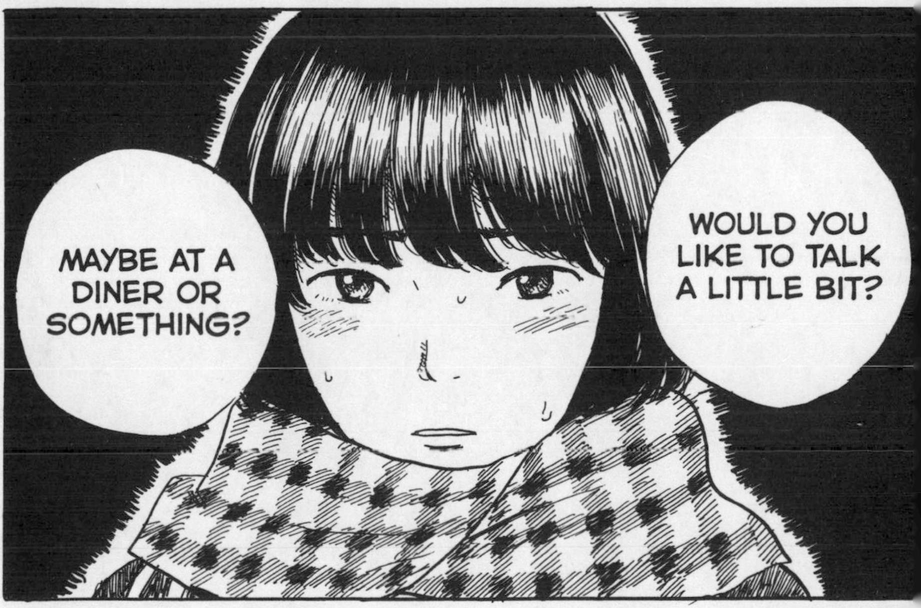
WOULD YOU LIKE TO TALK A LITTLE BIT?
MAYBE AT A DINER OR SOMETHING?

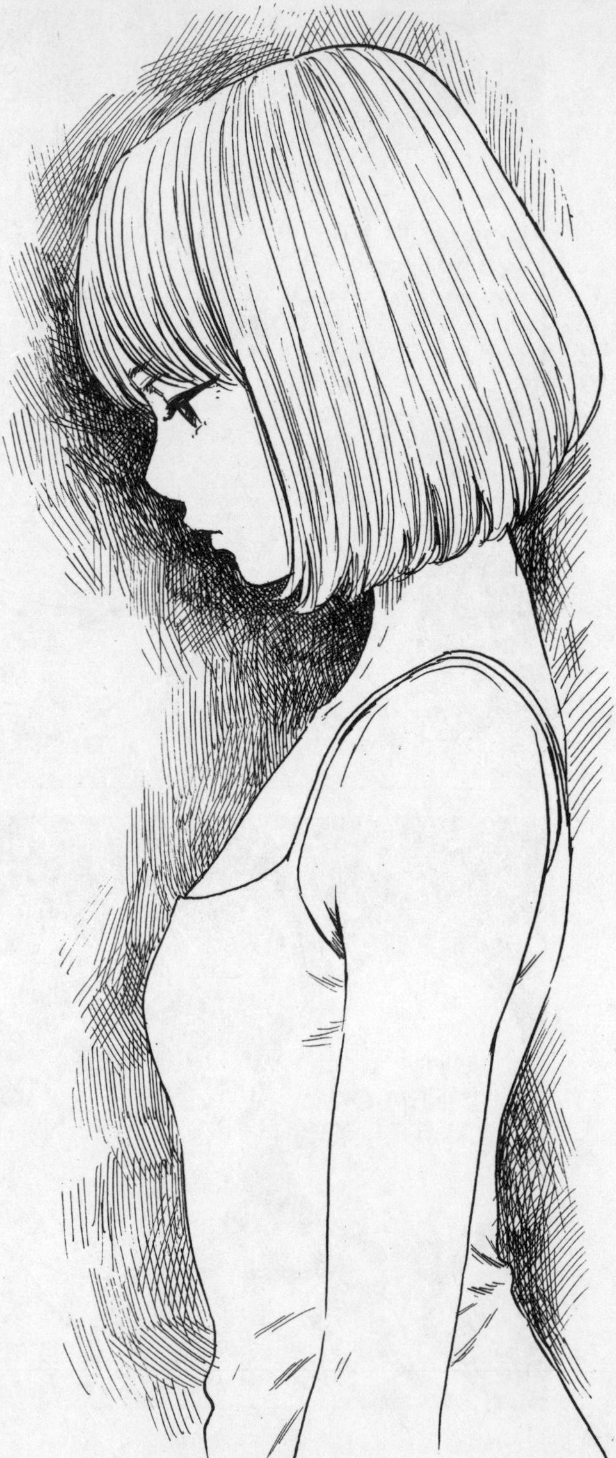

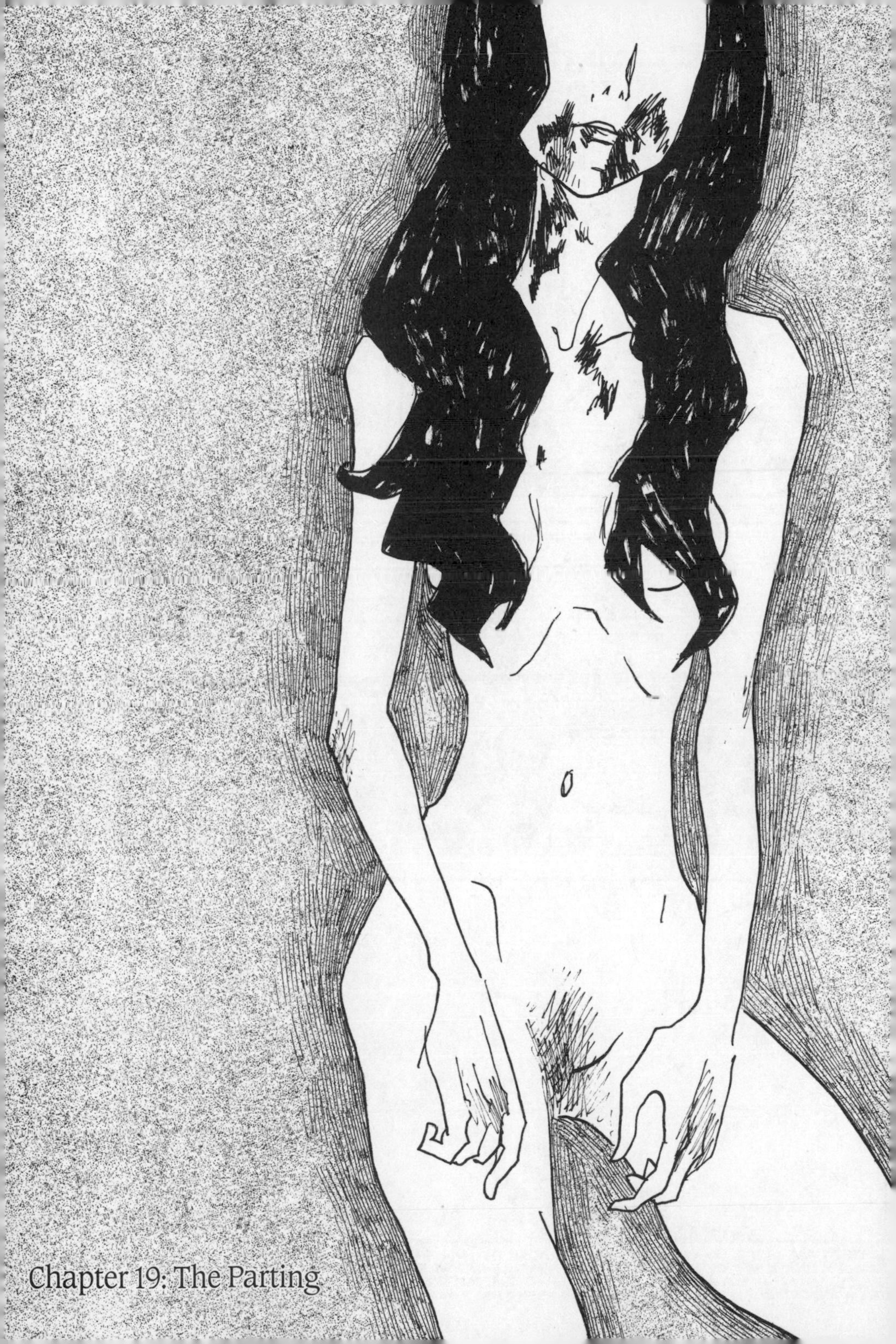

Chapter 19: The Parting

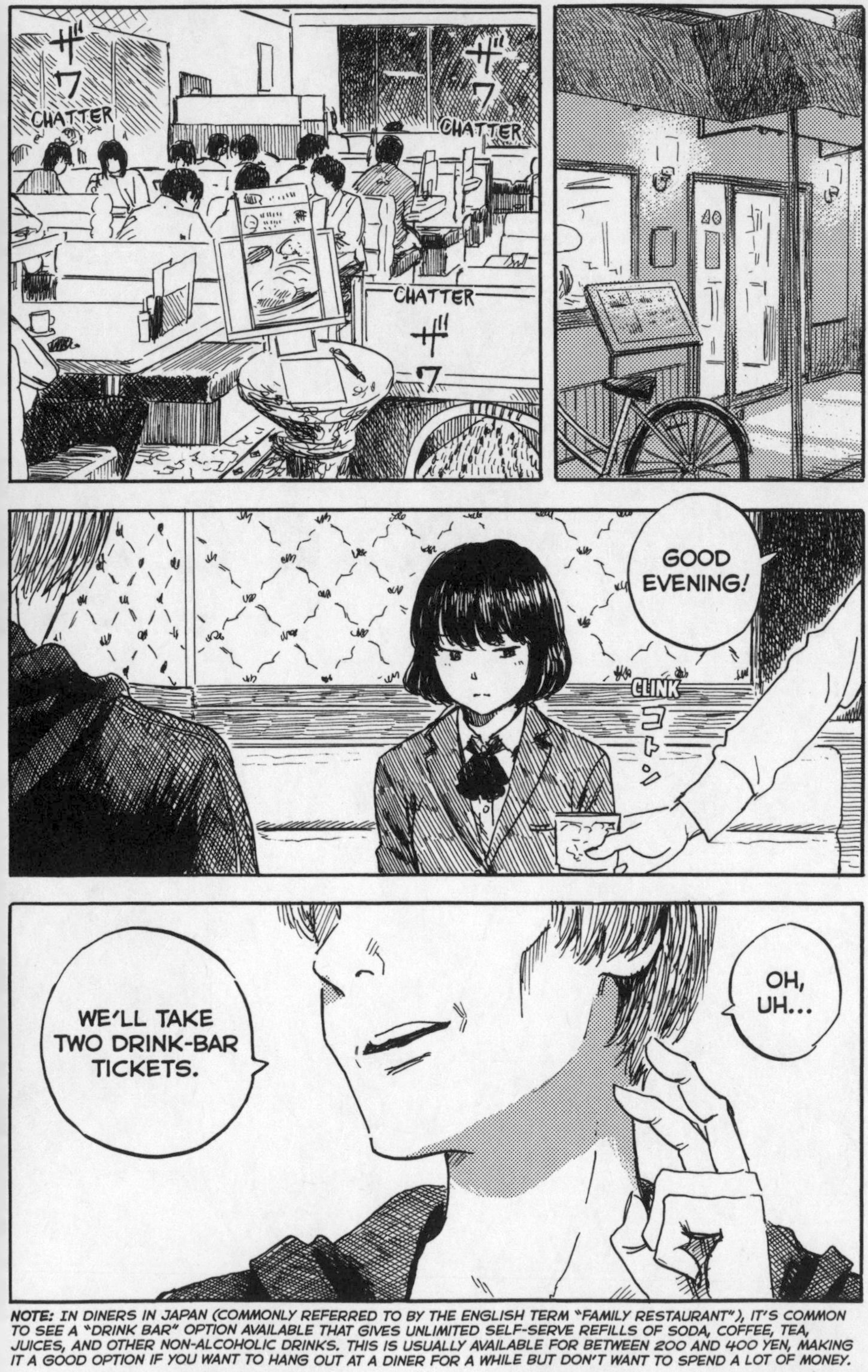
ザワ
CHATTER
ザワ
CHATTER
CHATTER
ザワ
GOOD EVENING!
CLINK
コトン
OH, UH...
WE'LL TAKE TWO DRINK-BAR TICKETS.

NOTE: *IN DINERS IN JAPAN (COMMONLY REFERRED TO BY THE ENGLISH TERM "FAMILY RESTAURANT"), IT'S COMMON TO SEE A "DRINK BAR" OPTION AVAILABLE THAT GIVES UNLIMITED SELF-SERVE REFILLS OF SODA, COFFEE, TEA, JUICES, AND OTHER NON-ALCOHOLIC DRINKS. THIS IS USUALLY AVAILABLE FOR BETWEEN 200 AND 400 YEN, MAKING IT A GOOD OPTION IF YOU WANT TO HANG OUT AT A DINER FOR A WHILE BUT DON'T WANT TO SPEND A LOT OF MONEY.*

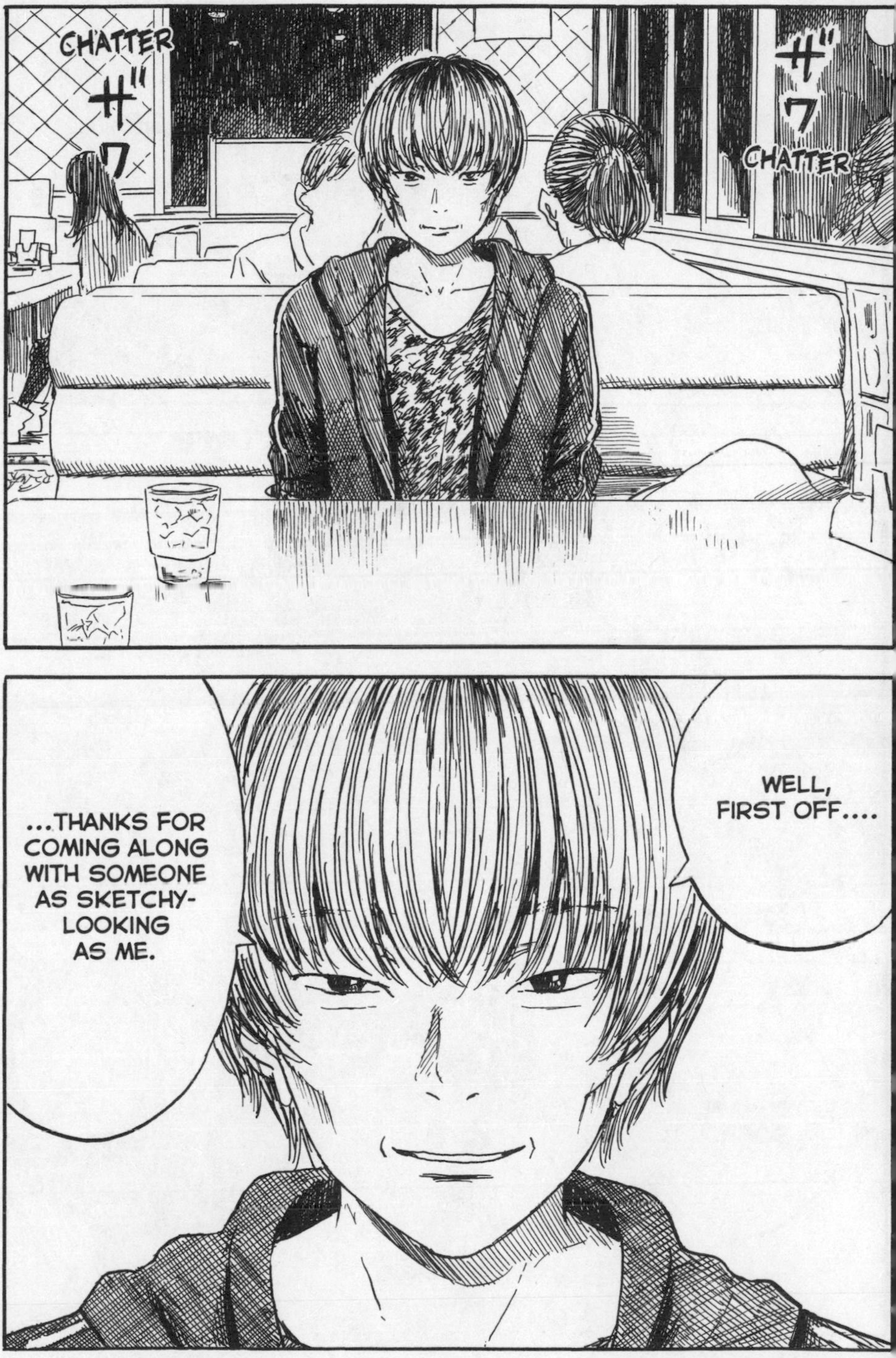
ザワ
CHATTER
CHATTER
ザワ
WELL, FIRST OFF....
...THANKS FOR COMING ALONG WITH SOMEONE AS SKETCHY-LOOKING AS ME.

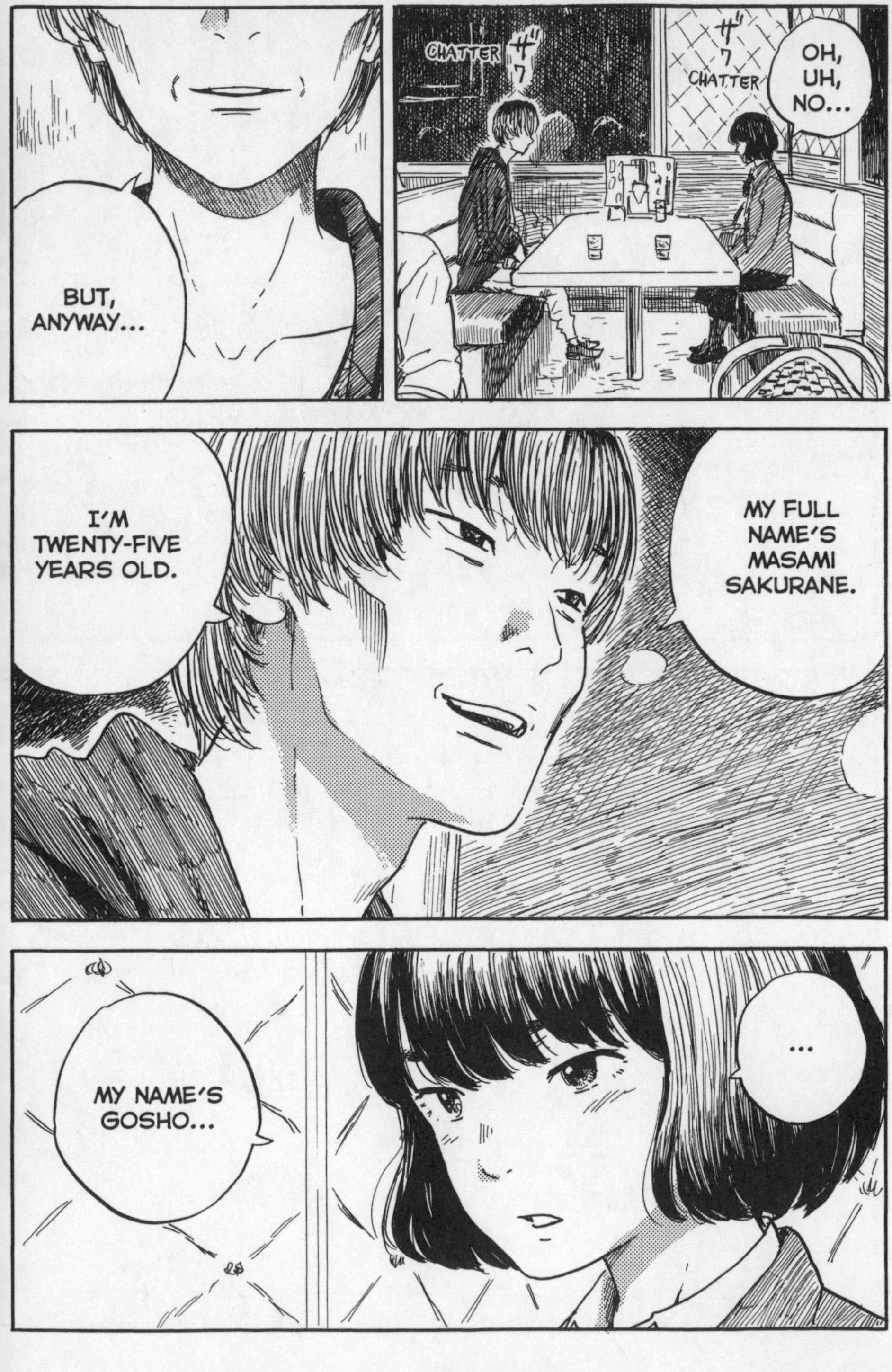
ザワ
CHATTER
ザワ
CHATTER
OH, UH, NO...
BUT, ANYWAY...
MY FULL NAME'S MASAMI SAKURANE.
I'M TWENTY-FIVE YEARS OLD.
...
MY NAME'S GOSHO...

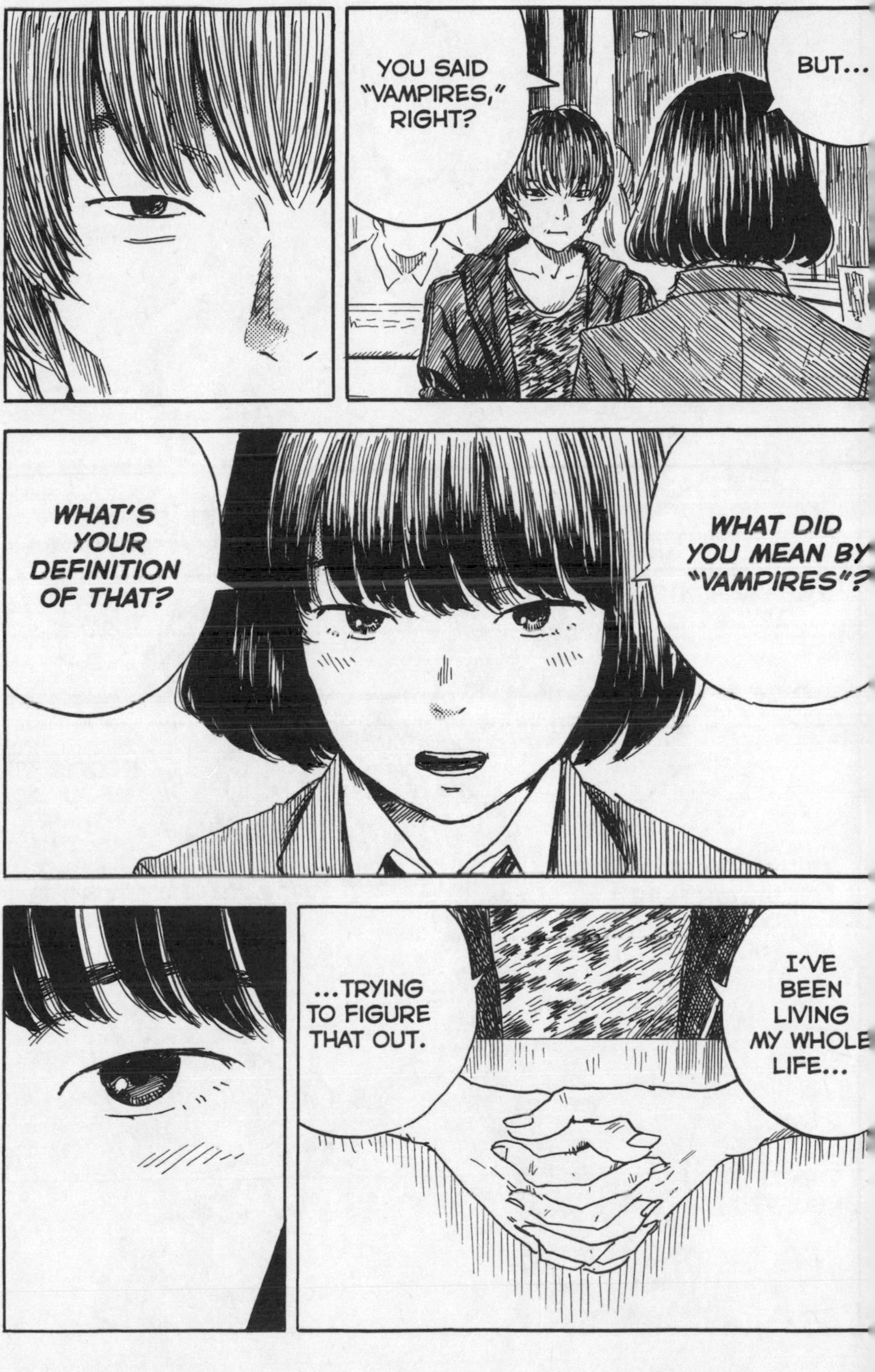
BUT...
YOU SAID "VAMPIRES," RIGHT?
WHAT DID YOU MEAN BY "VAMPIRES"?
WHAT'S YOUR DEFINITION OF THAT?
I'VE BEEN LIVING MY WHOLE LIFE...
...TRYING TO FIGURE THAT OUT.

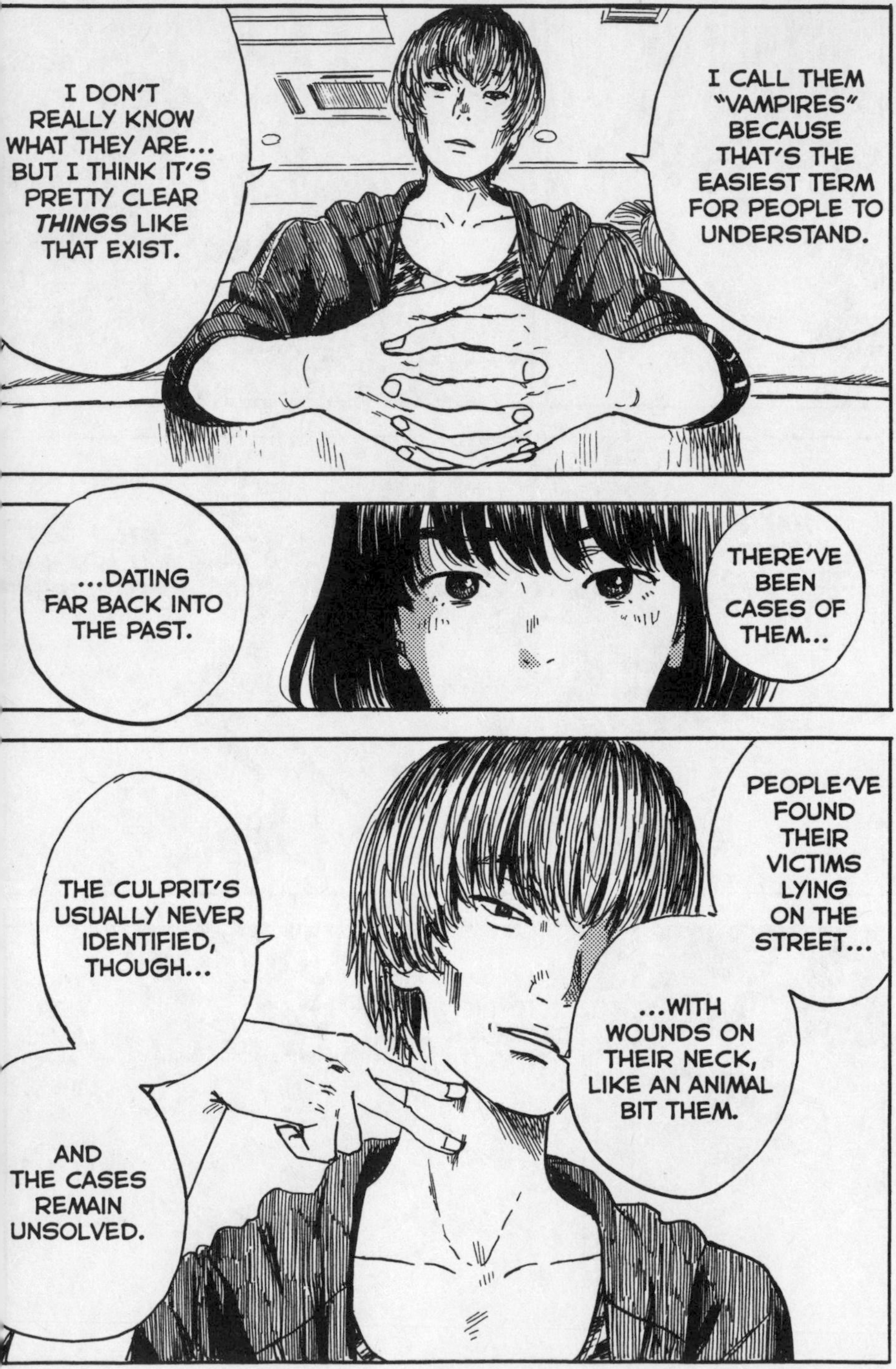
I CALL THEM "VAMPIRES" BECAUSE THAT'S THE EASIEST TERM FOR PEOPLE TO UNDERSTAND.
I DON'T REALLY KNOW WHAT THEY ARE... BUT I THINK IT'S PRETTY CLEAR *THINGS* LIKE THAT EXIST.
THERE'VE BEEN CASES OF THEM...
...DATING FAR BACK INTO THE PAST.
PEOPLE'VE FOUND THEIR VICTIMS LYING ON THE STREET...
...WITH WOUNDS ON THEIR NECK, LIKE AN ANIMAL BIT THEM.
THE CULPRIT'S USUALLY NEVER IDENTIFIED, THOUGH...
AND THE CASES REMAIN UNSOLVED.

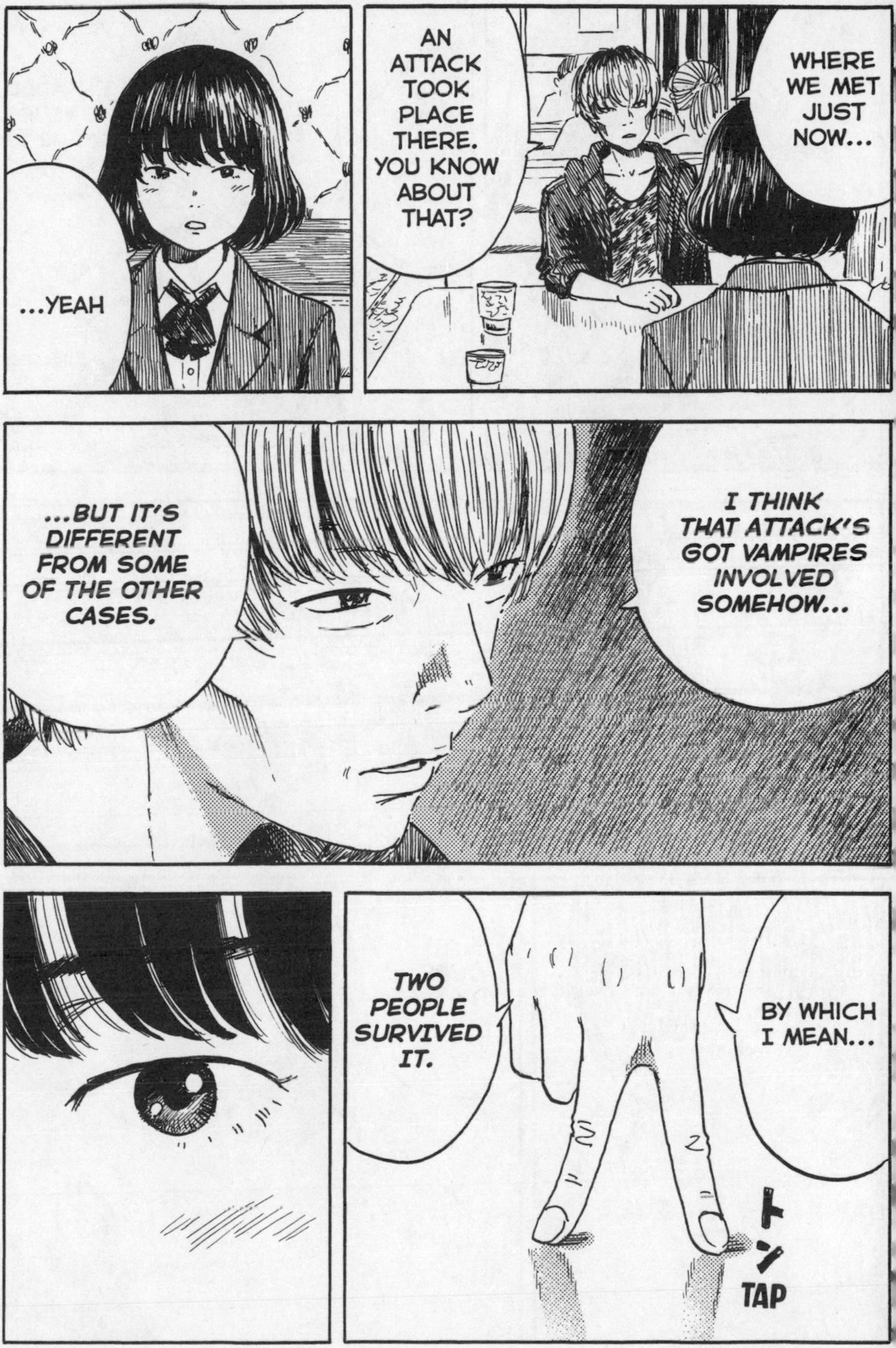
WHERE WE MET JUST NOW...
AN ATTACK TOOK PLACE THERE. YOU KNOW ABOUT THAT?
...YEAH
I THINK THAT ATTACK'S GOT VAMPIRES INVOLVED SOMEHOW...
...BUT IT'S DIFFERENT FROM SOME OF THE OTHER CASES.
BY WHICH I MEAN...
TWO PEOPLE SURVIVED IT.
トン
TAP

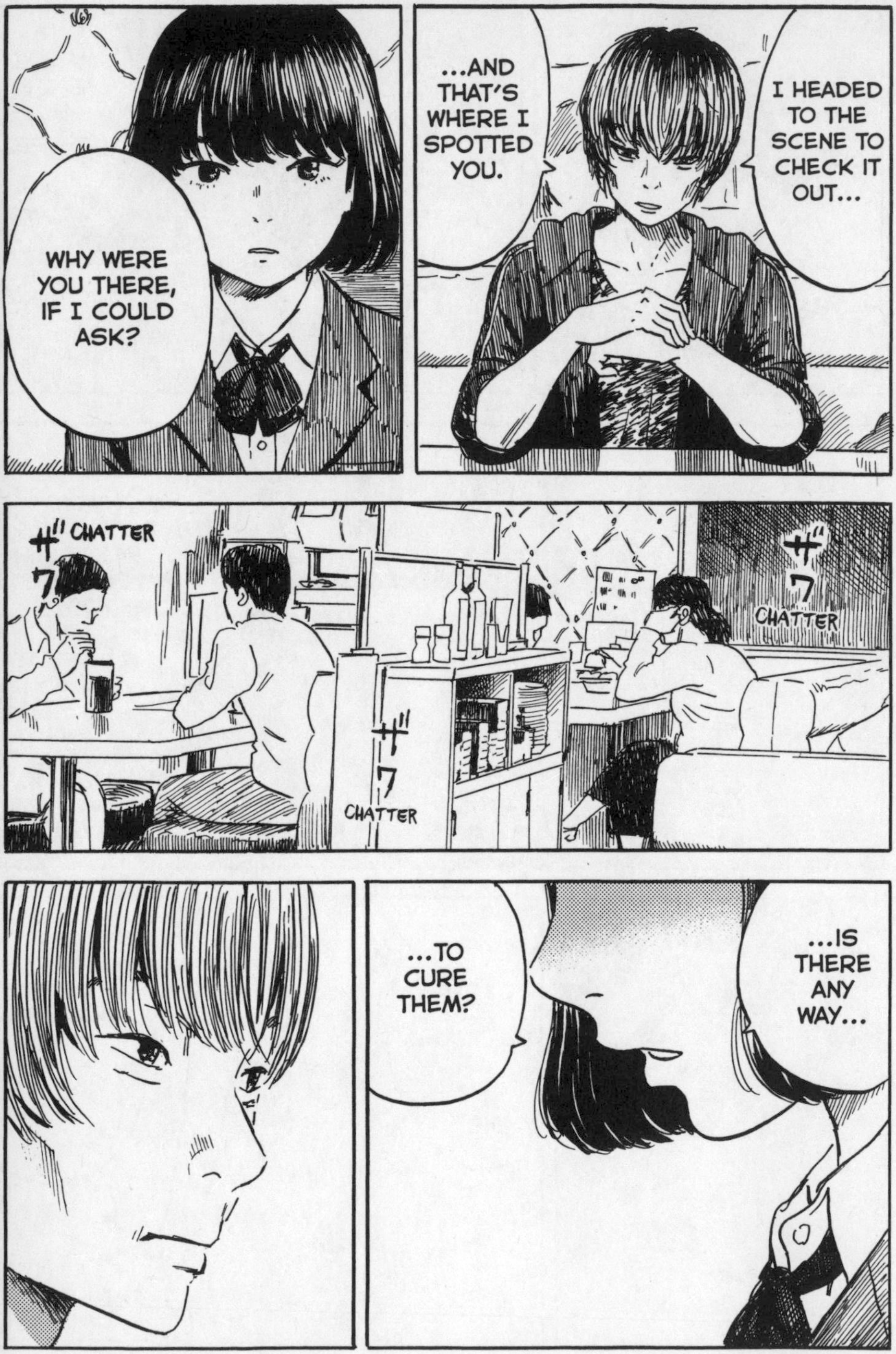
I HEADED TO THE SCENE TO CHECK IT OUT...
...AND THAT'S WHERE I SPOTTED YOU.
WHY WERE YOU THERE, IF I COULD ASK?
ザワ CHATTER
ザワ CHATTER
ザワ CHATTER
...IS THERE ANY WAY...
...TO CURE THEM?

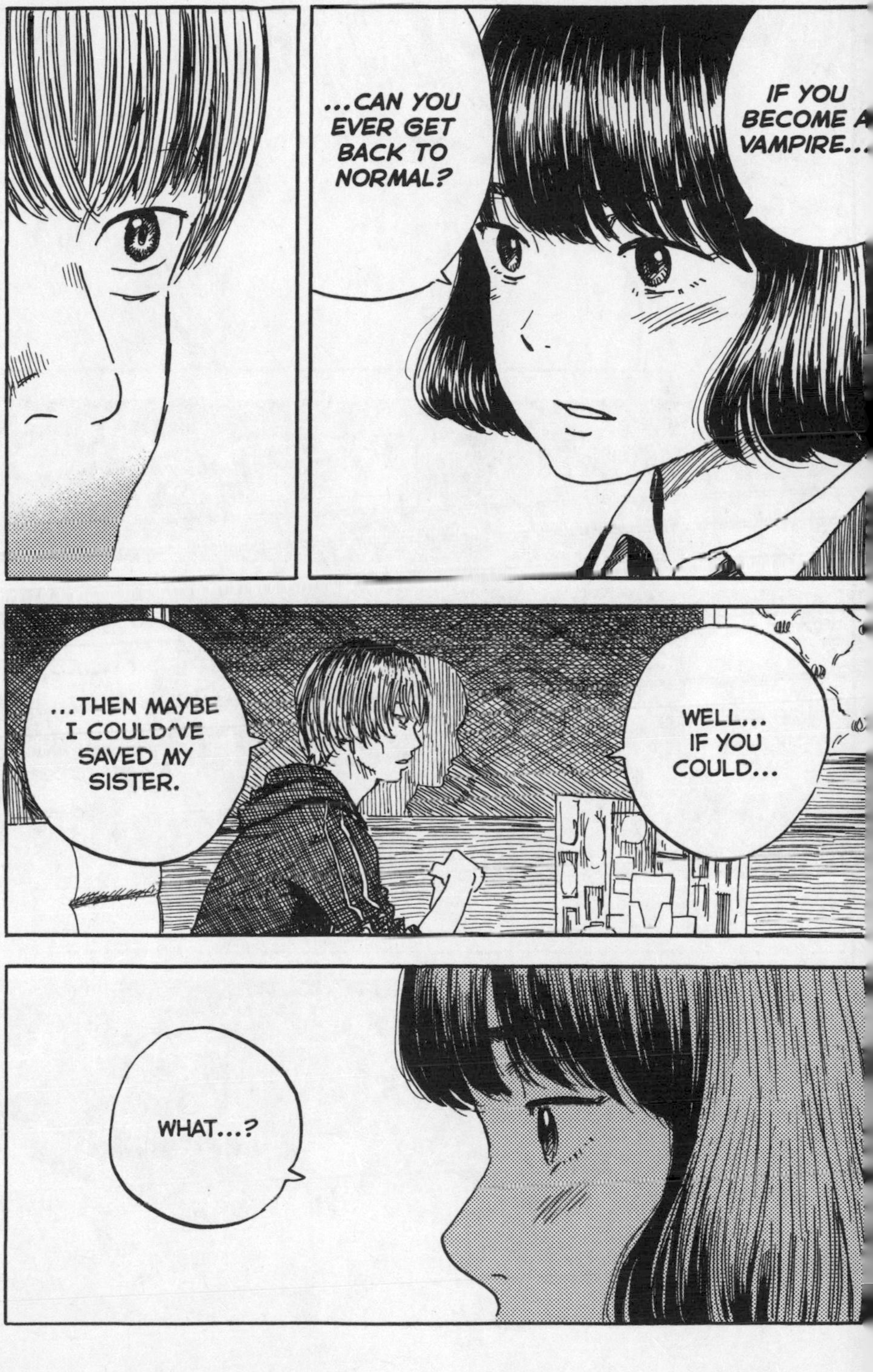
IF YOU BECOME A VAMPIRE...
...CAN YOU EVER GET BACK TO NORMAL?
WELL... IF YOU COULD...
...THEN MAYBE I COULD'VE SAVED MY SISTER.
WHAT...?

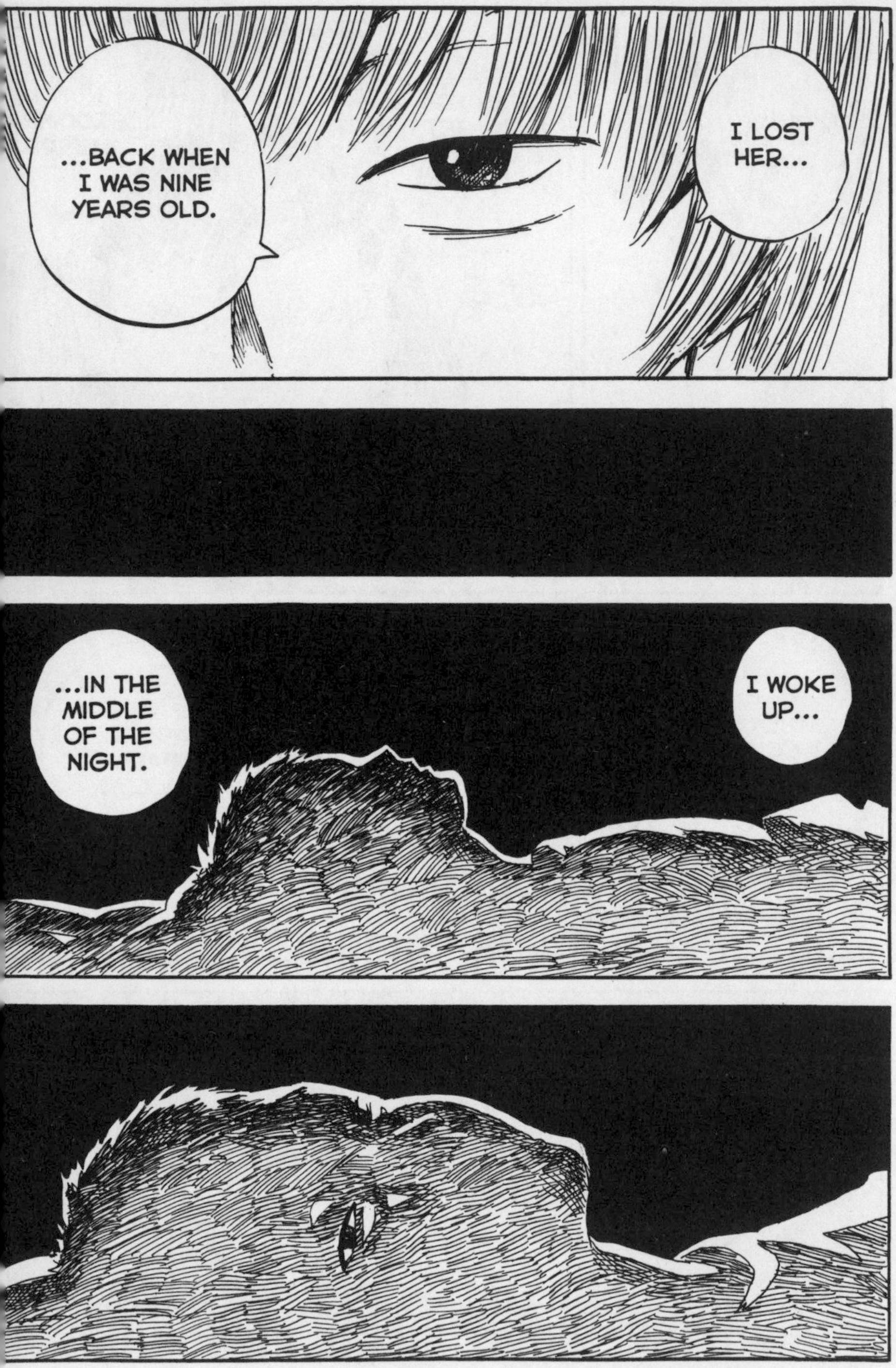
I LOST HER...
...BACK WHEN I WAS NINE YEARS OLD.
I WOKE UP...
...IN THE MIDDLE OF THE NIGHT.

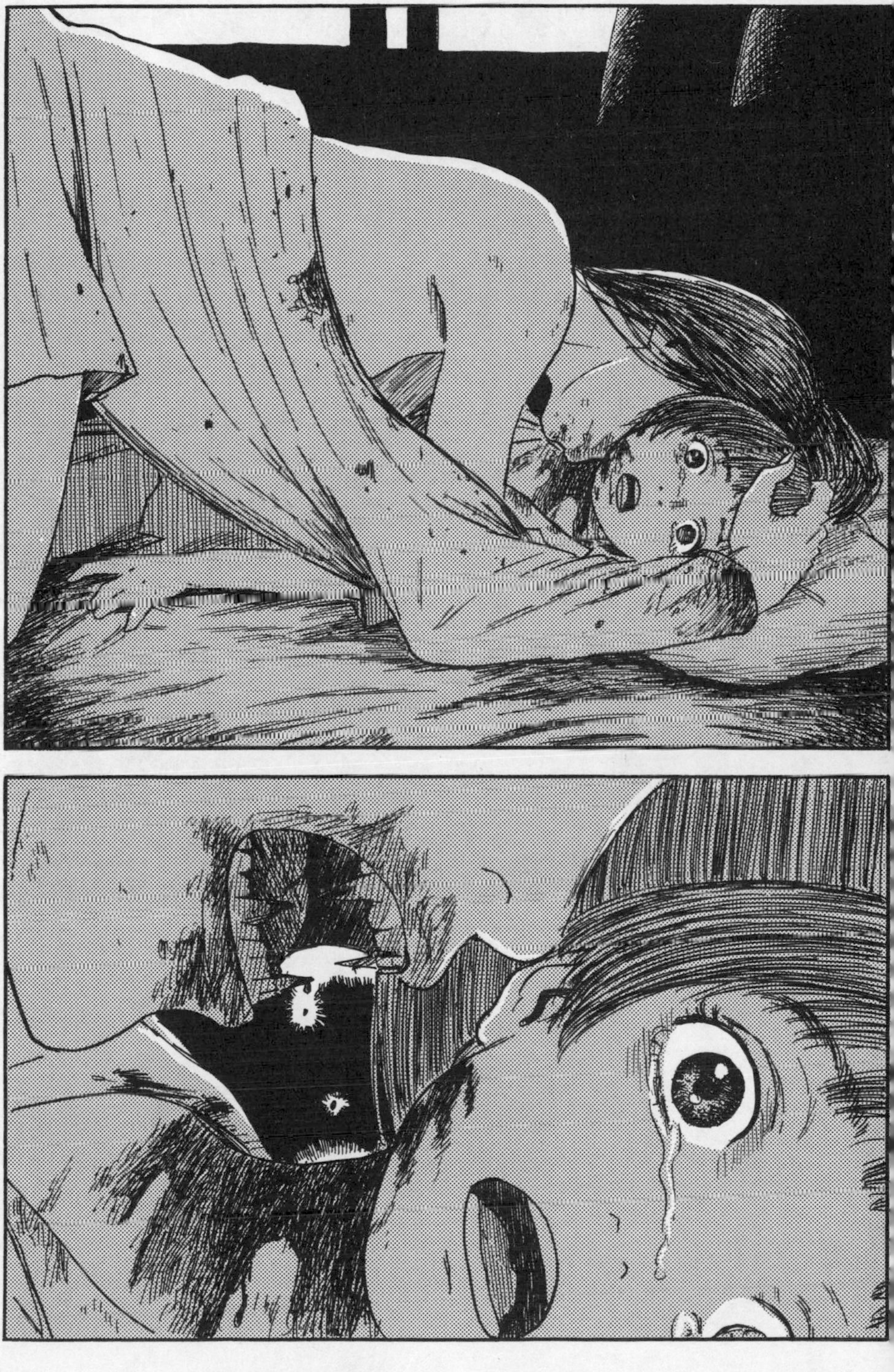

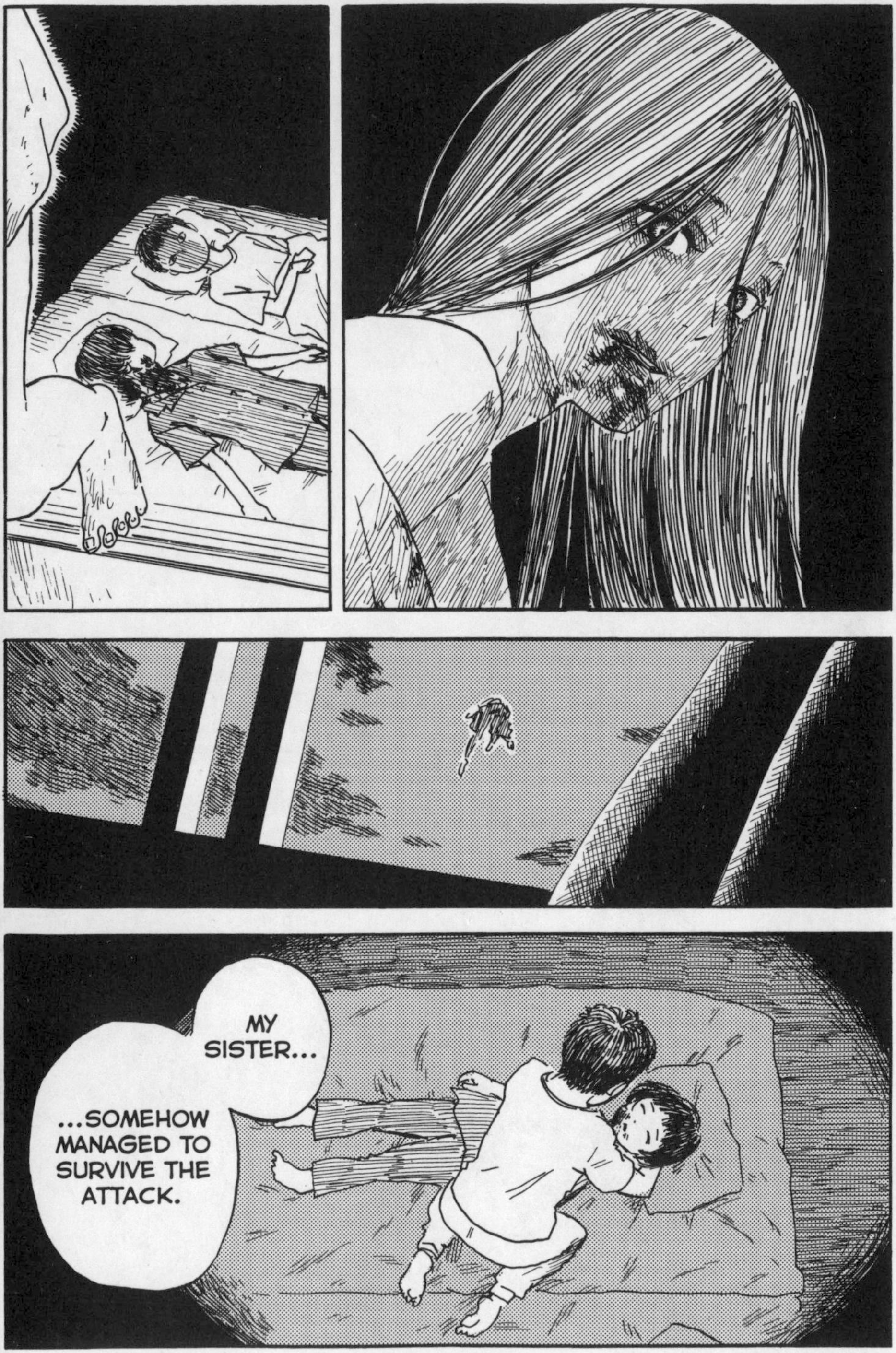
MY SISTER...
...SOMEHOW MANAGED TO SURVIVE THE ATTACK.

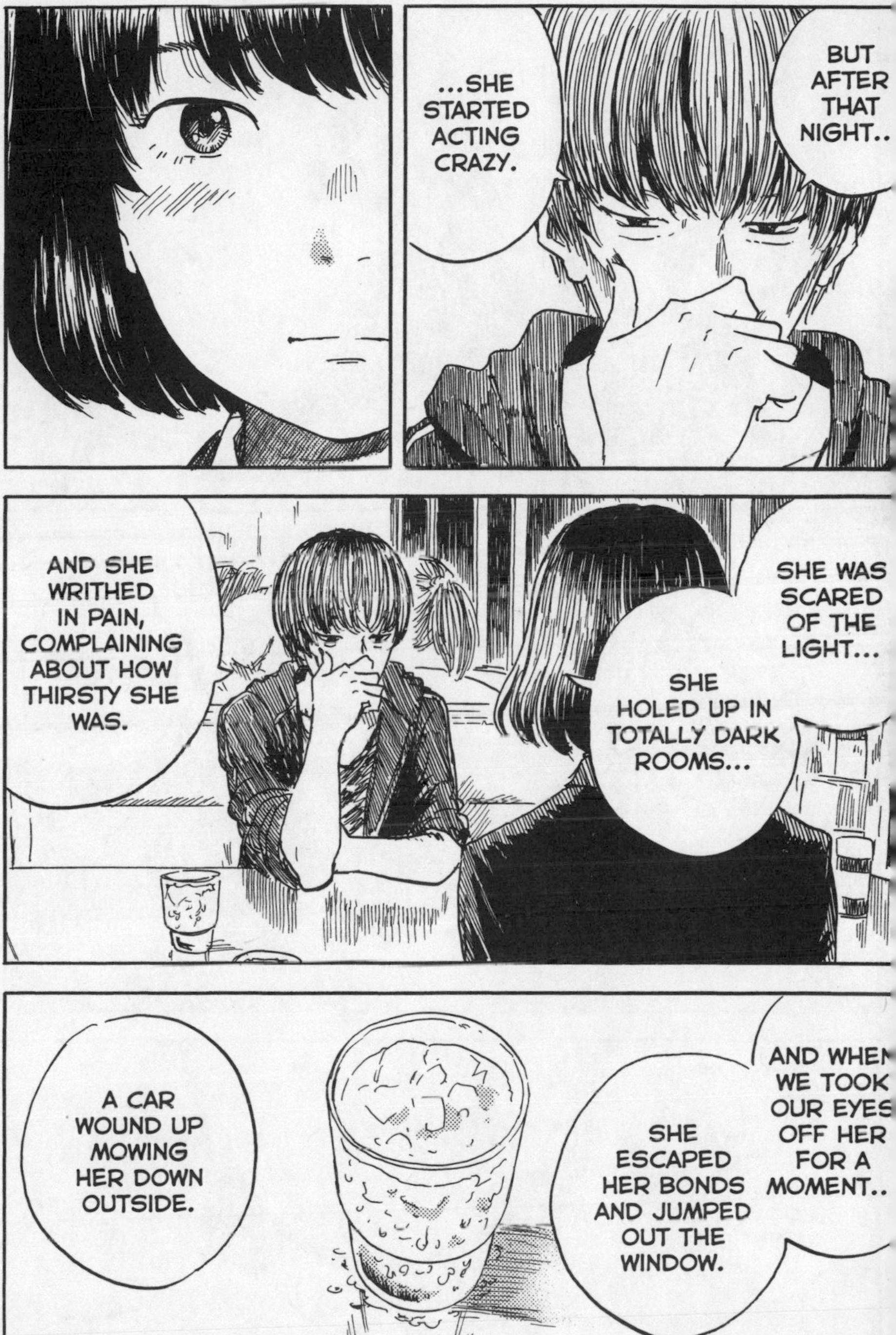
BUT AFTER THAT NIGHT..
...SHE STARTED ACTING CRAZY.
SHE WAS SCARED OF THE LIGHT...
SHE HOLED UP IN TOTALLY DARK ROOMS...
AND SHE WRITHED IN PAIN, COMPLAINING ABOUT HOW THIRSTY SHE WAS.
AND WHEN WE TOOK OUR EYES OFF HER FOR A MOMENT..
SHE ESCAPED HER BONDS AND JUMPED OUT THE WINDOW.
A CAR WOUND UP MOWING HER DOWN OUTSIDE.

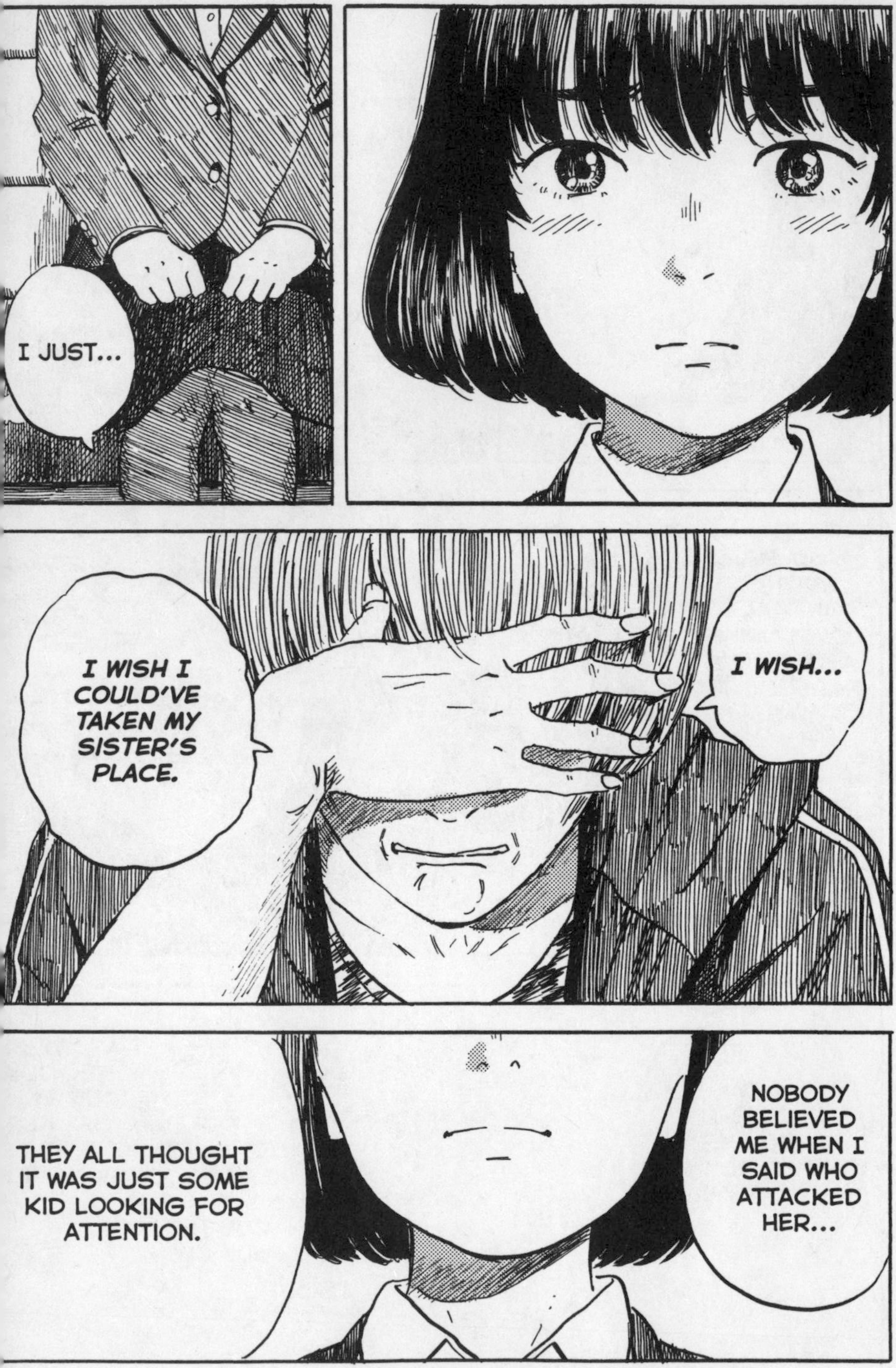
I JUST...
I WISH...
I WISH I COULD'VE TAKEN MY SISTER'S PLACE.
NOBODY BELIEVED ME WHEN I SAID WHO ATTACKED HER...
THEY ALL THOUGHT IT WAS JUST SOME KID LOOKING FOR ATTENTION.

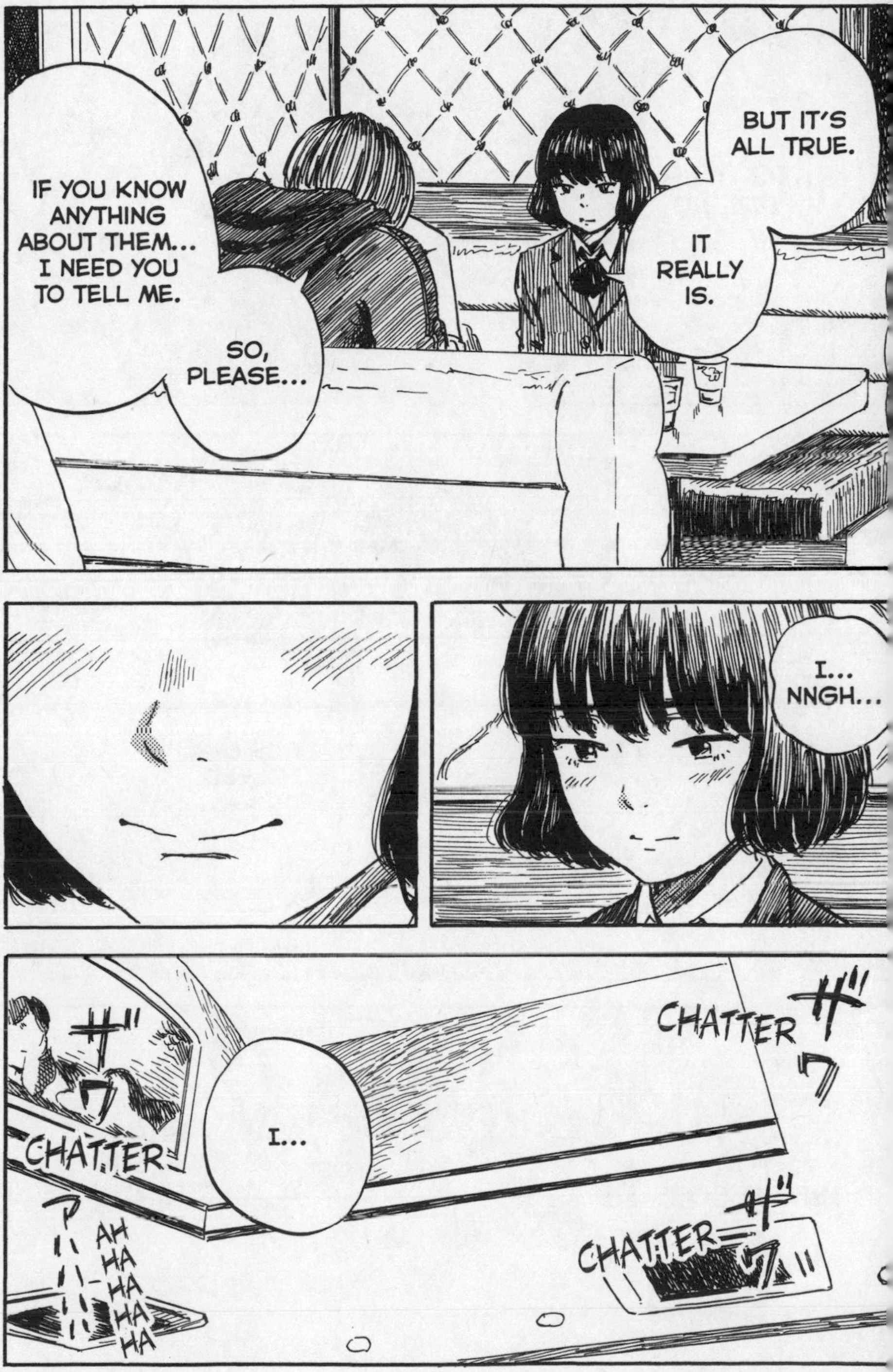
BUT IT'S ALL TRUE.
IT REALLY IS.
IF YOU KNOW ANYTHING ABOUT THEM... I NEED YOU TO TELL ME.
SO, PLEASE...
I... NNGH...
CHATTER ザワ
ザワ CHATTER
I...
CHATTER ザワ
AH HA HA HA HA

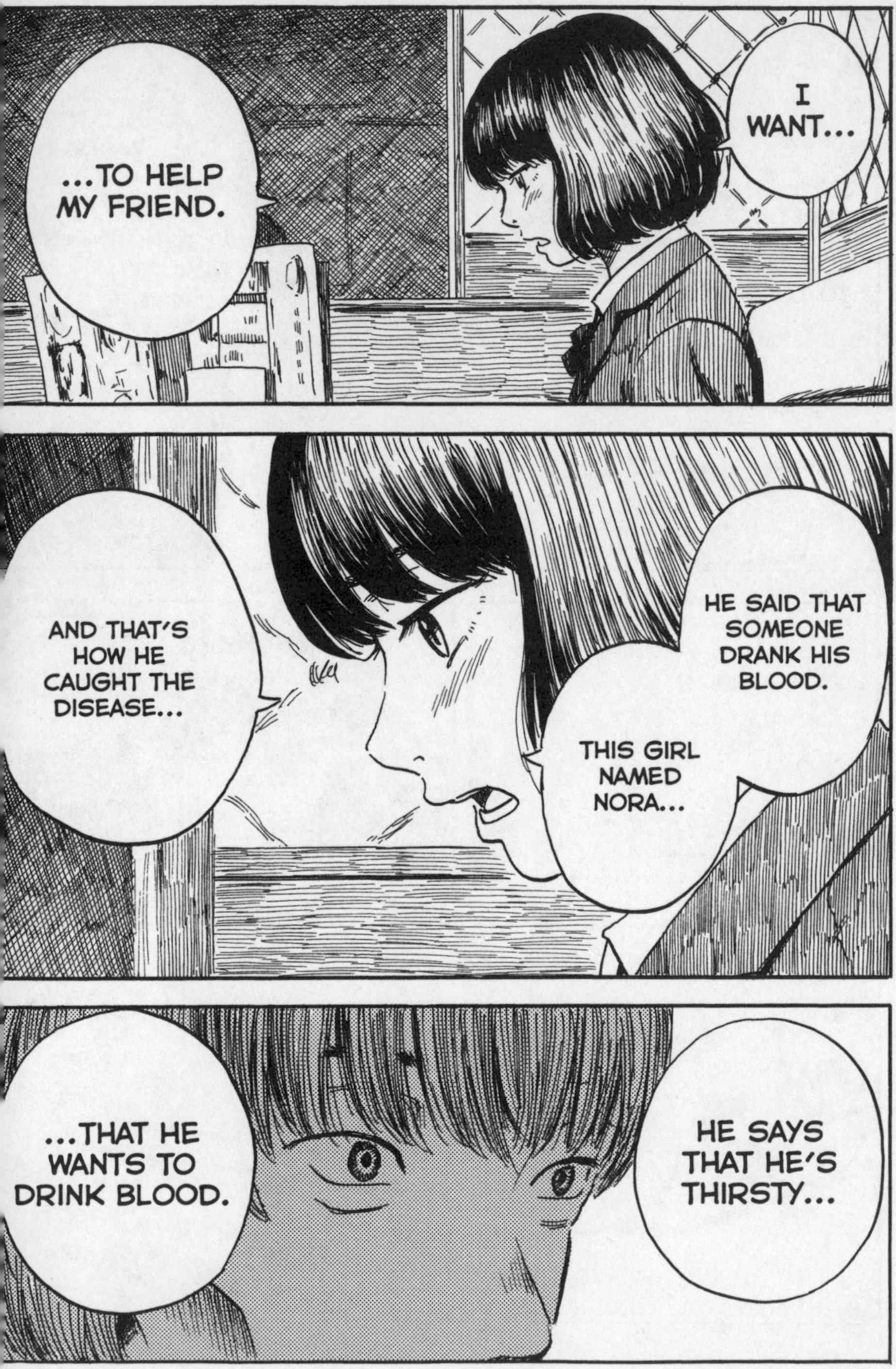
I WANT...
...TO HELP MY FRIEND.
HE SAID THAT SOMEONE DRANK HIS BLOOD.
THIS GIRL NAMED NORA...
AND THAT'S HOW HE CAUGHT THE DISEASE...
HE SAYS THAT HE'S THIRSTY...
...THAT HE WANTS TO DRINK BLOOD.

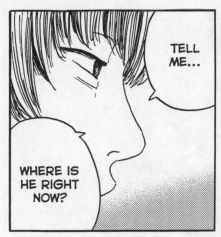

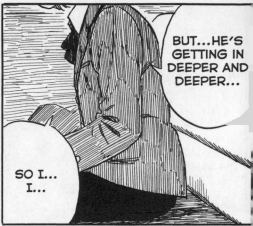

BUT...HE'S GETTING IN DEEPER AND DEEPER...
SO I... I...
TELL ME...
WHERE IS HE RIGHT NOW?
...I DON'T KNOW.
THEY SAID HE WAS KIDNAPPED BY...SOME CRAZY ORGANIZATION...
I...I HAVE NO IDEA...
...WHAT I SHOULD EVEN BE DOING...

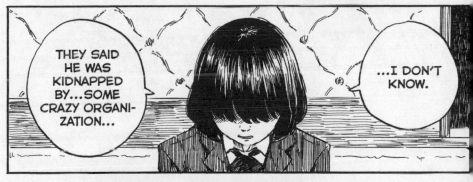

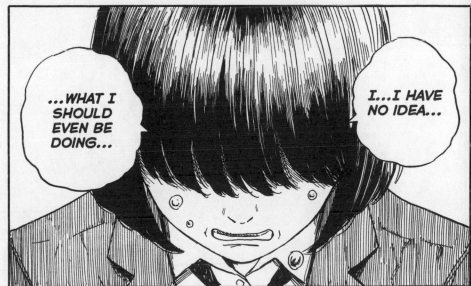

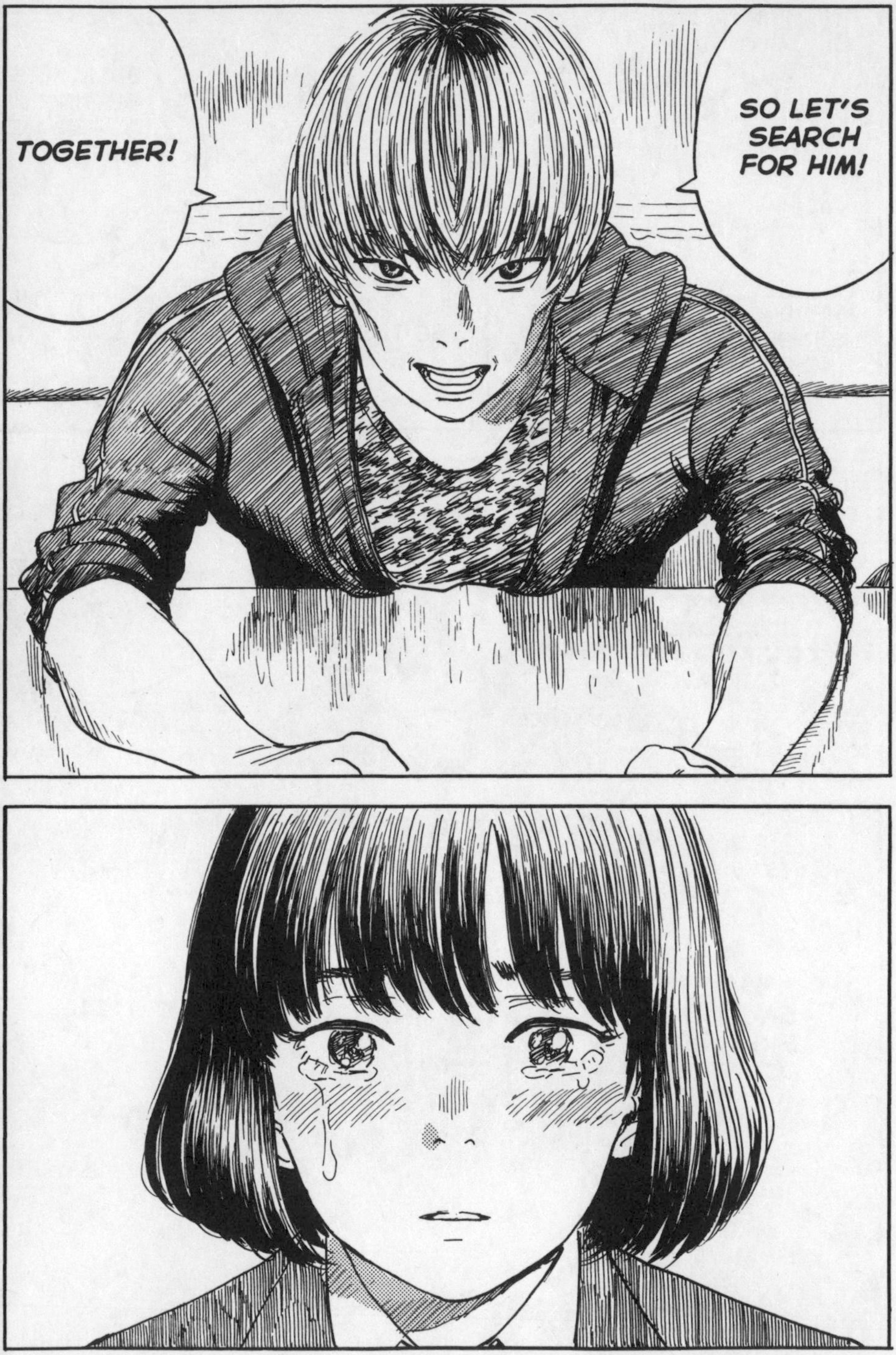
SO LET'S SEARCH FOR HIM!
TOGETHER!

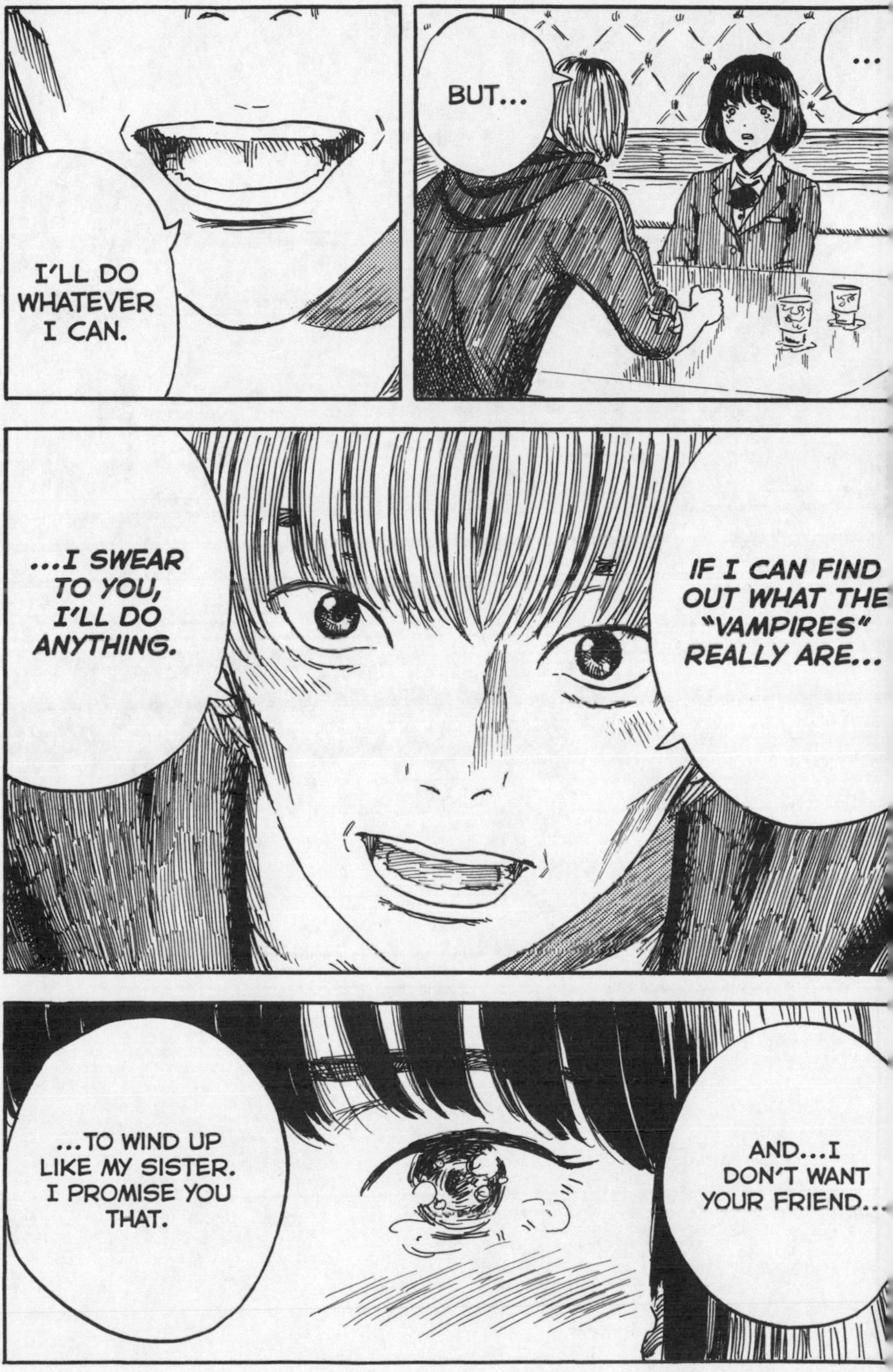
...
BUT...
I'LL DO WHATEVER I CAN.
IF I CAN FIND OUT WHAT THE "VAMPIRES" REALLY ARE...
...I SWEAR TO YOU, I'LL DO ANYTHING.
AND...I DON'T WANT YOUR FRIEND...
...TO WIND UP LIKE MY SISTER. I PROMISE YOU THAT.

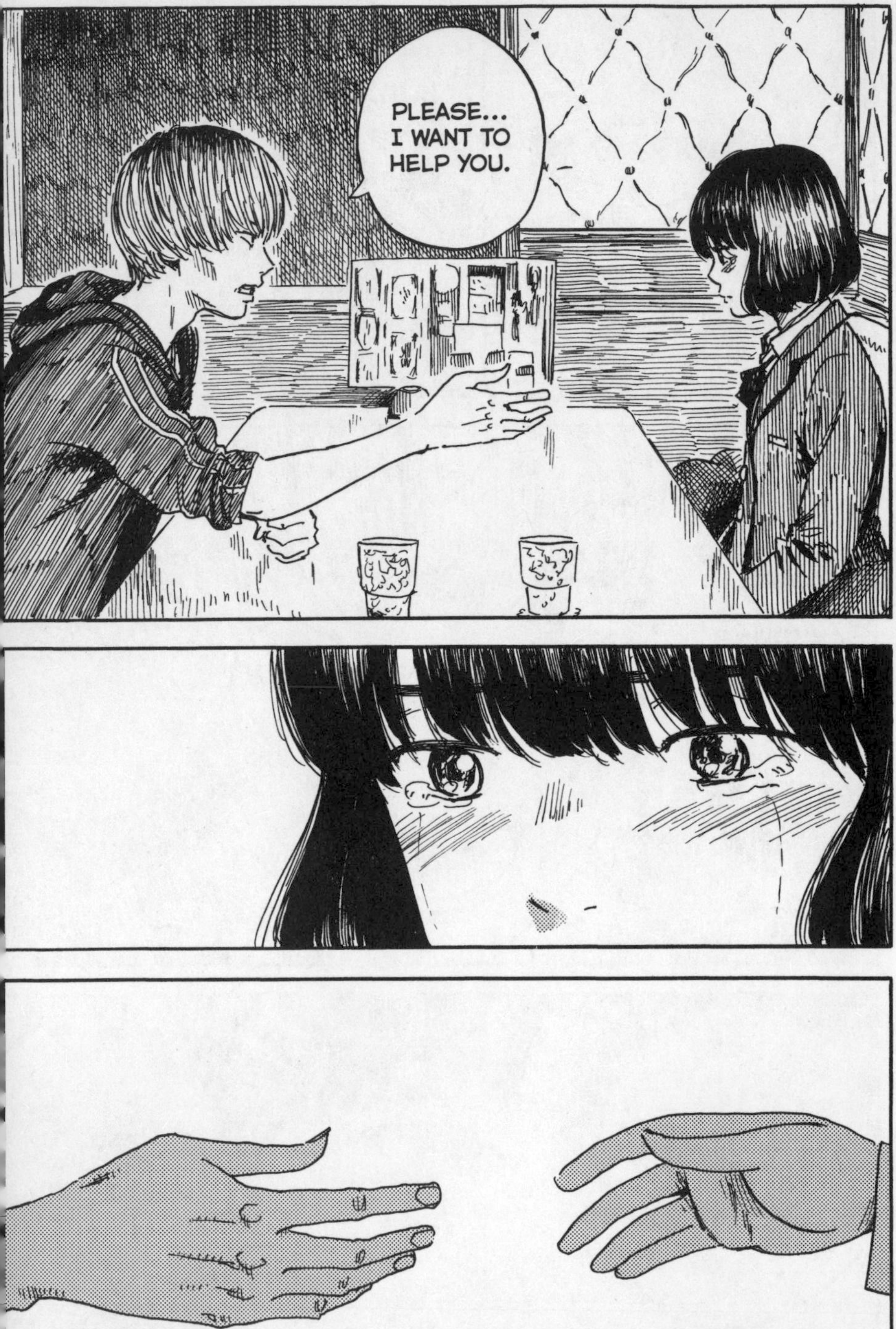
PLEASE... I WANT TO HELP YOU.

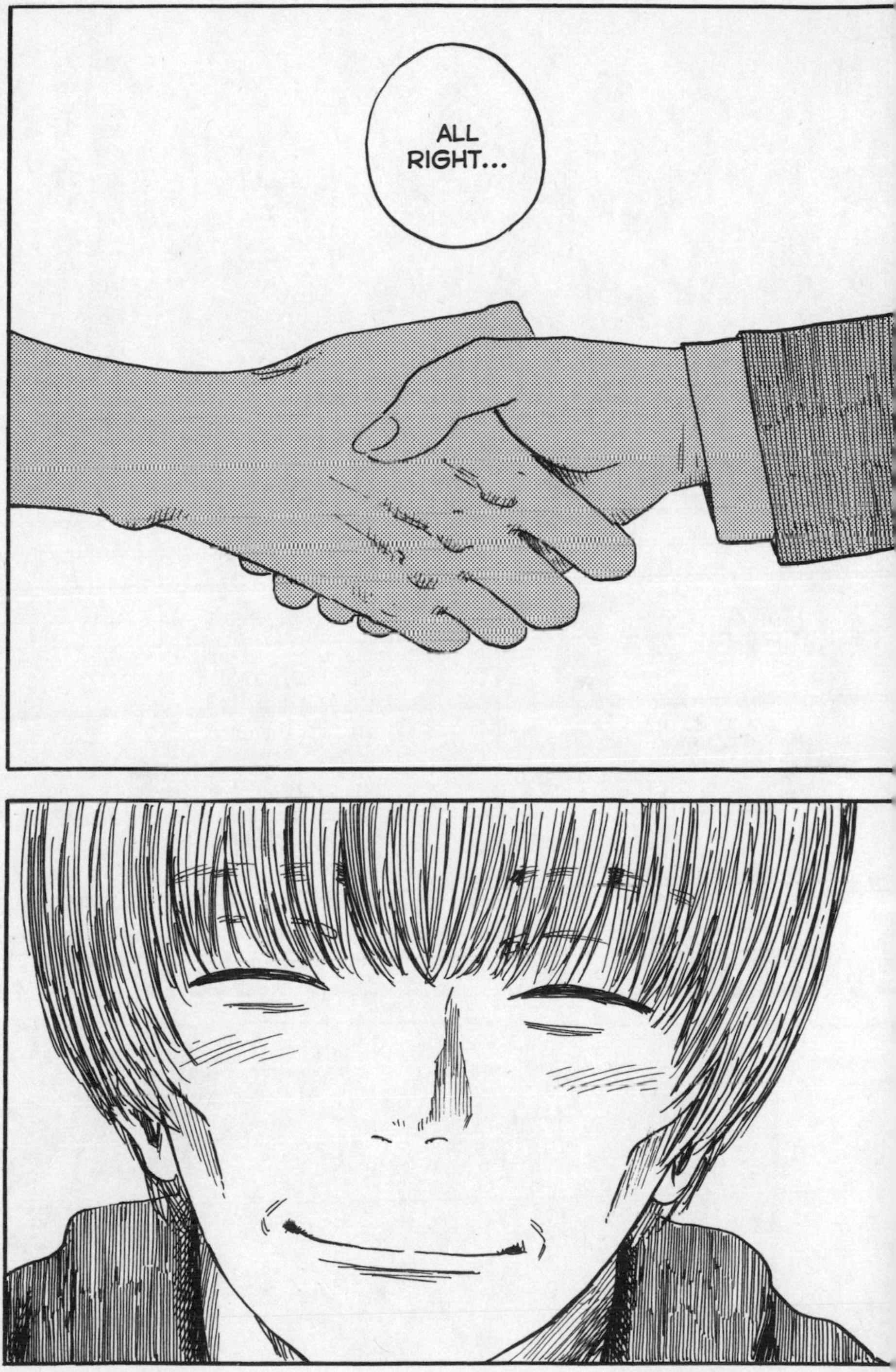
ALL RIGHT...

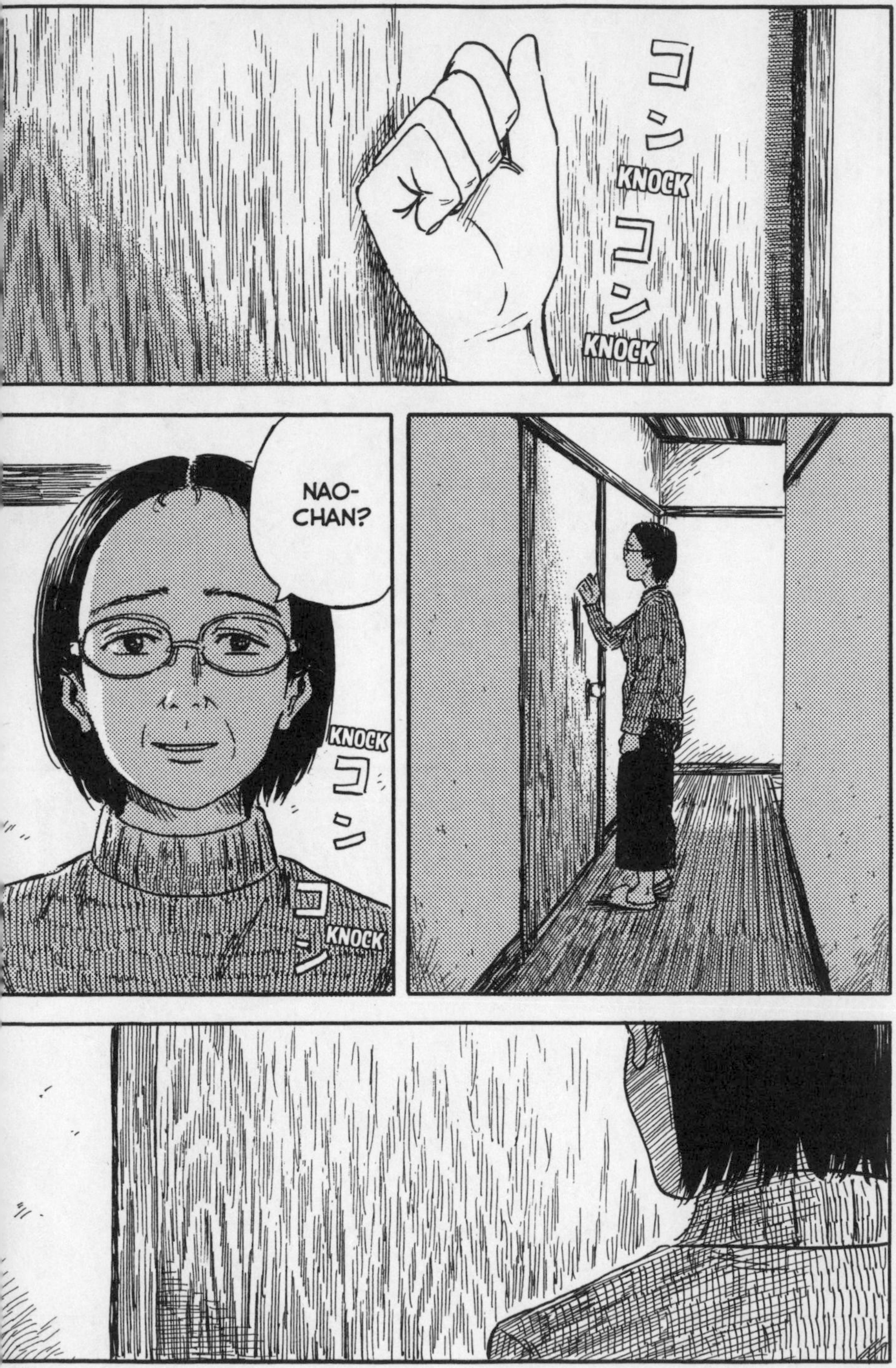
コン
KNOCK
コン
KNOCK
NAO-CHAN?
KNOCK
コン
コン
KNOCK

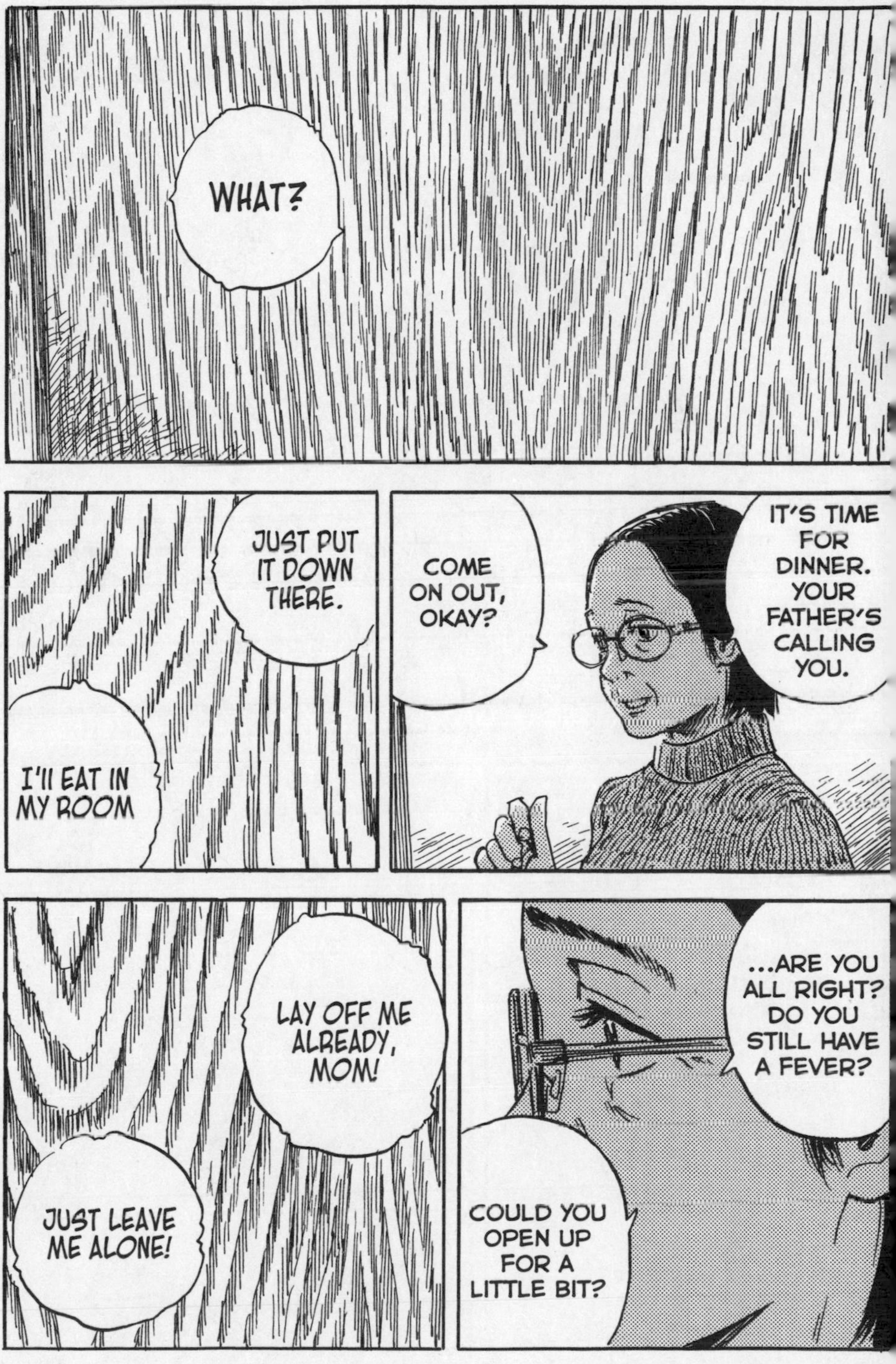
WHAT?
IT'S TIME FOR DINNER. YOUR FATHER'S CALLING YOU.
COME ON OUT, OKAY?
JUST PUT IT DOWN THERE.
I'll EAT IN MY ROOM
...ARE YOU ALL RIGHT? DO YOU STILL HAVE A FEVER?
COULD YOU OPEN UP FOR A LITTLE BIT?
LAY OFF ME ALREADY, MOM!
JUST LEAVE ME ALONE!

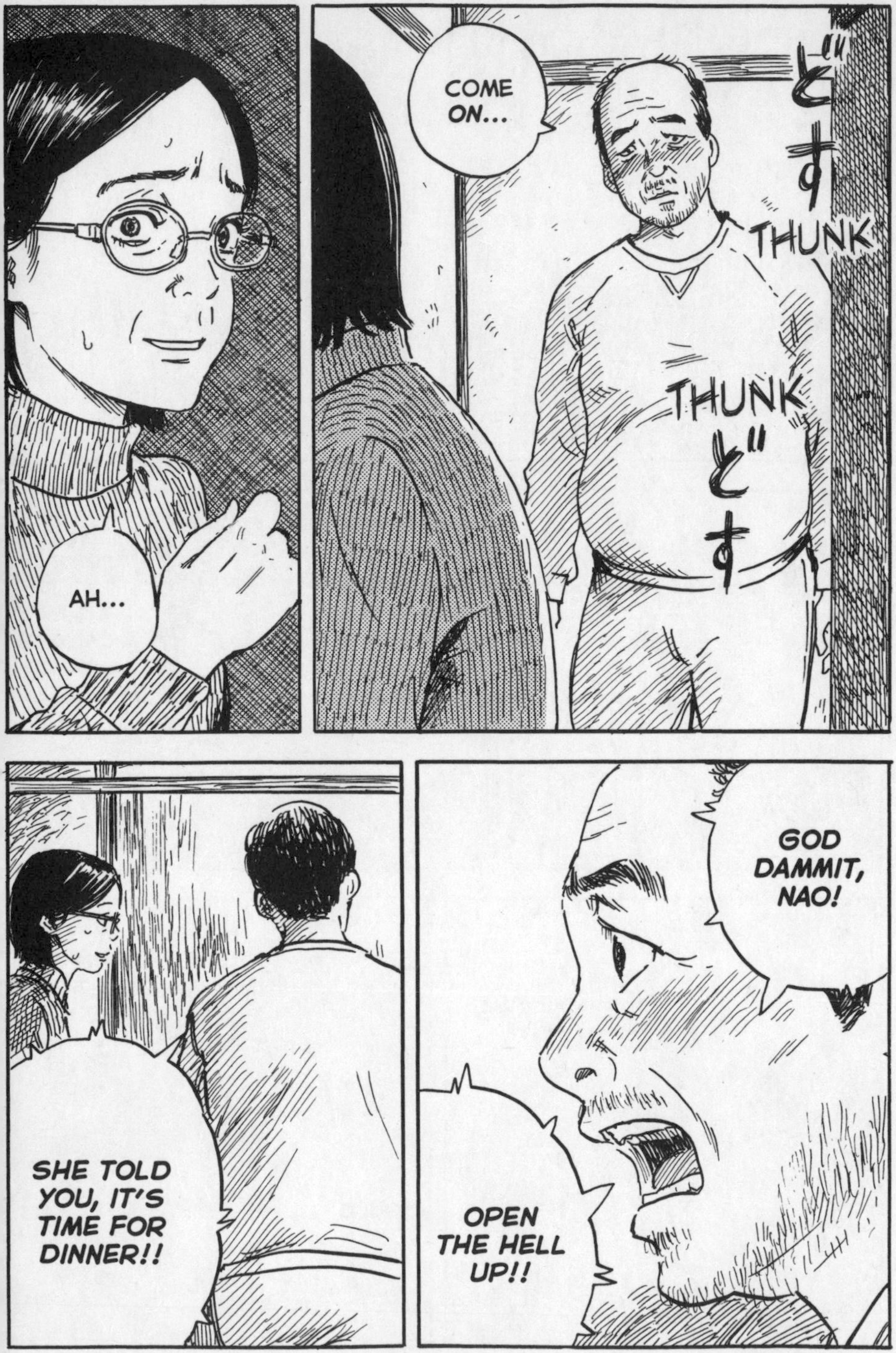
どす
THUNK
COME ON...
THUNK
どす
AH...
GOD DAMMIT, NAO!
OPEN THE HELL UP!!
SHE TOLD YOU, IT'S TIME FOR DINNER!!

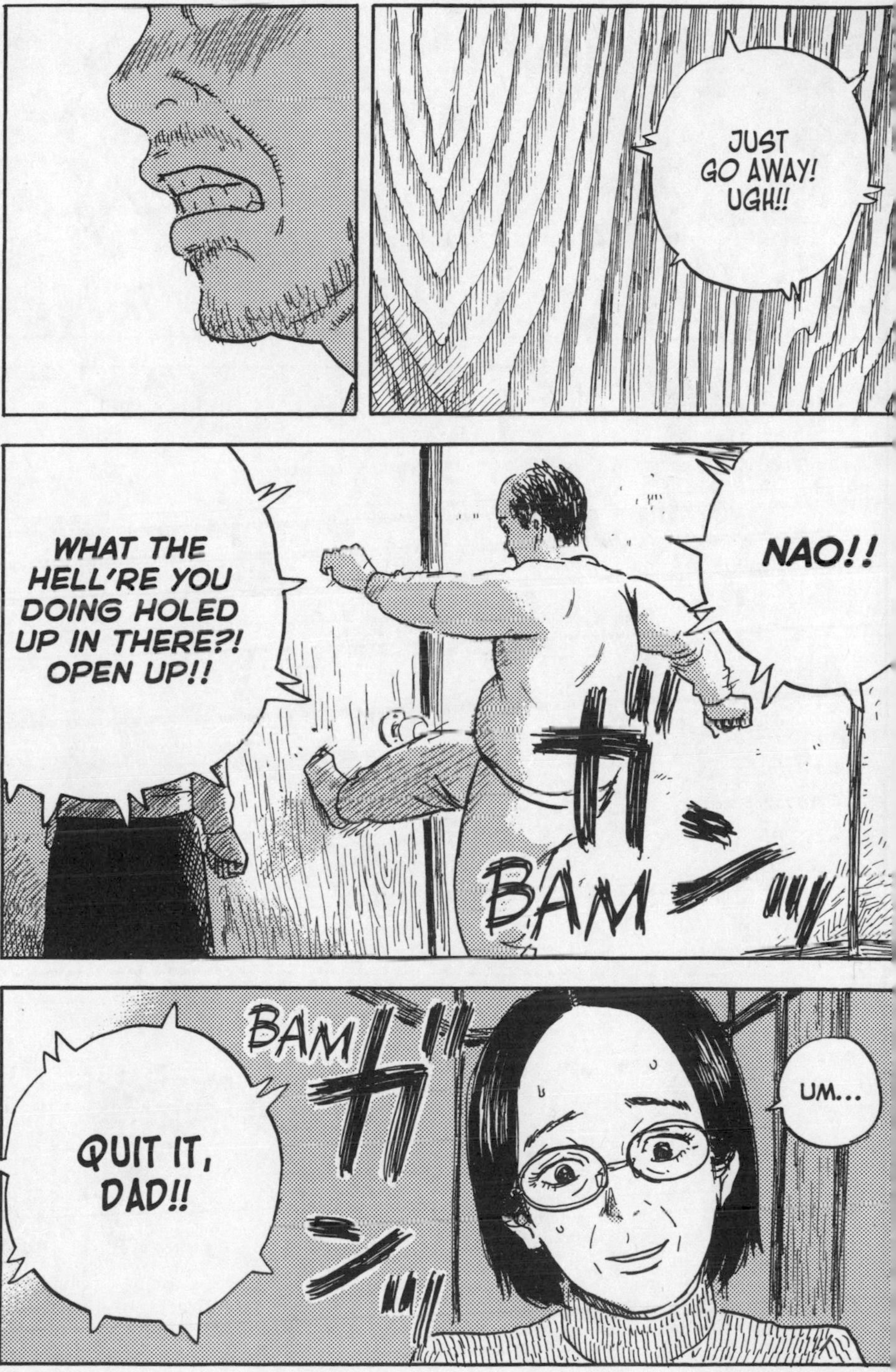
JUST GO AWAY! UGH!!
NAO!!
WHAT THE HELL'RE YOU DOING HOLED UP IN THERE?! OPEN UP!!
BAM
UM...
BAM
QUIT IT, DAD!!

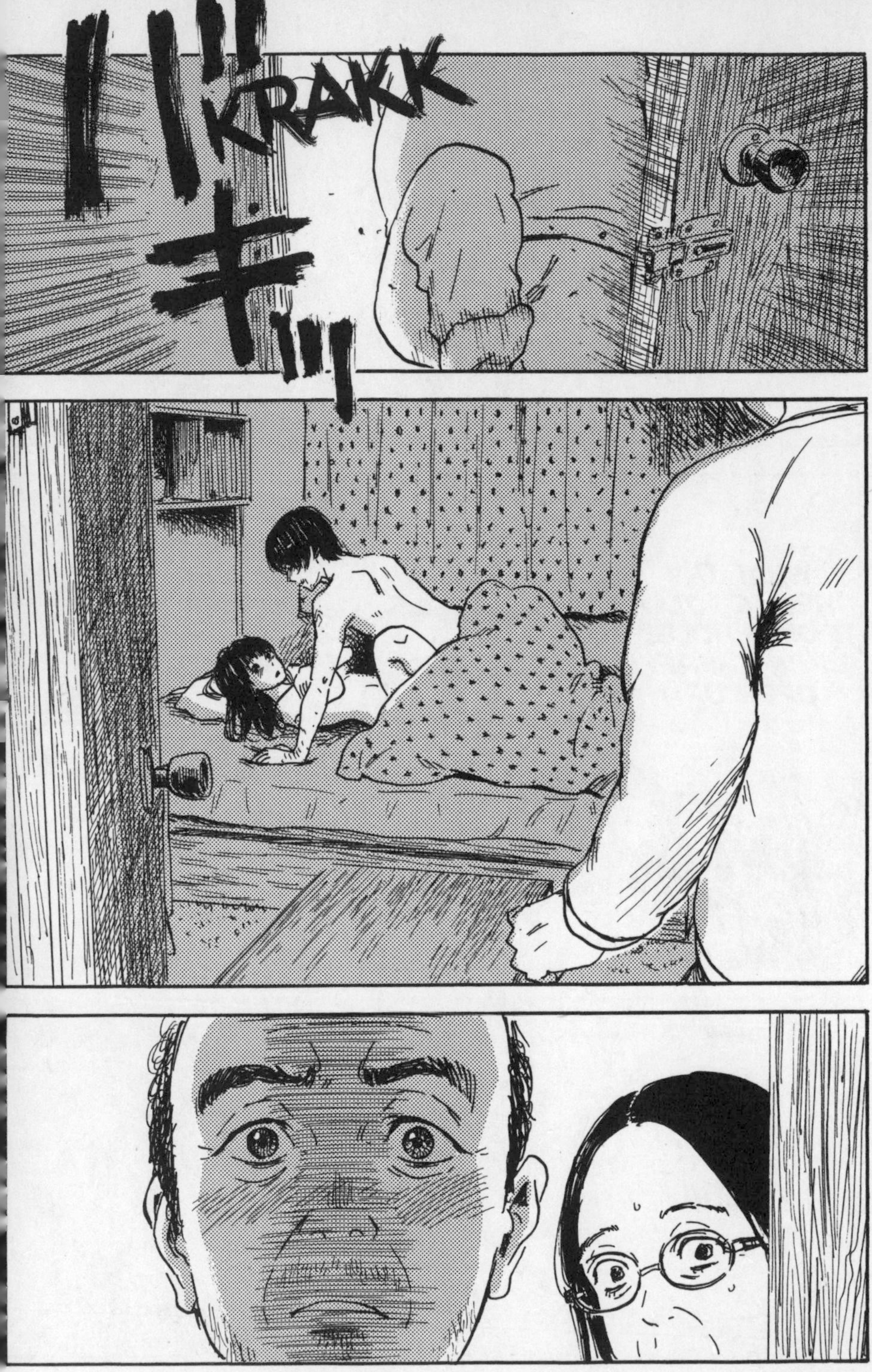
KRAKK

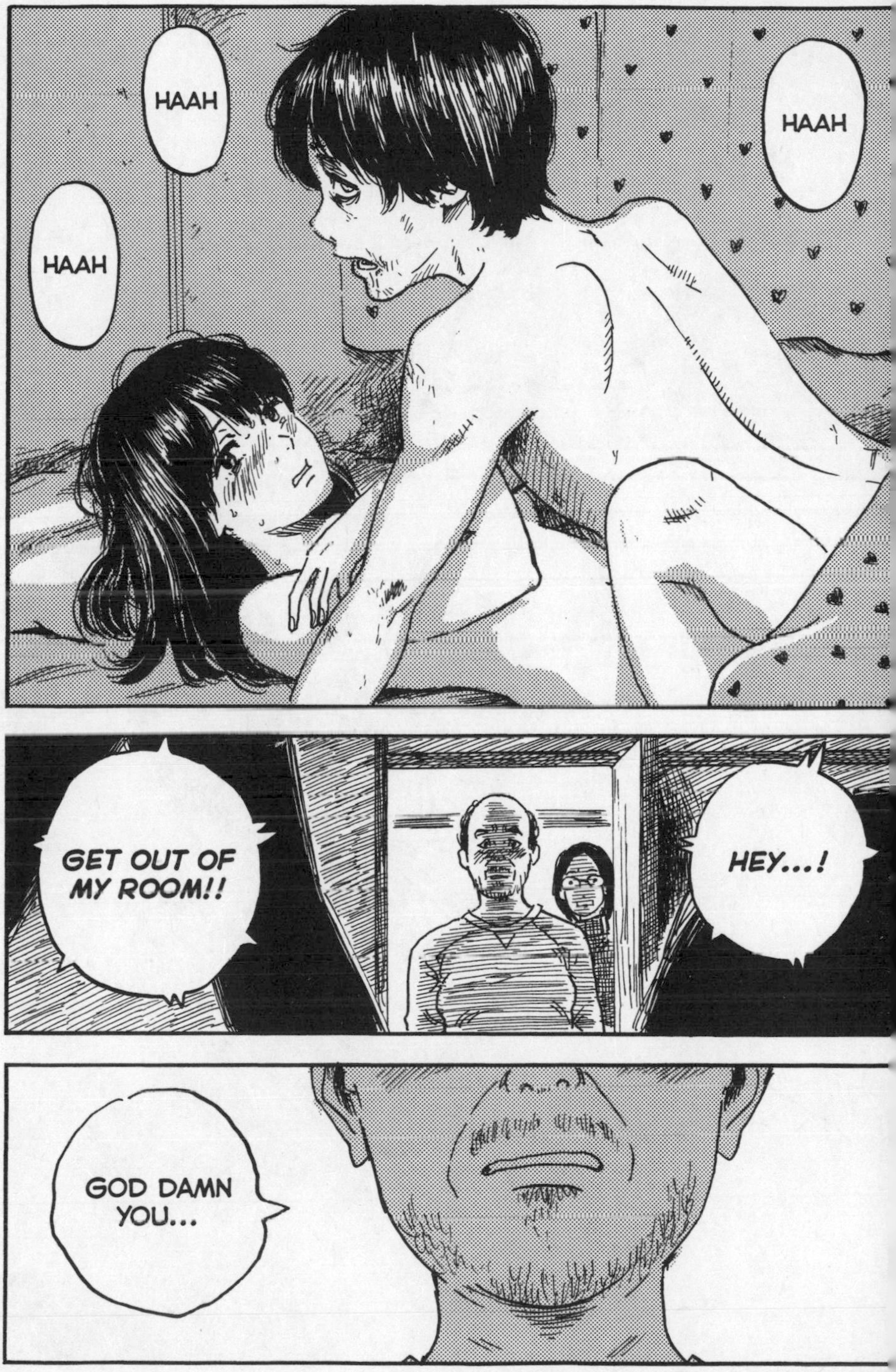
HAAH
HAAH
HAAH
HEY...!
GET OUT OF MY ROOM!!
GOD DAMN YOU...

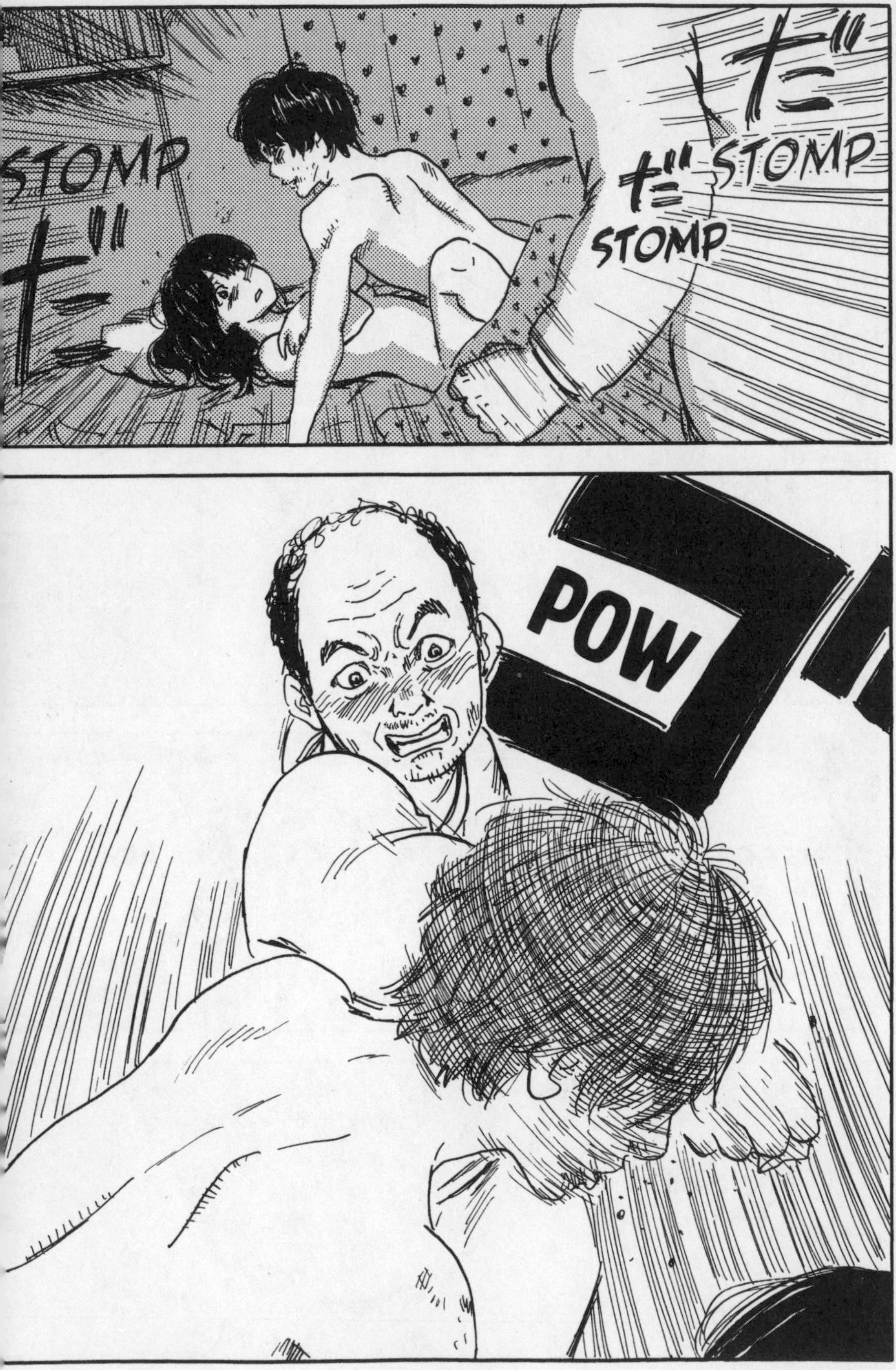
だ
STOMP
だ
STOMP
STOMP
だ
POW

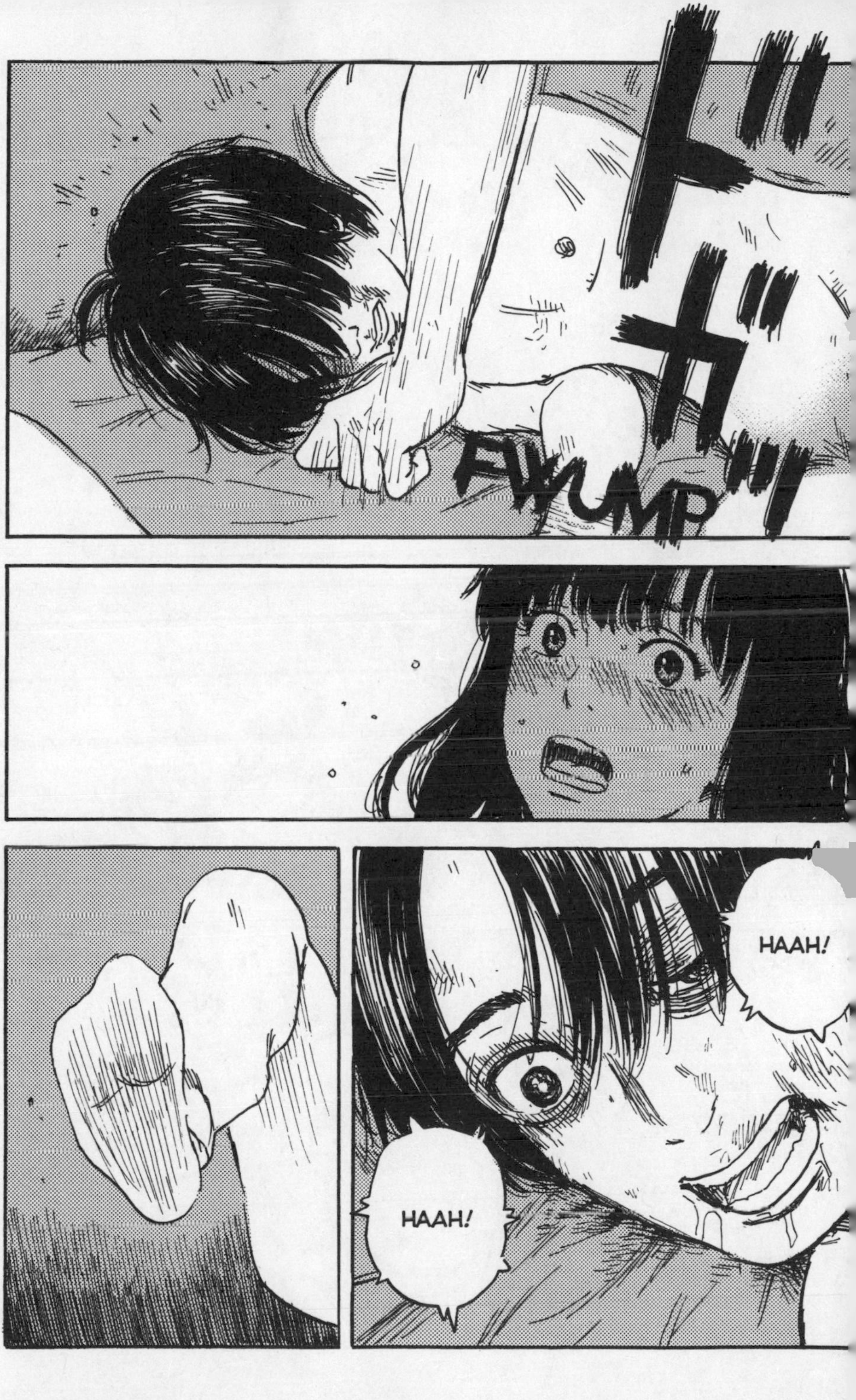
ドガ
FWUMP
HAAH!
HAAH!

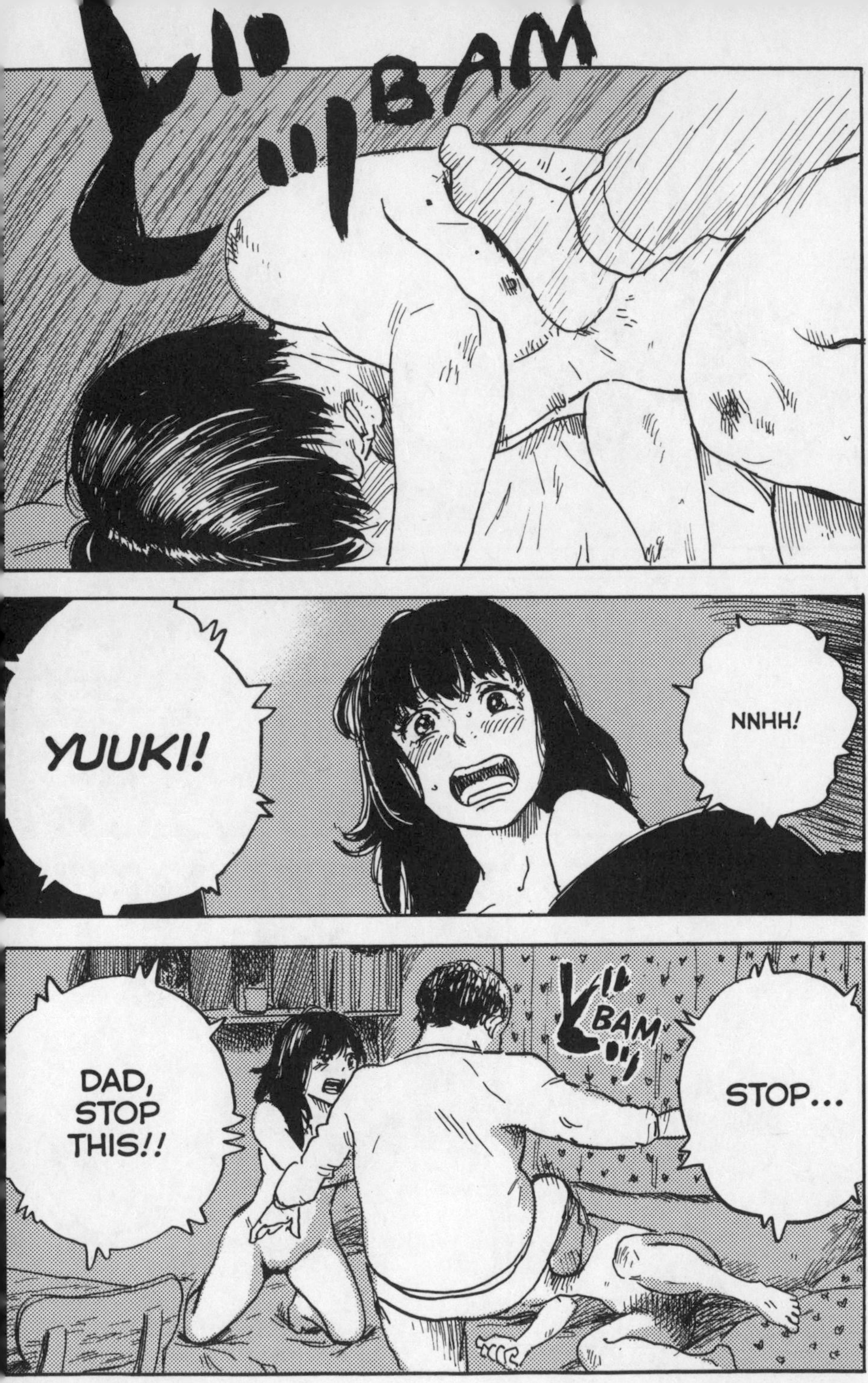
BAM
NNHH!
YUUKI!
STOP...
BAM
DAD, STOP THIS!!

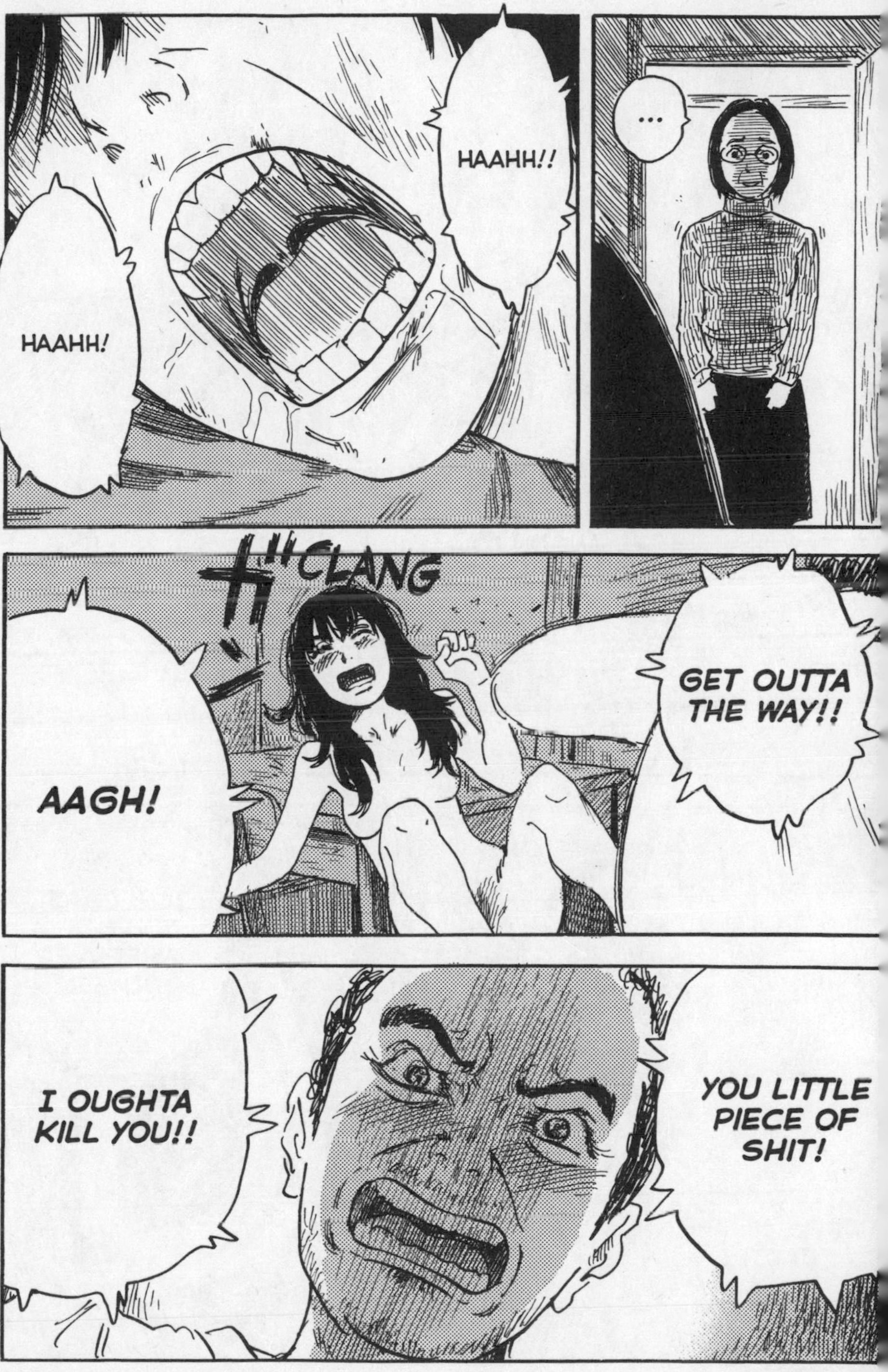
...
HAAHH!!
HAAHH!
GET OUTTA THE WAY!!
CLANG
AAGH!
YOU LITTLE PIECE OF SHIT!
I OUGHTA KILL YOU!!

YUUKI...
...YOU CAN'T ESCAPE.
I'LL CHASE YOU DOWN WHEREVER YOU GO...
...TO THE ENDS OF THE EARTH!

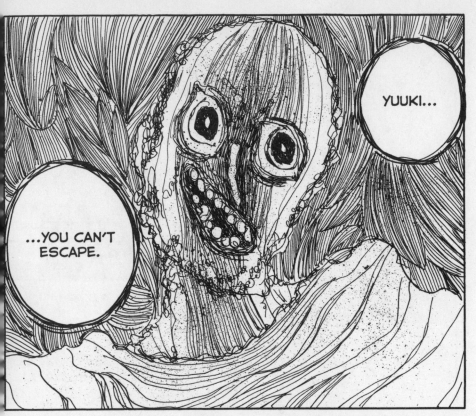

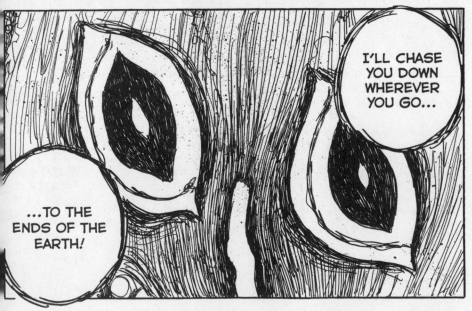

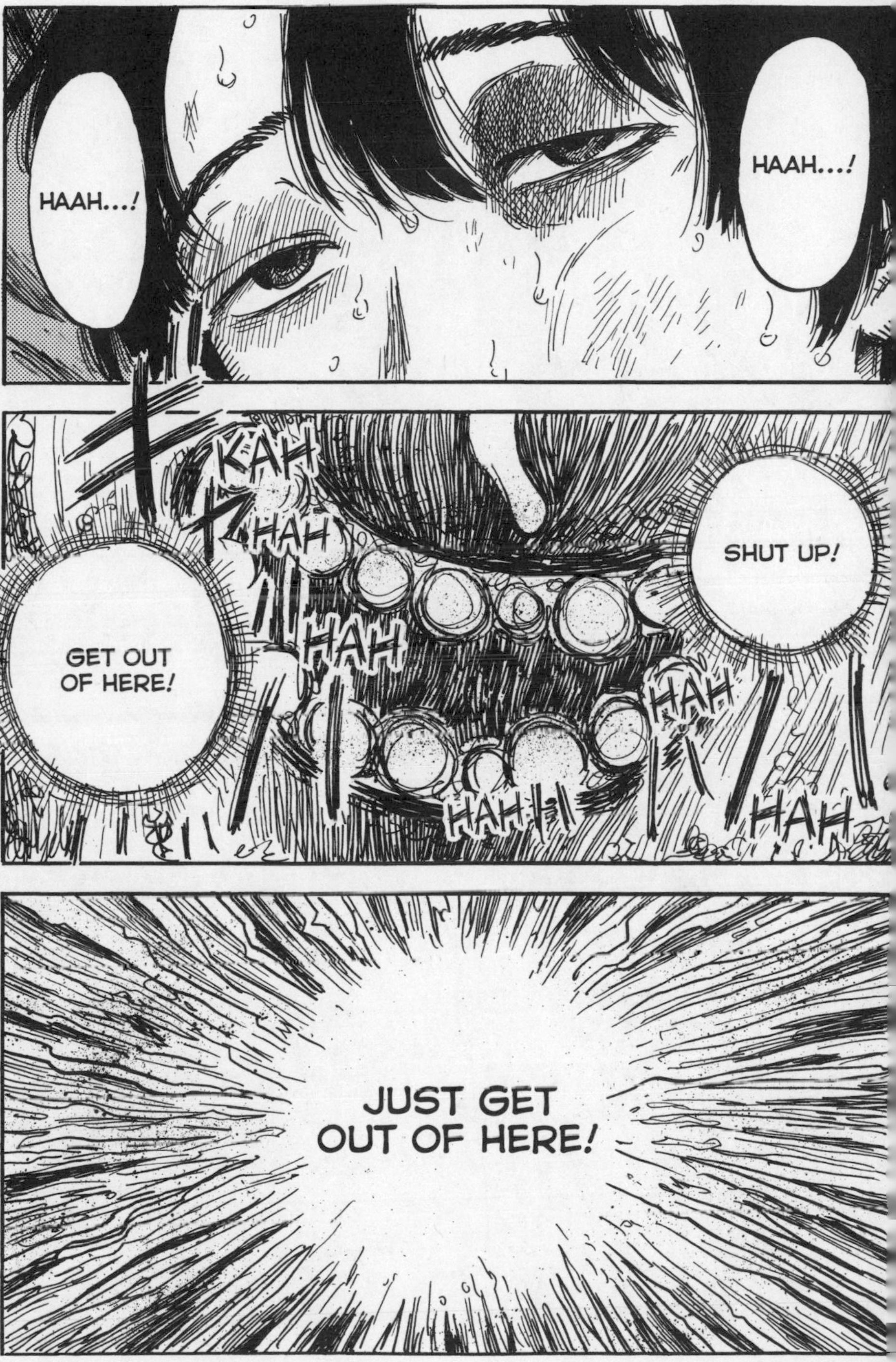
HAAH...!
HAAH...!
SHUT UP!
KAH
HAH
HAH
GET OUT OF HERE!
HAH
HAH
HAH
JUST GET OUT OF HERE!

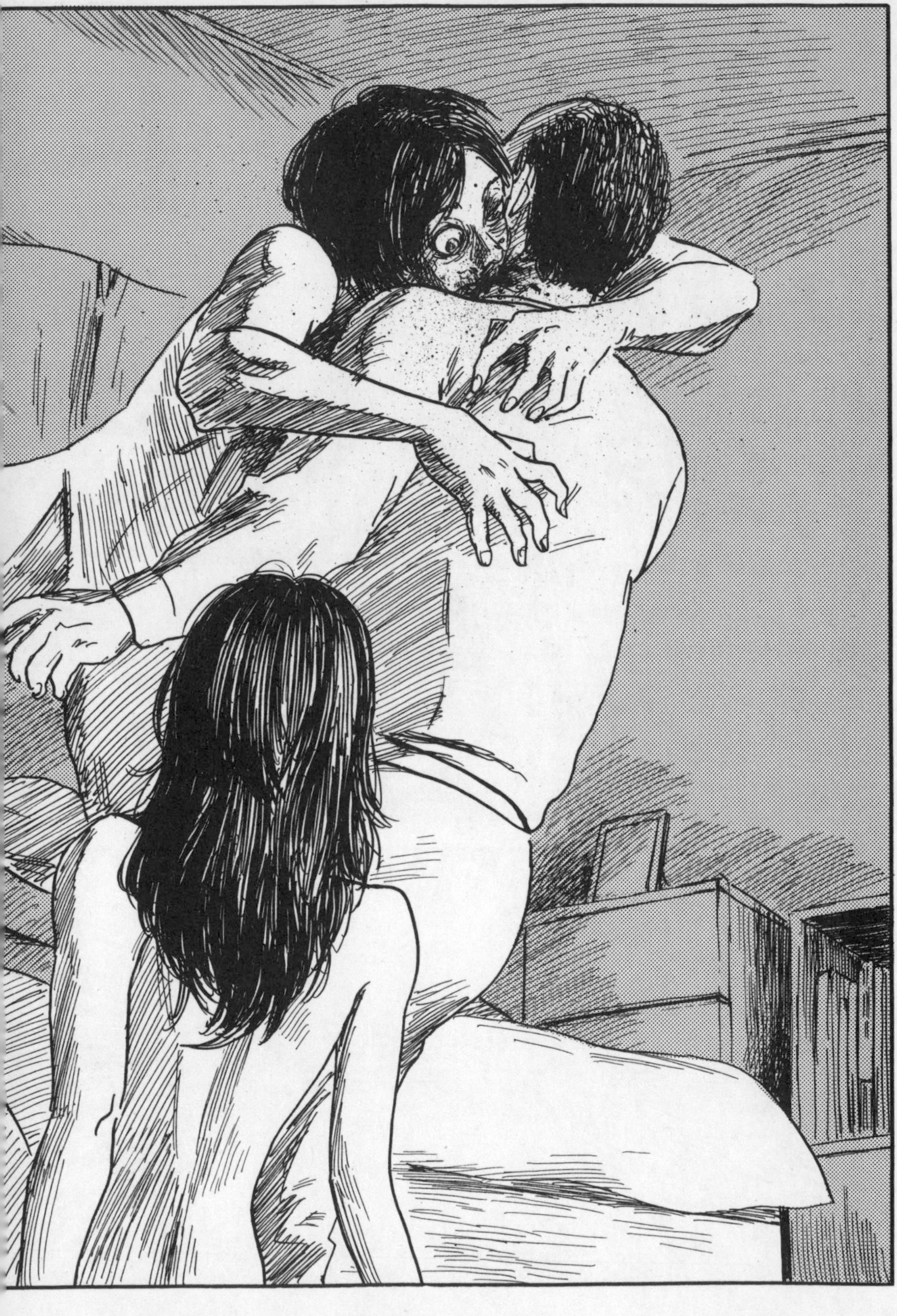

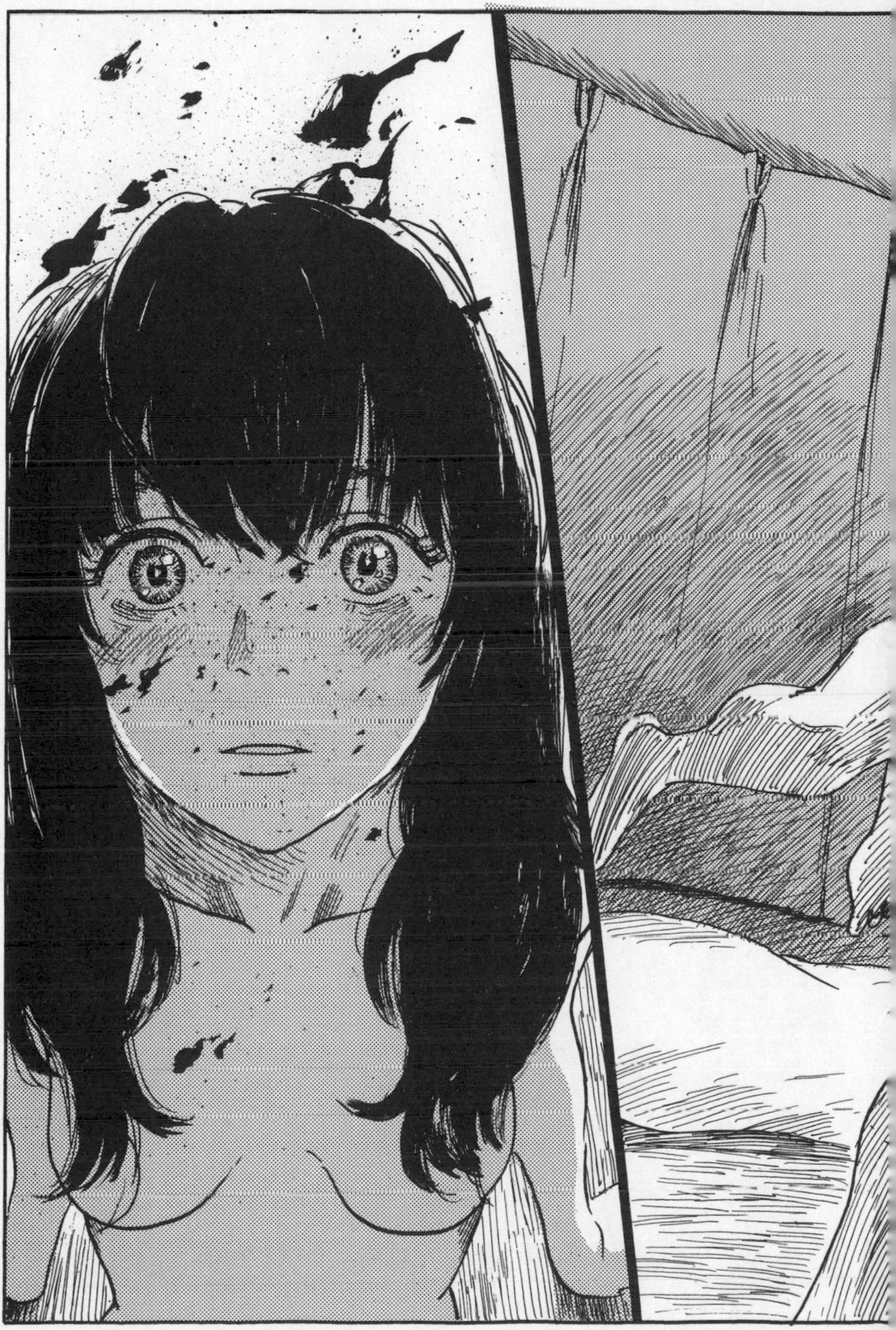

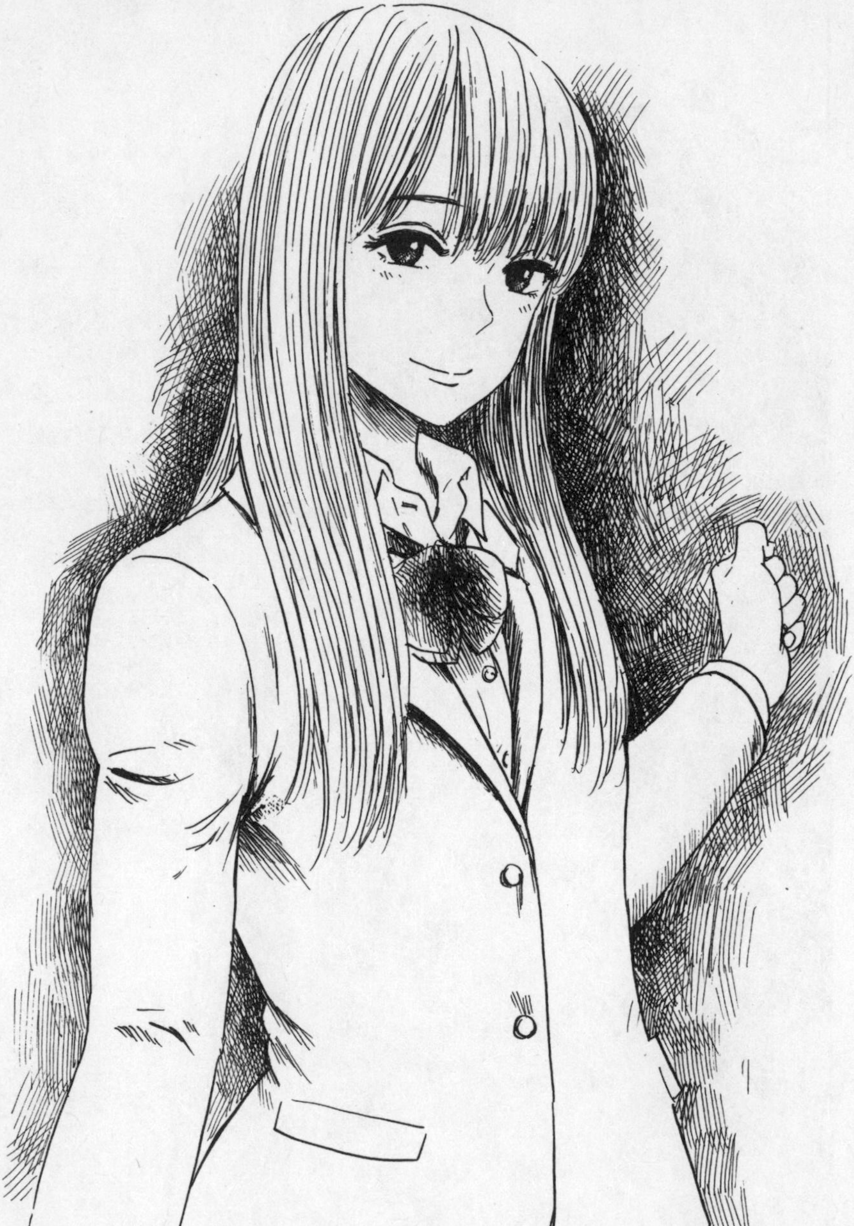

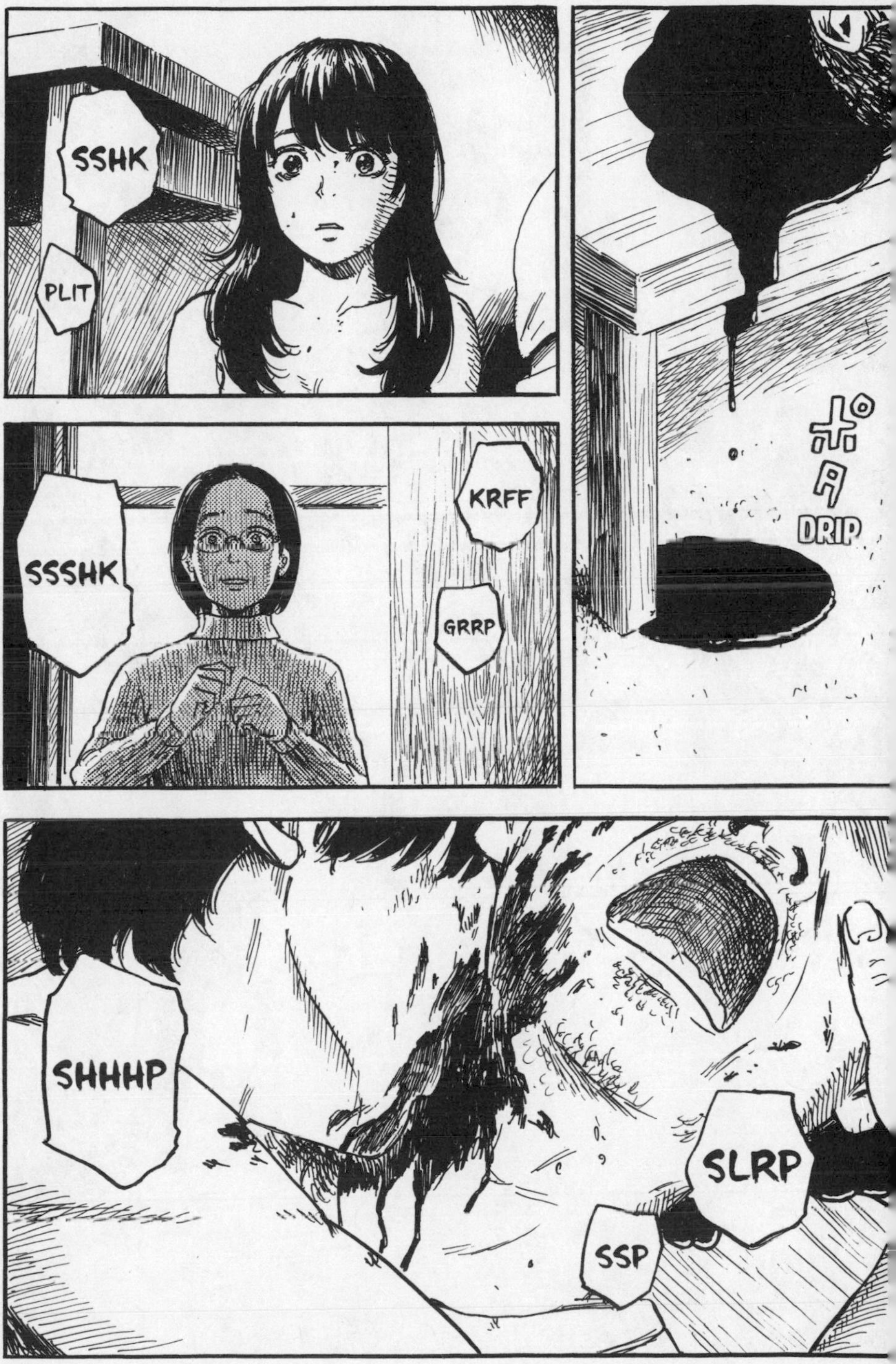
ポタ
DRIP
SSHK
PLIT
KRFF
GRRP
SSSHK
SLRP
SSP
SHHHP

Chapter 20: Such Sweet Sorrow

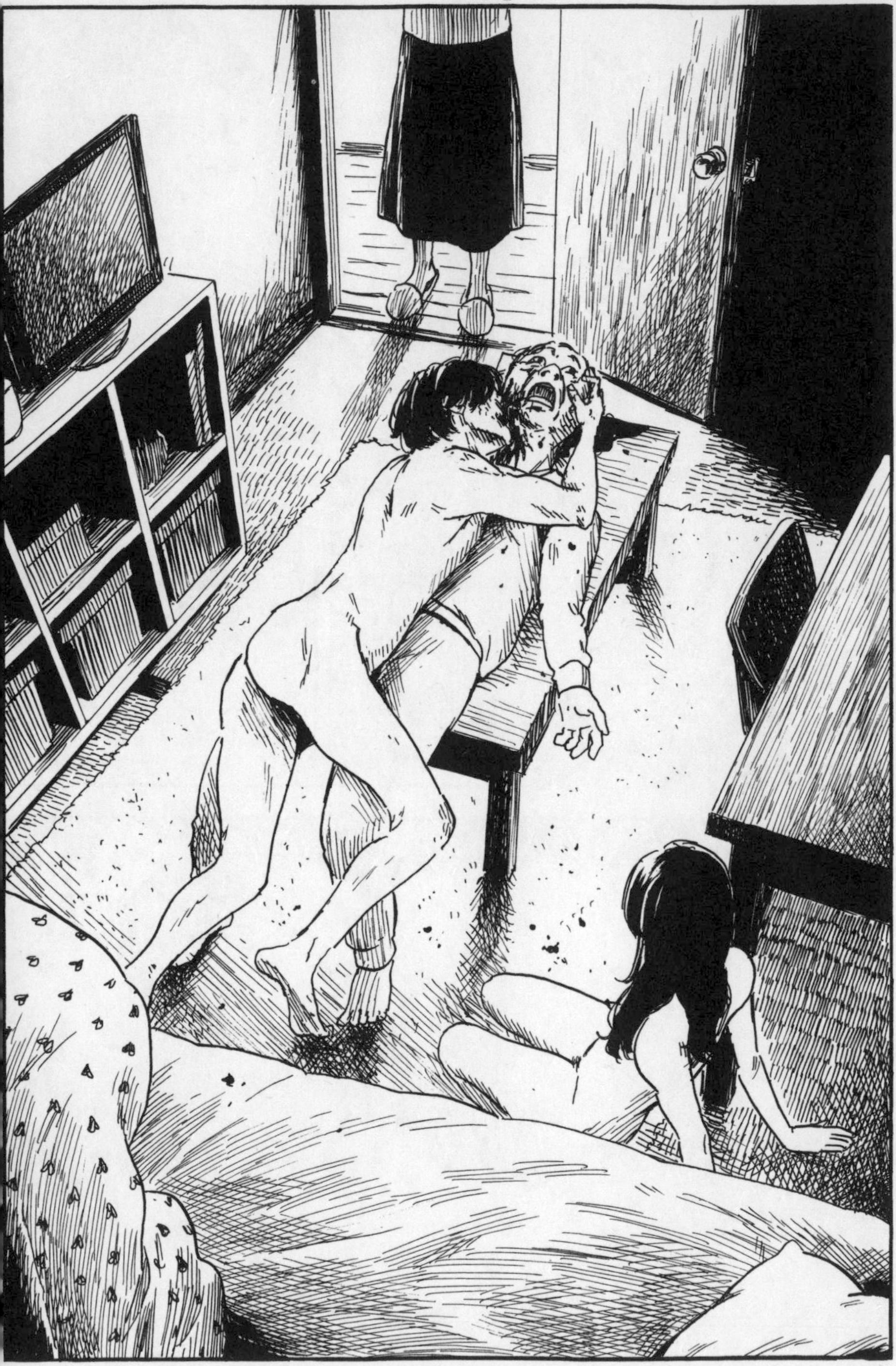

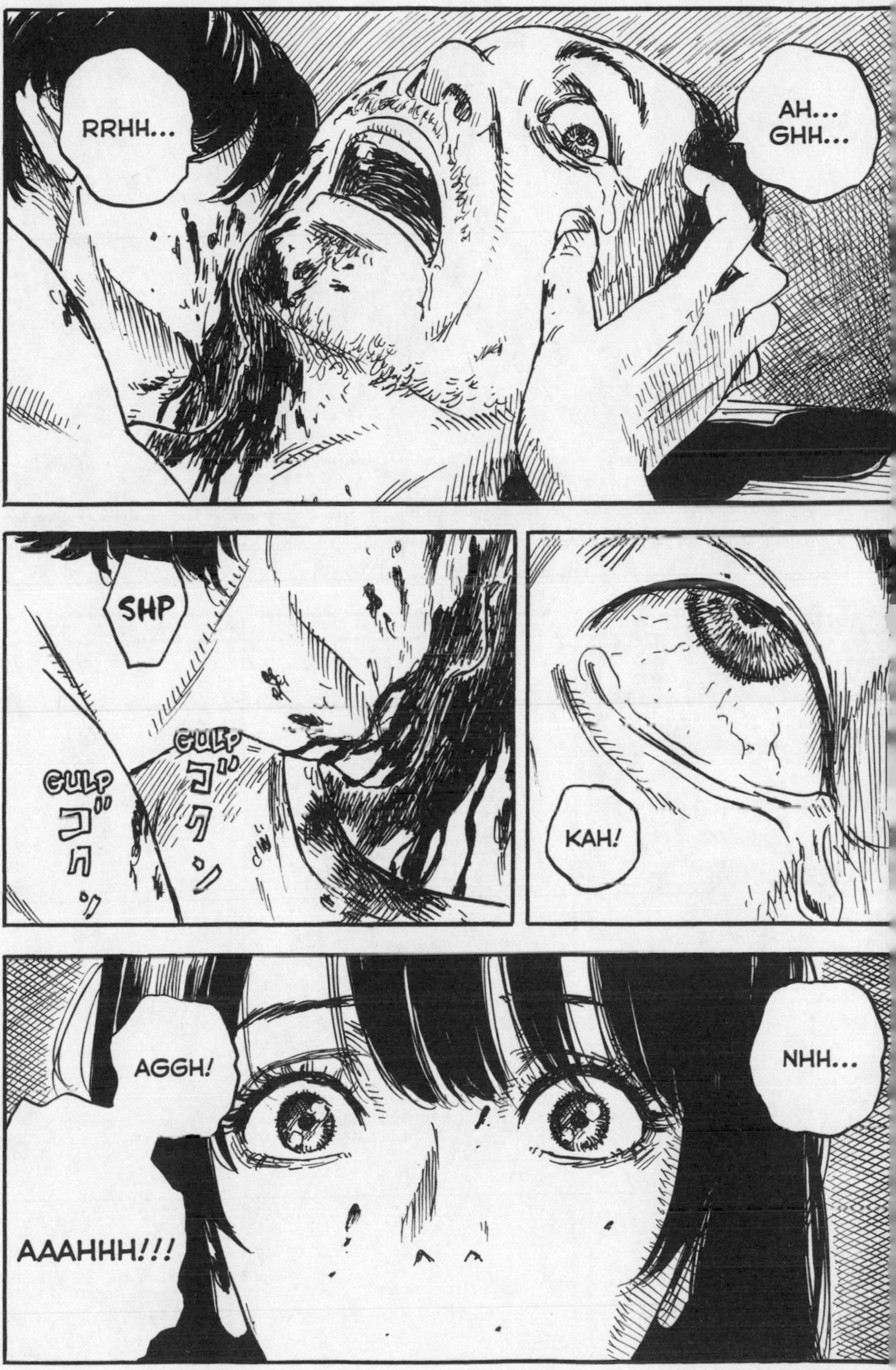
AH... GHH...
RRHH...
KAH!
SHP
GULP ゴクン
GULP ゴクッ
NHH...
AGGH!
AAAHHH!!!

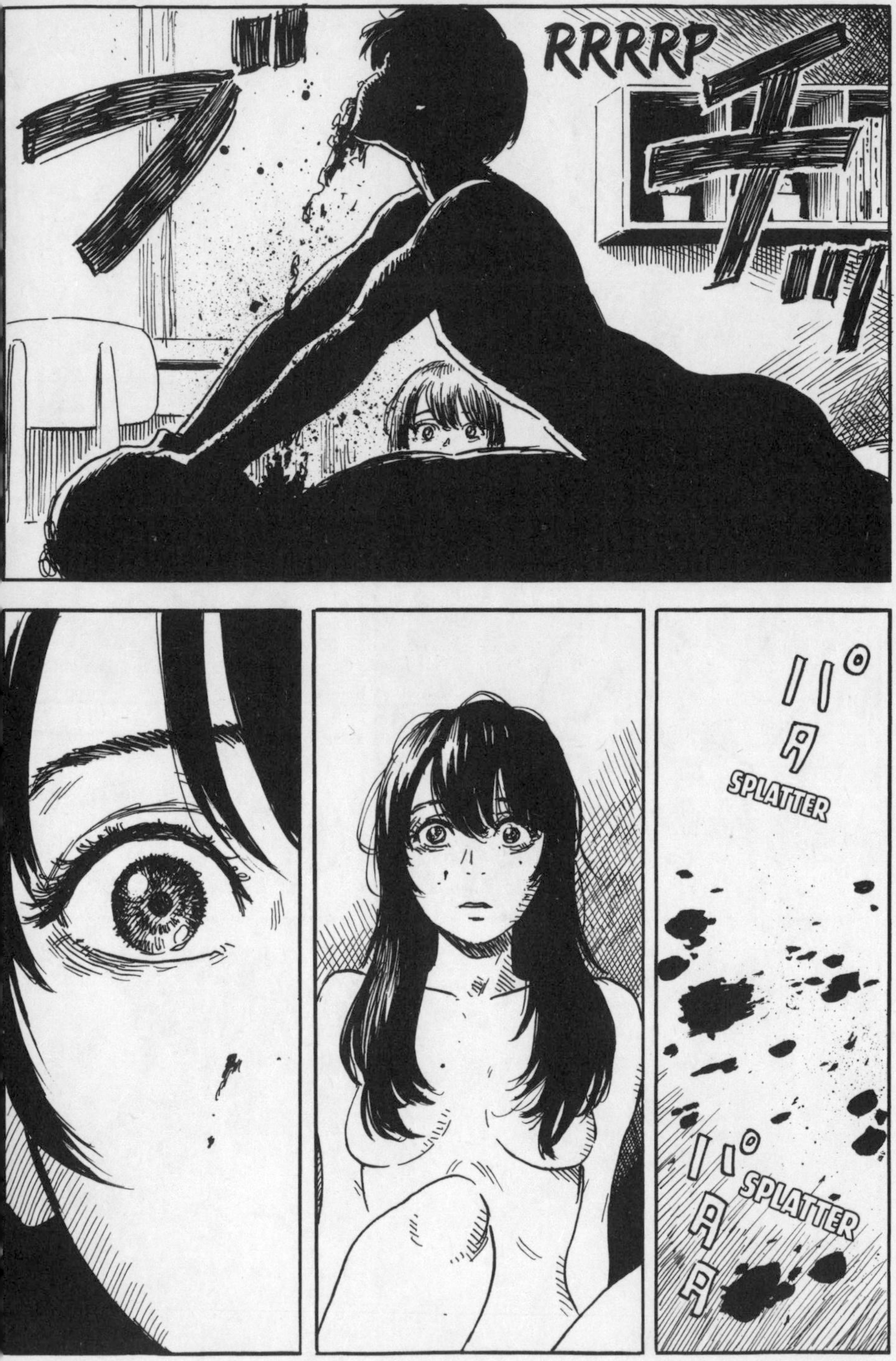
ブチッ
RRRRP
パタ
SPLATTER
パタタ
SPLATTER

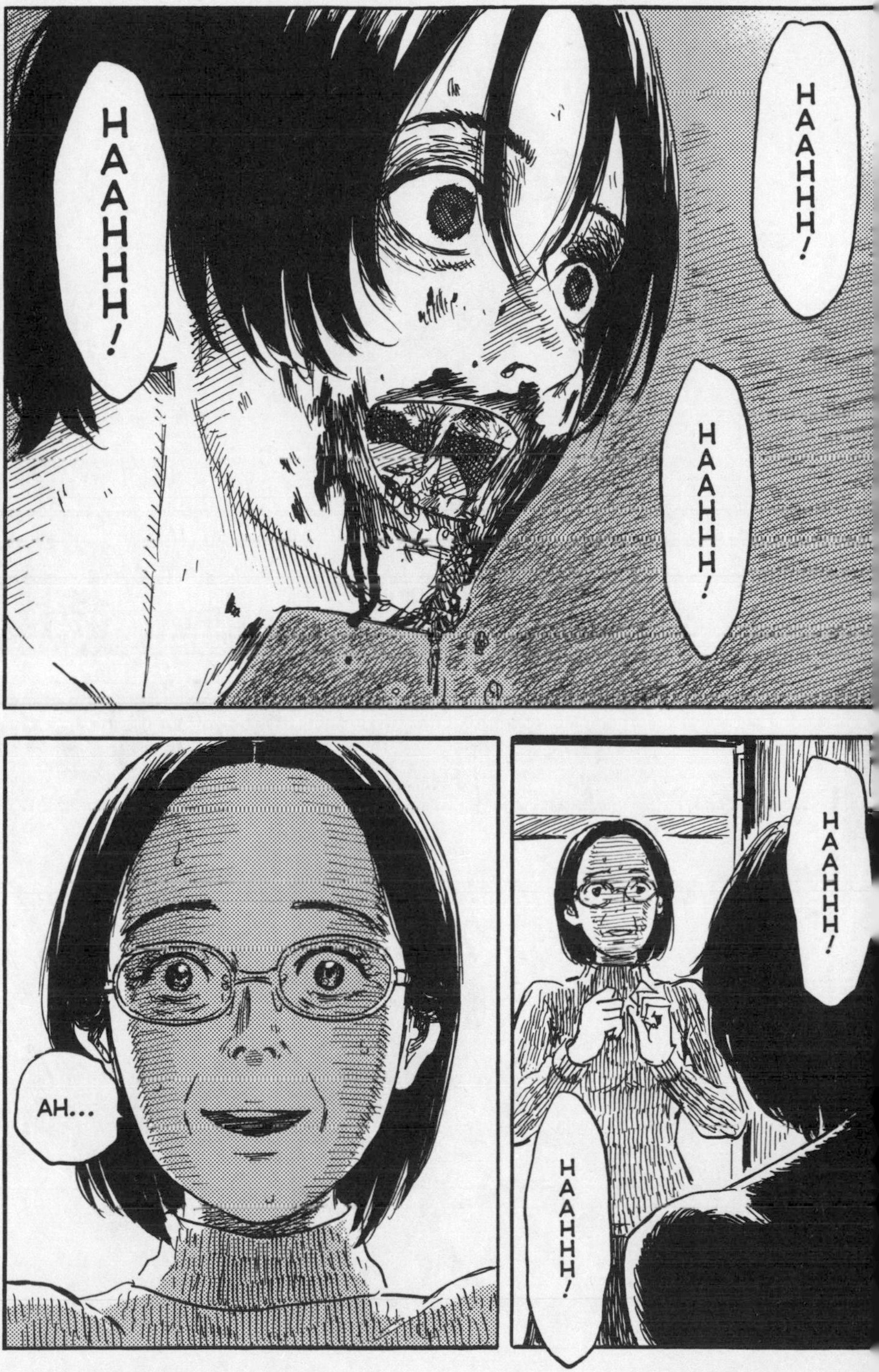
HAAHHH!
HAAHHH!
HAAHHH!
HAAHHH!
HAAHHH!
AH...

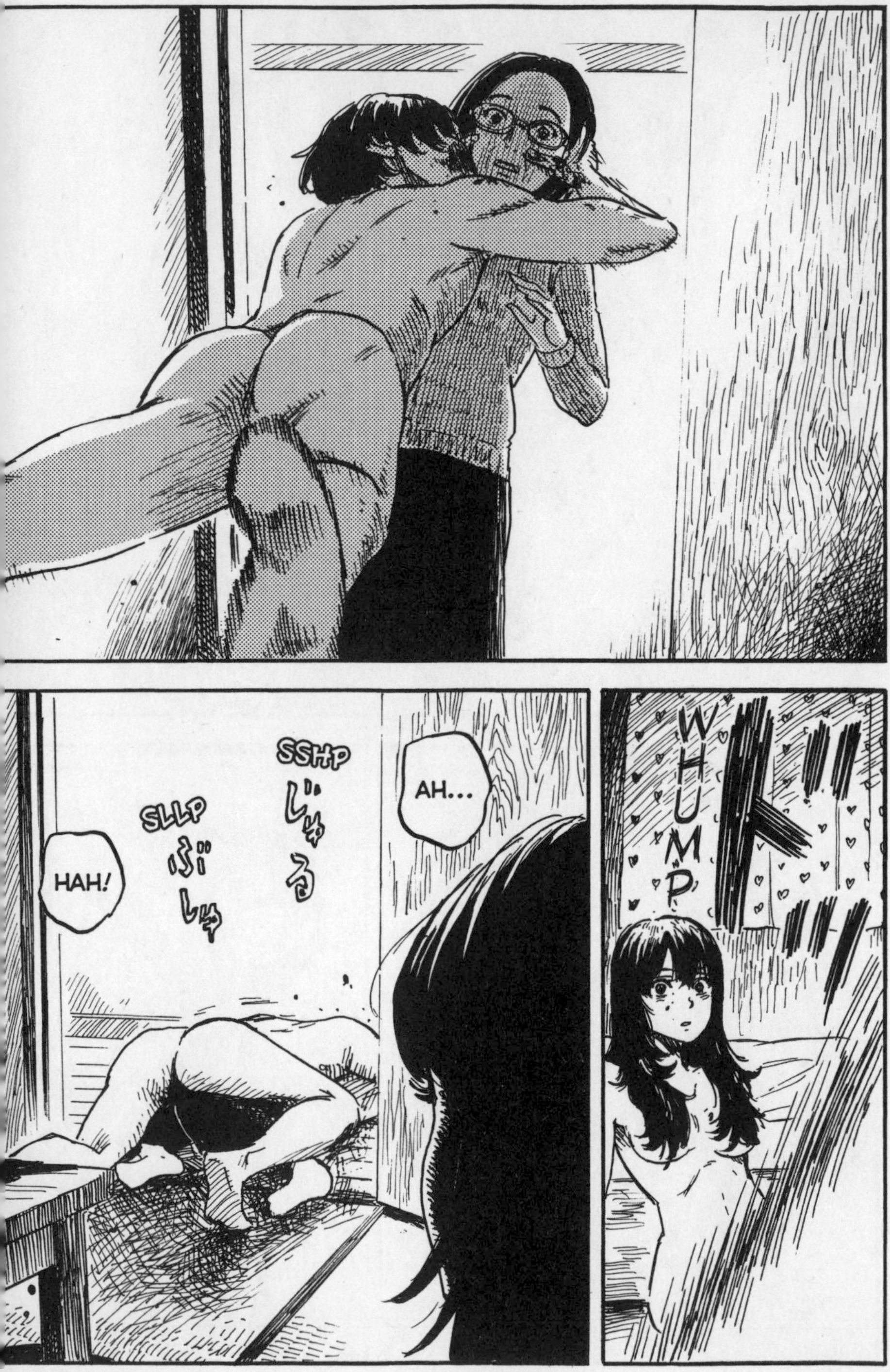
WHUMP
AH...
SSHP
じゅる
SLLP
ぶしゅ
HAH!

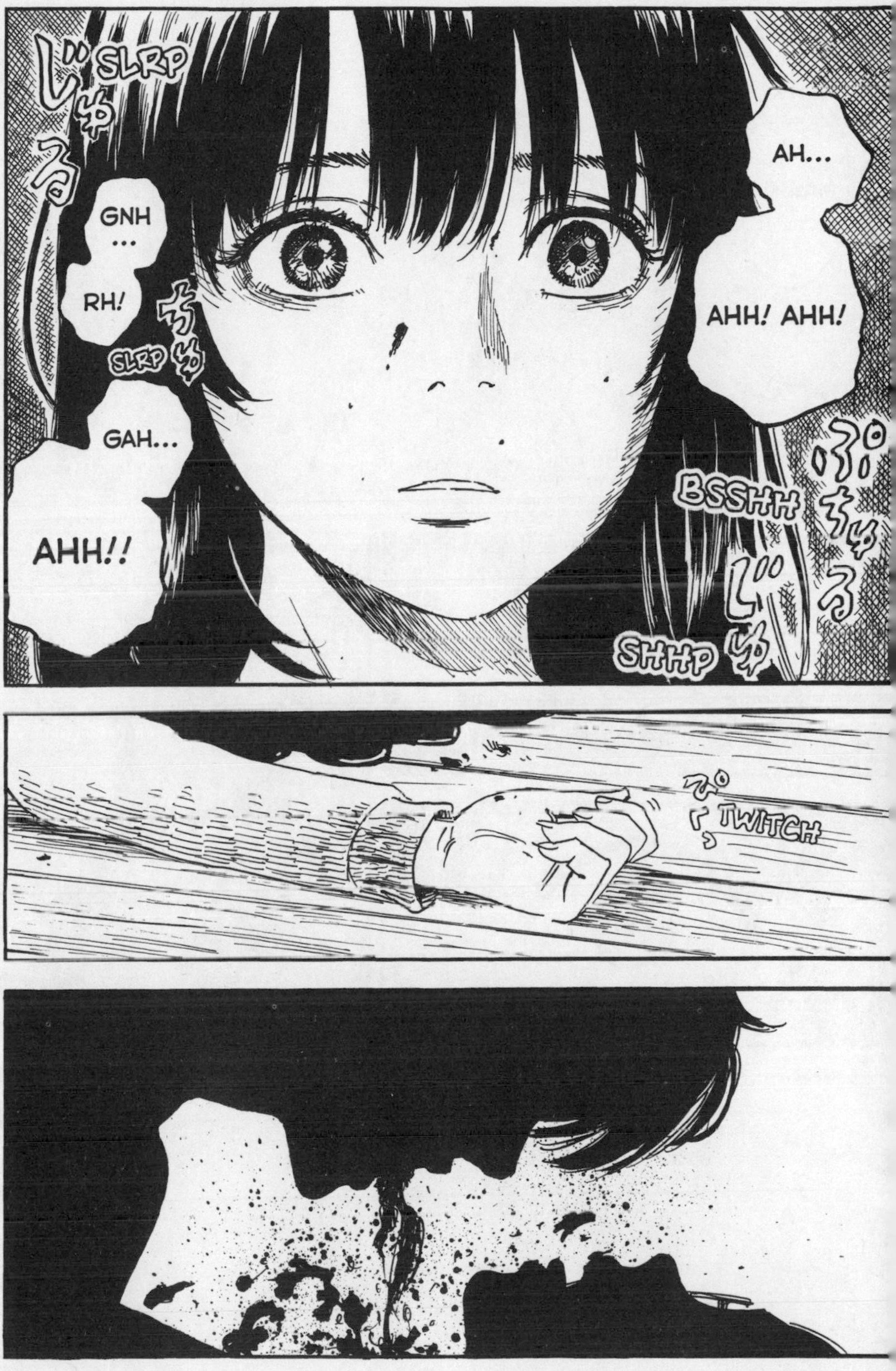
AH...
AHH! AHH!
ぷちゅる
BSSHH
じゅ
SHHP
じゅる
SLRP
GNH ...
RH!
ちゅ
SLRP
GAH...
AHH!!
ぴく
TWITCH

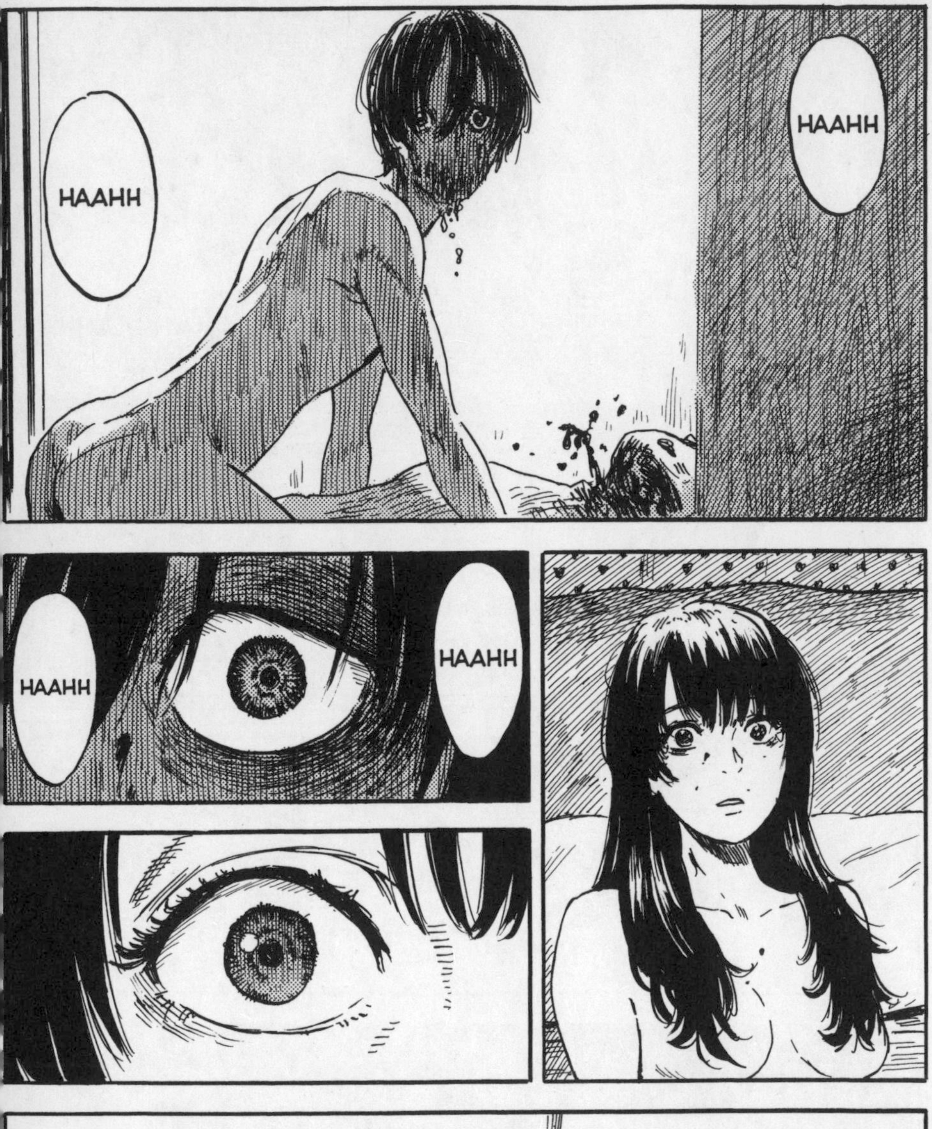
HAAHH
HAAHH
HAAHH
HAAHH

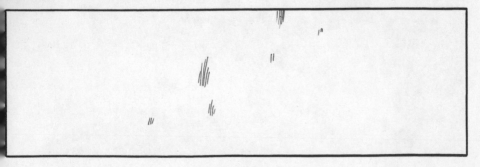

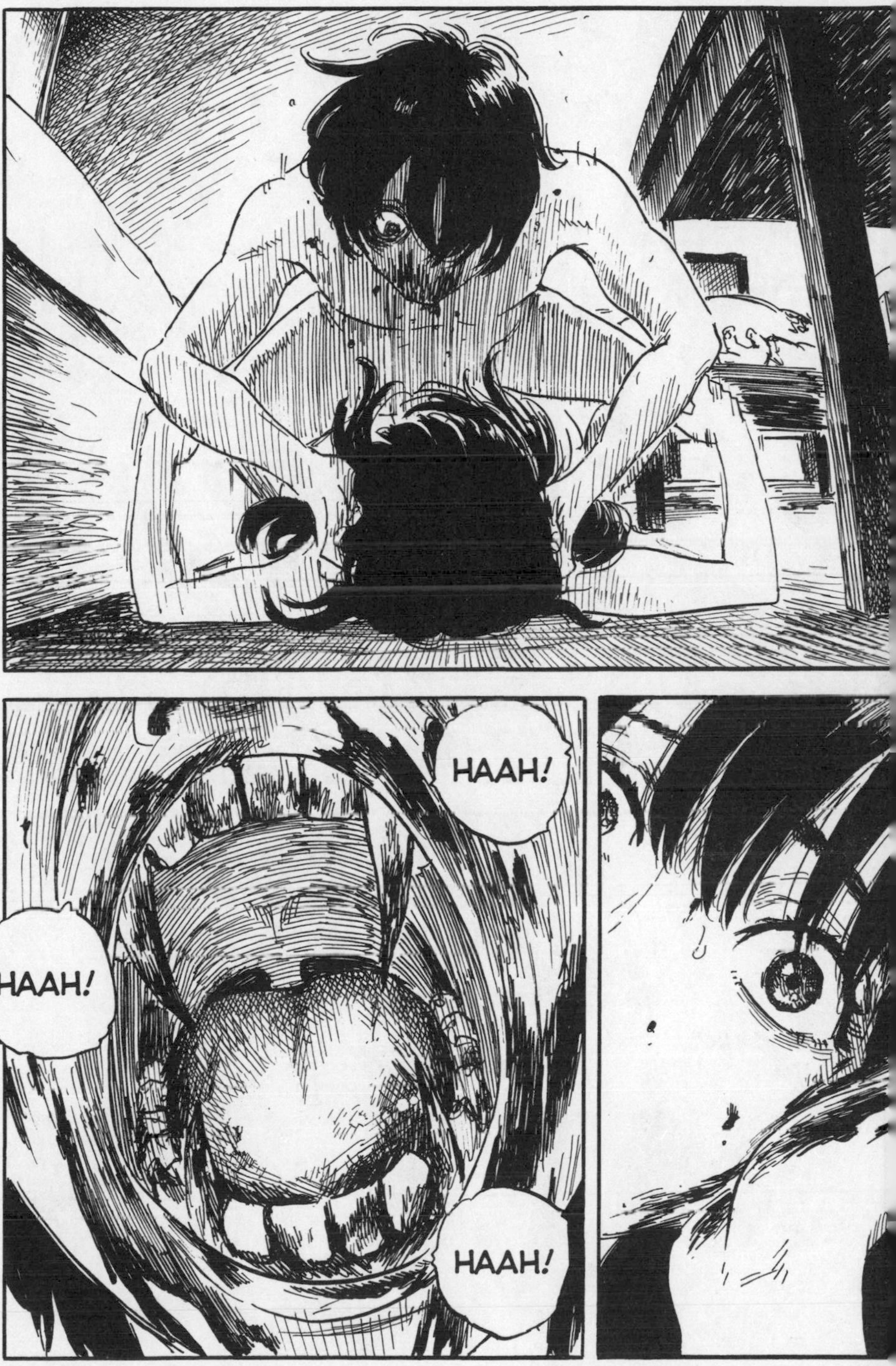
HAAH!
HAAH!
HAAH!

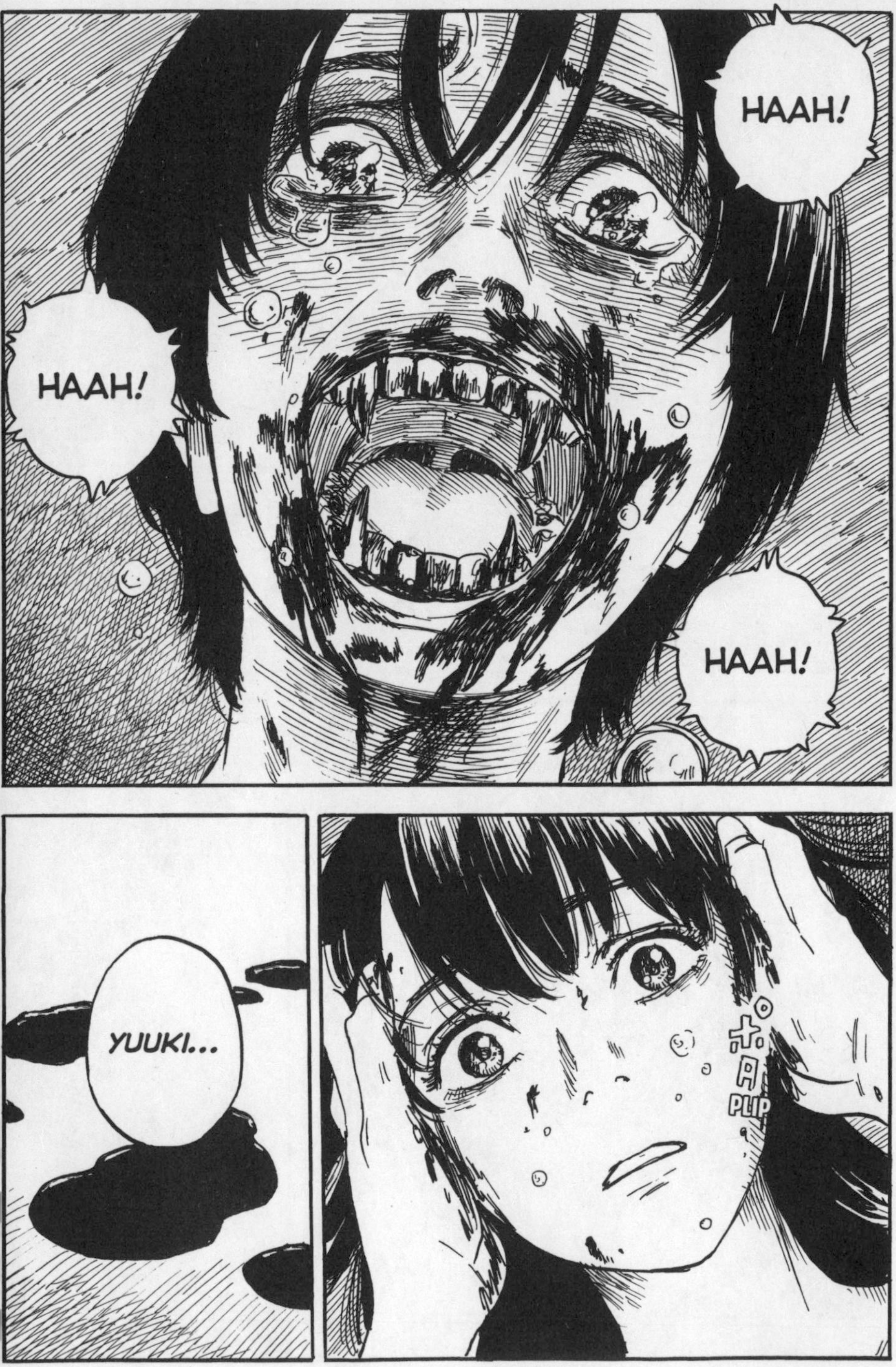
HAAH!
HAAH!
HAAH!
PLIP
YUUKI...

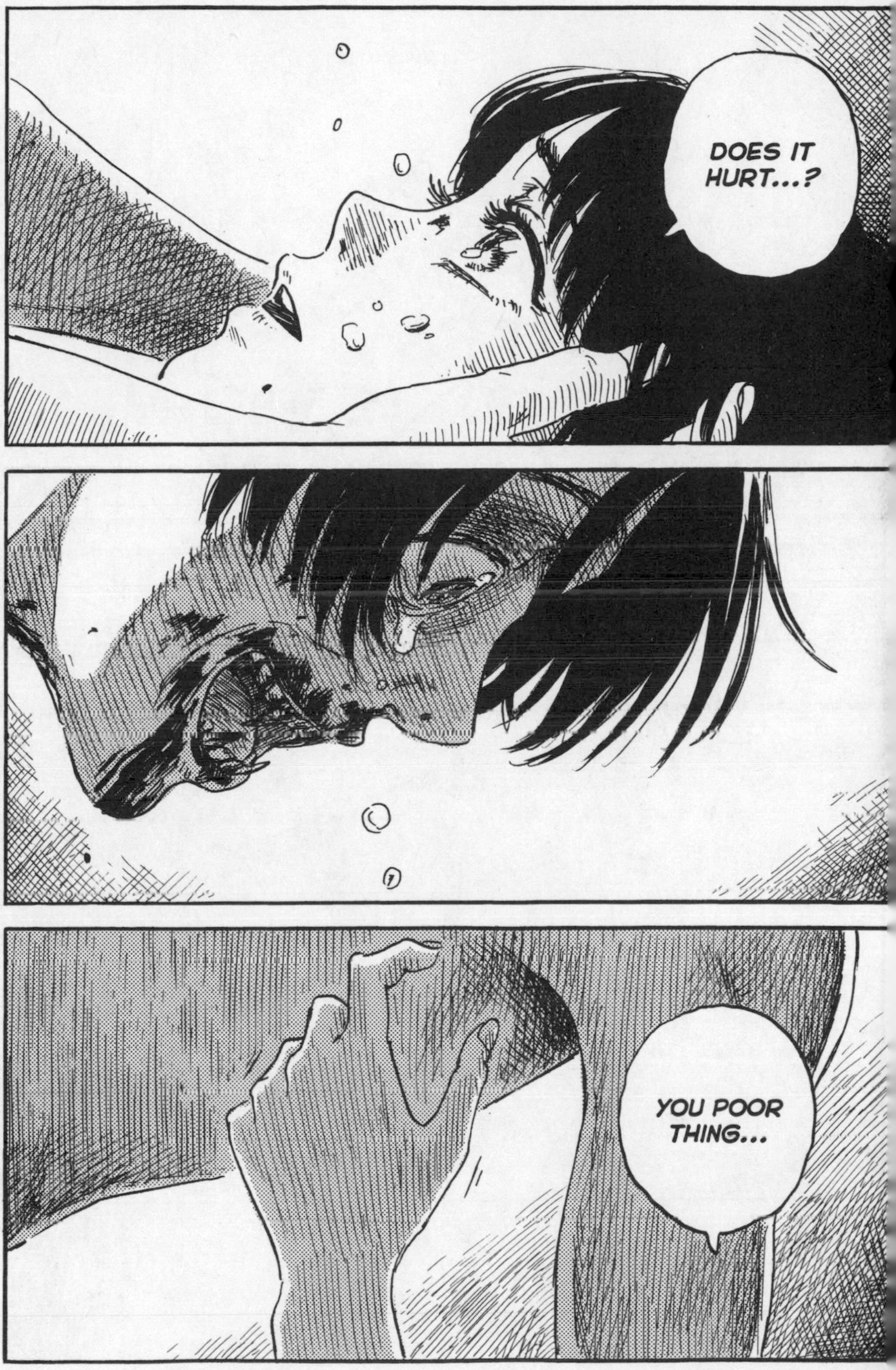
DOES IT HURT...?
YOU POOR THING...

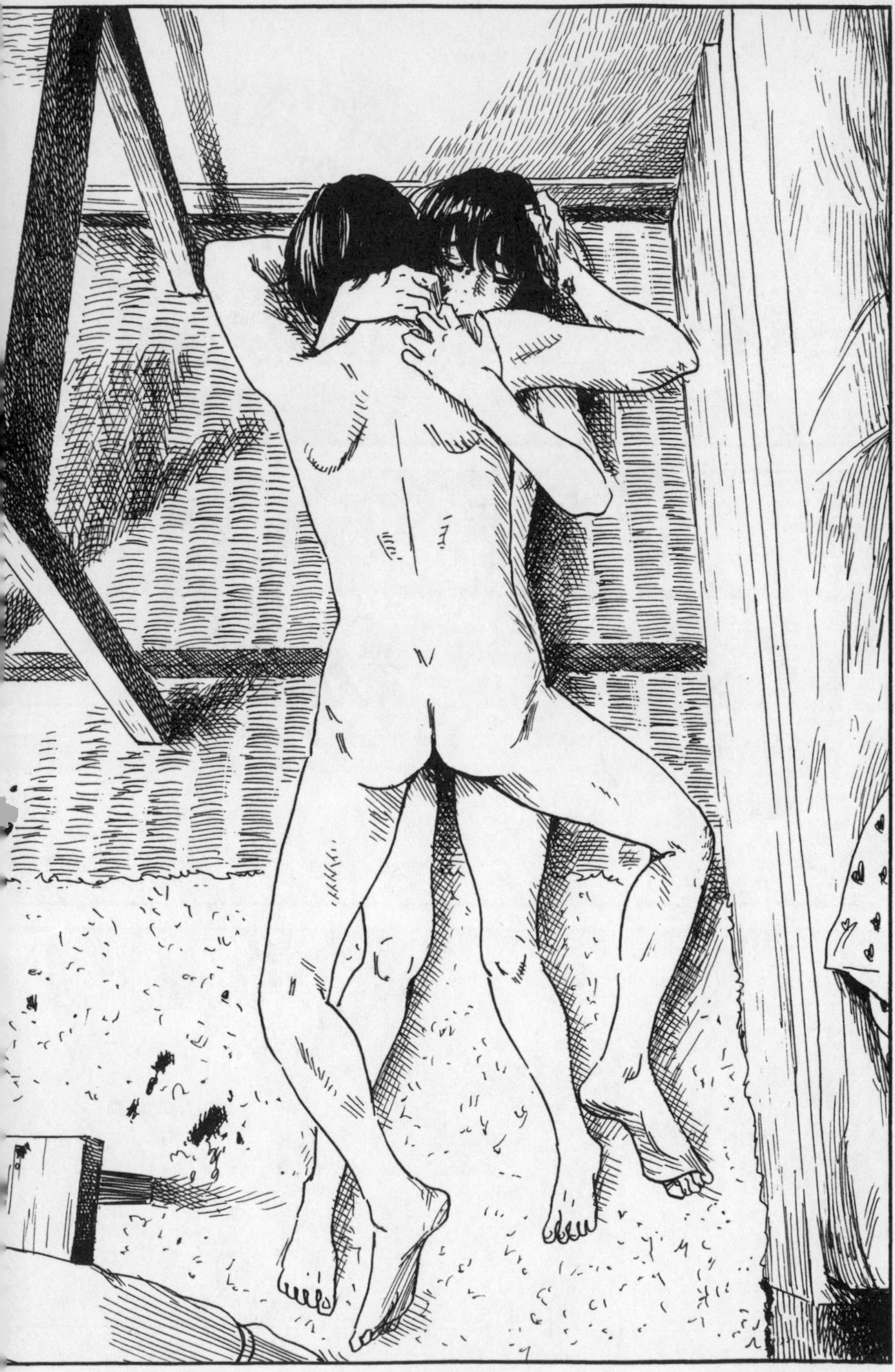

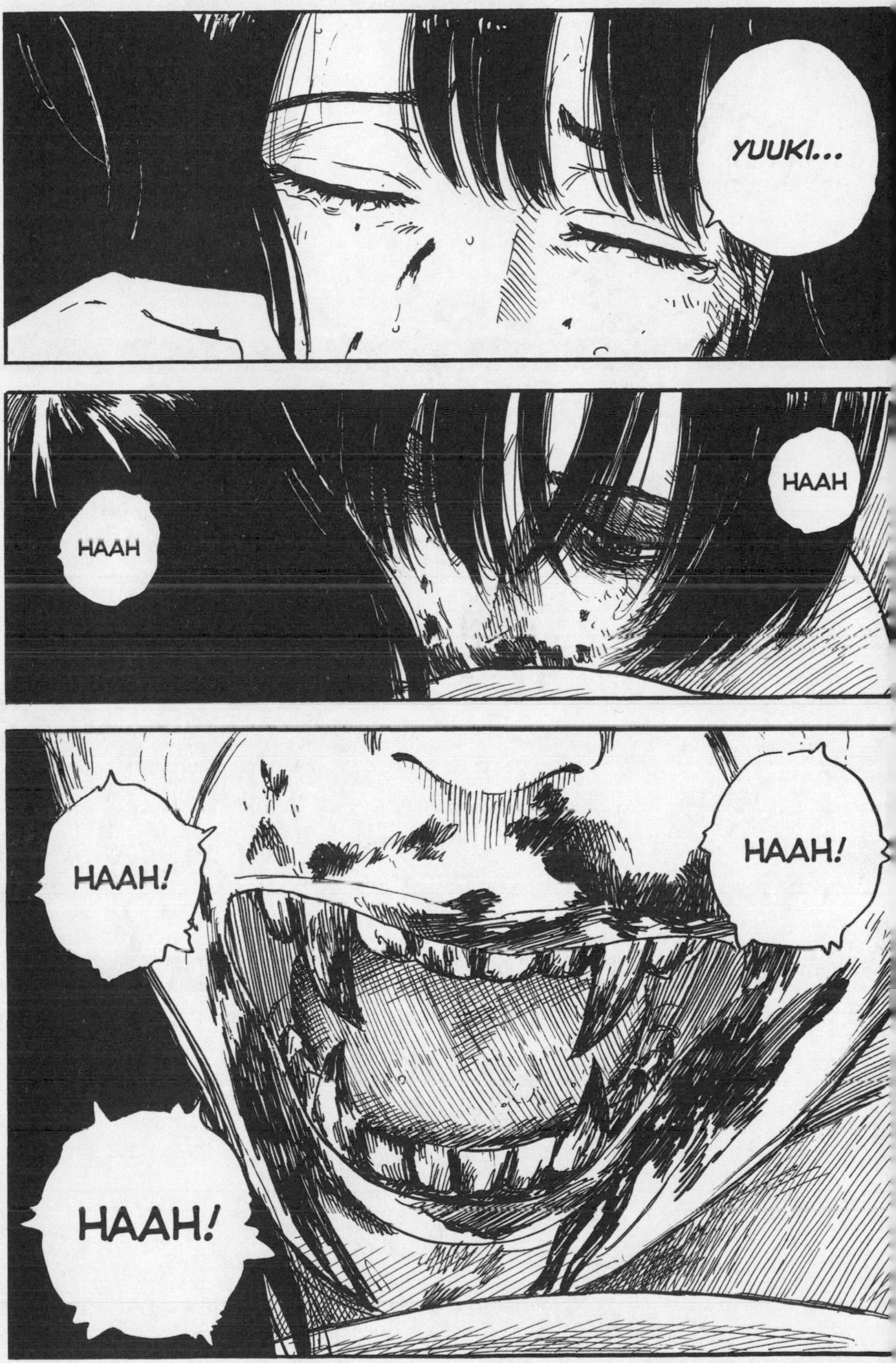
YUUKI...
HAAH
HAAH
HAAH!
HAAH!
HAAH!

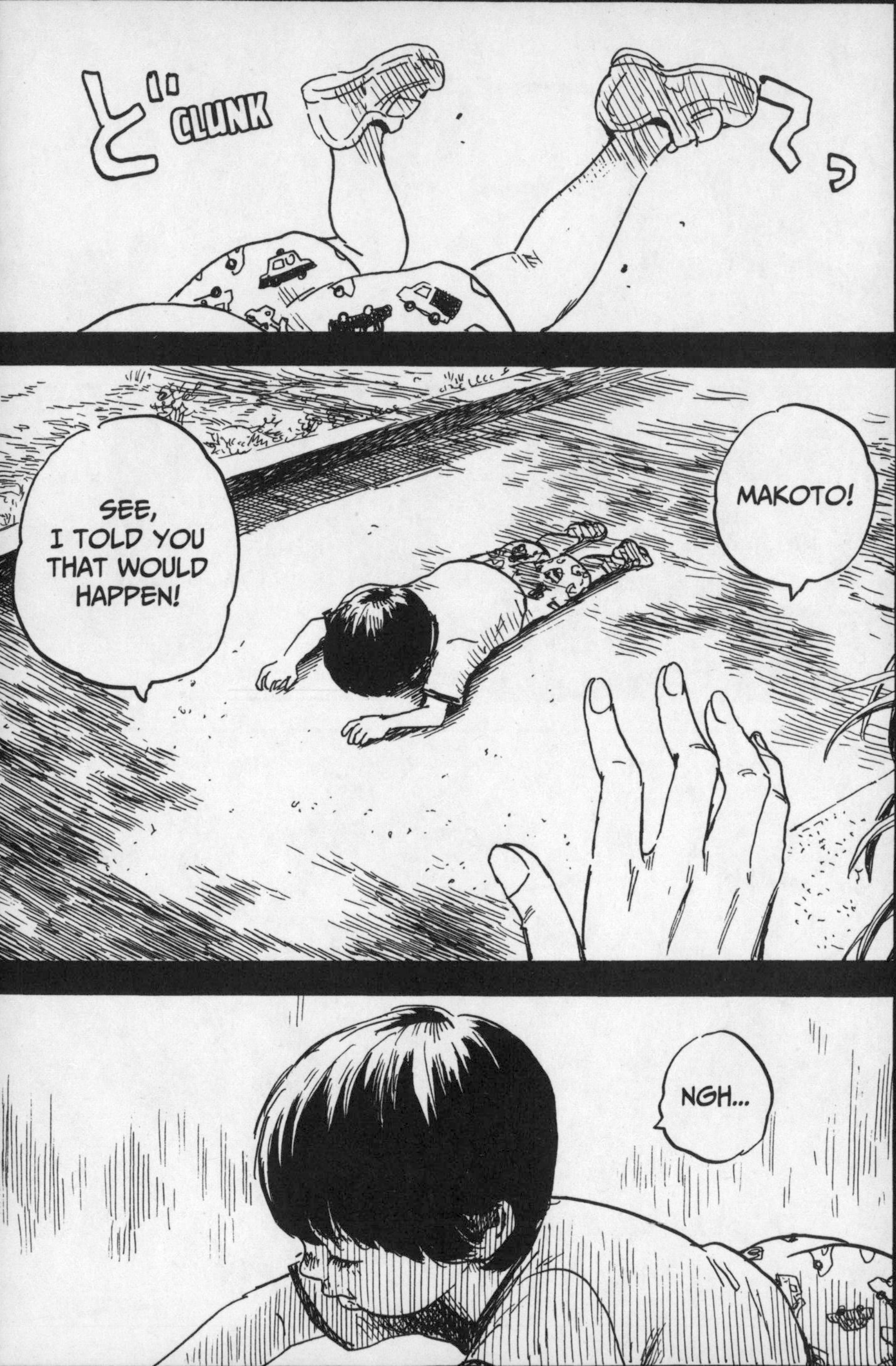
と
CLUNK
MAKOTO!
SEE, I TOLD YOU THAT WOULD HAPPEN!
NGH...

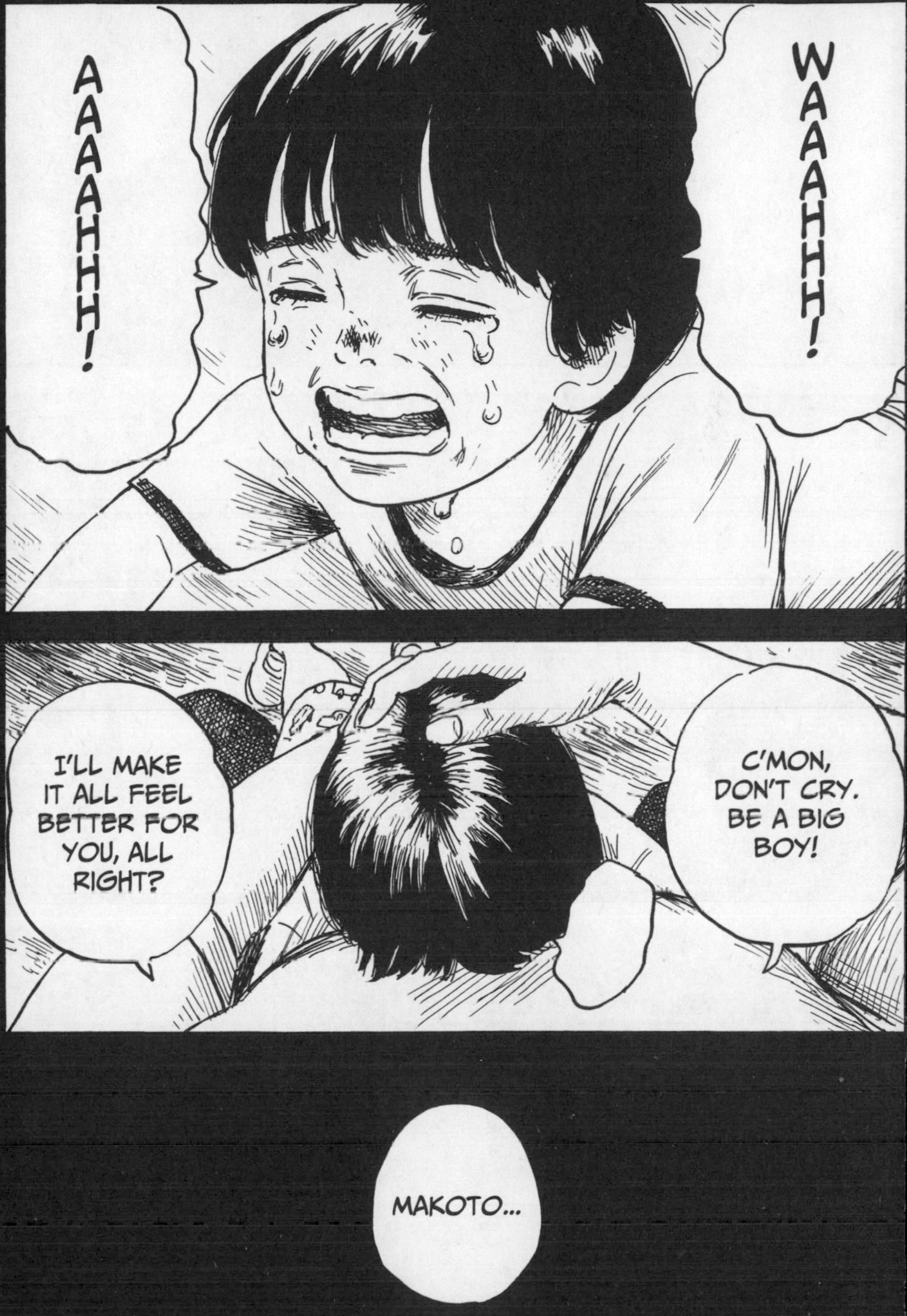
WAAAHHH!
AAAAHHH!
C'MON, DON'T CRY. BE A BIG BOY!
I'LL MAKE IT ALL FEEL BETTER FOR YOU, ALL RIGHT?
MAKOTO...

MAKOTO
...
ムク
LURCH
PHEW...

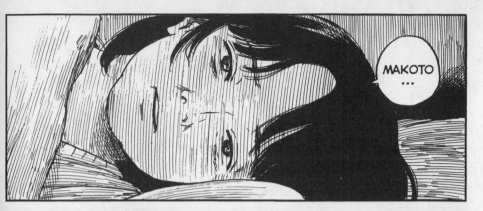

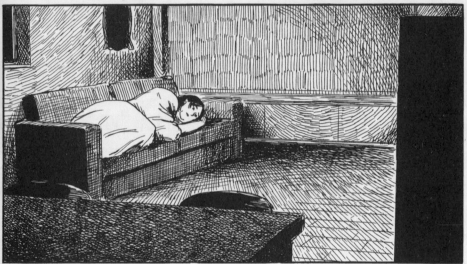

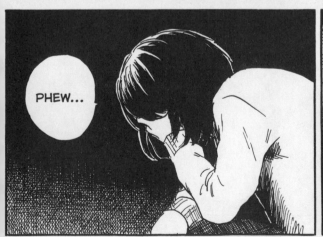

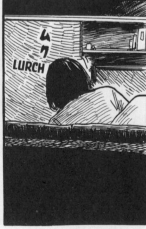

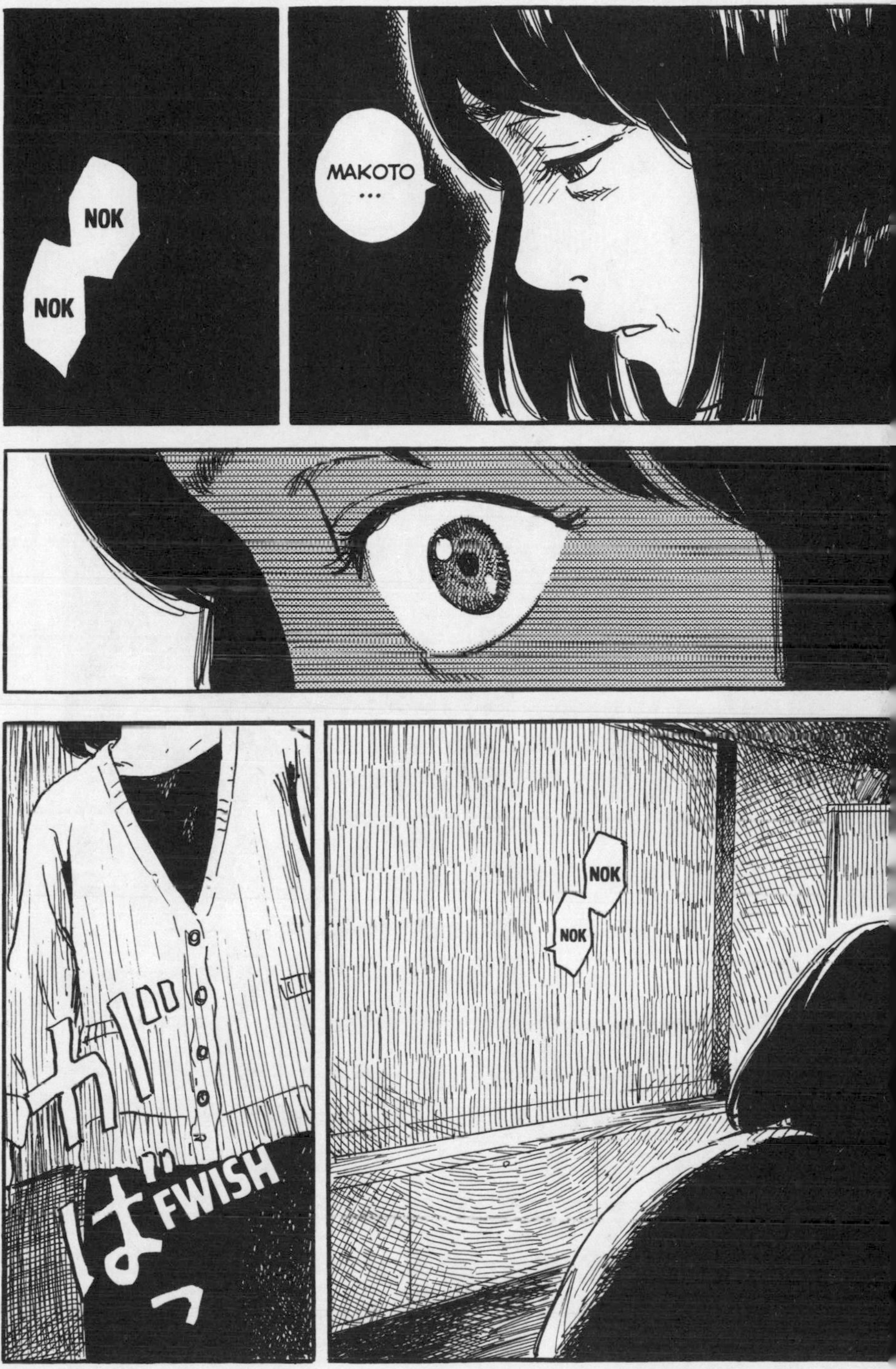
MAKOTO
...
NOK
NOK
NOK
NOK
FWISH

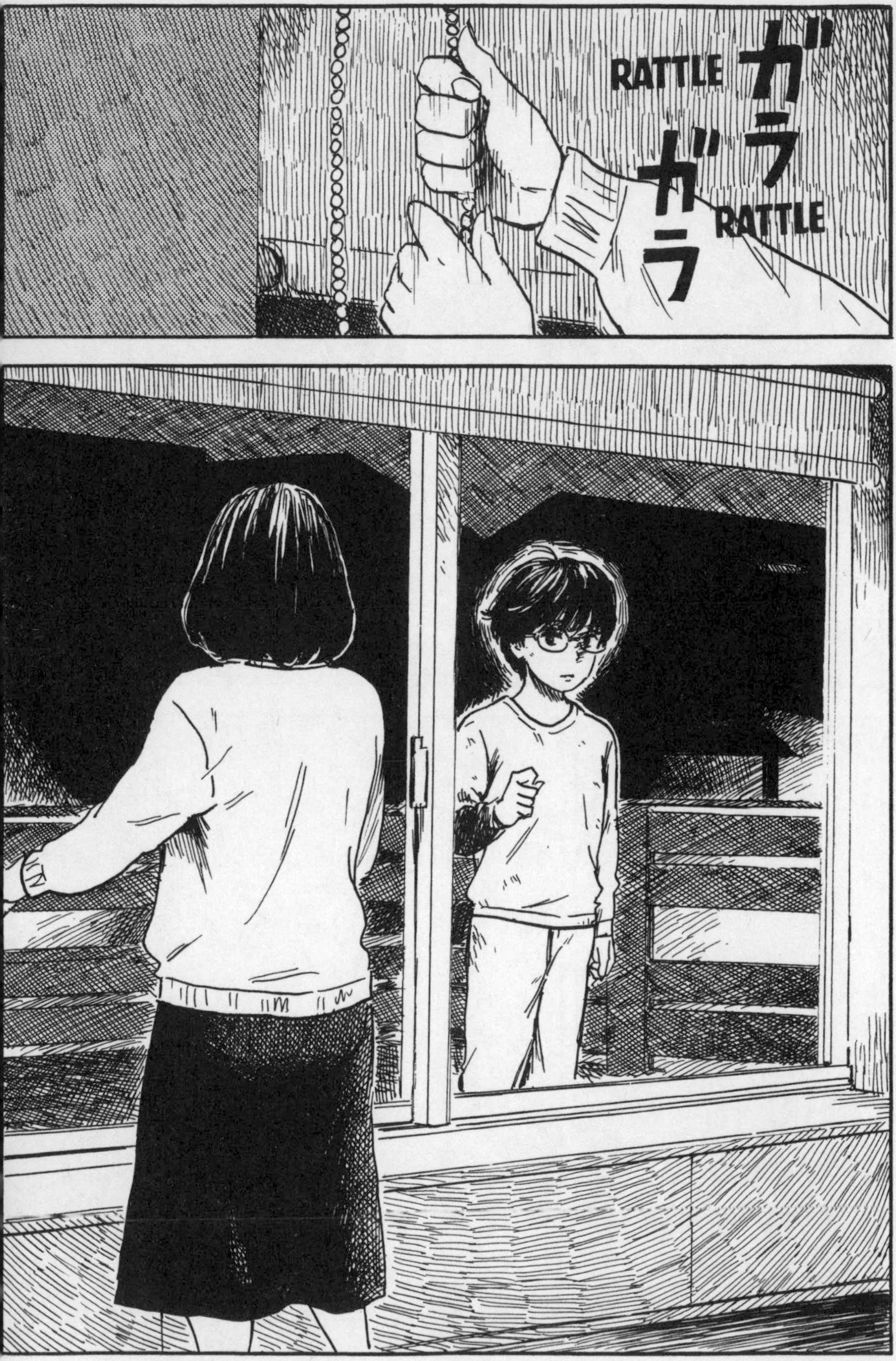
ガラ
RATTLE
ガラ
RATTLE

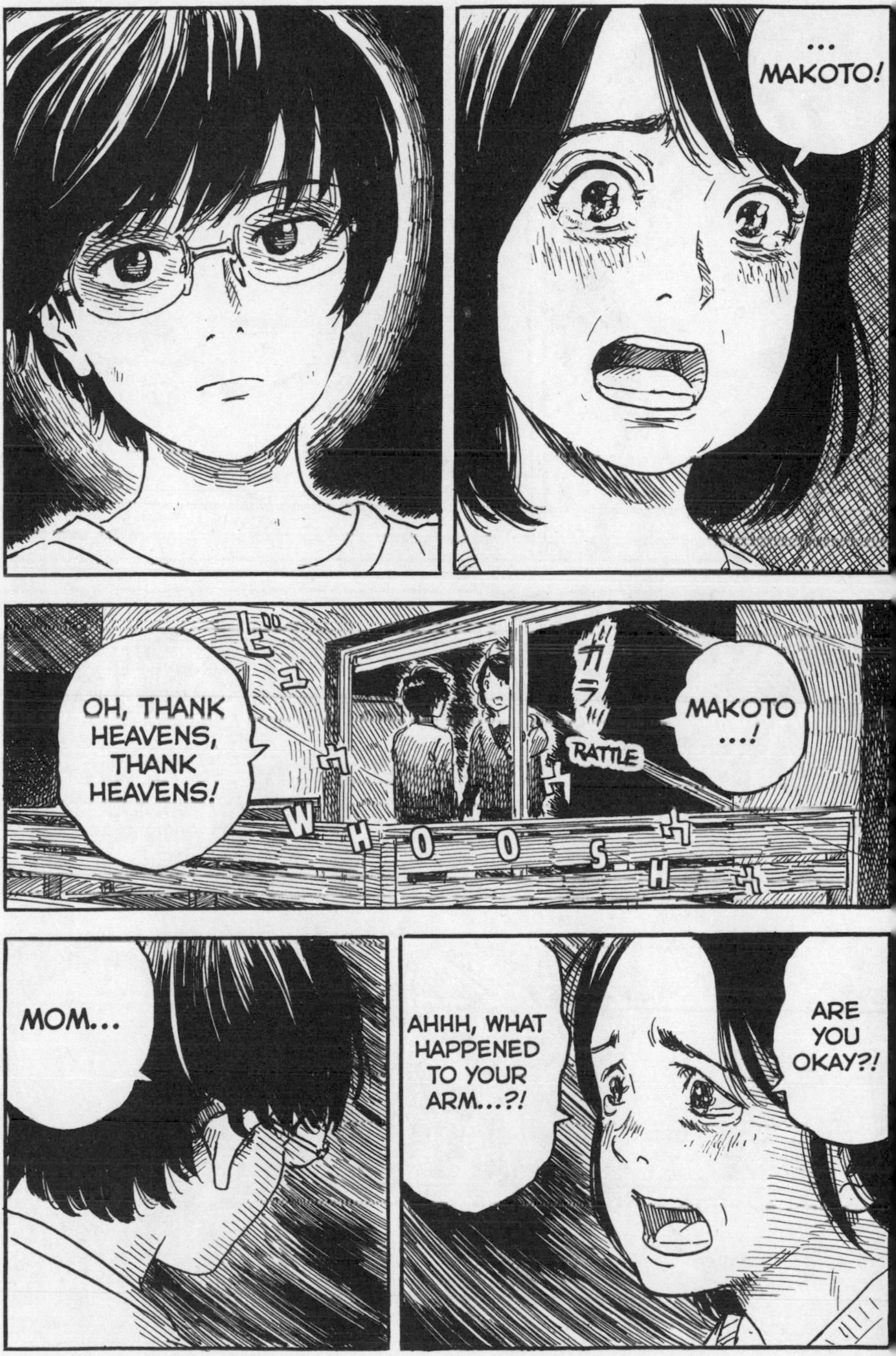
... MAKOTO!
MAKOTO ...!
RATTLE
WHOOSH
OH, THANK HEAVENS, THANK HEAVENS!
ARE YOU OKAY?!
AHHH, WHAT HAPPENED TO YOUR ARM...?!
MOM...

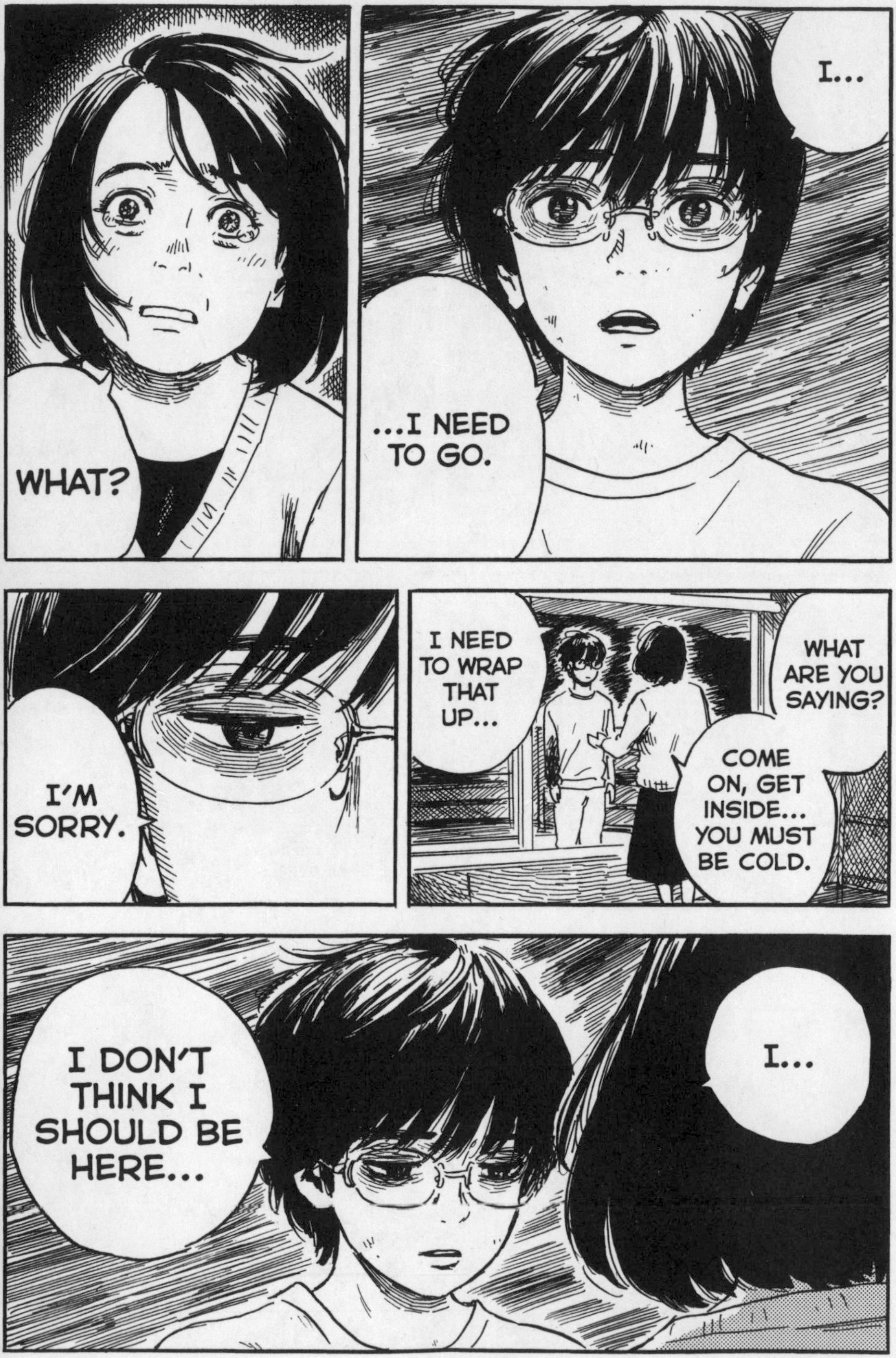
I...
...I NEED TO GO.
WHAT?
WHAT ARE YOU SAYING?
COME ON, GET INSIDE... YOU MUST BE COLD.
I NEED TO WRAP THAT UP...
I'M SORRY.
I...
I DON'T THINK I SHOULD BE HERE...

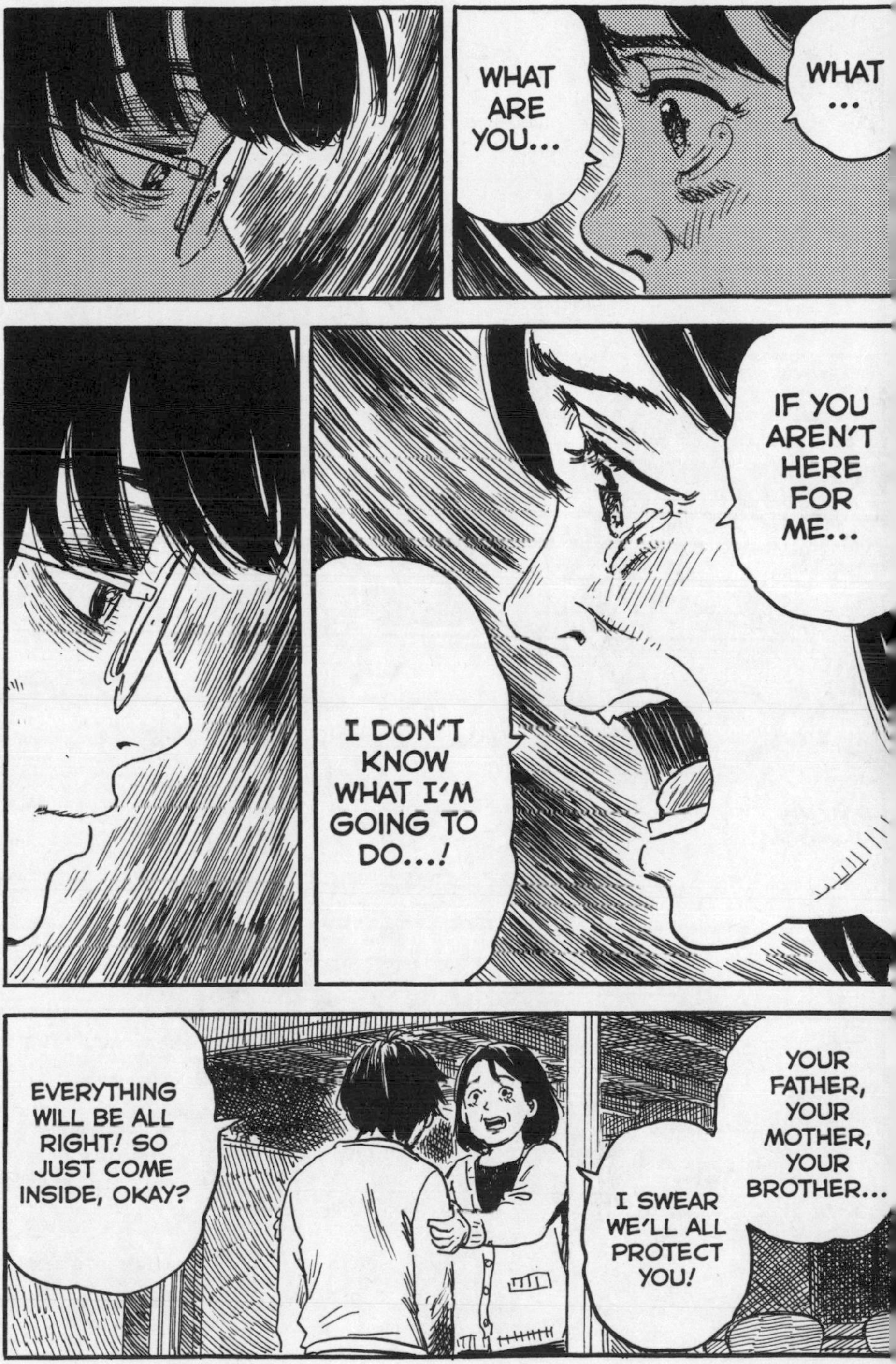
WHAT ...
WHAT ARE YOU...
IF YOU AREN'T HERE FOR ME...
I DON'T KNOW WHAT I'M GOING TO DO...!
YOUR FATHER, YOUR MOTHER, YOUR BROTHER...
I SWEAR WE'LL ALL PROTECT YOU!
EVERYTHING WILL BE ALL RIGHT! SO JUST COME INSIDE, OKAY?

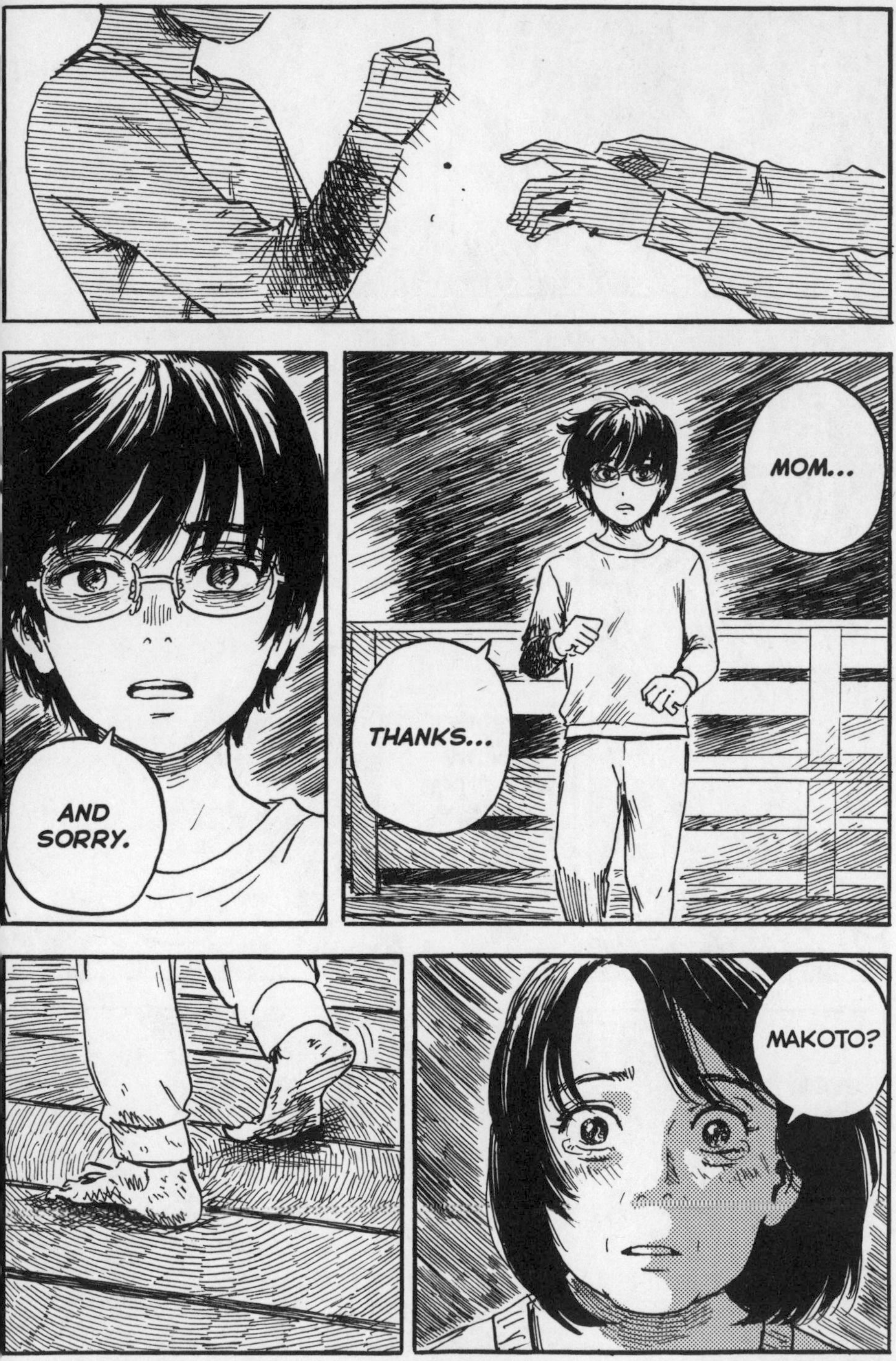
MOM...
THANKS...
AND SORRY.
MAKOTO?

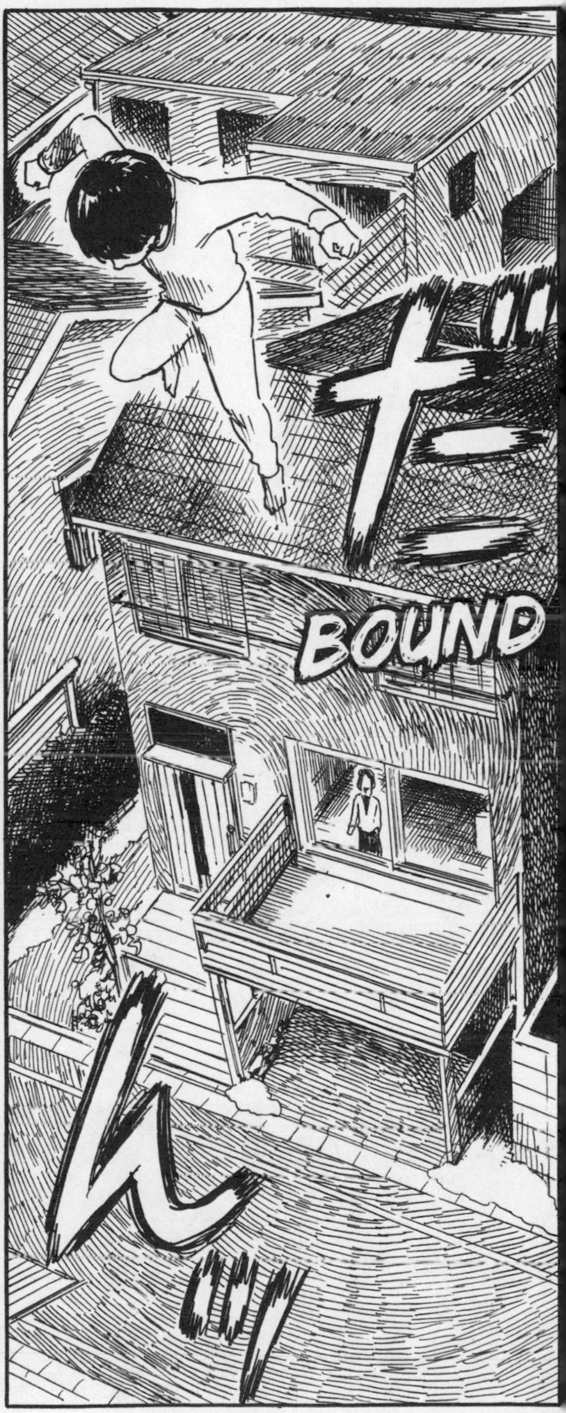
BOUND

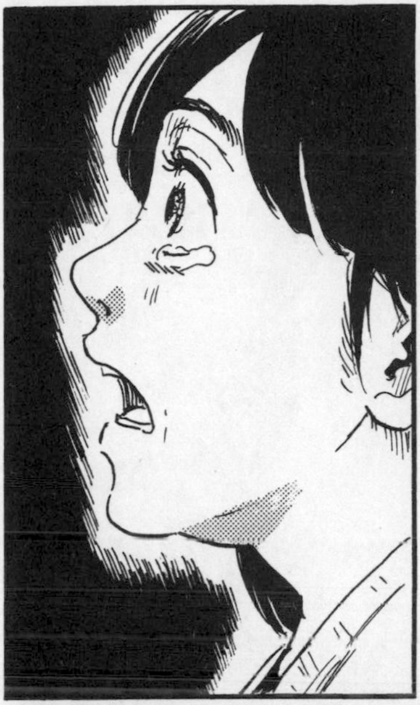

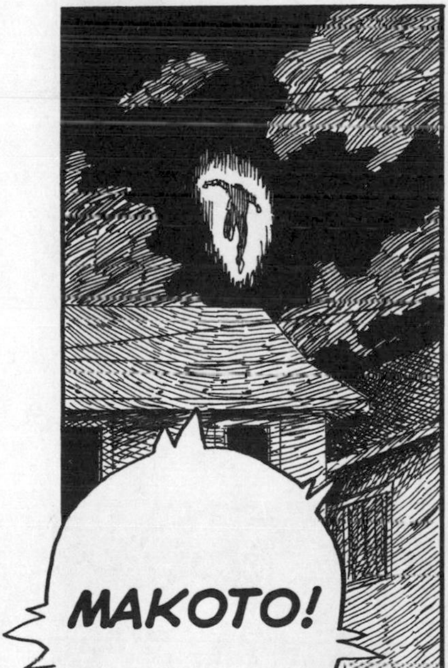
MAKOTO!

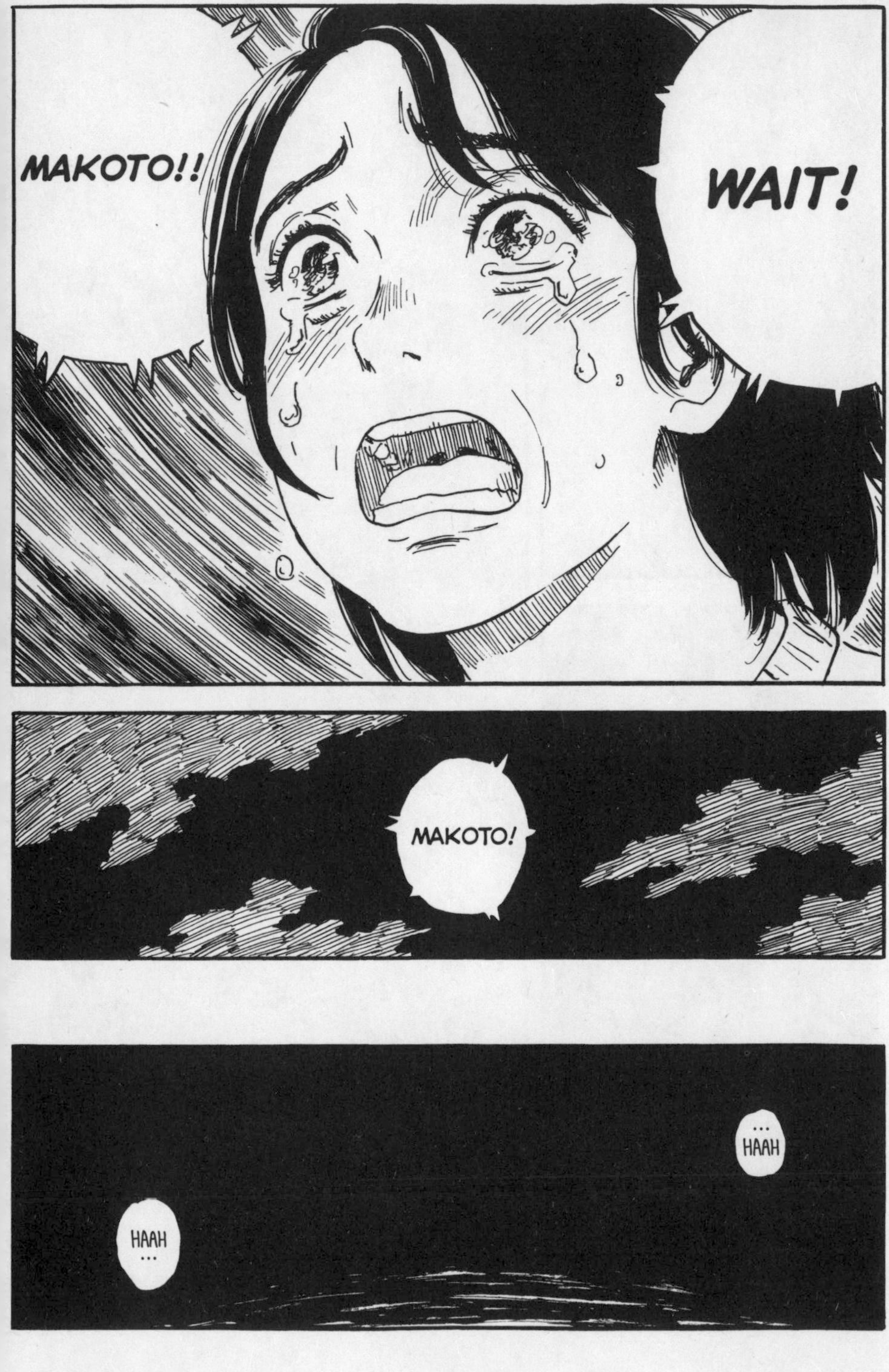
WAIT!
MAKOTO!!
MAKOTO!
... HAAH
HAAH ...

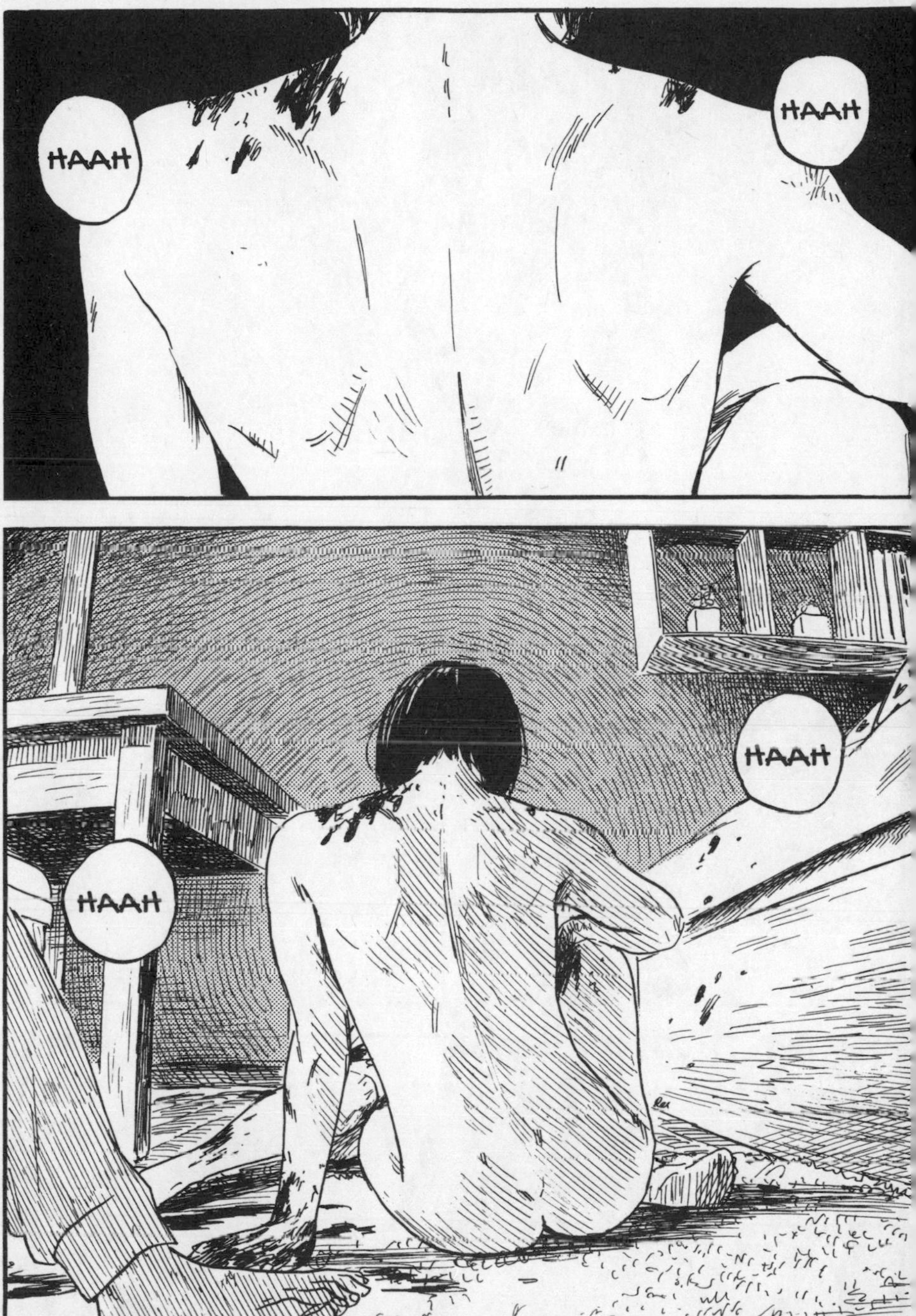

HAAH
HAAH
HAAH
HAAH

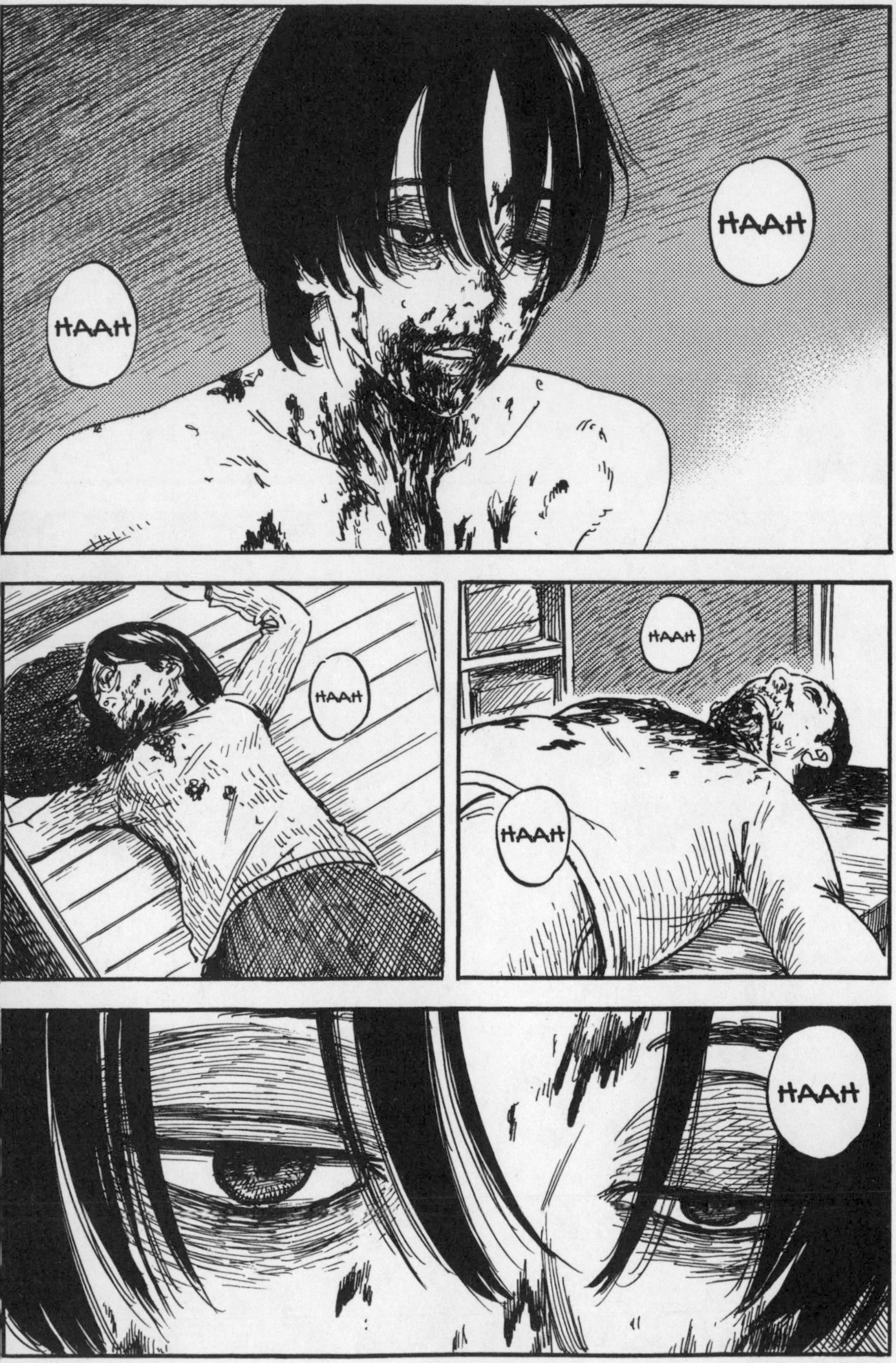
HAAH
HAAH
HAAH
HAAH
HAAH
HAAH

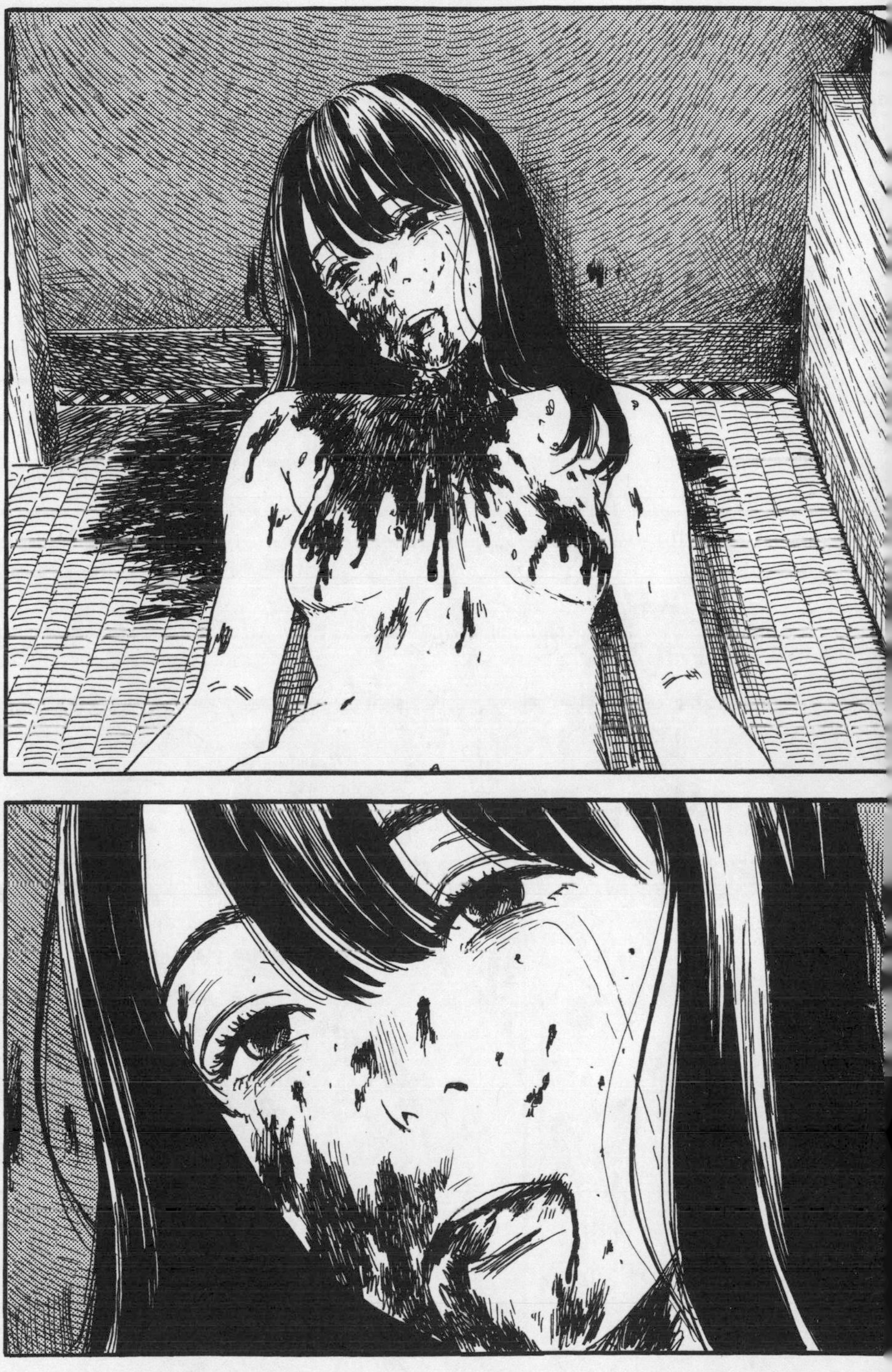

NAO...

NGH...

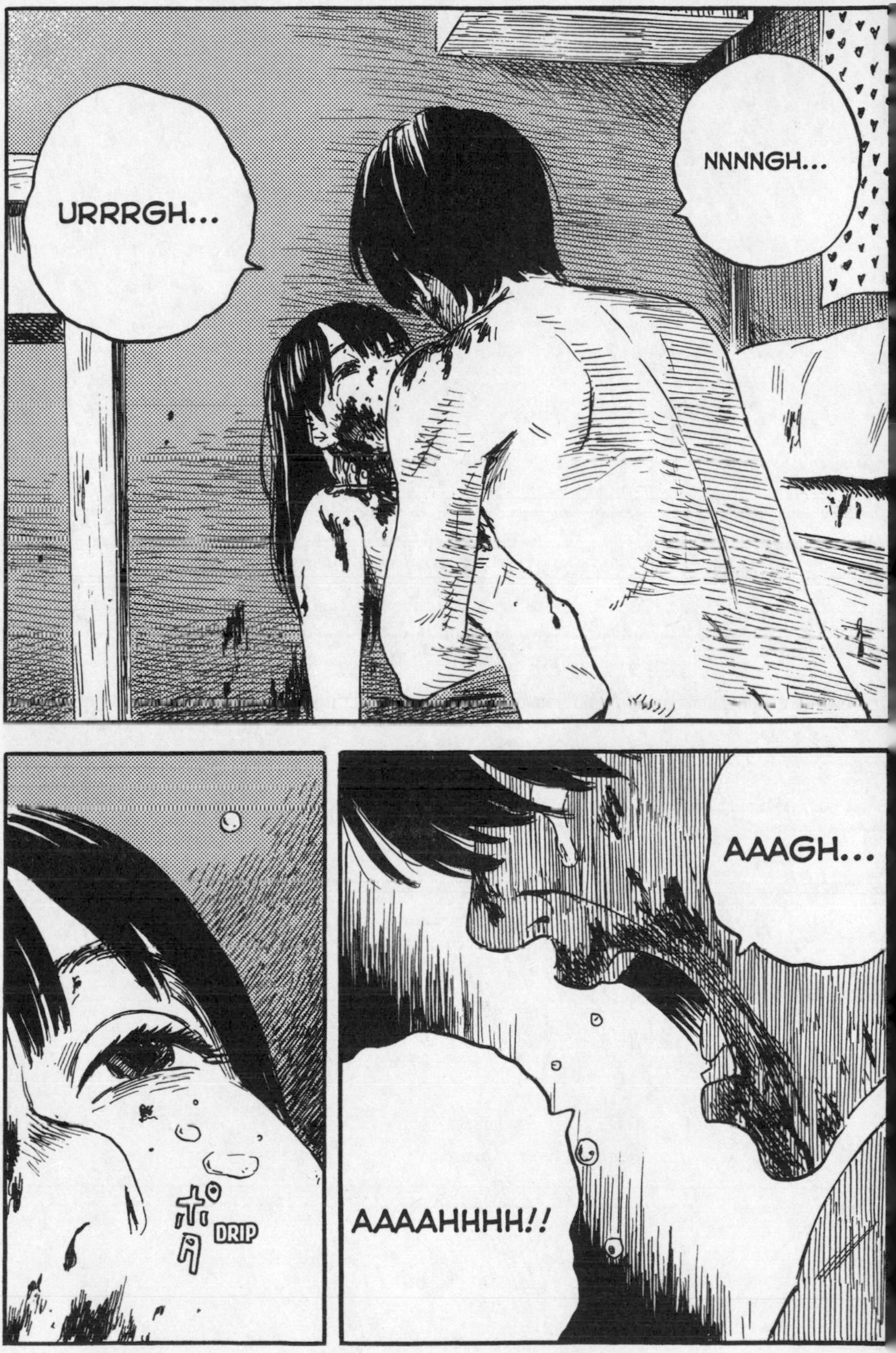
NNNNGH...
URRRGH...
AAAGH...
AAAAHHHH!!
ポタ
DRIP

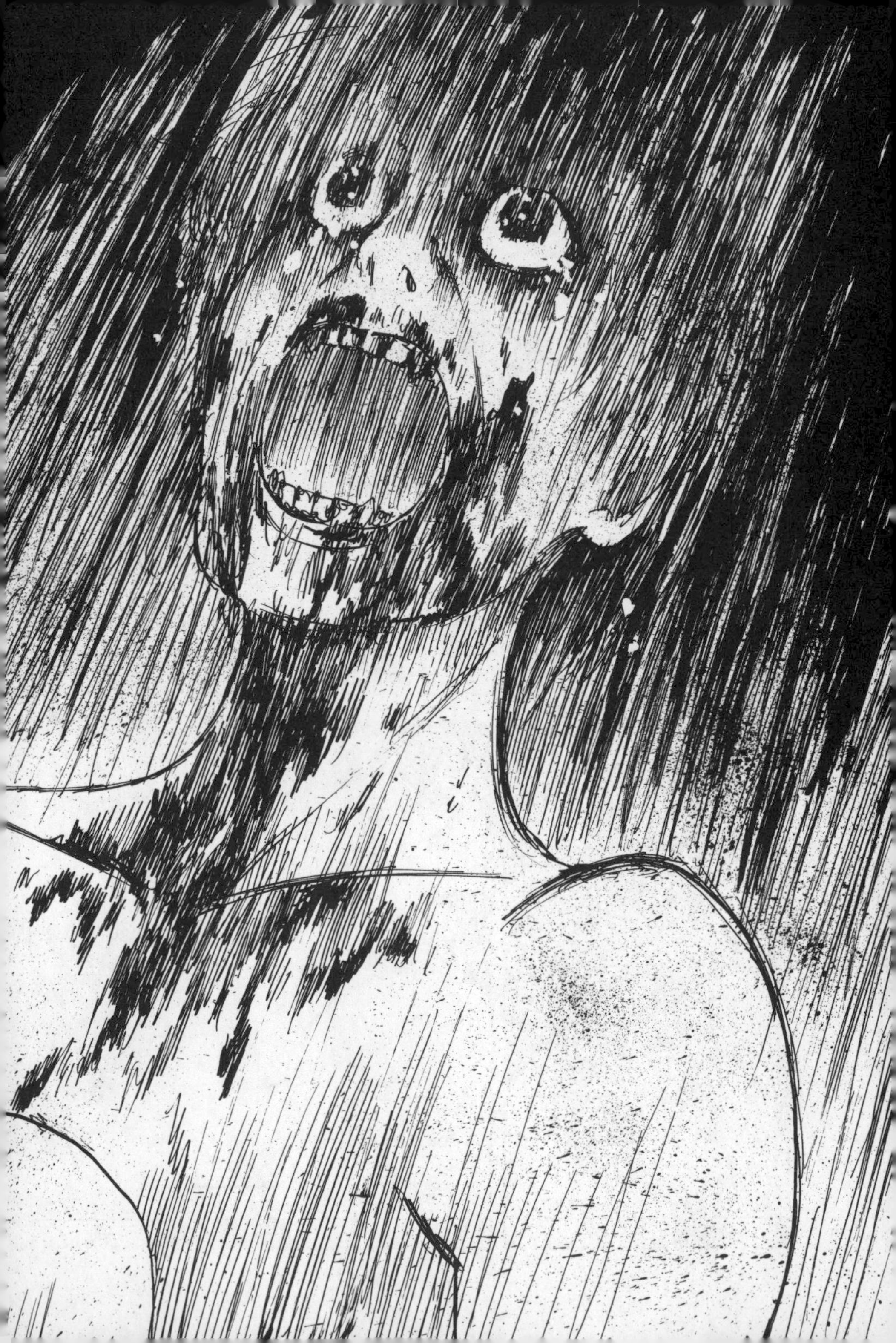

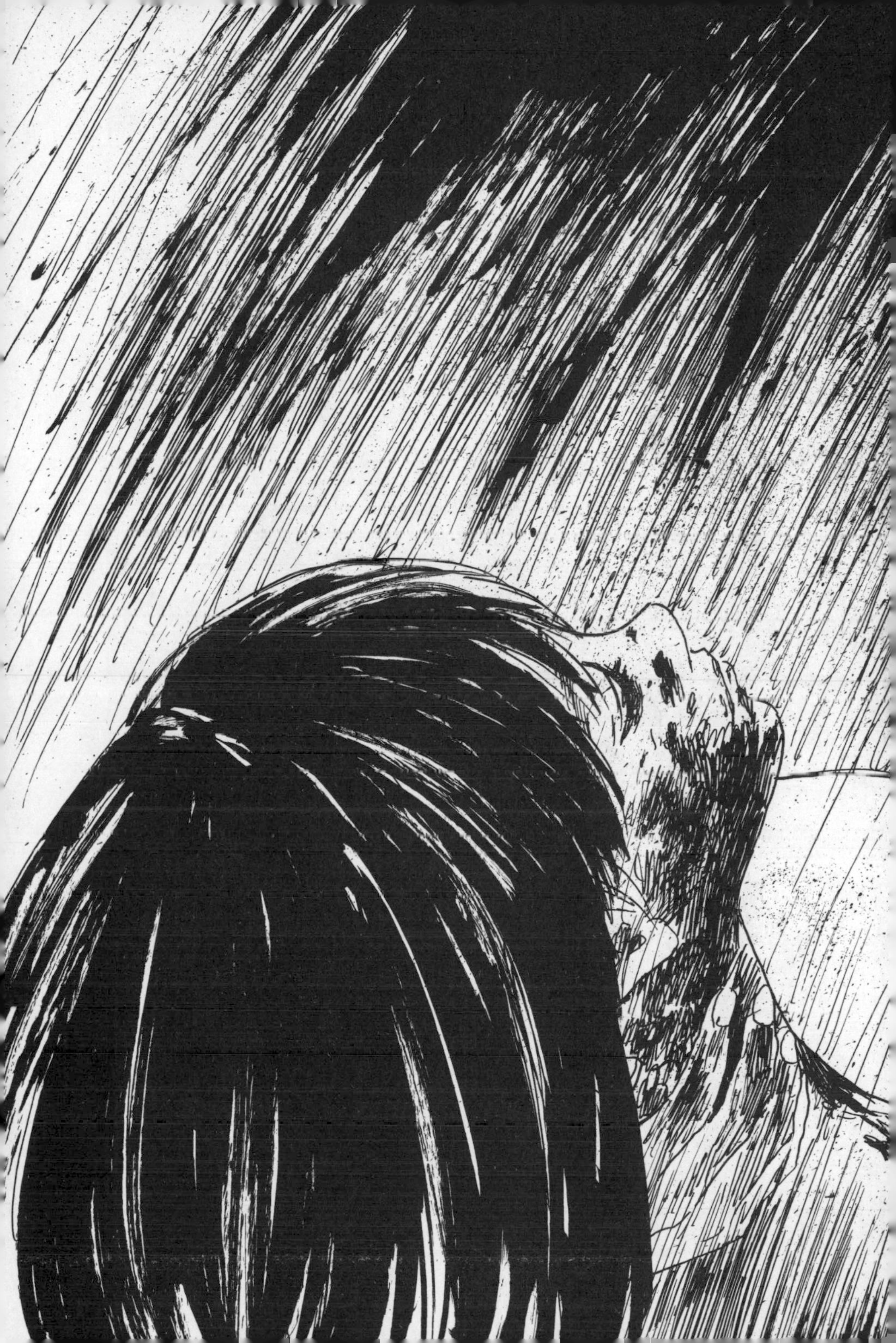

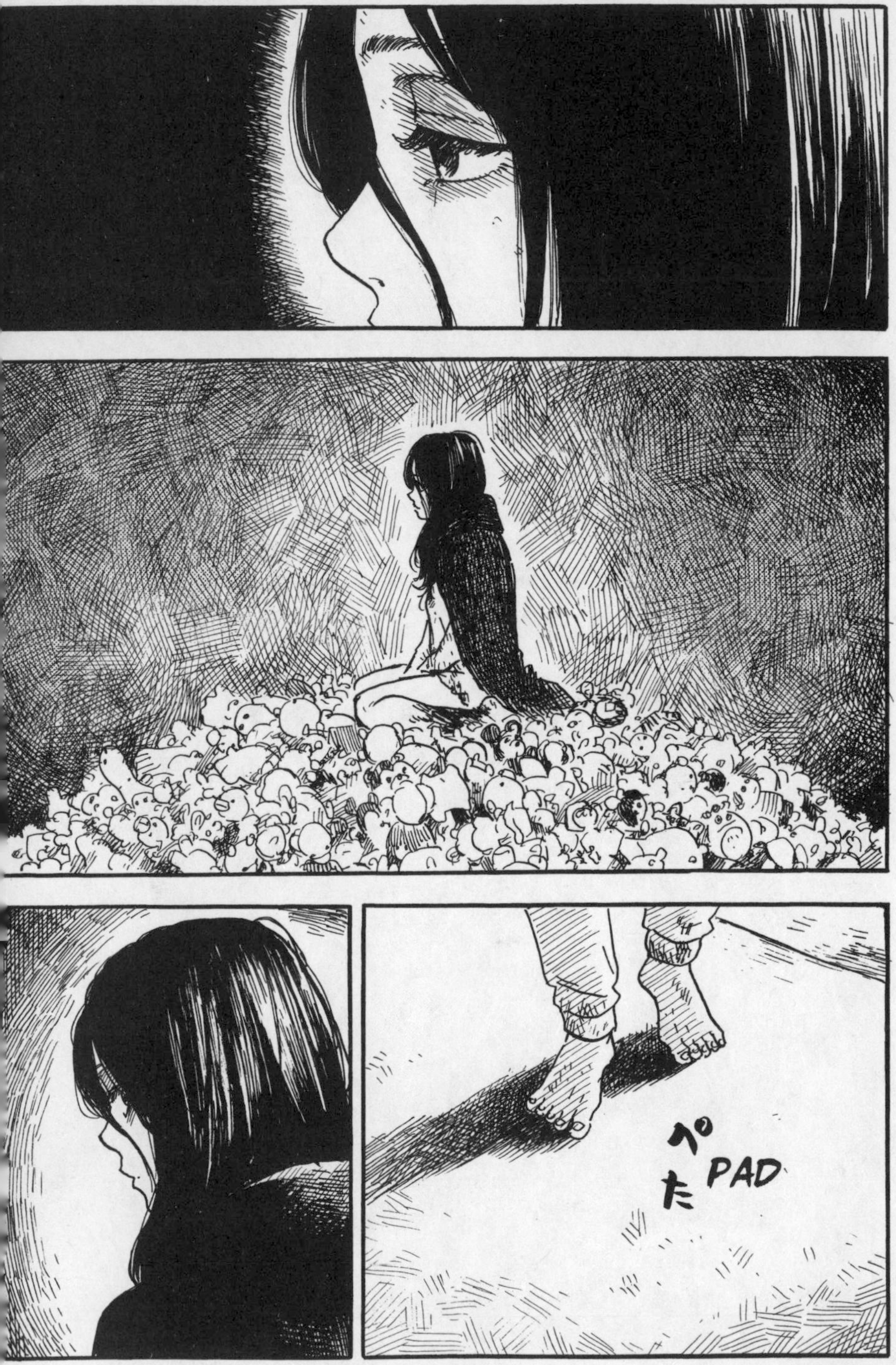
ぺた
PAD

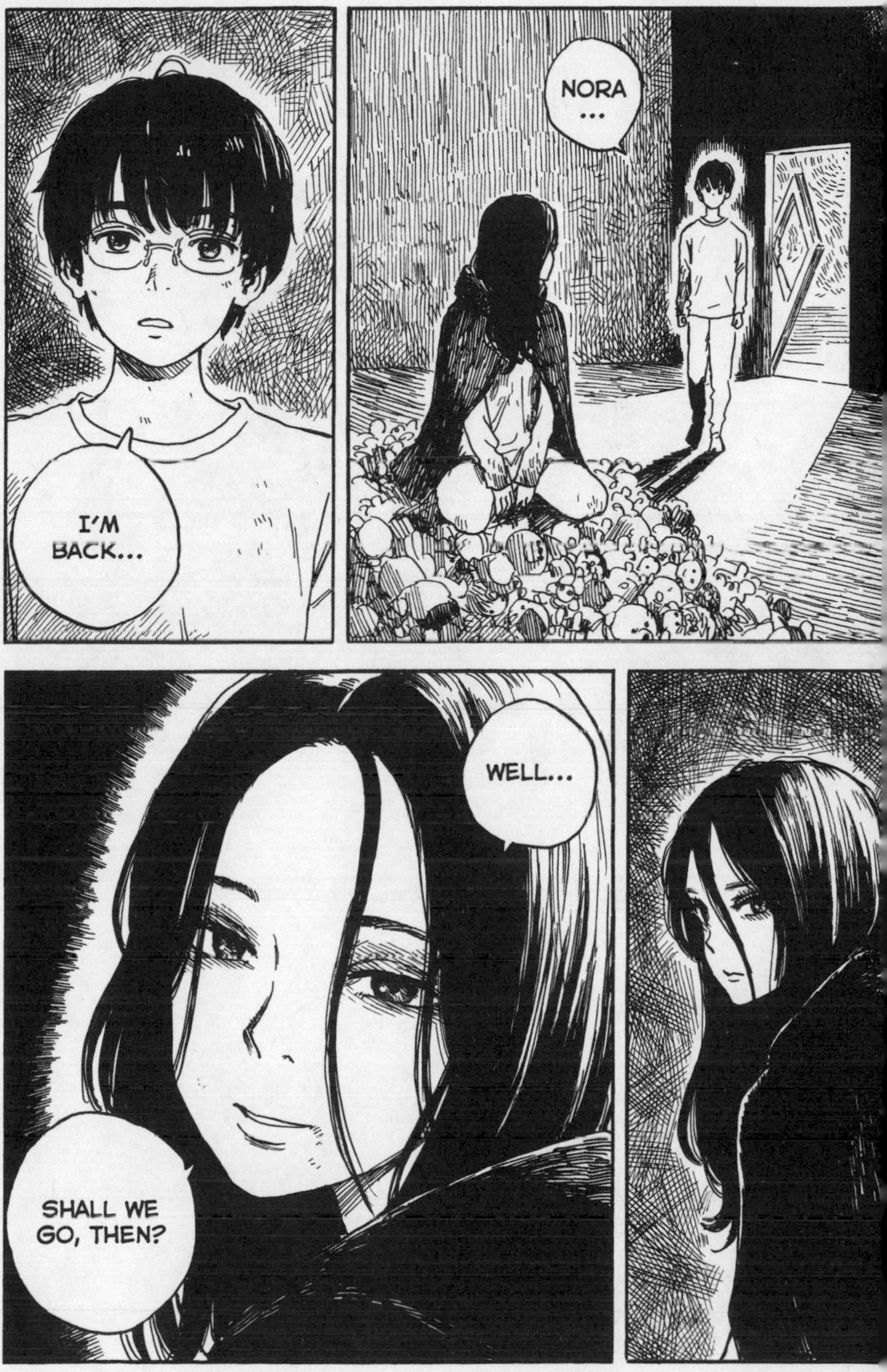
NORA ...
I'M BACK...
WELL...
SHALL WE GO, THEN?

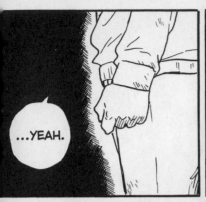

...YEAH.

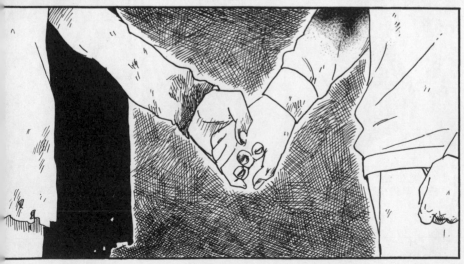

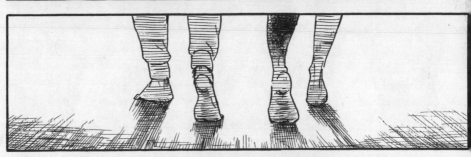

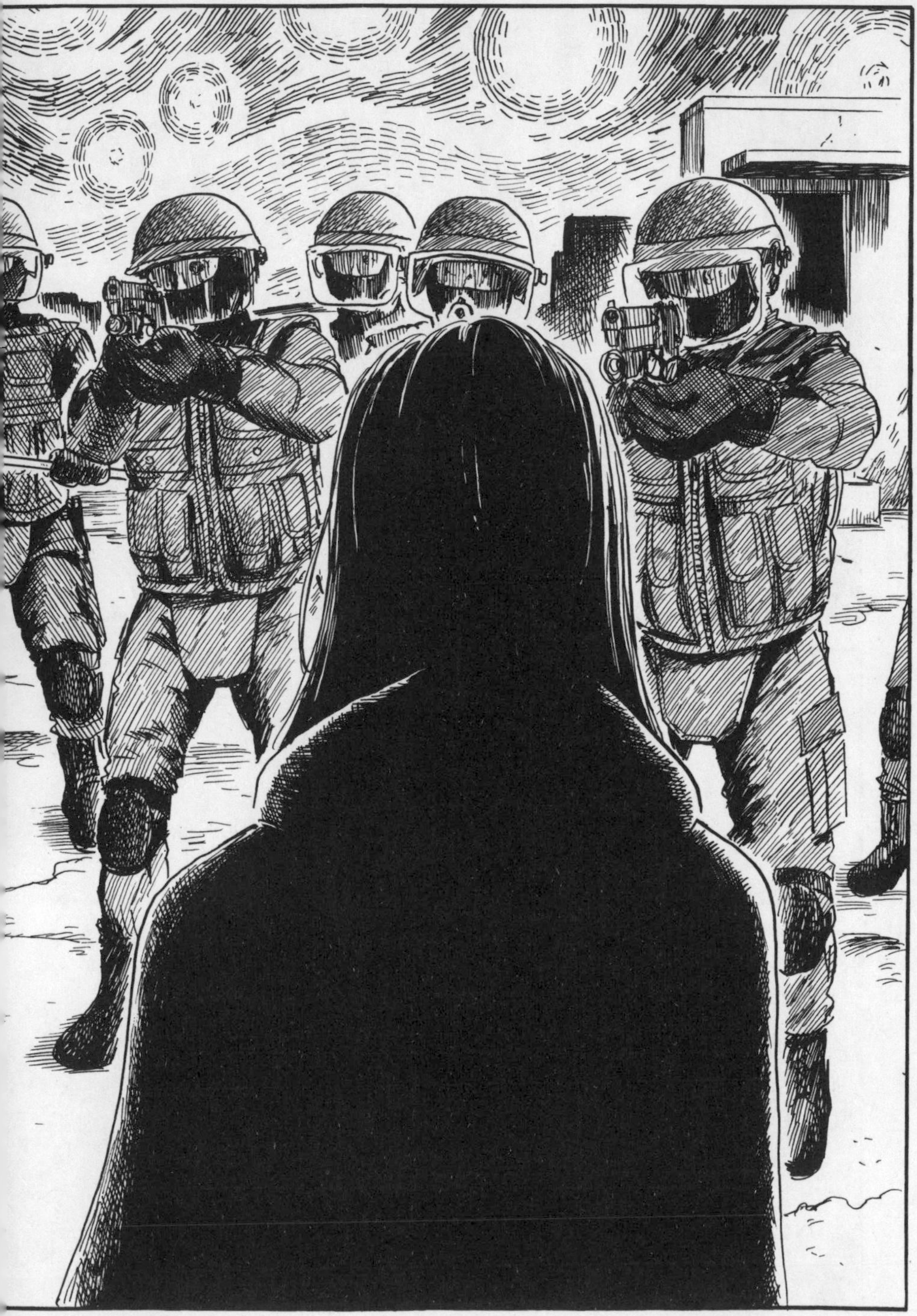

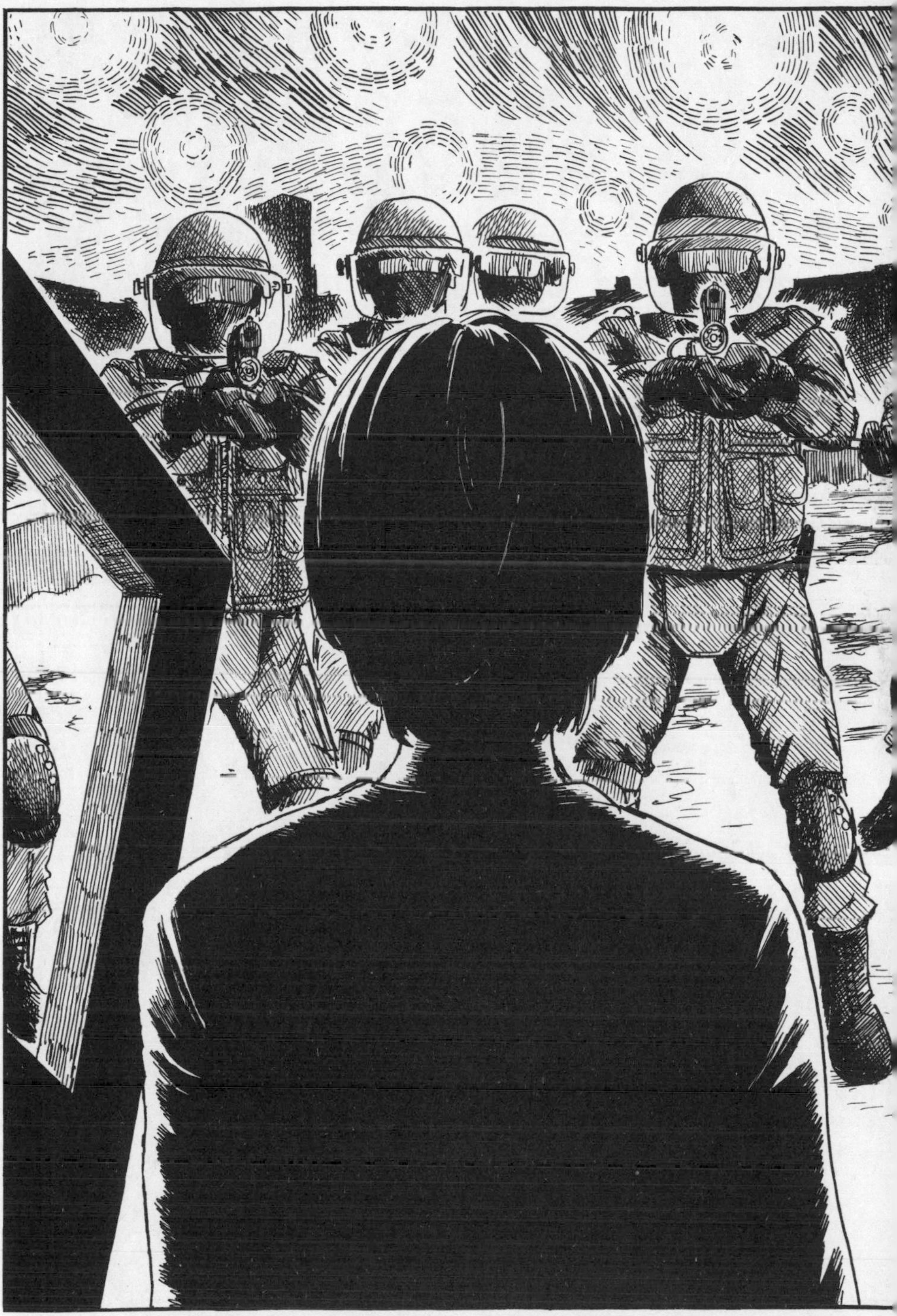

BLAM

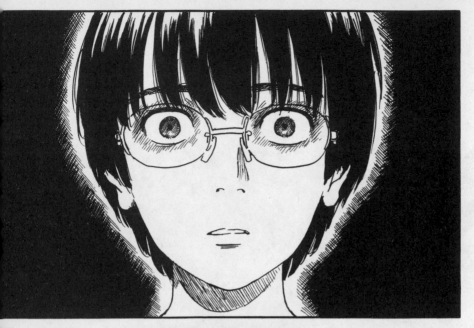

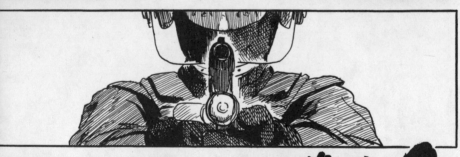

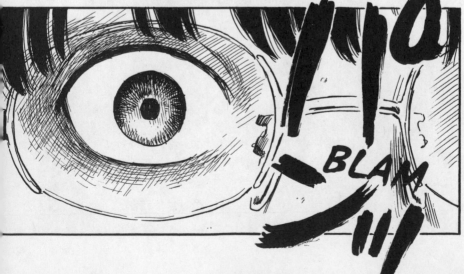

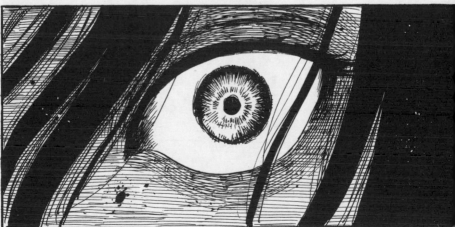

CONTINUED IN #5

"I'm pleasantly surprised to find modern shojo using cross-dressing as a dramatic device to deliver social commentary... Recommended."

-Otaku USA Magazine

The prince in his dark days

By Hico Yamanaka

A drunkard for a father, a household of poverty... For 17-year-old Atsuko, misfortune is all she knows and believes in. Until one day, a chance encounter with Itaru–the wealthy heir of a huge corporation–changes everything. The two look identical, uncannily so. When Itaru curiously goes missing, Atsuko is roped into being his stand-in. There, in his shoes, Atsuko must parade like a prince in a palace. She encounters many new experiences, but at what cost…?

New action series from Takei Hiroyuki, creator of the classic shonen franchise Shaman King!

In medieval Japan, a bell hanging on the collar is a sign that a cat has a master. Norachiyo's bell hangs from his katana sheath, but he is nonetheless a stray — a ronin. This one-eyed cat samurai travels across a dishonest world, cutting through pretense and deception with his blade.

By
Hiroyuki Takei

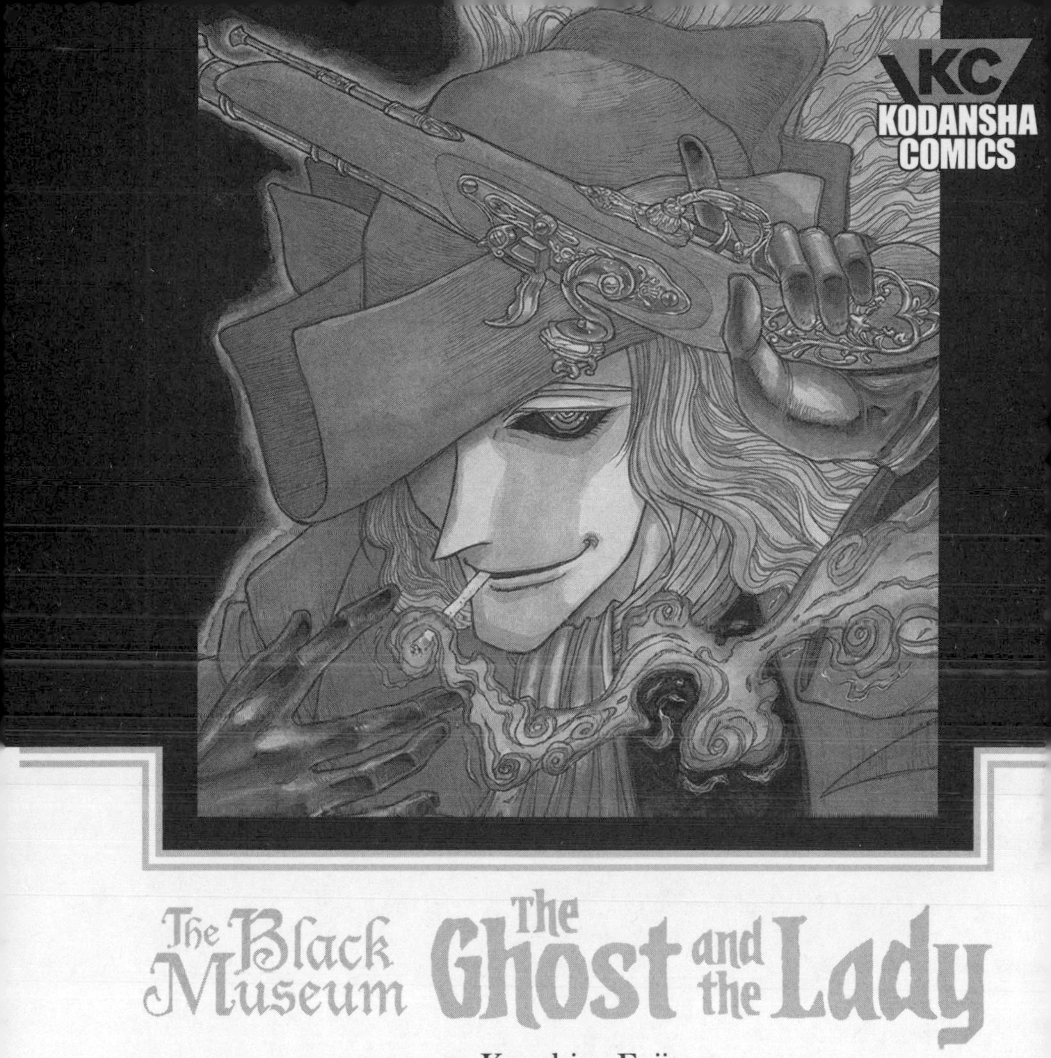
KC
KODANSHA
COMICS

The Black Museum: The Ghost and the Lady

By Kazuhiro Fujita

Deep in Scotland Yard in London sits an evidence room, where artifacts of the greatest mysteries in London history are kept. In this “Black Museum” sits two bullets, fused together after a head-on collision. This was the key piece of evidence in a case that brought together a supernatural Man in Gray and the famous nurse and activist Florence Nightingale – the only person who can see him. Surrounded by war and suffering, the lady enters into a desperate pact with this ghostlike man...

Praise for Kazuhiro Fujita’s *Ushio and Tora*

“A charming revival that combines a classic look with modern depth and pacing... **Essential viewing both for curmudgeons and new fans alike.”** — Anime News Network

“GREAT! The first episode of Ushio and Tora captures the essence of ‘90s anime.” — IGN

A Kodansha Comics Trade Paperback Original.

Published in the United States by Kodansha Comics, an imprint of Kodansha USA Publishing, LLC, New York.

Publication rights for this English edition arranged through Kodansha Ltd., Tokyo.

First published in Japan in 2016 by Kodansha Ltd., Tokyo, as Hapinesu volume 3.

ISBN 978-1-63236-393-0

Printed in the United States of America.

www.kodansha.us

9 8 7 6 5 4 3

Translator: Kevin Gifford
Lettering: David Yoo
Editing: Paul Starr
Kodansha Comics edition cover design by Phil Balsman